A-LEVEL FRENCH

COURSE COMPANION

William B Barratt
former Senior Lecturer at a college of Higher Education

Advisors:

Mike Buckby
Senior Research Fellow, Language Teaching Centre, York

Eileen Verlarde
Senior Chief Examiner, A-Level, JMB

First published 1992
by BPP (Letts Educational) Ltd
Aldine House, Aldine Place
142-144 Uxbridge Road
London W12 8AW
Revised 1993, 1994

Editorial Team
Christopher Norris, Angela Royal, Andrew Thraves

Design Team
Jonathan Barnard, Lesley Gilbert, Jordan and Jordan

Text: © William B Barratt 1992, 1993, 1994

Illustrations: Jordan and Jordan, Kathy Baxendate, Chris Evans

© BPP (Letts Educational) Ltd

British Library Cataloguing-in-Publication data
Barratt, William B
French : A-level course companion
I. Title
448

ISBN 1 85758 028 1

Printed and bound in Great Britain by
WM Print Limited, Walsall, West Midlands WS2 9NE
Reprinted 1993 and 1994 by Ashford Colour Press, Gosport, PO12 4DT

Note
Every effort has been made to trace all
copyright holders but, if any have been
inadvertently overlooked, the publishers will
gladly receive information enabling them
to rectify any error or omission in subsequent editions.

Preface

I would like to thank Mike Buckby, Senior Research Fellow at the Language Teaching Centre York, and Eileen Verlarde, Senior Chief Examiner for A-Level for JMB for much valuable advice during the planning stages of this book, for reading the text and for their many helpful suggestions. I am also grateful for the encouragement and advice of Hélène Burrows, Diane Fletcher and Andy Dobson who tried out a great deal of the material with their students at Halesowen College and Worcester Sixth Form College. I would also like to thank students in my own classes who have contributed their thoughts on ways of learning and what kind of material they find most beneficial. I am grateful too to Jean-Louis Drommi for his close scrutiny of the French text and his comments. Lastly I would like to thank the editorial staff of Letts Educational for their encouragement and the friendly working relationship fostered over the last eighteen months.

Acknowledgements

The author and publishers are grateful to the following for permission to reproduce their extracts and photographs.

Text
pp13–16 from *Collins-Robert English-French French-English Dictionary,* second edition (1987) reprinted by permission of Le Robert;
p 75 'The calming of the waters' (Marc 4, 5) from *L'Alliance Biblique Universelle* translation of the Bible, reprinted by permission of the Société Biblique Française;
p112 'Qu'est-ce qui est tendre…' (août 1990) reprinted by permission of *Nice-Matin*;
p115 'Le Sida – Fléau des années 90' (1 août 1990) reproduced by permission of *Modes et Travaux*;
p121 'Deux élèves japonais enterrés vivants' (23 juillet 1990) reproduced by permission of *Nice-Matin*;
p125 'Croyez-vous à la vie après la mort?' reproduced by permission of *Phosphore*;
p128 'Les dames du crime' (août 1990) reprinted by permission of *Modes et Travaux*;
p129 'L'Aventure en Amérique' (août 1990) reproduced by permission of *Modes et Travaux*;
p131 'Que faire en cas d'incendie' (8 septembre 1990) reproduced by permission of *50,000,000 de consommateurs*, published by the Institut National de la Consommation;
p132 'Hold-up' (août 1990) reproduced by permission of *Le Dauphiné Libéré – Vaucluse-Matin*;
p135 'Une crèche bilingue dès septembre, à Coulogne' (15 août 1990) reprinted by permission of *Littoral Nord;*
p179 'Les médias disent vrai?' (avril 1990) reproduced by permission of *Phosphore*;
p179 'Circuit de la drogue dans le monde' (août 1990) reproduced by permission of *Phosphore*;
p180 'Les Européens sont-ils de bons conducteurs?' (août 1990) reproduced by permission of *Phosphore*.

Photographs
p106 BPP (Holdings) Ltd
p123 Eurotunnel
pp144, 150, 158, 174 The Hulton Picture Company
p181 Ian Thraves

iv

Contents

Introduction

How to use this book

The material in this book has been designed to exemplify and practise the kinds of language task required by the Examination Boards for French at A and AS Level. The book also provides a bridge for the wide gap that exists between GCSE and A (or AS Level) French. It has also been devised with the needs of the self-learner in mind.

The sections on aims and objectives give an overall picture of what is needed to build on knowledge already acquired for GCSE French. Language-learning strategies deal with the ways in which you can consolidate and extend competence in the four language skills. This is followed by advice on how to organize your work and how to prepare for the examination.

The tables relating to the requirements of the Examining Boards and allocation of marks will give you a quick reference to what you need for the exam. They should be read in conjunction with the detailed syllabus for your particular Board, of which you should get a copy.

The section on dictionaries provides both an introduction to, and practice in, using larger dictionaries than you may have been accustomed to previously. The sections on vocabulary and gender provide a framework on which you can build to extend your knowledge of words and accuracy in using them.

The grammar section gives practical explanations and examples of the main points required to fill the gaps and extend your learning. Each section is followed by exercises, with answers in the key which follows. You can either work through this section systematically or dip into the parts you need. This section is derived from my long acquaintance with what is really essential in grammatical knowledge and where A-Level students need most help.

The sections on reading and writing skills deal with specific tasks. They are accompanied by examples from the Examining Boards' papers and model answers. This is followed by practice exercises and advice on how to improve each skill. You will benefit from working through all the sections here since many of the skills complement each other.

The literature section provides an introduction to literature for newcomers and covers both work in English and in French. There are model answers and advice on how to write answers to questions.

The topic section provides advice, guidance and several ideas for topic-work themes.

The section on oral work sets out the features common to most oral examinations and provides advice and practice material. This section should be studied in conjunction with the next one on pronunciation.

The listening section gives practical advice on how to deal with this part of the examination.

The verb table should not only be used as a reference tool but also as a learning aid, by photocopying and blanking out sections to be filled in as a check on learning.

The appendices contain a number of useful sources of further information that should complement much of the previous material.

The material as a whole in this book has been devised to represent many of the recurring themes at A and AS Level. Students will benefit therefore from working through as much of this as they can. Students will also find it beneficial if they can work with another person for many of the tasks. Not only is this more enjoyable but you will learn a great deal from each other.

A-Level aims

The broad aims of studying French at A Level are very similar to those at GCSE Level. The main differences lie in the breadth and depth of knowledge expected and the flexibility with which you can use this knowledge. The extension of your competence in French is closely linked with increasing maturity. By speaking and listening to the language, and by reading and writing it, you will be able to increase your knowledge of the world and society, discover and discuss the opinions of others and develop your own viewpoint and outlook. Study of a language becomes just as much a tool as it is a target. The A-Level examination will test your ability to handle ideas as well as your ability to speak, understand, read and write French.

One important difference between studying French at GCSE and A Level is the responsibility put upon you as learner. You cannot be told or shown everything you need in order to pass the A-Level examination. There will inevitably be an element of the unexpected. You will have to develop your own habits for studying and apply these consistently, so that you take charge of your own education, creating learning opportunities for yourself. Guidance and help with this task will be found in this book.

A typical description of some of the aims of an A-Level syllabus in French is given on page vi:

1 To develop the candidates' intellectual and critical faculties by encouraging the acquisition and development of:
   (a) awareness of the use of language
   (b) an imaginative and creative approach to language
   (c) learning strategies and study skills
   (d) awareness and understanding of themselves, of other individuals and of society

2 To enable the candidates to attain sufficient command of language skills in order to:
   (a) communicate easily and with confidence in a French-speaking environment
   (b) understand and appreciate spoken and written French from a variety of sources and in registers including colloquial, informative and literary
   (c) seek and convey information, report and express ideas and feelings in various modes such as conversation, discussion, personal and analytical writing

3 To form a sound base of the language and learning skills required for further study (of French and other languages) whilst continuing its use in work and leisure.

4 To encourage first-hand contact with the culture and civilization of France or French-speaking communities through, for example:
   (a) exchange of letters, cassettes or magazines, etc
   (b) travel and residence where possible

5 To further the candidates' appreciation of language by helping them to understand culture and civilization (both British and French) from the viewpoint of the respective peoples.

6 To foster interest in the views of French-speaking people on current issues.

You will see from the above that study of French at A Level is as much about extending you as a person as it is about acquiring knowledge.

Increasing your confidence and competence in using a foreign language has an immediate and valuable practical purpose in everyday life. Despite the growth of English as a world-wide language, you can only really get to know and understand people from another country and their way of life by communicating with them in their own language, whether for pleasure or for commercial purposes.

A-Level examination objectives

Just as at GCSE level, the A-Level examination objectives are based upon the four skills of speaking, listening, reading and writing.

Speaking

Objectives for spoken French at A Level are an expansion of the skills expected at GCSE. A typical description of what is required at GCSE level might be: 'to seek and provide information, to take part in conversational interchange, to express opinions in French in a range of situations within the candidates' own experience'. At A Level you will be expected to 'extract more detailed information by following up initial questions' or to 'marshall ideas in order to persuade' to 'counter the opinions of another person' or 'present orally the substance of an English or French text'. The important differences therefore, at A Level, are: being able to pick out and manipulate ideas; making use of the spoken language for a greater variety of purposes; and often taking the initiative yourself and explaining how and why. There is also much more unpredictability at A Level. Topics are no longer closely defined. You will have the chance though of talking about something that interests you and that you have prepared. Role-play, general conversation and talking around a prepared topic figure in the oral examination of each Board. The oral exam tends to be a little longer at A Level, from 15 to 30 minutes, depending on the Examination Board.

Listening

The main differences in objectives for listening skills at A Level relate to the ability to pick out relevant ideas as well as facts; to summarize or extract the main points of what you have heard. You will hear a greater variety of speakers and kinds of interchange than at GCSE level and some of the spoken passages will be longer. Questions are usually framed in English to be answered in English. Ways of testing listening comprehension do vary however and you may be asked to give answers in French, transcribe parts of what you have heard, or list points mentioned in sequence.

Reading and writing

There are some important differences in objectives for reading and writing at A Level: you will be required to translate from and into French; and you will do more writing in French of various kinds. The written element in French normally counts for more in the overall weighting of marks.

Passages are usually taken from magazines, newspapers and other contemporary sources. Most Boards set questions in English to be answered in English but questions in French are also a possibility. Summary in English of a passage (or a section of it), is a new skill that you will have to develop. You may have to translate selected extracts into English or give a brief résumé or paraphrase in French. The emphasis is again on being able to deal with ideas and opinions as well as factual items. Some Boards have longer passages for translation into English. Retranslation is also a task required by some Boards (i.e. translating into French a short passage in English based closely on what you have just read).

Writing in French can take the form of an essay, presenting points for and against a certain issue, or a composition of a more imaginative kind. Writing letters or reports in French is required by some Boards. There is also the possibility, with most Boards, of an extended piece of writing in French on a selected subject done in your own time and presented as coursework.

Studying French literary texts, or books on certain aspects of French life and culture, are also features of most A-Level syllabuses. In both cases you are required to read texts in French and answer questions in English or French according to the requirements of the Board. Wide reading of this kind comes as a bit of a shock after GCSE but, if thoroughly done, it has a beneficial effect on your competence in writing and understanding French. You will be able to extend your vocabulary, meet and develop new ideas and use the language, you have acquired by this process, in essay and composition work.

Grammar, structures and vocabulary

The grammar and structures required for GCSE form the basis for what you need at A Level with two important considerations. Firstly, many of the points of grammar that formerly you needed only to recognize (e.g. certain pronouns and tenses) will now be required for active use in writing and speaking. Secondly, the range of grammatical items will need to be extended. This is particularly the case with verbs and tenses . You will have to extend the range of verbs you are familiar with in the present tense and also make some additions to tense, mood and voice. For example, the subjunctive is not required by some boards at GCSE level or only the present subjunctive by others. You will need to use both the present and the perfect subjunctive as well as recognize its other two tenses.

Most GCSE Examination Boards publish a defined content of their syllabus which lists grammar, structures, vocabulary and expressions as well as functions and notions of language required for their examination. Send off for your copy. It is an extremely useful document for A-Level students as a check list, a quick reference and a learning aid. You will get something of a boost when you find out how much you already know! Defined content syllabuses are pretty indigestible for all but the most gifted GCSE students but they become easier to assimilate as you grow in confidence with all the bits and pieces of French you have learned.

The vocabulary needed for A Level is far broader than that for GCSE and no definitive list can be made. It is important to get into the habit of keeping a vocabulary book right from the start of the course. Many words are going to be more for productive use, others you will need just to understand. More will be said about this in the section on language-learning strategies.

The AS-Level examination

The AS-Level examination is meant to be a natural extension of the skills acquired at GCSE Level for those students who have obtained grade C or above and wish to continue their study of French during their sixth-form course. The attainment level is identical with that of A Level but the content is half that of an A-Level syllabus and should require half the contact time. The broad aims and examination objectives are similar to those already outlined. An AS-Level course is meant to extend over two years. The reduced content of the syllabus is reflected by fewer items in each examination paper and, consequently, a shorter examination time. Writing in French is required for AS Level by three of the Boards but not by the other five. Marks are usually assigned equally to the skills of listening, reading and speaking. A coursework topic is available as an option, set against reading comprehension, in two of the syllabuses. The listening, reading and speaking parts of the AS-Level exam are usually identical with all or part of the A-Level examination.

Language-learning strategies

Gaining competence in a foreign language often appears a slow process. It is difficult to see how far you have come because there is no accurate way of measuring the 'distance' in the short term. This is partly because of the 'maturation factor' in language learning. It seems that we have to allow time for the brain to order and assimilate what has been fed into it before it can be retrieved and used as language. This is probably true of all attempts to assimilate knowledge but it appears more obvious with foreign-language learning. This is perhaps because knowing a foreign language involves several skills, often needed at once and also because language is unpredictable for the most part. We can never be sure of what we are going to hear or read any more than we can know beforehand what we will say or write. One thing is certain: it is important to be consistent and persistent in your learning habits – a little at a time over a long period is better than hectic bursts of activity.

Another effect, that you might notice, is the impression of reaching a plateau or threshold in your learning and the feeling that you can't get any further. This pause effect is quite normal and connected with the maturation factor already mentioned. You *will* move off but only imperceptibly at first.

Using a foreign language is a skill which has to be practised otherwise it fades or 'stiffens up'. The phrase often heard on older people's lips, 'My French/German/Spanish is a bit rusty' is very evocative of this phenomenon. It helps a great deal therefore if you set yourself targets and procedures for study: learning so many words a week; devoting a set amount of time to each of the language skills; reading through and adding to your literature or grammar notes; consulting books of criticism; reading background or topic material.

It helps enormously if you can work with a friend, particularly one following the same course as you. One advantage of this is being able to practise your oral skills together. You will also be able to plug the gaps in each other's knowledge. Grammar points often seem clearer when explained by someone on the same level as yourself. If you both come to a dead end on the same point, it probably needs clearing up with the whole class and will give your teacher something to focus on. You can also test each other's vocabulary.

If no learning companion is available, finding someone to whom you can teach basic conversational French can be quite helpful. Having to explain things to someone else sharpens up your own understanding and grasp of the language.

Skills

Listening

This is possibly the most neglected skill and the one that can be most obviously deficient to Examiners marking papers. If French is used a lot in the classroom for all the activities that don't specifically need English your exposure to spoken French will be increased. Some class-time will be devoted to listening to taped material in the classroom. Nevertheless, you will need to create your own opportunities for practising listening skills at other times.

You have immediate access to French voices by tuning to either side of BBC Radio 4 on long wave. There are at least three radio stations that can be received in Britain. France-Inter the national station 160 khz, and Europe 1, a commercial station 180 khz, will give you the best reception, depending on what part of the country you live in. You can listen casually, just letting the language flow over you or you can make a point each day of listening to something specific. If you have never listened to French announcers before you will probably be alarmed at the speed of their speech. This is particularly the case with news bulletins and weather forecasts because the news-reader is using a printed text that he or she has to fit into a given time. Speed of delivery does vary however and it is partly a case of tuning in your ear. Other items like interviews and discussions are at a slower pace. For example, France-Inter has a 'What the papers say' slot between morning news bulletins and a series of relaxed interviews with people from all walks of life during the morning and at the end of the afternoon. It is also worth listening to advertisements on the commercial stations as well as the government-directed ones on France-Inter.

By recording ten minutes of a programme, you can listen to it as many times as you like. Try with the beginning of a news bulletin that lists the main items first or with part of an interview. Listen to it a couple of times and make a list of the items talked about. You probably won't be able to understand every word; it is not essential to do so. Select a shorter section and try writing down words or phrases that you can catch. Have a dictionary at hand. Each time you listen you should be able to fill in a bit more. As you improve at this, try making a transcript of a short section. Take the tape and specific problems to your teacher for explanation.

There are commercially produced tapes available, often accompanied by a transcript of the tape. Cassettes Radio France publish a catalogue of tapes taken from their programmes. The newspaper *Authentik* (*l'Authentique en Français*), published 5 times a year in Dublin produces a tape with transcript and exercises. A recent new publication *La Vie Outre-Manche* appears monthly and has an accompanying tape of readings from its articles (*see* appendix 3, page 210). There are several useful things you can do once you have a tape with a transcript:

1   Try listening several times to the tape while following the printed version with your eye. If you have not done this before you will be surprised by the way words merge or seem swallowed because of linking, use of liaisons, stress and intonation patterns.

2   Make a few photocopies of the transcript. With Tippex block out every seventh or so word. Listen again and see if you can fit in the words in your mind, or write them in. You could also select verbs, nouns or adjectives for blocking out.

3   You could also try reading the text over the taped voice, with the volume turned low. This helps to practise intonation and stress patterns.

You can use this book's tape and transcript in these ways. Another source of taped material are the BBC's schools programmes. They offer a wide range of live interviews, designed for different levels, and are accompanied by a booklet. It is often helpful to select a level below the one you are doing. This has the effect of reinforcing what you have perhaps only partially remembered.

You could try your local library. They often have tapes that accompany courses. Your local university or polytechnic is sure to have a language laboratory and might allow you to use it in conjunction with their tape library. Exchanging live recorded tapes with a French school or friends in France is another possibility.

Watching French films with subtitles on television can be very helpful. Satellite TV and video recording bring a further range of possibilities. News, interviews and discussions are good starting points. Commercials, documentaries, soap-opera series, films that you have already seen and are dubbed in French are relaxing ways of listening. (Where do you think the word 'dubbed' comes from?) There are usually current series of language programmes on TV for older learners. Try the beginners' courses. You will be surprised how much you know and how much you will re-learn or reinforce.

Speaking

There are two aspects to this skill: practising saying or reading French to get your tongue round words and perfect a smooth flow; practising responding to a spoken cue and reacting to a spoken situation.

Working with a tape is the best way of practising pronunciation on your own. The voice-over already mentioned is one way. A taped text, with gaps in for you to repeat or anticipate what is said is a mechanical but still useful exercise. This also works well in a language laboratory because you are 'closer' to the sound of your own voice wearing ear-phones.

It is possible to do basic role-plays on your own by imagining the other person and just reacting to the English cues. Some people use their pets as stand-ins to create the illusion of talking to someone. You can also rehearse situations in your head while travelling in the bus or train. Internal rehearsal is something we might at times do in English and is a well-known feature of day-dreaming. Try some day-dreaming in French. Research has shown that successful language learners are in-the-head rehearsers.

As well as role-plays, 'explaining some aspect of life in your own country' is something that you can do in your head by taking subjects like: opening times of banks; pubs; post-offices; the meanings of abbreviations such MOT, PYO, VAT; how cricket is played; what happens on Christmas day and so on. Short news items from newspapers fulfil the same function.

You can record one part of a role-play on tape leaving a gap for your response, perhaps with a response added as a further reinforcement. If you work through a tape several times you will begin to memorize the dialogue and be able to retrieve phrases that can be used in other situations.

Taking turns to play the parts with a friend is better still, since you will tend to learn from one another. You could try using some GCSE role-plays to begin with. Put some play-acting into this activity. It helps to make the situation more convincing as well as more enjoyable.

Most role-plays centre on (a) giving or asking for information or (b) on resolving a situation or problem. A simple way of practising role-plays with a friend, is to have two cards; one with the cues in English, the other with full responses in French (the part normally played by an examiner). The roles can then be exchanged. Another way is to have both roles, labelled A and B respectively, fully written out in French and English alternately on two cards or on a sheet that folds down the middle. You then have the possibility of either just reading the French or of playing the role from the English version. This method is a bit restrictive. There is often an element of the unexpected in A-Level role-plays. You may be contradicted, challenged to prove something, have to apologize or deal with the displeasure or seeming indifference of your role-play opposite.

Your opportunities for speaking and listening to French can be increased by: joining a local '*Cercle Français*' or other French club; using your French Assistant(e); or joining an evening class. There are also many intensive language days and courses all over the country, many are organized by ALL (The Association for Language Learning, *see* appendix 2) others by local universities, polytechnics and Colleges of Further Education. There are also many '*Stages d'été*' in France as well as the possibility of finding part-time employment there. The '*Service Culturel*' of the French Institute will provide a full list of courses and the Central Bureau for Educational visits and Exchanges has information about jobs and other activities (*see* appendix 2).

Reading and writing

You will be required to do more writing in French at A Level than you did for GCSE and, of the four skills, writing has slightly more marks assigned to it in the examination. The writing section of the exam will test your ability to produce French with a minimum of spelling and grammatical errors and to express and order your ideas clearly. Marks are given for accuracy and expression, so both are important. You will need to check your written French for mistakes in a routine way and establish a system for checking spelling, gender, agreement and tense (*See* page 88 for specific guidance). This is particularly important with coursework in French since this will not be corrected for you by your teacher before being sent to the Examination Board for marking.

Apart from the written tasks you do as assignments there are other ways in which you can practise writing French with a practical purpose.

Firstly correspond regularly with a pen-friend. When deciding on a correspondant, you might like to bear in mind that French is a language used by people every day in many other parts of the world apart from France: in Canada; large parts of the African continent; Madagascar and islands in the Indian ocean; in some of the Caribbean and South Pacific islands (e.g.Tahiti); as well as in parts of Switzerland, Belgium, Luxemburg and the Lebanon.

You could also write letters to France to gather information for your topic work or to pursue interests or hobbies that will almost certainly be represented by clubs or organizations in France. It is also worth contacting your local Chamber of Commerce or LX centre (government-sponsored Language and Export Centres, *see* appendix 2) to discover what firms in your area are doing business with France, or French-speaking countries and who might find your services helpful.

The reading you do for A Level covers a wide range of texts. If you choose a literary option, you will be dealing with plays and novels. Non-literary options will introduce you to various aspects of French life and culture. Topics in language work are explored through newspaper and magazine articles, brochures, surveys and marketing reports which cover aspects, issues and concerns of everyday life.

There are three kinds of reading process that you might need: **skimming** (reading quickly through a text to find out what it is about); **scanning** (to find particular information); and **reading** (closely to extract full detail).

In practice scanning and skimming go together, particularly in the early part of your sixth-form course. You need a lot of practice before you can do them efficiently. You will complain at first that you are always having to read carefully because you find it difficult to come to grips with the meanings of words and phrasing of sentences at the same time. It is worth bearing in mind not every word necessarily counts in a text and it is sometimes better to skip over obstacles rather than keep coming to a dead halt.

You will get quite a bit of practice from the reading you do in class and from set texts. You will also have to read using your own initiative in connection with any topic work you do. This might involve regular dips into magazines and newspapers as well as into books where you are looking for relevant passages or details.

You should also try to be as wide-ranging as possible in choosing what you read in French. Bilingual texts of all kinds are now commonplace: labels; instructions and directions for installation; holiday and tourist brochures. See what your local tourist bureau has to offer in French. You can improve your reading skills, enlarging and consolidating your other language skills, by actively looking out for this kind of material.

Your place of study will probably subscribe to magazines and newspapers. The *Authentik* publication (*see* page 208) has a good range of articles from the French press. The French monthly magazine for 16 to 18-year-olds *Phosphore* is an excellent publication; informative and relevant to this age group, written in a language you will be able to understand (*see* appendix 4).

Some popular magazines, especially in the feminine press, are now available in French and English. Examples are: *Cosmopolitan*; *Anna* (a German publication, but appears in French and English); *Elle*; and *Marie-Claire*. These magazines nearly all produce a different version for the British market. *Anna* however has a certain number of articles and adverts that are the same or similar in both languages. Having both versions not only gives you the possibility of comparing language but also of scanning or skimming and checking with the English version and of trying translations both ways yourself. In the case of different versions, it is interesting and enlightening to compare the choice of material chosen for the respective countries.

Check what your local library, college or polytechnic has to offer. Many English detective stories, as well as other novels, have been translated into French. Try dipping into some that you are already familiar with in English. You should also find helpful the bilingual texts in the series *Les Langues Pour Tous* published in France by Presse Pocket. The latter are often taken from the classics of English literature and are intended for French students studying English. If you are also doing English Literature at A Level you might find a translation of one of your set texts and you might '*faire d'une pierre deux coups*'!

The ability to read and understand French more and more easily has positive advantages. It enables you to pursue and develop your hobbies and interests through the medium of French. Whether you are keen on fishing, windsurfing, stamp-collecting or environmental issues there will be plenty of organizations in France with whom you can get in touch and whose publications or magazines you can acquire. The tables on pages xii–xiii give a language-task breakdown for Boards examining at A and AS Levels. Make sure you read carefully the detailed syllabus for your particular Board. Get hold of a copy!

Examination Boards: Addresses

AEB The Associated Examining Board
Stag Hill House, Guildford, Surrey GU2 5XJ

Cambridge University of Cambridge Local Examinations Syndicate
Syndicate Buildings, 1 Hills Road, Cambridge CB1 2EU

JMB Joint Matriculation Board
Manchester M15 6EU

London University of London Examinations and Assessment Council
Stewart House, 32 Russell Square, London WC1 5DN

Northern Northern Ireland Schools Examinations and Assessment Council
Ireland Beechill House, 42 Beechill Road, Belfast BT8 4RS

Oxford Oxford Delegacy of Local Examinations
Ewert House, Ewert Place, Summertown, Oxford OX2 7BZ

Oxford and Oxford and Cambridge Schools Examination Board
Cambridge (a) Purbeck House, Purbeck Road, Cambridge CB2 IPU
(b) Elsfield Way, Oxford OX2 7BZ

Scottish Scottish Examinations Board
Ironmills Road, Dalkeith, Midlothian EH22 1LE

WJEC Welsh Joint Education Committee
245 Western Avenue, Cardiff CF5 2YX

Studying advice

Your work will be more purposeful and effective if you can get yourself organized from the beginning. You could start with a loose-leaf folder and some dividers. Main divisions will be: language, listening grammar, literature, topic, and vocabulary. These can then be further sub-divided where necessary.

Language This should be divided into the main skills tested by your particular Examination Board. Start with writing in French. Include here notes from class discussions on various topics, useful phrases and vocabulary and any copies of texts used. Over the period of your course, add assignments, essays (or other pieces of work) and themes for essays that might figure in the examination. If you work out model answers to the latter, reduce these to a series of headings so that they will be easier to memorize. Under 'language' you could also include sections for: translation both ways; paraphrase; cloze exercises; summary; reading comprehension; and any exercises you have done.

Listening This should include a note of the theme of passages that you heard plus your written answers, noting any words whose sound you found difficult. Also, include a note of any weekly listening practice done by yourself and what it was about.

Grammar This section should contain notes on explanations done in class, with examples, and any exercises you have done.

Literature This section would include your summary of the action and characters for each text, notes on the author and his or her background (either from classwork or your own research), as well as essays done and possible themes for further questions. You might also include *brief* quotations that usefully illustrate particular points.

Topic Here you should include your outlines for possible themes of research and the sources consulted and any notes on these as well as copies of texts or visual material.

continued page xiv

Analysis of examination syllabuses — A Level

Key for syllabus analysis
O   Required in detail at A Level
*   Dictionaries permitted
**   One of a choice of options
[1] See note 1 below

	AEB	Cambridge	JMB	London **[2] (Syllabus A)	NISEC	Oxford
Written examination papers (% total mark)	1 Listening 20 (1 h) 2 Reading 20 (2 h) 3 Writing 20 (2½ h) 4 Topic 20 (2½ h)	3 Listening 20 (1 h) 4 Reading /Writing 25 (2½ h) 5 Essay 10 (1½ h) 7 Literature 20 (3 h)	1 Literature 20 (3 h) 2 Reading /Writing 35 (3 h) 3 Listening 20 (1h 20 min)	1 Listening 15 (45 mins) 2 Literature 25 (2 h) 4 Writing /essay 20 (2½ h) 5 Translation/ reading 20 (2 h)	2 Listening 15 (45 mins) 3 Reading/ Writing 30 (2½ h) 4 Prose essay 20 (2½ h) 5 Literature 20 (2½ h)	2 Reading Writing (2 h) 3 Listenin (1 h) 4 Writing + 10 (1½–3h)
Oral examination (% total mark)	5 Oral 20 (20 min)	1/2 Oral 25 (20 min)	Oral 20 (15 min)	6 Oral 20 (20 mins)	1 Oral 15 (20 mins)	1 Oral (30-35
Course-work topic (% total mark)		6 Coursework (see note 1) 20	1 Topic** 25			5 Coursev (see not
Listening tasks						
1 Questions and answers in English	O	O	O	O	O	
2 Questions and answers in French		O	O			O*
3 Summary in English		O	O			O*
4 Gist identification			O			
5 Completing 'gapped' transcript		O	O			
6 Retranslation			O			
7 Discrepancies in transcript			O			
8 Non verbal responses: Multiple; choice; True/false; Grid-filling; Sequencing		O	O			
Reading and writing tasks						
1 Questions and answers in English	O	O		O	O	
2 Questions and answers in French						O*
3 Questions in French on an English text	O	O				
4 Summary in English		O				
5 Summary in French	O	O			O	
6 Comparison between two texts		O				
7 Cloze tests			O			
8 Paraphrasing in French			O			O*
9 Translation into English (full passage)	O			O	O	
10 Translation into English (short extract)			O			O*
11 Translation into French (full passage)					O	
12 Translation into French (short extract)	O			O		
13 Retranslation			O	O		
14 Explanation of context		O				
Writing tasks						
1 Essay in French: pre-set topics		O				O*
2 Writing from stimulus	O	O		O	O	
3 Discursive writing			O	O	O	
4 Descriptive writing			O	O	O	
5 Narrative			O	O		
6 Imaginative writing			O	O		
7 Dialogue			O	O		
8 Letter writing			O	O	O	
9 Report making					O	
10 Writing based on video						O*
11 Writing a short article						
Topic: literary and non-literary						
1 Examined literary questions and answers in English			O	O	O	
2 Examined literary questions and answers in French		O	O			O*
3 Examined non-literary questions and answers in English				O		
4 Examined non-literary questions and answers in French	O			O		O*
5 Coursework in French		O	O			O
6 Extended essay in English						
7 Extended essay in French		O				
Oral tasks						
1 General conversation	O	O	O	O	O	
2 Conversation on topic/book	O	O	O	O		O*
3 Conversation on stimulus material	O			O	O*	O*
4 Role-play		O				
5 Reporting		O				O*
6 Interpreting and eliciting information						O*

Notes 1 Options for A-Level Coursework: 1 item coursework + 2 exam questions (2 h); **or** 2 items coursework + 1 exam question (1 h)
2 London A-Level, Syllabus B: 1 Listening (45 mins) **10%** 2 Topic (2 h) **20%** 3 Guided writing (1½ h) **15%** 4 Translation into French (1½ h) **15%** 5 Translation into English and reading comprehension (2 h) **20%** 6 Oral (20 mins) **30%**

			AS Level							
Oxford and Cambridge (see note 4)	**SEB** (Scottish Higher Certificate)	**WJEC**	**AEB**	**Cambridge**	**JMB**	**London**[**²] (Syllabus A)	**NISEC**	**Oxford**	**Oxford and Cambridge**	**WJEC**
Listening 20 (h) Reading 20 Writing** 20 (h) Literature/ Civilization 20 (¾ h) 20	**1** Reading 30 (1¾ h) **2** Listening/ Writing 20 (1 h) **3** Essay 13.3 (1¼ h) **4** Cloze test 6.6 (½ h)	**1** Reading 20 (2½ h) **2** Writing 20 (3 h) **3** Listening 20 (1 h) **5** Literature/** 20 (2½ h) **5** Extended language 20 (1½ h)	**1** Listening 35 (1 h) **2** Reading 35 (1¼ h)	**3** Listening** 30 (40 mins) **4** Reading 30 (1 h)	**1** Listening 30 (1 h 10 mins) **2** Reading 30 (2 h)	**1** Listening 25 (45 mins) **2** Reading 25 (1 h) **3** Writing 15 (1 h)	**1** Listening 30 (45 mins) **2** Reading/ Writing 40 (1½ h)	**2** Reading 35 (1½h) **3** Listening 35 (1 h)	**1** Listening 20 (1 h) **2** Reading 40 (2½ h)	**1** Listening 40 (1 h) **2** Reading 40/20 (2½ h)
al 20 (0 min) 20	**4** Oral 30 (15 min)	**4** Oral 20 (15-20 min)	**3** Oral 30 (20 min)	**1** Oral 40 (20 min)	Oral 40 (15 min)	**4** Oral 35 (20 min)	**1** Oral 30 (20 min)	**1** Oral 30 (20 min)	**3** Oral 40 (30 min)	**3** Oral 20/40 (10/15-20min)
oject**		**5** Project** 20		**2** Topic 30	**2** Topic** 30					
O*		O	O	O	O	O	O		O*	O
	O*			O				O*	O*	
				O	O			O*		
					O					
O*				O					O*	
O*	O*	O	O	O	O	O*	O		O*	O
								O*		
O*				O					O*	O
	O*	O*					O			
				O						
O	O									
O	O*									
O*										
O*	O*	O						O*	O*	O
O		O*								
		O*								
				O						
		O*								
		O*								
O		O*								
O	O*	O*								
O	O*	O*								
O		O*					O*	O		O*
		O*					O*	O		
		O*						O		
O		O								
		O								
O										
O		O								
					O					
				O						
										(option 1)
		O*	O	O	O		O			O*
O*	O	O*	O	O	O	O*		O*	O*	O*
O*	O		O				O*	O*	O*	
O*		O*			O	O*			O*	O
					O					
		O*				O*		O*		O*

3 Oxford writing/coursework options: 2 items coursework; 2 exam questions (3h); 1 item coursework + 1 exam question (1½h); 1 exam question (1½h) + viewing test (1½h); 1 item coursework + viewing test (1½h)

4 Oxford & Cambridge 'writing' – choice of two from: free composition; prose composition; use of French; project option (in place of 1 exam question)

Vocabulary You might want to include this section within topics or you may prefer to keep a separate book for this purpose. Whichever you choose, have some way of dividing words from their meanings so that you can cover up one side for learning purposes. You might want to list words under themes. For example: pollution; health; poverty; population; transport; education; war; racial problems; and national characteristics. This depends on the requirements of your Board. You may wish to list words under the headings of: people; emotions; things; and ideas. For learning purposes, make a distinction between active and passive words (i.e. between those you are going to need to use and those which only need to be recognized). It is helpful to put *un* or *une* in front of each noun so that you can memorize the gender at the same time and to give plural or feminine forms if these are irregular.

Using your system

Once you have got a system working it makes it easier to file material regularly. When you do this, think about the best place to put each piece of work. This will make you read through what is already there. Make a regular habit of looking through the sections of your file but don't just be content with reading through. For example, when looking at the material on essays ask yourself 'How would I say this?' or 'What's the word for?'. Look these up and add them to your system. Also, add any other articles you come across that deal with similar or related themes and underline useful words or expressions in them.

When you have accumulated several pieces of written French, in the form of exercises, start listing the kinds of mistakes you have been making (e.g. label them T for tense, Gen for gender, Gr for grammar, V for vocabulary, A for agreement, and S for spelling). In this way you will discover where you tend to make most mistakes and be able to take effective action.

This process will sometimes refer you back to the grammar section. You may have to look the point up in this book or elsewhere. Try to find exercises to practise the point and discuss it with a teacher or friend. If retranslation (or translation into French) is one of the skills needed, make a list of reoccuring structure words like: 'yet'; 'ago'; 'according to'; 'because of'; 'thanks to'; and so on. Also make a list of grammar points that reoccur in cloze exercises.

In the literature section, go over essays you have done and improve them with the help of the teacher's corrections. You can then reduce these to note form for memorization and revision purposes. Note the weak points in your essays: retelling the story to no purpose; not discussing the real question; and not using references to the text to support your arguments. You can improve on these aspects!

Make a regular habit of learning vocabulary, enlisting the help of a friend to test you if possible. If you highlight words that cause difficulty, you will automatically re-read these every time you look down a column. Explore and add further vocabulary by investigating different themes.

Revision

If you have been working on a regular basis, as suggested above, you will have been doing the kind of revision necessary for effective language learning. You will feel less inclined to try and cram everything into the few weeks before the exam. Part of the secret is making effective use of time available **during your course**. Set yourself a target of a number of hours per week (say 10–15) which will include doing work set as well. Keep a log over a couple of weeks and treat yourself to time off if you have achieved your target. For example, those 45 or so minutes while you are waiting for tea can soon add up and swell your total.

Examiners are always drawing attention to lack of basic knowledge of vocabulary and grammar. One excellent way of dealing with this is to get hold of a detailed GCSE syllabus and to read through the lists of language tasks, communication strategies and vocabulary by topic areas – the one available from the Northern Examining Association is a good example. You will find that you already know a lot of it but you will also find blank spots and things that you only half-know. Doing this will plug the gaps in your understanding and reinforce what you are already familiar with.

Well before the examination, say two months, work out a revision timetable. Make a list of priorities based on how long ago you did something and on the kinds of mistakes you are tending to repeat. Go through these systematically with the most distant and most persistent faults first, ticking off what you have covered on a wall chart. In the run-up to the exam you should only be dealing with minor or very persistent stumbling blocks.

Do not concentrate on a particular area the day before the exam. **Take time off to do something completely different**.

During the exam, it helps to increase your liquid intake to combat loss of water through perspiration. Increasing the amount of sugar and carbohydrate you eat also helps to compensate for lower blood sugar levels and that empty feeling in your stomach that are commonly experienced at these times.

On the day of an oral exam, make sure you arrive in plenty of time. Make a conscious effort to think in French and hold conversations with yourself in the time before.

In the exam

You should already be familiar with the format and layout of each paper for your particular Board. Nevertheless read through each part carefully, paying special attention to the instructions when there are choices or options available and highlighting them.

1   Read through **all** the questions. Don't just pick the first one you think you can answer.
2   Read each word in the question and underline or highlight key words.
3   Beware of plunging right away into questions that seem a bit like ones you have done before. You can probably use much of the original material but you might have to change the emphasis or order of things.
4   Questions usually have more than one part. Make sure you give sufficient attention to each part.
5   Spend 5–10 minutes planning out your answer.
6   Where passages in French are involved, read these several times. You are bound to meet words you do not understand. Don't panic at this. Some of these might come to you later or you might only need to work out an approximate meaning which will become clearer after several readings. You might not need to know the full meaning of some of them at all! If you highlight the words you don't know, it is helpful when a retranslation follows. By searching through the highlighted items you might be able to guess at a word you need. **Note**: avoid using red or green for your underlining. Examiners use these colours for marking and re-marking.
7   Allocate enough time to do each part of the paper. If you have only a short time left at the end with one question to do, spend time on this (in note form if necessary), rather than on polishing up the ones you have already done. You can get no marks for a question if you have written nothing and the ones you have done will not compensate enough. It is important to look at the number of marks allotted to each question. It gives you an idea of how much detail is needed and a guide to how much time it is profitable to spend on that question. Obviously it is foolish to spend a lot of time on a question that has only 5 marks when an essay for example has 35.
8   Leave time at the end for checking through what you have written. Make sure you have underlined titles, used inverted commas where required, checked spelling and punctuation. Apply a language-accuracy check to your written French (*see* page 88).

Part I Vocabulary

1 Common word patterns

Learning words and their meanings is an on-going process. We continue to meet words in English that we haven't seen or heard before. Some of these are committed to memory straight away, others are forgotten completely. Some will look familiar when you meet them again but you can't quite remember what they mean. You may find concrete words (i.e. words standing for objects) easier to memorize because you have a picture in your mind to go with them. Abstract words (i.e. ones standing for an idea) are often more difficult to store in your mind. They are best remembered when associated with a word you already know.

Broadly speaking, words in English and in foreign languages fall into three categories: **active words** (i.e. words you can understand straight away and use in writing and speaking); **passive words** (i.e. ones that you can recognize when you see or hear them but that you cannot retrieve instantly from your memory store); and **deducible words** (i.e. that you can work out the meaning of because of what you already know of the language). There is probably a gradual movement of words from the third category towards the first category, depending on how often you use or meet them. The gradual assimilation process in language learning already mentioned also plays its part.

Recording and learning vocabulary

It is essential to have a vocabulary book in which you write down new words as you meet them. Write in two columns (one for the word and one for its meanings) so that you can cover up one side of the page and try to recall one and the other. Be selective in what you write down. Some words are more commonly used than others. Keep one half of the book for words that you may only need to recognize, the other for words that you are more likely to need to use. This decision is not always easy to make on your own. Your teacher is the best guide. It helps to write a short phrase illustrating the meaning, particularly with abstract or idiomatic uses. For example:

que de – what a lot of
Que de bruit! – What a lot of noise!

It is helpful to put *un* or *une* in front of nouns so that you learn the gender at the same time. You could also try writing masculine words in blue and feminine ones in red. You also need to note any irregularities in plurals or feminine endings and with verbs the group it belongs to together with the past participle, if this is odd. Write clearly because your visual impression is a part of the memorizing process. Record words on a regular basis and also read through your vocabulary book often, preferably getting a friend to test you. If you highlight words that you have difficulty with, every time you read through your vocabulary book your eye will be caught by these and you will be doing a bit of automatic revision.

How do we remember French words and what they mean? Some are easy because they look just like the English word and have roughly the same meaning. These are called **cognates**. Others are deceptive because they look like the English word but have a very different meaning. The term *faux amis* – 'false friends' has been coined for these (*French False Friends* C W E Kirk-Greene, Routledge and Kegan Paul). Other words contain a clue within them. If for example you already know the word *chaud* you might guess that *chaleureux* has got something to do with it. Some words you will remember because of some peculiarity or funny association. The word *poubelle* – dustbin, is one of these and *quincaillerie* – ironmonger's shop, sounds a bit like its meaning. *Caoutchouc*, meaning the substance 'rubber', is not as easily forgotten as its spelling! You might even remember some words because of where you have written them on the page! One thing is certain: the more words you learn, the more you will be able to recognize and guess at others.

Here are some more strategies for learning vocabulary:

Opposites

Learning words as pairs of opposites can also be effective. You may find both words in the same text but more often you will have to look one of them up. A monolingual dictionary is useful for this purpose. You will soon find that there are often several possibilities for the opposite of a word. Adjectives have the widest range; verbs and nouns fewer possibilities. Here are some of the commoner examples:

Adjectives

> *bon – mauvais, meilleur – pire, vrai – faux, dur – tendre/mou, pareil – différent, naturel – artificiel, absurde – logique, modéré – excessif, raisonnable – exagéré, courageux – lâche, faible – fort, supérieur – inférieur*

Nouns

> *espoir – désespoir, puissance – faiblesse, vérité – mensonge, augmentation – réduction, les possédants – les non-possédants* (the haves and the have-nots), *hausse – baisse, patronat – ouvriers, cadres – exécutants*

Verbs

> *augmenter – diminuer, avancer – reculer, conserver – jeter, parler – se taire, économiser – gaspiller*

Check the meanings of the above if you don't recognize them. Check the feminine forms of the adjectives. Find a phrase to use them in.

Word families

Grouping words around a theme, or building word families, can also be a helpful memorizing process. There is some evidence to suggest that we store words in our own language in fields or areas of meaning (*Words in the Mind*, J Aitchison, Blackwell). Therefore, it would seem sensible to use this existing pattern to create word families in another language. For example, words to do with politics:

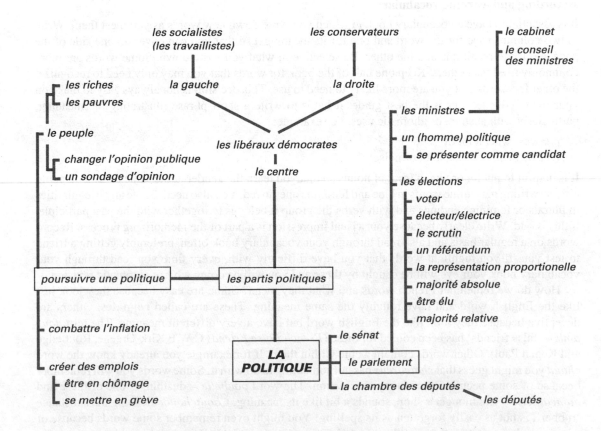

The above example is a fairly detailed one. You might find that a simplified version works better for you. You could also try colour-coding parts of your diagram.

Another variation of family grouping is synonym building. This can help you to think of alternative words to use instead of always sticking to the same word or expression. (*See also* page 126.)

Adjective 'size'

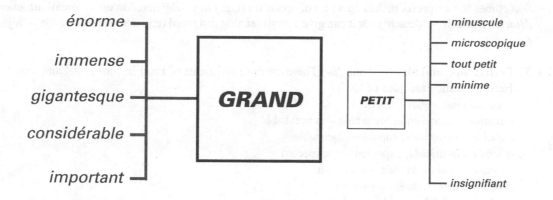

Verb 'saying'

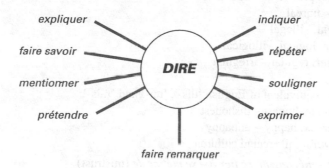

Common patterns of words in French and English

Knowing and recognizing patterns of words in French, and their similarities with English ones, can be a great help in vocabulary building and give you access to more words. It gives you a big advantage in reading comprehension because you can work out meanings more easily. It helps in writing because you can deduce and generate words yourself. It also helps with paraphrase and language exercises, helping you to manipulate words with greater facility. The beginnings and endings of words (i.e. the prefixes and suffixes) are the keys to this skill.

Prefixes

1   **Prefix: 'ré-', 're-', or 'r-'** This changes the meaning of many verbs to 'again', 'once more' or 'back'. Here are some examples:

voir – revoir:
J'espère la revoir cet été – I hope to see her again this summer

s'insérer – se réinsérer:
Après cinq années en prison il est difficile de se réinsérer à la société
After 5 years in prison it is difficult to readapt to social life

appeler – rappeler:
Je ne me rappelle plus son nom – I can't remember his name any more
Rappelle-moi demain – Call me back tomorrow

avoir – ravoir:
Est-ce que je peux ravoir mon livre? – Can I have my book back?

2   **Prefix: 'de-' or 'dé-'** This has the same value as the 'un-' prefix in English but also of 'de-' and 'dis-'.

Déboutonnez votre chemise – Unbutton your shirt
J'ai vite défait le paquet – I quickly undid the parcel

La Lozère est un département très dépeuplé – The Lozère is a very depopulated 'département'
Il faut désarmer tous les pays du monde – We must disarm all the countries of the world
Sometimes the *de*-prefix makes up a pair of opposites (e.g. *faire – défaire*, 'do up' – 'undo' *attacher – détacher*, 'attach' – 'detach'). Or it can give a new meaning to a word (e.g. *détourner un avion* – 'hijack a plane').

3 **Prefix: *'in-'* and also *'ir-'* and *'il-'*** These are the equivalents of English 'un-', 'in-' and 'non-'. Here are some examples of *'in-'*:
égal – inégal, equal – unequal
cassable – incassable, breakable – unbreakable
capable – incapable, capable – incapable
✓*attendu – inattendu*, expected – unexpected
connu – inconnu, known – unknown
direct – indirect, direct – indirect
visible – invisible, visible – invisible

Note
'in' + vowel is pronounced as *'ine'* (as in *'mine'*, *'fine'*)
'in' + consonant is pronounced as *'in'* (as in *'vin'*, *'pin'*)

Here are some examples of *'ir-'* and *'il-'*:
✓ *réel – irréel*, real – unreal
légal – illégal, legal – illegal
logique – illogique, logical – illogical
régulier – irrégulier, regular – irregular

4 **Prefix: *'mal-'*** The equivalent of English 'dis-', 'un-' and 'mis-':
honnête – malhonnête, honest – dishonest
heureux – malheureux, happy – unhappy
✓*des enfants maltraités* – ill-treated children

Note also *content – **mé**content, se fier à – se **mé**fier de* (mistrust)

5 **Prefix: *'pre-'*** Equivalent of English 'for-', 'pre-'. Here are some examples:
✓*Il est impossible de prédire l'heure de son arrivée* – forecast, fortell
On n'avait pas prévu toutes les difficultés – We hadn't foreseen all the difficulties
✓*Un préjugé c'est une opinion préconçue* – Prejudice is a preconceived opinion

✓**6** **Prefixes: *'sur-'* and *'sous-'*** These work just like the English 'under-', 'over-':
la surproduction
les régions surpeuplées
les pays sous-développés
Note also
✓ *souligner* – underline, stress
Un film russe avec sous-titres – A Russian film with subtitles

✓**7** **Prefix: *'mi-'*** Equivalent of half, part. Here are some examples:
la mi-temps dans un match – half-time
s'arrêter à mi-chemin – half-way
répondre à mi-voix – in a low voice, whisper
les yeux mi-clos – half-closed eyes

Suffixes

1 **Suffix: *'-tion'*** There are a large number of words in French and English with this suffix. Many have more or less the same meaning. They are **all feminine gender words**. For example:

situation – position – compétition – variation – intention – contradiction

Others don't have exactly the same spelling or suffix in English:
traduction – translation
punition – punishment
réparation – repairs

Others have different meanings to the word they look like in English:

manifestation – demonstration

✓ *formation* – training

✓ *revendication* – claim, demand

✓ *Les revendications des manifestants étaient légitimes. Ils demandaient une augmentation de salaire* – The claims of the demonstrators were well-founded. They were asking for a wage increase.

2 Suffix: '-té' and '-tié' Roughly the equivalents of '-ty' in English but also of '-ness' and '-ship'. For example:

beau – beauté

solidaire – solidarité

égal – égalité

pauvre – pauvreté

libre – liberté

✓ *sain – santé*

✓ *gai – gaieté*

ami – amitié

propre – propreté

Note

(a) *propriété* means property

(b) words with the *'-té'*, *'-tié'* suffixes, of abstract meaning, are all **feminine**

3 Suffix: '-eur' This comprises a large group of words to do with size, colour, human and abstract qualities. They are mostly of feminine gender. Thay have no single corresponding suffix in English. For example:

blanc – blancheur

grand – grandeur

chaud – chaleur

haut – hauteur

rouge – rougeur

profond – profondeur

la couleur – une odeur

Note

le bonheur – happiness

le malheur – unhappiness

un honneur – an honour

Also in *'-eur'* there are a large number of words denoting occupations and professions, mainly of masculine gender:

un employeur

un professeur

✓ *un producteur* (films, industry)

✓ *un metteur en scène* (producer, theatre)

✓ *un réalisateur* (producer, television)

Look up the section on gender for the **feminine** equivalents of these.

4 Suffix: '-er' This is another common suffix denoting occupation, often the equivalent of '-er' in English. For example:

épicier

policier

banquier

hôtelier

cuisinier

fermier

5 Suffix: '-able' This makes a verb into an adjective. Here are some examples:

faire – faisable

imaginer – imaginable

manger – mangeable

laver – lavable

réparer – réparable

trouver – trouvable (introuvable)

Note

potable – drinkable

eau potable – drinking water

6 Suffix: *'-ette'* This ending indicates a smaller version of something and is always feminine. For example:

un cigare – une cigarette

une fille – une fillette

une tarte – une tartelette

une fourche (gardening) *– une fourchette* (eating)

un banc – une banquette (seat in train, car)

Note

un banquet – banquet (ceremonial dinner)

7 Suffix: *'-eux' '-ieux'* These suffixes are equivalent to the English '-ous'. Here are some examples:

mystérieux

courageux

sérieux

dangereux

furieux

contagieux

précieux

furieux

montagneux

religieux

8 Suffix: *'-aire'* This is the English '-ar' and '-ary':

populaire

un salaire

vulgaire

nécessaire

une secrétaire

extraordinaire

élémentaire

primaire

un anniversaire

un millionnaire

9 Suffix: *'-que'* This is the English '-c', '-ck', '-cal', and '-k':

automatique

classique

une attaque

une remarque

économique

logique

une banque

plastique

romantique

tragique

une brique

physique

10 Suffix: *'-er'* These verbs in French are '-ate' verbs in English:

faciliter

exagérer

imiter

compliquer

faciliter

abdiquer

améliorer

compenser

11 Suffix: '-e' This ending in French is the consonant ending (no '-e')in English:
le calme
modeste
une insulte
un adulte
moderne
une lampe
le pilote
rapide
une plante

12 Suffix: '-ant' This present participle ending in French is the '-ing' in English:
charmant
✓ *choquant*
dégoûtant
intéressant
préoccupant (worrying)
provoquant
amusant
insultant
brillant

13 Suffix: '-ment' This adverbial ending in French is the '-ly' in English:
absolument
rarement
sûrement
généralement
gravement
énormément
sincèrement
complètement
immédiatement

Note (*see also* page 72)
évident – évidemment
constant – constamment
récent – récemment
fréquent – fréquemment

Near cognates

These are words that come from the same root in both languages but have acquired a French or an English 'look' as the case may be:

1 French **'gu-'**, English 'w-' (a small group):
la guerre
Guillaume (*le prénom*)
une guêpe – wasp
guetter – keep watch, look out
un guerrier – warrior

2 Initial **'e-'** in French, initial 's' in English:
école
étable
étage (d'un bâtiment)
étudiant
étrangler
estomac
étranger
état
✓ *épeler* – spell

The French word might be a bit 'buried' in the English one. Can you work out what the following mean?

regarder le petit écran

Il fait si chaud! On va s'étouffer ici

✓*une carte à grande échelle*

✓*Marie Antoinette est morte sur l'échafaud*

l'écureuil est un animal très agile

3 **'-êt', '-ât', 'ôt'** in French, '-est', '-aste', 'ost' in English:

une bête

une tempête

un hôte

✓*la crête (d'une montagne)*

la pâte (dentifrice)

la hâte

le mât (d'un bateau)

une fête

Having pointed out a number of parallels between French and English words, the following stumbling blocks should be noted:

4 **Nouns**

un psychologue – psychologist

un scientifique – scientist

un sociologue – sociologist

un psychiatre – psychiatrist

un photographe – photographer

un homme politique – politician

un géographe – geographer

5 **Adjectives**

pessimiste – pessimistic

optimiste – optimistic

évoquateur – evocative

réaliste – realistic

bénéfique – beneficial

bénévole (un groupe bénévole) – voluntary group

conservateur (le parti politique) – conservative

Exercices

1 Cherchez dans le cercle à droite le contraire des adjectifs suivants:

grand	premier	vrai
bon	sale	faible
dur	pauvre	long
sage	privé	doux
nouveau	jeune	stupide

mauvais	fort	sec
tendre	ancien	propre
petit	vieux	court
méchant	riche	intelligent
dernier	faux	public

2 Dites la même chose d'une façon différente. Par exemple:

Ce n'est pas correct – C'est incorrect

Il n'est pas content – Il est mécontent

(a) Il n'est pas honnête

(b) Cette marque n'est pas connue en France

✓ (c) Cette occasion n'est pas ordinaire

(d) Cette date n'est pas possible

(e) Il n'est pas heureux

(f) Cette information n'est pas utile

✓ (g) Ce rendez-vous n'est pas convenable

✓ (h) Je ne suis pas optimiste

(i) Cette viande n'est pas tendre

✓ (j) Ce n'est pas bon marché

3 Completez ces phrases:
  le bonheur et le
  en hiver et en
  grand-père et
  en bas et en
  entrer et
✓ le pour et le
  le chaud et le
  le matin et l(e)
  mon neveu et ma
  jour et
✓ faire et
  une photo en noir et
  le bien et le
  le début et la
  frère et
  arriver et
  question de vie ou de
  pile ou

4 Dites le contraire sans employer le négatif:
  (a) Je regarde peu la télévision
  (b) Je vais quelquefois à Paris
  (c) C'est loin d'ici
  (d) J'adore les frites
  (e) Il fait déjà jour
  (f) A la fin de l'après-midi
  (g) Cette eau est pure
  (h) Au premier étage
  (i) Le chef est de mauvaise humeur
  (j) Cette fourchette est propre

5 Without using a dictionary, make a collection of French words ending in '*-tion*' that have the same spelling as their English counterparts. Find at least one for as many letters as possible of the alphabet. Do this with a friend or make it a team game and compare your lists afterwards. Score nought for getting the same word as the other team. Check the meanings in a dictionary

6 Do the same thing with words that end in '*-ty*' in English and '*-té*' in French (e.g. *éternité* – eternity, *rapidité* – rapidity).

7 Repeat the same activity, this time with '*-er*' verbs that closely resemble English verbs (e.g. *danser* – dance, *changer* – change, *avancer* – advance).

8 'Le chat de ma tante' Use one of two phrases: *Le chat de ma tante est adorable/ bilingue/ charmant* or *Ma tante a un chat adorable / bilingue / charmant* (the second one practises position of adjectives) and work through the alphabet. You can leave out very difficult letters. This works well as a team game. You must be ready to justify the adjective used (e.g. *le chat de ma tante est affecté parce qu'il prend toujours ses repas dans la salle à manger*).

9 Other variations on this are: *Le chat de ma tante sait* + verb (e.g. **arranger** *les fleurs*); or + adverb (e.g. *Le chat de ma tante chante* **affreusement**).

10 Combien des appareils cités ci-dessous est-ce que vous possédez dans votre maison? Faites trois listes:
  (a) Ceux qui sont indispensables
  (b) Ceux qui sont assez utiles
  (c) Comparez votre liste avec celle de votre voisin

  Un adoucisseur d'eau, un aspirateur, une cafetière électrique, un congélateur, un couteau électrique, une cuisinière électrique, une essoreuse, un fer à coiffer, un fer à repasser, un flash électronique, une perceuse électrique, une friteuse électrique, un gaufrier, un

grille-pain automatique, une hotte de cuisine, une huche à pain, un lave-vaisselle, une machine à coudre, une machine à éplucher les pommes de terre, une machine à tricoter, un mixer à main, un moulin à café électrique, un pèse-personne, un radio-réveil, un rasoir électrique, un réfrigérateur, une rôtissoire électrique, une tondeuse à gazon, une trancheuse électrique, une tronçonneuse, un four à micro-ondes, un sèche-linge, un magnétoscope, une caméra vidéo, un lecteur de disques compacts à laser, un micro-ordinateur, une chaîne hi-fi, un lave-linge, une baignoire à remous.

2 Dictionaries

A good dictionary is an essential tool for all language learners. It is worth spending some time and money over your choice. You will need to use it during language lessons, when working on your own and, increasingly, during the exam itself, depending on the rules of the Examination Board. It is important that you are familiar with using your copy and what it can do for you. Some Examining Boards specify a monolingual dictionary (i.e. a French–French one as used by native speakers). More often though a bilingual dictionary is allowed (i.e. a French–English, English–French one). Both types of dictionary are useful and ideally you should have both.

The very small pocket dictionary that you probably had for GCSE has a very limited use at A Level. When considering buying a larger dictionary, check when it was printed or last revised. Dictionaries get out of date very quickly.

A reliable bilingual dictionary will help with eveything you need including translation from English into French. A monolingual one lacks an English–French section but has many other advantages. It will help you to think more in the language since meanings are explained in French. It will help you to write more accurate and appropriate French because you will often be able to use or adapt phrases, descriptions and definitions from the text of the dictionary. It will also give you synonyms and perhaps antonyms (opposites) which are helpful when attempting paraphrasing tasks.

Dictionaries
Collins–Robert English–French French–English Dictionary, 2nd edition, 1987 Collins (bilingual)

Dictionnare du Français (1980), Larousse (monolingual)
Dictionnaire de la Langue Française (1975), Clé (monolingual, 2 vols)
Petit Larousse Illustré (1992), Larousse, Dictionary and encyclopedia (monolingual)

Contents of a dictionary

Preface or Introduction – Avant-propos

This is usually contained in the first few pages. It explains the theory behind the selection of words, their meanings, and the conventions of spelling/ordering of words adopted by the compilers of the dictionary. An explanation of the abbreviations used is often included here also. This section can be very helpful in getting you to know how to use the dictionary.

List of abbreviations – Abbréviations

These are the abbreviations used in the text of the dictionary itself. They may be included in the introduction. The more important ones will be dealt with below. Some dictionaries also have under the heading of 'abbreviations' a list of acronyms, *sigles* in French. More recently, published dictionaries have omitted this kind of list since it gets out of date rapidly. Instead they include the more common acronyms, like HLM *(habitation à loyer modéré),* within the text of the dictionary itself. You need to be familiar with many of the French acronyms in everyday use.

Phonetic guide to pronunciation – Système phonétique et transcription

In table form, this lists the vowels and consonants with their phonetic symbols in square brackets [ ] and examples of pronunciation. A monolingual dictionary might also give the range of spellings that can represent each sound. This can be useful, for example for 'sorting out' the spellings for the four nasal sounds in French. A bilingual dictionary will also have a corresponding section for the sounds of English.

Grammar section

Most dictionaries have a complete list of regular and irregular verbs. Bilingual ones sometimes have a grammar outline. Monolingual dictionaries usually just have a verb list but often deal with some grammatical usage in the text. For example, under the entry *dans* you could find a summary and comparison of the various uses of *dans* and *en* meaning 'in'. Monolingual dictionaries sometimes have lists of prefixes and suffixes used in the construction of words. From these you can see patterns for turning verbs into nouns, nouns into adjectives and for changing the sense of a verb by a prefix. This is a helpful back-up to the Vocabulary and Common Patterns sections of this book.

Other sections

Some recently published bilingual dictionaries contain a section on language structures useful in essay-writing, debating and discussion. It gives examples of phrases and expressions for a variety of language functions. This can be a particularly valuable section and should be consulted in conjunction with the relevant sections of this book.

Some monolingual dictionaries have a *travaux pratiques* section with exercises designed to expand and enhance use of language with the help of the dictionary. Since these exercises are designed for native speakers they can prove difficult for learners. They are nevertheless worth looking at later in your course.

Using a dictionary

French–English section

The main working part of a dictionary is the alphabetical list of words. To be able to use the dictionary quickly and efficiently you need to know the layout and conventions of this section.

Usually, words are listed together with their plurals or the feminine form if these are irregular or, in some bilingual dictionaries, with the parts of a verb. With verbs some dictionaries refer you by number to an irregular verb list. Next, in square brackets, there is a phonetic transcription of the sound of the word. For example:

cheval, -aux [ʃ(ə)val, o] *faux, fausse* [fo, fos]

Grammatical abbreviations

This is followed by a grammatical abbreviation telling you what part of speech the word is. You will need to be familiar with the lists on page 12:

English	French
a. – adjective	adj. – *adjectif*
adv. – adverb	adv. – *adverbe*
{n. – noun	n. – *nom* } one or
{s. – substantive	s. – *substantif* } other is used
v.tr.– verb transitive	v.tr.– *verbe transitif*
v.i. – verb intransitive	v.i. – *verbe intransitif*
v. – verb	v. – *verbe*
f.– feminine	f. – *féminin*
m. – masculine	m.– *masculin*
pl – plural	pl – *pluriel*

Definitions

Following the abbreviation for the part of speech, there is either a definition of the word, if it is a monolingual dictionary, or an English equivalent in a bilingual one. When definitions are very numerous, they may be divided under Roman numerals (I, II, III etc.) or under numbers (1, 2, 3, etc.). These may again be subdivided under either letters or figures. It saves time when there are many meanings to skim through the main divisions for the most appropriate context for the word you are looking up. Do not just select the first meaning you see on the page. Words with a smaller number of entries are usually just numbered 1, 2, 3, etc. and are much easier to scan.

Not finding a word

It is helpful initially, if you know from the context whether the word is a noun, adjective or verb. However, if you cannot find it listed, it is possibly the plural of a noun/adjective or, even more likely, the past participle/past historic tense of a verb. In this case, you will have to look through infinitives that start with the first three letters of the word. Failing this consult a list of irregular verbs. Don't forget all the compounds of irregular verbs! Check if there is a prefix to the verb. If the word starts with '*re*' it might just be the prefix of a common verb like *faire* (e.g. *refaire* – to remake, re-do; the past historic of which is *je refis, il refit, ils refirent* etc.).

Using the English–French section

Consulting this section to find the right word is a more hazardous process. There are obvious snags to translating word for word. You will most often want to use the English–French section when doing a translation from English to French. Try to resist this temptation when writing an essay, a letter or a report in French. You will derive more benefit and write more accurately if you get used to using a monolingual dictionary.

If you do have to consult the English–French section, the guidelines mentioned previously should still be followed. In addition:

(a) Check the meaning in the French–English section. You should get back to the same word.

(b) Look at the examples given of the word in use. These will give you a better feel for the meaning and you might be able to use or adapt the example phrase. Consulting a monolingual dictionary will give you a further check on the word.

(c) Look at any abbreviations that follow the word: (v.) is vulgar (pop. – *populaire* in French); (fam.) means the word is familiar, (*fam. familier* in French); (sl.) means slang (arg. – *argot* in French); (pej.) means pejorative or insulting (*péj.* in French). The Collins–Robert dictionary has a grading system of asterisks (from one to three) indicating the degree of offensiveness or familiarity of a word. You should exercise great care in the use of such words. Most of them will rarely be suitable for most of the writing tasks at A Level. Other abbreviations might indicate technical, medical, scientific usage and so on. Make sure that the word you are choosing is not too technical or restricted for the context.

(d) Take great care when dealing with English verbs followed by a preposition. The latter can change the meaning of a verb completely. Take the verb 'to run' as an example. French *courir* might be a suitable equivalent in some cases: I ran to catch the bus – *j'ai couru pour attraper l'autobus,* but sentences like 'my car ran into a tree', 'the police ran him in', 'I ran into him yesterday' will all require different verbs in French. A verb like 'run' has a large number of entries, with several sub-sections. When there are a number of prepositional uses listed, it is worth remembering these are listed alphabetically by preposition. This can save time when skimming.

There are some extracts from a current dictionary on pages 13–16 illustrating the points made above and with further explanations: **Source** *Collins–Robert French Dictionary*, 2nd edition 1987.

Noun: forme

1 Phonetic symbols: pronunciation guide.

2 *nf* means noun feminine.

3 (*a*) to (*h*): division of categories of meaning in order of frequency of use from general to specific.

4 ( ) indicate synonyms, words with approximate same meanings in French.

5 ( ) and [ ] indicate area and context of usage, followed by nearest English equivalent in that context.

6 Example in French with meaning in English.

7 Italics indicate specific case e.g. *chapeau sans forme* – 'shapeless hat'.

8 *V* means *voyez* – 'see also' refers you to another example of 'form' under the entry *haut*.

9 * one asterisk or fam. means familiar, conversational or casual use.

forme [fɔʀm(ə)] *nf* (**a**) *(contour, apparence)* form, shape. cet objet est de ∼ ronde/carrée this object is round/square ou is round/square in shape; en ∼ de poire/cloche pear-/bell-shaped; elle a des ∼s gracieuses she has a graceful form ou figure; vêtement qui moule les ∼s clinging ou figure-hugging garment; une ∼ apparut dans la nuit a form ou figure ou shape appeared out of the darkness; n'avoir plus ∼ humaine to be unrecognizable; sans ∼ *chapeau* shapeless; *pensée* formless; prendre la ∼ d'un rectangle to take the form ou shape of a rectangle; prendre la ∼ d'un entretien to take the form of a talk; prendre ∼ *[statue, projet]* to take shape; sous ∼ de comprimés in tablet form; sous la ∼ d'un vieillard in the guise of ou as an old man; sous toutes ses ∼s in all its forms.

(**b**) (*genre*) *[civilisation, gouvernement]* form. les ∼s d'énergie the forms of energy; ∼ de vie (*présence effective*) form of life, life-form; (*coutumes*) way of life; une ∼ de pensée différente de la nôtre a different way of thinking from our own; les animaux ont-ils une ∼ d'intelligence? do animals have a form of intelligence?

(**c**) (*Art, Jur, Littérat, Philos*) form. soigner la ∼ to be careful about form; poème à ∼ fixe fixed-form poem; poème en ∼ d'acrostiche poem forming an acrostic; remarques de pure ∼ purely formal remarks; *aide, soutien* de pure ∼ token (*épith*), nominal; pour la ∼ as a matter of form, for form's sake; en bonne (et due) ∼ in due form; (*fig*) sans autre ∼ de procès without further ado; faites une réclamation en ∼ put in a formal request; *V* fond, vice.

(**d**) (*convenances*) ∼s proprieties, conventions; respecter les ∼s to respect the proprieties ou conventions; refuser en y mettant des ∼s to decline as tactfully as possible; faire une demande dans les ∼s to make a request in the correct form.

(**e**) (*Ling*) form. mettre à la ∼ passive to put in the passive; ∼ contractée contracted form; ∼ de base base form.

(**f**) (*moule*) mould; (*Typ*) forme; *[cordonnier]* last; *[modiste]* (dress) form; (*partie de chapeau*) crown; *V* haut.

(**g**) (*Sport, gén: condition physique*) form. être en ∼ to be on form, be fit, be in good shape; hors de ∼ off form, out of form; en grande ∼ in top ou peak form; retour de ∼ return to form; baisse de ∼ loss of form; retrouver la ∼ to get back into shape ou back on form, get fit again; la ∼ revient his form's coming back; être en pleine ∼ to be right on form*.

(**h**) (*Mus*) ∼ sonate sonata form.

Adjective: courant

1 Feminine form.

2 Phonetic pronunciation with phonetic form e.g. 't' is pronounced.

3 (*a*) to (*d*) meanings with synonyms in French and their English meanings.

4 *V* refers you to other entries under *chien, compte, eau* etc. because there are many meanings under 'running' – the physical action.

courant, e [kuʀɑ̃, ɑ̃t] **1** *adj* (**a**) *(normal, habituel)* dépenses everyday, standard, ordinary; (*Comm*) *modèle, taille, marque* standard. l'usage ∼ everyday ou ordinary ou standard usage; en utilisant les procédés ∼s on gagne du temps it saves time to use the normal ou ordinary ou standard procedures; il nous suffit pour le travail ∼ he'll do us for the routine ou everyday business ou work; *V* vie.

(**b**) (*fréquent*) common. ce procédé est ∼, c'est un procédé ∼ it's quite common practice ou quite a common procedure, it's quite commonplace; ce genre d'incident est très ∼ ici this kind of incident is very common here, this kind of thing is a common occurrence here.

(**c**) (*en cours, actuel*) *année, semaine* current, present; (*Comm*) inst. ou instant (*Brit*), (*Comm*) votre lettre du 5 ∼ your letter of the 5th inst. ou instant (*Brit*) ou of the 5th of this month; *V* expédier, monnaie etc.

(**d**) (*qui court*) *V* chien, compte, eau etc.

14 Dictionaries

Verb: marquer

marquer [maʀke] (1) 1 *vt* (a) (*par un signe distinctif*) *objet personnel* to mark (*au nom de qn* with sb's name); *animal, criminel* to brand; *arbre* to blaze; *marchandise* to label, stamp.

(b) (*indiquer*) *limite, position* to mark; (*sur une carte*) *village, accident de terrain* to mark, show, indicate; [*horloge*] to show; [*thermomètre*] to show, register; [*balance*] to register. marquez la longueur voulue d'un trait de crayon mark off the length required with a pencil; j'ai marqué nos places avec nos valises I've reserved our seats with our cases; j'ai marqué ce jour-là d'une pierre blanche/noire I'll remember it as a red-letter day/black day; marquez d'une croix l'emplacement du véhicule mark the position of the vehicle with a cross; la pendule marque 6 heures the clock points to *ou* shows *ou* says 6 o'clock; (*Couture*) des pinces marquent/une ceinture marque la taille darts emphasize/a belt emphasizes the waist(line); une robe qui marque la taille a dress which shows off the waistline; cela marque (bien) que le pays veut la paix that definitely indicates *ou* shows that the country wants peace, that's a clear sign that the country wants peace.

(c) *événement* to mark. un bombardement a marqué la reprise des hostilités a bomb attack marked the renewal *ou* resumption of hostilities; des réjouissances populaires ont marqué la prise de pouvoir par la junte the junta's takeover was marked by public celebrations; pour ~ cette journée on a distribué ... to mark *ou* commemorate this day they distributed ... .

(d) (*écrire*) *nom, rendez-vous, renseignement* to write down, note down, make a note of. ~ les points *ou* les résultats to keep *ou* note the score; on l'a marqué absent he was marked absent; j'ai marqué 3 heures sur mon agenda I've got 3 o'clock (noted) down in my diary; il a marqué qu'il fallait prévenir les élèves he noted down that the pupils should be told, he made a note to tell the pupils; qu'y a-t-il de marqué? what does it say?, what's written (on it)?

(e) (*endommager*) *glace, bois* to mark; (*fig: affecter*) *personne* to mark. (*influencer*) ~ son époque to put one's mark *ou* stamp on one's time; la souffrance l'a marqué suffering has left its mark on him; visage marqué par la maladie face marked by illness; visage marqué par la petite vérole face pitted *ou* scarred with smallpox; la déception se marquait sur son visage disappointment showed in his face *ou* was written all over his face.

(f) (*manifester, montrer*) *désapprobation, fidélité, intérêt* to show.

(g) (*Sport*) *joueur* to mark; *but, essai* to score. ~ qn de très près to mark sb very closely *ou* tightly.

(h) (*loc*) ~ le coup* (*fêter un événement etc*) to mark the occasion; (*accuser le coup*) to react; j'ai risqué une allusion, mais il n'a pas marqué le coup* I made an allusion to it, but he showed no reaction; ~ un point/des points (sur qn) to be one up/a few points up (on sb); ~ la mesure to keep the beat; ~ le pas (*lit*) to beat *ou* mark time; (*fig*) to mark time; ~ un temps d'arrêt to pause momentarily.

2 *vi* (a) [*événement, personnalité*] to stand out, be outstanding; [*coup*] to reach home, tell. cet incident a marqué dans sa vie that particular incident stood out in *ou* had a great impact on his life.

(b) [*crayon*] to write; [*tampon*] to stamp. ne pose pas le verre sur ce meuble, ça marque don't put the glass down on that piece of furniture, it will leave a mark.

Noun: turn

turn [tɜːn] 1 *n* (a) (*movement: of wheel, handle etc*) tour *m*. to give sth a ~ tourner qch (une fois); to give a screw a ~ donner un tour de vis; with a ~ of his head he could see ... en tournant la tête il voyait ...; (*Culin*) done to a ~ à point; V hand.

(b) (*change: of direction, condition*) tournure *f*; (*bend: in road etc*) tournant *m*, virage *m*; (*Ski*) virage *m*. to make a ~ [*person, vehicle*] tourner; [*road, ship*] virer; 'no left ~' 'défense de tourner à gauche'; take the next left ~ prenez la prochaine (route) à gauche; (*walk*) to go for *or* take a ~ in the park aller faire un tour dans le parc; the milk is on the ~ le lait commence à tourner; at the ~ of the century en début (*or* en fin) de siècle; (*specifically*) fin dix-neuvième et début vingtième *etc*; at the ~ of the year vers la fin de l'année, en fin d'année; (*fig*) at every ~ à tout instant; things took a new ~ les choses ont pris une nouvelle tournure; events took a tragic ~ les événements ont pris un tour *or* une tournure tragique; [*events*] to take a ~ for the worse s'aggraver; to take a ~ for the better s'améliorer; the patient took a ~ for the worse/better l'état du malade s'est aggravé/amélioré; V tide.

(c) (*Med: crisis*) crise *f*, attaque *f*; (*fright*) coup *m*. he had one of his ~s last night il a eu une nouvelle crise *or* attaque la nuit dernière; she has giddy ~s elle a des vertiges; it gave me quite a ~*, it gave me a nasty ~* ça m'a fait un coup*.

(d) (*action etc*) to do sb a good ~ rendre un service à qn; to do sb a bad ~ jouer un mauvais tour à qn; that's my good ~ for the day j'ai fait ma bonne action *or* B.A.* pour la journée; (*Prov*) one good ~ deserves another un prêté pour un rendu (*Prov*); it has served its ~ ça a fait son temps.

(e) (*esp Brit: Theat etc*) numéro *m*. to do a ~ faire un numéro; V star.

(f) (*Mus*) doublé *m*.

(g) (*in game, queue, series*) tour *m*. it's your ~ c'est votre tour, c'est à vous; it's your ~ to play (c'est) à vous de jouer; whose ~ is it? (*gen*) c'est à qui le tour?; (*in game*) c'est à qui de jouer?, c'est à qui le tour?; wait your ~ attendez votre tour; they answered in ~ ils ont répondu chacun à leur tour, ils ont répondu à tour de rôle; they played in ~ *or* by ~s ils ont joué à tour de rôle; I feel hot and cold by ~s *or* in ~ j'ai tour à tour trop chaud et trop froid; and he, in ~, said... et lui, à son tour, a dit...; (*answering*) et lui, il a répliqué ...; ~ (and ~) about à tour de rôle; to take it ~ (and ~) about to do sth, to take ~s at doing sth, to take it in ~(s) to do sth faire qch à tour de rôle; take it in ~s! chacun son tour!; to take ~s at the wheel se relayer au volant; to take a ~ at the wheel faire un bout de conduite*; (*Mil etc*) ~ of duty tour *m* de garde *or* de service; (*fig*) to speak *or* talk out of ~ commettre une indiscrétion.

(h) (*tendency etc*) tendance *f*, tournure *f* d'esprit, mentalité *f*. to be of *or* have a scientific ~ of mind avoir l'esprit *or* une tournure d'esprit scientifique; to be of *or* have a cheerful ~ of mind être d'une disposition *or* d'une nature joyeuse; to have a strange ~ of mind avoir une mentalité bizarre; ~ of phrase, ~ of style tournure, tour *m* de phrase; there's an old-fashioned ~ to her speech sa façon de parler a un tour démodé; to have a good ~ of speed être rapide.

---

1 *vt* means transitive verb (has a direct object).

2 (*a*) to (*h*) meanings with French synonyms in brackets, followed by context and examples of usage.

3 Specialized contexts indicated by whole word or abbreviations in brackets, e.g. *couture* means 'dressmaking' or (fig) is the figurative use.

1 *n* means noun.

2 (*a*) to (*h*) various meanings of 'turn' followed by the English synonym and its French equivalent.

3 *cpd* means compound nouns from 'turn' arranged alphabetically 'turnabout' to 'turntable'.

4 *V* means *voyez* 'see also' under entry for 'turn-up' hyphenated compound nouns listed alphabetically.

5 *vt* means verb transitive for meanings (*a*) to (*g*).

6 *vi* means verb intransitive for meaning (*a*) to (*d*).

$\overline{2}$ *cpd* turnabout *V* turnabout; turnaround *V* turnaround; turncoat renégat(e) *m(f)*; turndown *V* turndown; turnkey geôlier *m*, -ière *f*; turnoff *V* turnoff; turn-on *V* turn-on; turnout *V* turnout; turnover *V* turnover; turnpike (*barrier*) barrière *f* de péage; (*US: road*) autoroute *f* à péage; turnround = turnaround; (*US Aut*) turn signal clignotant *m*; turnstile tourniquet *m* (*barrière*); turntable *[record player]* platine *f*; (*for trains, cars etc*) plaque tournante; turntable ladder échelle pivotante; turn-up *V* turn-up.

3 *vt* (**a**) *handle, knob, screw, key, wheel* tourner; (*mechanically etc*) faire tourner. ∼ it to the left tournez-le vers la gauche; ∼ the wheel right round faites faire un tour complet à la roue; what ∼s the wheel? qu'est-ce qui fait tourner la roue?; (*Aut*) he ∼ed the wheel sharply il a donné un brusque coup de volant; you can ∼ it through 90° on peut le faire pivoter de 90°; ∼ the key in the lock ferme (la porte) à clef; *V* somersault.

(**b**) *page* tourner; *mattress, pillow, collar, the soil, steak, record* retourner. to ∼ one's ankle se tordre la cheville; it ∼s my stomach cela me soulève le cœur, cela m'écœure; *V* inside, upside down.

(**c**) (*change position of, direct*) *cor, object* tourner (*towards* vers); *gun, hose, searchlight* braquer (*on sb* sur qn); *thoughts, attention* tourner, diriger (*towards* vers). to ∼ a picture to the wall tourner un tableau face au mur; ∼ the switch to 'on' ouvrez le commutateur; ∼ the knob to 'high' tournez le bouton jusqu'à 'fort'; ∼ it to 'wash' mettez-le en position 'lavage'; to ∼ the lights low baisser les lumières; ∼ your face this way tourne le visage de ce côté-ci; he ∼ed his back on us (*lit*) il nous a tourné le dos; (*fig*) il s'est mis à nous battre froid; he ∼ed his back on the past il a tourné la page (*fig*); as soon as he ∼s his back, as soon as his back is ∼ed dès qu'il a le dos tourné; without ∼ing a hair sans sourciller, sans broncher; (*fig*) to ∼ the other cheek tendre l'autre joue; he ∼ed his hand to writing il s'est mis à écrire; he can ∼ his hand to anything il sait tout faire; (*fig*) I'm trying to ∼ an honest penny j'essaie de me faire de l'argent honnêtement; (*fig*) to ∼ the tables renverser les rôles, retourner la situation (*on sb* aux dépens de qn); he ∼ed his steps to the sea il a dirigé ses pas vers la mer; they ∼ed his argument against him ils ont retourné son raisonnement contre lui; they ∼ed him against his father ils l'ont fait se retourner contre *or* ils l'ont monté contre son père; *V* account, advantage, heat *etc*.

(**d**) (*deflect*) *blow* parer, détourner. he ∼ed the beggar from the door il a chassé le mendiant; nothing will ∼ him from his purpose rien ne l'écartera *or* ne le détournera de son but; to ∼ sb from doing dissuader qn de faire.

(**e**) (*shape*) *wood, metal* tourner. a well-∼ed leg une jambe faite au tour; (*fig*) well-∼ed phrase expression bien tournée.

(**f**) (*go round*) to ∼ the corner (*lit*) tourner au *or* le coin de la rue; (*fig*) passer le moment critique; *[patient]* passer le cap; he has *or* is ∼ed 40 il a 40 ans passés; it's ∼ed 3 o'clock il est 3 heures passées.

(**g**) (*transform*) changer, transformer (*into* en); (*translate*) traduire (*into* en); *milk* faire tourner. she ∼ed him into a frog elle l'a changé en grenouille; they ∼ed the land into a park ils ont transformé le terrain en parc; the experience ∼ed him into an old man cette expérience a fait de lui un vieillard; an actor ∼ed writer un acteur devenu écrivain; (*fig*) ∼ your talents into hard cash faites travailler vos talents pour vous, tirez à tirer parti de vos talents; to ∼ a book into a play/film adapter un livre pour la scène/l'écran; to ∼ verse into prose mettre de la poésie en prose; to ∼ sth black noircir qch; it ∼ed him green with envy cela l'a fait verdir de jalousie, il en était vert de jalousie; we were ∼ed sick by the sight le spectacle nous a rendus malades; to ∼ a boat adrift faire partir un bateau à la dérive; *V* loose *etc*.

4 *vi* (**a**) (*move round; rotate, revolve*) *[handle, knob, wheel, screw, key]* tourner; *[person]* se tourner (*to, towards* vers), (*right round*) se retourner. ∼ to face me tourne-toi vers moi; he ∼ed and saw me il s'est retourné et m'a vu; he ∼ed to me and smiled il s'est tourné vers moi et a souri; he ∼ed to look at me il s'est retourné pour me regarder; he ∼ed to lie on his other side il s'est tourné pour changer de côté; the earth ∼s on its axis la terre tourne autour de son axe; (*fig*) my head is ∼ing j'ai la tête qui tourne; his stomach ∼ed at the sight le spectacle lui a retourné l'estomac *or* soulevé le cœur; (*depend*) to ∼ on sth dépendre de qch, reposer sur qch; it all ∼s on whether he has the money tout dépend s'il a l'argent ou non; to ∼ tail (and run) prendre ses jambes à son cou; he would ∼ in his grave if he knew ... il se retournerait dans sa tombe s'il savait ...; *V* toss, turtle.

(**b**) (*move in different direction*) *[person, vehicle, aircraft] (change course*) tourner; (*reverse direction*) faire demi-tour; *[ship]* virer; *[road, river]* faire un coude; *[wind]* tourner, changer; *[tide]* changer de direction. (*Mil*) right ∼! à droite, droite!; to ∼ (to the) left tourner à gauche; ∼ first right prenez la première à droite; they ∼ed and came back ils ont fait demi-tour *or* fait volte-face et ils sont revenus (sur leurs pas); the car ∼ed at the end of the street (*turned round*) la voiture a fait demi-tour au bout de la rue; (*turned off*) la voiture a tourné au bout de la rue; (*Aut*) there's nowhere to ∼ il n'y a pas d'endroit où faire demi-tour; the car ∼ed into a side street la voiture a tourné dans une rue transversale; our luck has ∼ed la chance a tourné pour nous; the conversation ∼ed on the election la conversation en est venue à l'élection; the dog ∼ed on him le chien l'a attaqué; they ∼ed on him and accused him of treachery ils s'en sont pris à lui et l'ont accusé de trahison; (*fig*) to ∼ against sb se retourner contre qn; (*fig*) he didn't know which way to ∼ il ne savait plus où donner de la tête; he ∼ed to me for advice il s'est tourné vers *or* adressé à moi pour me demander conseil; where can I ∼ for money? où pourrais-je trouver de l'argent?; he ∼ed to politics il s'est tourné vers la politique; he ∼ed to drink il s'est mis à boire; our thoughts ∼ to those who ... nos pensées vont à *or* se tournent vers ceux qui ...; *V* tide.

(**c**) (*become*) to ∼ into devenir; he ∼ed into a frog il se changea *or* se métamorphosa en grenouille; he ∼ed into an old man overnight il est devenu vieux en l'espace d'une nuit; to ∼ to stone se changer en pierre, se pétrifier; his admiration ∼ed to scorn son admiration se changea en *or* tourna au *or* fit place au mépris; (*fig*) his knees ∼ed to water *or* jelly ses genoux se sont dérobés sous lui; the weather has ∼ed cold le temps s'est rafraîchi; to ∼ black noircir; to ∼ angry se mettre en colère; to ∼ traitor (*Mil, Pol*) se vendre à l'ennemi; (*gen*) se mettre à trahir; to ∼ communist devenir communiste; to ∼ Catholic se convertir au catholicisme; to ∼ professional passer *or* devenir professionnel.

(**d**) *[leaves]* jaunir; *[milk]* tourner; *[weather]* changer.

◆turn about, turn around 1 *vi* [*person*] se retourner, faire volte-face; [*vehicle*] faire demi-tour; [*object*] tourner. (*Mil*) about turnI demi-tour!
　2 *vt sep* (a) (*lit*) tourner (dans l'autre sens).
　(b) (*fig*) (*change mind, tactics etc*) to turn sb around faire changer d'avis à qn; to turn things around renverser la situation.
　3 turnabout n, turnaround n V turnabout, turnaround.
◆turn aside 1 *vi* (*lit, fig*) se détourner (*from* de).
　2 *vt sep* détourner.
◆turn away 1 *vi* se détourner (*from* de).
　2 *vt sep* (a) head, face, eyes, gun détourner. turn the photograph away from the light tourne la photographie de telle façon qu'elle ne soit pas exposée à la lumière.
　(b) (*reject*) person (*gen*) renvoyer, (*stronger*) chasser; *salesman at door* envoyer promener; *offer* refuser, rejeter. they're turning business or customers away ils refusent des clients.
◆turn back 1 *vi* (a) [*traveller*] revenir, rebrousser chemin, faire demi-tour; [*vehicle*] faire demi-tour.
　(b) to turn back to page 100 revenir à la page 100.
　2 *vt sep* (a) (*fold, bend*) bedclothes, collar rabattre; *corner of page* relever, replier.
　(b) (*send back*) person, vehicle faire faire demi-tour à.
　(c) clock, hands of clock reculer (*to* jusqu'à). (*fig*) if only we could turn the clock back si seulement on pouvait remonter le (cours du) temps; it has turned the clock back 50 years cela nous (*or* vous *etc*) a fait revenir en arrière de 50 ans.
◆turn down 1 *vt sep* (a) (*fold, bend*) bedclothes rabattre, retourner; *collar* rabattre. to turn down the corner of the page corner la page.
　(b) (*reduce*) gas, heat, lighting, radio, music baisser.
　(c) (*refuse*) offer, suggestion, loan, suitor rejeter, repousser; *candidate, volunteer* refuser.
　(d) (*place upside down*) playing card retourner (face contre table).
　2 turndown n, adj V turndown.
◆turn in 1 *vi* (a) [*car, person*] to turn in to a driveway entrer *or* tourner dans une allée.
　(b) his toes turn in il a les pieds tournés en dedans.
　(c) (*: go to bed*) aller se coucher.
　2 *vt sep* (a) to turn in the ends of sth rentrer les bouts de qch; to turn one's toes in tourner les pieds en dedans.
　(b) (*: surrender, return*) borrowed goods, equipment rendre (*to* à); *wanted man* livrer (à la police); *stolen goods* apporter à la police.
◆turn off 1 *vi* (a) [*person, vehicle*] tourner.
　(b) [*heater, oven etc*] to turn off automatically s'éteindre automatiquement.
　2 *vt sep* water fermer; *tap* fermer; *light* éteindre; *gas* éteindre, fermer, (*at main*) all services couper; *radio, television, heater* éteindre, fermer, arrêter. (*Rad, TV*) he turned the programme off il a fermé *or* éteint le poste; (*Aut*) to turn off the engine couper l'allumage, arrêter le moteur; the oven turns itself off le four s'éteint tout seul *or* automatiquement; (*fig*) the way he smiled turned me off‡ sa façon de sourire m'a totalement rebuté *or* (*stronger*) m'a dégoûté‡.
　3 turn-off n V turn-off.
◆turn on 1 *vi* (a) [*heater, oven etc*] to turn on automatically s'allumer automatiquement.
　(b) (*Rad, TV*) allumer le poste.
　2 *vt sep* (a) tap ouvrir; *water* faire couler; *gas, electricity* allumer; *radio, television, heater* allumer; (*at main*) all services brancher; *engine, machine* mettre en marche. to turn on the light allumer; (*fig*) to turn on the charm‡ (se mettre à) faire du charme‡.
　(b) (*: excite: gen*) exciter. she ∼s him on elle l'excite; this music turns me on‡ cette musique me fait quelque chose‡; (*fig*) to be turned on‡ (*up-to-date*) être branché‡ *or* dans le vent; (*by drugs*) planer‡; (*sexually*) être (tout) excité *or* émoustillé‡ (*by* par).
　3 turn-on‡ n V turn-on.
◆turn out 1 *vi* (a) (*from bed*) se lever; (*from house*) sortir; [*guard*] (*aller*) prendre la faction; [*troops etc*] aller au rassemblement. not many people turned out to see her peu de gens sont venus la voir.
　(b) [*car, pedestrian*] to turn out of a driveway sortir d'une allée.
　(c) his toes turn out il tourne les pieds en dehors, il a les pieds en canard.
　(d) (*transpire; end*) se révéler, s'avérer. it turned out that she

7 ◆ Symbol for 'phrasal verbs' — i.e. those taking a preposition in English — arranged by alphabetical order of pronoun.

Exercices

1　Vérifiez la prononciation des mots suivants. Soulignez les mots de même prononciation.
　　(a)　vert, verre, vers
　　(b)　pour, pur, peur
　　(c)　sûr, sur, sœur
　　(d)　fait, fée, fête
　　(e)　désert, dessert, des serres
　　(f)　foie, foi, fois
　　(g)　volet, voler, volée
　　(h)　veille, vieille, viol
　　(i)　thon, ton, temps
　　(j)　feindre, fendre, fondre

2　Parmi les mots suivants lesquels riment l'un avec l'autre.
　　(a)　rhum, rhume, somme
　　(b)　alcool, sol, colle
　　(c)　femme, madame, thème
　　(d)　dent, dans, dent

3 Vérifiez dans un dictionnaire la prononciation des mots suivants:

solennel	le Christ
évidemment	album
condamner	Adam
baptême	Degas
Jésus Christ	équateur

4 (i) Vérifiez le genre des mots suivants

    (ii) Employez-les dans une phrase pour en faire ressortir la signification.

tour	poste
mort	poêle
mode	voile
critique	Champagne
vase	champagne

5 Check the meanings of the following which contain particular uses of common verbs. What would you write down in French and English as a reminder of the phrase? (e.g. en vouloir à quelqu'un?)

    (a) Ah! Ce prof, il m'agaçait continuellement, *il m'en voulait*, hein.

    (b) Quand il nous a vus, *il s'est sauvé*.

    (c) *Je tiens* beaucoup *à* vous voir ce soir.

    (d) Cet ouvre-boîte, je ne sais pas comment *m'en servir*.

    (e) On peut *se passer d'*eau durant trois jours mais on peut *se passer de* nourriture durant trois semaines.

    (f) Ah, *je m'en doutais* qu'il le ferait!

    (g) *Il s'est privé* de cigarettes pour toute une semaine.

    (h) Pour le physique *il tient de* son père.

    (i) Est-ce que *vous croyez en* Dieu?

    (j) *Il ne croit plus au* Père Noël

    (k) Ce nouveau prof, *qu'en pensez-vous*?

    (l) Depuis qu'elle est partie *je pense* souvent *à* elle.

6 Vérifiez l'accord de l'adjectif dans les exemples suivants:

une chemise *bleu marine*

un corsage *mauve*

une jupe *bleu clair*

des chaussettes *marron*

de l'eau *frais*

une tranche *épais*

7 Attention aux 'faux amis' qui suivent:

    (a) Son doigt avait été sectionné

    (b) Il aimait regarder cette dame à la dérobée

    (c) J'ai trouvé une bague de diamant

    (d) On va déguster ces huîtres

    (e) Il va rester définitivement en France

    (f) Il faut observer les convenances

    (g) Au café j'ai demandé une blonde

    (h) Les étudiants donnent souvent des leçons particulières

    (i) Où est-ce qu'il a suivi sa formation?

    (j) J'ai suivi avec intérêt l'exposé de cette jeune Suédoise

    (k) Je ne me suis pas rendu compte des difficultés qu'il m'avait signalées

    (l) C'est une jeune fille très sensible

    (m) C'est un garçon très sérieux

    (n) Il m'a eu. Il m'a joué un sale tour

    (o) J'ai un chien dressé pour chercher les truffes

Anecdote The following ingenious translation was offered in the old GCE exam for the French phrase, – *Il était assis au fond de la pièce à l'ombre* – 'He was fond enough of his bit in the dark.' How do you think the candidate arrived at this interpretation? What better translation could you find?

8 Même jeu. Trouvez un mot français pour le mot anglais en italique
   (a) What are *his motives*?
   (b) An *experienced* journalist
   (c) A *demonstration* in front of the town hall
   (d) A *disaster area*
   (e) A *sensible* idea
   (f) *He's going on a course* in Lyon
   (g) *I draw* my money on Fridays
   (h) It gives me *vertigo*
   (i) I have nothing to say *on this issue*
   (j) I've always kept a *diary*
   (k) How do you hope to become a *photographer* if you haven't got a *camera*?

9 Trouvez un verbe ou une phrase pour traduire les mots en italique:
   (a) *Carry* straight *on*
   (b) The coach *carries* 30 passengers
   (c) The plan is difficult to *carry out*
   (d) I was *carried away* with excitement
   (e) I've *run out* of sugar
   (f) I *ran into* him in the supermarket
   (g) He was *run over*
   (h) Don't *run away with* the idea that you can *run* this place
   (i) Is the engine *running?*
   (j) He is *running as* town councillor
   (k) I'll *look after* you
   (l) I'll *look into* it
   (m) I'll *look in* tomorrow
   (n) She *looks sad*
   (o) *I look up to* him
   (p) She's a *good-looker*
   (q) It *looks like* rain

10 Traduisez en anglais le passage suivant en faisant ressortir:
   (a) un style plutôt familier;
   (b) un style soigné.

   Marc était au restaurant avec son amie/son flirt/sa poule Annie. Ils avaient bien mangé/bouffé/s'étaient bien nourris et Annie avait consommé/avalé/bu deux bouteilles de gros rouge/pinard/vin de table. Elle était maintenant complètement paf/ivre/soûle et, soudain, elle a commencé à gueuler/hurler/parler très fort. Enfin le restaurateur leur a demandé de partir/décamper/ficher le camp. Ils ont trouvé ça rigolo/marrant/amusant.

11 Comment ça s'écrit en français et en anglais?
   Vérifiez l'orthographe des mots suivants en soulignant les mots anglais:
   example – exemple
   character – caractère
   miroir – mirror
   adresse – address
   apartment – appartement
   utensil – ustensile
   crystal – cristal
   alcool – alcohol
   eccentric – excentrique
   millionnaire – millionaire
   contrat – contract
   agression – aggression

12 Utiliser des mots ou des expressions empruntés à une autre langue est un procédé bien connu et en perpétuelle évolution. Le passage suivant a été conçu pour montrer, d'une manière artificielle mais amusante, un bon nombre de mots français qui peuvent être utilisés en anglais. Souvent, un mot emprunté diffère légèrement mais parfois totalement de son sens original. A l'aide d'un dictionnaire, vérifiez la signification en français et en anglais des mots soulignés. Lesquels ont plus ou moins le même sens? Lesquels sont différents? Dans ce dernier cas trouvez un mot français plus convenable. Cherchez aussi un synonyme français pour les mots marqués d'un astérisque.

Cul-de-sac to an affaire

Yvonne sat at the banquette, in the buffet restaurant, with her <u>suave</u>* fiancé Charles. She wore a <u>cerise</u> <u>blouse</u> on her après-ski <u>costume</u>. She viewed the menu and ordered <u>blancmange</u> for dessert. She was no gourmet and gastronomic rendez-vous frequently gave her a <u>migraine</u>*. As for Charles he was suffering from a profound malaise. They left their chaperon, a blonde Swiss au-pair girl, at the café with an apéritif, while they went off to Charle's pied-à-terre for their tête-à-tête*. His apartment was full of bizarre <u>bric-à-brac,</u> mostly <u>brassières</u> and other outré articles of <u>lingerie</u> for which he had a penchant*. For these reasons he liked her to be dressed in a tulle <u>négligé</u>, despite her protestations that it was too risqué for a débutante. Their <u>affaire</u> was still in its early stages. Today Yvonne went into the <u>boudoir</u> to change, while Charles lay on the chaise-longue, inhaling eau de Cologne from a <u>chiffon</u> scarf.

Pardon me if I seem <u>brusque</u>* or <u>gauche</u>*, he said. I am no bourgeois voyeur, as you might imagine. In fact I am an émigré Russian prince <u>engaged</u> in <u>espionage</u>* to restore the ancien régime by a coup d'Etat. Our marriage will have no mésalliance for your family. But life is an inscrutable game of roulette, and I have reached the <u>cul-de-sac</u>* of my rôle. Take my attaché case. Inside you will find a <u>solitaire</u>. Give it to the au-pair girl who has always been my <u>paramour.</u>

Auberon Waugh

3 Gender

Knowing whether a noun is masculine or feminine in French, is one of the more difficult things to acquire for someone who has not learned the language from an early age. Gender has no real connection with sex. Nouns simply fall into one of two groups in French. Some languages have a third group called neuter nouns. There is no logic to these divisions. In English we lost these distinctions a long time ago. However, we still tend to think of ships and countries as feminine. You would say 'Britain and her (or possibly 'its') sovereignty', but never 'his' sovereignty. There are some gender oddities in French:

(a) *Pierre est **une** personne que je connais très bien* (*Personne* is always feminine).
(b) *Mon père a été **la** victime d'une attaque*
(c) *Il n'est pas **la** dupe de tout le monde*
(d) *Mme Cresson était **le** premier Premier ministre féminin*
(e) ***Un** soldat* usually performs the duty of ***une** sentinelle*

The best way to remember gender is to learn it with the noun; by putting *le* or *la*, *un* or *une* into your memory with the word or by combining the noun with an adjective when you learn it. (e.g. *de l'eau chaude*.) The next best thing is is to make up some basic rules together with the most common exceptions.

Basic Rules

1 Gender by meaning

Feminine	Exceptions
1 Names of countries and rivers ending in a mute '-e' *la Pologne, la Russie, la Loire*	*le Mexique, le Rhône*
2 Most abstract nouns: *la peur, la foi* (faith), *la douleur*	*le courage, le vice*
3 Names of females: *une nièce, une grand-mère, une chatte, une chienne*	*un ange* – angel, *un témoin* – witness, are always masculine Also *écrivain, auteur, médecin, professeur* etc., which have been traditionally male occupations

	Masculine	**Feminine**

4 Names of countries and rivers not ending in mute '-*e*':
le Brésil
le Canada
le Cher (river)
le Loir (river)

5 Names of trees, minerals, and metals: *la bauxite*
le chêne – oak
le pin
le sable
le charbon – coal
le cuivre – copper

6 Seasons, months, days of week, points of compass, and decimal weights and measures:
le printemps
le mois de janvier
le lundi
le nord
un kilo
un gramme

2 Gender by derivation

Masculine	**Feminine**

1 Words and expressions not originally nouns:
un oui
un non
un pourboire
le savoir-faire
un devoir

2 Nouns from verbs not ending in mute '-*e*':   Nouns from verbs ending in mute '-*e*':
un refus   *la marche*
un emploi   *la visite*
le choix   *la chasse*
un espoir

3 Compound nouns made up of two nouns take the gender of the first noun. The great majority
of these are masculine: **But**
un chou-fleur   *une basse-cour* – back yard
un chef-d'œuvre   *une porte-fenêtre* – French window

4 Compound words made up of verb + noun. These are all masculine and there are many of them:
un tourne-vis
un tire-bouchon
un pare-soleil – sun-visor
*un **par**apluie* – works on the same principle, as does *un **par**achute*.
The verb is *parer* to 'ward off', 'protect from'

3 Gender by ending

1 All words with the suffix '-*tion*' are **feminine.** There are very many of these:
une installation
la composition
la position
etc.

2 Nearly all words ending in '-*té*', and '-*tié*' are **feminine** if they are abstract in meaning:
une amitié
la santé,
la propriété
la capacité
etc.

These are numerous.
Exception: *le traité*

3   Nearly all words ending in *'-eur'* are **feminine** if **abstract**:
   la couleur
   la froideur
   la grosseur
   la profondeur

Exceptions

un honneur
le bonheur
le malheur

4   *Gender pairs*

Masculine	**Feminine**
1 *'-eur'* (role or occupation)	*'-euse', '-trice'*
un acteur	*une actrice*
un instituteur	*une institutrice*
un inspecteur	*une inspectrice*
un vendeur	*une vendeuse*
2 *'-er, '-ier'*	*'-ère', '-ière'*
le plancher	*la lumière*
le papier	*la misère* – poverty
un fermier	*une fermière*

Exceptions

le caractère	
le mystère	*la mer*

3 *'-eau', '-il'*	*'-elle', '-lle'*
le chapeau	*une chapelle*
le bateau	*une rondelle* - slice
un château	*une fille*
un fil (de coton)	
le cil – eyelash	

Exceptions

	une eau
	la peau – skin

4 *'-t'*	*'-tte', '-te'*
le mot	*la patte* – paw
le pot	*la pâte*
le chocolat	*une allumette*
le sujet	*la crête*
le but	*la planète*
	une capote
	une anecdote

Exceptions

un vote	*la forêt*
le pilote	*la dent*
un antidote	*la plupart*
	la part

5 *'-c'*	*'-che'*
le lac	*la tâche* – stain, spot
le bac – ferry or exam	*la cloche*
un flic	
un choc	

le manche – handle
un reproche – reproach, blame

6 *'-age'* (as a suffix)   *'-age'* (not a suffix)
le village   *la cage*
le courage   *la rage*
un reportage   *la page*

Exception

un âge

7 *'-oir'*   *'-oire'*
le miroir   *la gloire*
un mouchoir   *une histoire*
un couloir – corridor

Exceptions

un laboratoire
un observatoire,
le conservatoire
un ivoire – ivory

8 *'-é'*   *-ée'*
le dé – dice   *une journée*
le marché   *une année*
                                                            la matinée

Exceptions

le lycée
le musée

9 *'-on'*   *-onne'*
un bâton   *une couronne*
le son   *une consonne* – consonant
le béton – concrete
le ton
un ballon

10 *'-acle', '-ecle'*   ***
un miracle
un obstacle

Exception

un cercle   *une débâcle* – disaster, rout

11 *'-ège'*   ***
le piège – trap
un collège
le cortège – Procession

12 *'-ème'*   ***
le poème
le thème
le problème

Exception

                                                            la crème

13 *'-o'*   ***
le numéro
un zéro
un écho

14 *'-ou'*   ***
un caillou – pebble
un fou
un trou
un chou

15 ***

'**-esse**'
la paresse
une ivresse – drunkenness
la messe – mass, religious service
une masse – weight

16 ***

'**-ie**'
la maladie
une colonie
une tragédie
la folie

Exceptions

un incendie
le génie – genius, spirit

17 ***

'**-ine**'
la colline
une mine
la cantine

18 ***

'**-une**'
la fortune
la rancune – grudge, rancour

19 ***

'**-ure**'
la nature
une voiture
la couture – dressmaking

20 ***

-ance', '**-anse**'
la vengeance
la chance
la danse

21 ***

'**-ence**', '**-ense**'
la prudence
la défense
la décence

Exception

le silence

17 '**-isme**'   ***
le communisme
le socialisme
le réalisme
le romantisme

The above guidelines to gender are designed as **basic reference points.** The main endings have been covered together with those exceptions it is felt you are likely to meet. You should note other exceptions as you come across them.

5 Words that change their meaning according to gender

There are about a hundred of these in French, of which you are likely to meet only a small number. Some common words are included but very often the other word in the pair is fairly rare. For example, I learned many years ago that *la mousse* means 'moss' but that *le mousse* means 'cabin boy'. It wasn't until recently that I read in a northern French newspaper *'Le mousse perdu d'un bateau dans la Manche'*. I don't think I had ever come across the word before in print let alone in spoken French. Here are some of the commonest of these words. It is worth remembering that even if you get the gender wrong it would hardly be noticed in speech and in most cases the context makes the meaning clear enough.

Masculine	Feminine
le livre – book	*la livre* – pound (money, weight)
le tour (de France) – round trip	*la Tour Eiffel* – tower
le mode d'emploi (pour les médicaments)	*la mode (pour les vêtements)*
un poste de télévision	*la poste où on achète des timbres etc.*
un critique (la personne dont le métier est de critiquer les livres, films etc.)	*une critique c'est le livre ou l'article dans lequel on écrit ses jugements*
un mémoire (une note ou un rapport sur q.c.)	*la mémoire (la faculté de se rappeler i.e. On a une bonne ou une mauvaise mémoire)*
un somme (petit sommeil)	*la somme (qu'il faut payer)*
le vase (dans lequel on met des fleurs)	*la vase (ce qui se trouve souvent au fond des lacs ou rivières)* – mud, silt
le physique – physical appearance	*la physique* – physics
le voile – v**e**il *(Les Musulmanes le portent)*	*la voile* – s**a**il
le poêle – sto**ve**	*la poêle* – frying p**an**

Part II Grammar Section

As already mentioned in the section on aims, the grammar that you learned for GCSE should provide a sound basis for what you need at A and AS Level with two important considerations: (a) many grammar points, only needed previously to be recognized and understood for reading and listening, now come into active use for speaking and writing; (b) the range of grammatical considerations needs to be expanded and in some cases extended, particularly with verbs.

The knowledge and understanding of grammar that you gained for GCSE was probably restricted by the use you needed to make of it. A lot of language was needed for transactional purposes. For example, the *je, tu* and *vous* parts of the verb were used more frequently in speaking and writing than *nous, il* and *elle*. The plural forms *ils* and *elles* were needed even less. Similarly your use of the imperfect may have been restricted to *j'étais* and *j'avais*, even though you had learned the other parts. The part of the conditional you used most was probably *je voudrais*. The result of this is that the overall picture you have of French grammar is bitty and uneven.

For A Level, you need to have a good basic framework of grammar so that you know the main parts and their names and can fit the new rules that you come across into an overall pattern.

The grammar section that follows is **not** intended to be a complete grammar of the French language. The aim is to provide a description and an explanation for learning and reference of the main grammatical features that need to be understood and put into use at A and AS Level. Broad rules and guidelines will be given; not necessarily all the exceptions and oddities. You will find these in a complete grammar reference book. Good books to consult are:

H Farrar (1973), *A French Reference Grammar, 2nd Edition,* OUP
J E Manion (1952), *A Grammar of Present-Day French, 2nd Edition,* Harrap
L Byrne and E Churchill (1956), *A Comprehensive French Grammar,* Blackwell
W Rowlinson (1991), *French Grammar,* OUP

The most conspicuous area with probable gaps in knowledge is the verb: this comes first. The verb is the main working part of a sentence. Getting it right earns you more credit and makes the rest of the sentence fall into place more readily.

Tense

Getting an 'overall picture' of the system of tenses is an important part of learning languages. Once acquired for one language it can be applied to learning other ones. Tense is to do with time. There are three basic aspects of time, common to all languages: past, present and future. These are exemplified in the former Soviet slogan 'Lenin lived, Lenin lives; Lenin will live.' Even if the prediction does not fulfil itself the slogan covers the full range of time.

You can then make adjustments to the way you look at past time: actions that began in the past or were completed in the past (the perfect tense in French) in contrast to actions that were continuous or repeated themselves (the imperfect tense). If you take a step further back into the past, before something else happened, the pluperfect is used. Similarly, referring to the future, you can make a prediction that someone will have done something (before something else) and the future perfect is used. 'Will', put into reported speech, becomes 'would' (he said he would arrive early) and the conditional or future in the past is needed.

Contents of the Grammar Section

1 Theory

1 Present tense – *Le présent*

Use

The present tense is used in French as it is in English except that:

(a) French has only one present tense form where English has three:

   (i)   *Je trouve mon travail difficile* – I find my work difficult
                             – I am finding my work difficult
                             – I do find my work difficult

(b) French uses a present tense where English has a perfect continuous tense for an action started in the past but still happening now:

   (i)   *Il habite Birmingham depuis dix ans* – He has been living in Birmingham for ten years
  (ii) *Je t'attends ici depuis une heure* – I've been waiting for you here for an hour

This present tense is usually signalled by *depuis* but *il y a* and *voici* can also introduce the same idea:

 (iii) *Il y a un an maintenant que je travaille là-bas* – I've been working there for a year now
 (iv) *Voici trente minutes que je t'attends!* – I've been waiting for you for half an hour!

The question 'How long have you/has he/she been...' is usually introduced by *Depuis combien de temps* or *Depuis quand*.

If you take a step back into the past with this continuous idea, you get in English:
'She said she **had been** waiting for me for an hour'

In French you need a continuous past tense, so the **imperfect** is used:
Elle a dit qu'elle m'attendait depuis une heure.

Formation

The present tense is usually encountered early in a French course because the present seems a logical place to start. Unfortunately the present tense in French is the most complicated in terms of irregularities. Many of these irregular verbs are amongst the most frequently used in the language. It is helpful to divide the present tense into two groups: regular and irregular.

Regular verbs

These fall into three groups according to the ending of the infinitive (this is the part you find when you look up a verb in the dictionary).

1 **'*-er*' verbs** The biggest group, containing about 90 per cent of the verbs in the language. All verbs in '*-er*' belong here. There is an example on page 27:

je chante	*nous chantons*
tu chantes	*vous chantez*
il chante	*ils chantent*
elle chante	*elles chantent*

2 **'-ir' verbs** These make up about 350 verbs. **Note** there are several commonly used verbs in '-ir' which are irregular (e.g. *venir; ouvrir; dormir* etc. — *see* verb list, page 203).

je ralentis	*nous ralentissons*
tu ralentis	*vous ralentissez*
il ralentit	*ils ralentissent*
elle ralentit	*elles ralentissent*

3 **'-re' verbs** Again there are a number of common irregular verbs in '-re' that do not belong to this group (e.g. *boire; lire; naître* — *see* verb list).

je descends	*nous descendons*
tu descends	*vous descendez*
il descend	*ils descendent*
elle descend	*elles descendent*

Spelling and pronunciation

There are two main difficulties with the present tense: knowing which letters are pronounced and which are silent. The following should be noted about the three regular groups:

(a) All persons of the singular sound the same –
je descends, tu descends , il descend (final '-ds' or '-d' are silent)
(b) The final '-ent', the third person plural, is not pronounced –
il parle and *ils parlent* sound the same
You can tell the third person singular from third person plural in verbs beginning with a vowel or silent 'h', because of the liaison or slur in the latter;
elle arrive but *elles arrivent* and *il habite* but *ils habitent* — the 's' sounds like a 'z'

Some deviations in the regular verbs

Again it is a question of spelling and pronunciation. The endings remain regular but the rest of the verb changes slightly.

(a) **Double 't' and 'l'**, e.g. *jeter* – to throw and *projeter* – to project:

Je jette	*Vous jetez*
Tu jettes	*Nous jetons*
Il jette	*Ils jettent*
Elle jette	*Elles jettent*

The example above shows a double consonant before a silent ending. *Jette* rhymes with *fillette*. In *jetons* and *jetez* the 'e' sounds like the 'e' in '*le*'.

With *appeler* and *rappeler*, double the 'l' in the same way. The pronunciation of 'e' follows the same pattern.
(b) **Verbs with an 'e' syllable before the '-er' ending**, e.g. *lever, répéter, amener, espérer, acheter* etc. change the sound of the 'e' by adding or changing an accent.

J'achète	*Nous achetons*	*Je répète*	*Nous répétons*
Tu achètes	*Vous achetez*	*Tu répètes*	*Vous répétez*
Il achète	*Ils achètent*	*Il répète*	*Ils répètent*
Elle achète	*Elles achètent*	*Elle répète*	*Elles répètent*

You will notice that the accent changes, appears or disappears, according to whether the ending is silent or not. Can you see a similarity of pattern with the previous group?

(c) **Verbs in '-oyer', '-uyer',** e.g. *envoyer, employer, essuyer, ennuyer,* all change 'y' to 'i' before a silent ending:
J'envoie but *Vous envoyez*
Il essuie but *Vous essuyez*

(d) **Verbs in '-ger',** like *changer, arranger, manger,* all have an extra 'e' before the first person plural ending:
Nous arrangeons

(e) **Verbs in '-cer'** have a cedilla beneath the '*c*' in the same place:
Nous avançons

The rule here is that before '*a*', '*o*' or '*u*', '*c*' and '*g*' are pronounced as a hard '*c*' as in *Calais* and '*g*' as in *gare* so an '*e*' or cedilla needs to be added to keep the soft '*s*' or '*zh*' sound. An '*e*' or '*i*' would make the following '*c*' or '*g*' soft anyway. So you only get cedillas before '*a*', '*o*' or '*u*' if the '*c*' has to remain soft. For example:

> *Mâcon (en Bourgogne)* but *un maçon (un homme qui construit des bâtiments avec des briques)*

Irregular Verbs

You could start to give rules about the peculiarities of the present tense of irregular verbs. For example, **four** have a third person plural ending in '*-ont*': *Ils ont (avoir)*; *Ils sont (être)*; *Ils font (faire)*; and *Ils vont (aller)* — **three** have a second person plural in '*-es*': *Vous dites*; *Vous faites*; *Vous êtes*.

This soon gets complicated, however, and bogged down with exceptions. The only way to get to grips with them is to learn them by saying them over to yourself using a verb table. If you photocopy a table where, for example, the present tense is written out in full, you can blank out selected parts of verbs, photocopy them and then try writing in the missing parts.

One helpful fact to remember is that, having learned to say and spell the present tense of, say, *mettre* – put or place, all the compound verbs (those formed by adding a prefix) become accessible to you. For example: *promettre* – promise, *permettre* – permit, *admettre* – admit, *soumettre* – submit, *transmettre* –transmit, *commettre* – commit.

Compound verbs are often fairly close in appearance to English verbs with a similar meaning. (What does *compromettre* mean? — *Ce scandale va compromettre cet homme politique.*) This extension of learning one verb also applies to all the other tenses that you will meet.

Exercices

1 Traduisez en français:

    (a) Do you watch television every night?
    (b) Do you do your homework while you are watching television?
    (c) Are you waiting for the six o'clock train?
    (d) No, I'm waiting for my friend
    (e) Is he working in London?
    (f) I am thinking of her while I write this letter
    (g) Is he going to come with us?
    (h) Does he speak Russian?
    (i) I am writing to thank you for the present
    (j) What are you doing this evening?

2 Traduisez:

    (a) Depuis combien de temps est-ce qu'il habite Bruxelles?
    (b) Ça fait deux semaines que je reçois des coups de téléphone mystérieux
    (c) Cela fait deux ans que nous nous écrivons
    (d) Depuis quand est-ce qu'il la connaît?
    (e) Voici deux mois que j'attends une lettre

3 Traduisez:

    (a) How long have you been waiting for me?
    (b) I've been here since six o'clock
    (c) They have been writing to one another for years
    (d) She has been in England for years
    (e) That makes five years I have known you

2 Perfect tense – *Le passé composé*

Use

This is probably the most frequently used tense in French after the present. 'Perfect' means 'finished', so this tense is used for actions completed in the past. English verbs have three ways of indicating this idea:

> You found your bag!
> You have found your bag
> You did find your bag

In French, *Vous avez trouvé votre sac* would be used for all of these. The French name *passé composé* means that it is a made up verb with two parts: *avoir* — the auxiliary verb — and the past participle, just like the English 'have found'. Most verbs in French form their perfect tense with *avoir*, the rest with *être*. You need to know two things then to form the perfect tense:

(a) Is it an *avoir* or an *être* verb?
(b) What is the past participle?

Formation

Avoir or être

(a) Most verbs take avoir:
   Vous avez commencé?
   Ils ont trouvé l'adresse.

(b) About 16 verbs, very frequently used, take *être* to form the perfect tense:

aller	– venir
arriver	– partir
monter	– descendre
entrer	– sortir
mourir	– naître
tomber	– rester
devenir	– revenir
rentrer	– retourner

So *je suis arrivé* can mean 'I have arrived' and *elle est partie* 'she has left'. These verbs are best remembered as pairs of opposites as shown above. There are 'about' 16 because by prefixing '*re-*' to many of them their number increases. For example, *remonter* – to go back up/go up again.

These verbs belong to such a group, not because of some conspiracy on the part of the French to make their language difffficult for foreigners, but because they are all 'intransitive' when used with *être* – that is they can't have a direct object. You can't 'go something or someone' or 'fall something or someone' (*see also* pages 31 and 50)

A few of them however can be used with a direct object (transitively) in which case they do take *avoir* and undergo a slight change of meaning:

(i) *J'ai monté vos valises, monsieur* – I've taken your suitcases up
(ii) *Le voleur a sorti un revolver* – The thief got out a gun
(iii) *J'ai rentré les chaises du jardin* – I've taken in the chairs from the garden

Descendre and *retourner* can also be used like this.

(c) All reflexive verbs take *être* to form the perfect tense. The reflexive pronoun is kept with all the persons:

(i) *Je me suis levé à 6 heures* – I got up at six o'clock
(ii) *Nous nous sommes promenés jusqu'à 10 heures* – We walked until ten o'clock
(iii) *Vous vous êtes bien amusés?* – Did you have a good time?

Past participles

It is essential to know this part of the verb. It should be memorized together with the infinitive as a group. The following outline rules are useful:

(a) All '*-er*' verbs have a past participle ending in '*é* '. This sounds identical with the infinitive ending '*-er*', so beware when writing!

(b) Regular '*-re*' and '*-ir*' verbs have a past participle ending in '*-u*' and '*-i*' respectively. The trouble is remembering which are the regular '*-re*' and '*-ir*' verbs.

(c) All the other past participles have to be learned. There are certain patterns:

pouvoir	– *pu*
savoir	– *su*
devoir	– *dû*
recevoir	– *reçu*
vouloir	– *voulu*
falloir	– *fallu*
pleuvoir	– *plu*

Unfortunately, others are 'non-conformist':

(i) **souffrir** *J'ai souffert le martyr pour apprendre ces verbes* – I went through agonies to learn these verbs
(ii) **lire** *Il a beaucoup lu* – He has read a lot

(iii) *courir*   *J'ai couru partout pour trouver ce vin* –
        I've been all over the place to find this wine

(iv) *croire*   *Elle ne m'a pas cru* – She didn't believe me

Learning the past participles requires an effort. Try working backwards by copying out 20 to 30 past participles and then see if you can write down the infinitive beside each one. Remember that having learned one it might give the pattern for several compounds:

    ouvrir – *ouvert*

    offrir – *offert*

    couvrir – *couvert*

It is also helpful to say the English past participle in your mind when you are learning:

    offert – offered

    couvert – covered

Exercices

1   Try hanging the 16 *être* verbs in the following acrostic:

A A D D E M M N P R R R S T V
R
R
I
V
E
R

2   La famille de Jean-Paul est nombreuse mais ce soir il est resté seul dans le salon. Où sont ses parents, ses sœurs Marie-Claude, Sandrine, Claudette et Alice, son frère Albert et le chat?

    Voici des notes pour vous aider:

        Maman – montée dans sa chambre – papa descendu dans la cave – Alice pas encore rentrée– Sandrine allée à la disco – Albert pas revenu depuis ce matin – Claudette sortie avec ses amis – Marie-Claude rentrée à 6h, restée 5 minutes, repartie – la chatte tombée de la fenêtre, morte

    Jouez le rôle de Jean-paul. Qu'est-ce qu'il s'est dit?
    Exemple: Maman est montée dans sa chambre. Papa...

3   Traduisez
    (a) Has he left?
    (b) Did he stay a long time?
    (c) He went up to his room
    (d) He hasn't gone out
    (e) Did he arrive on time?
    (f) I got back late
    (g) He fell over outside the café
    (h) I have returned the books
    (i) My friends have returned
    (j) I have brought down your luggage
    (k) He got out a pen
    (l) I was born in Scotland

4   **Role-play** Pour faire le rôle de M. Camembert, préparez des réponses détaillées; pour le rôle du policier préparez vos questions.

    M. Camembert, au commissariat, fait sa déposition. Voici les notes qu'il a préparées:

        levé 6h – descendu – pris un café – sorti de la maison – entré dans un tabac – arrivé à la gare, pris le train de 7h15 – descendu à la gare St Lazare – arrivé au bureau – monté au 5e – resté toute la journée

    The police officer also wants the following details: the precise times of the above actions, did he get dressed or washed even? Did he eat nothing? What did he buy in the tabac? Did anyone see him go into the office building? What did he do at lunchtime? Did he leave the office during the day?

5   (i) Il a conduit (from conduire) means 'conducted', 'led', 'driven'. Can you find French cognates for the verbs on page 31?

reduced –
seduced –
introduced –
produced –
deduced –
constructed –

(ii) Also, find the French for 'translated' and 'destroyed'. 'Well cooked' is bien cuit. What is the infinitive of this verb?

3 Past participle agreement

Rules

1 The 16 or so *être* verbs all agree with the subject of the verb. The suffixes '-*e*', '-*s*' or '-*es*' may need to appear on the end of the past participle:

   (i)   *Elle est partie*
   (ii) *Marie et son amie sont arrivées*
   (iii) *Ils sont revenus*

A woman writing a letter would have to put *Je suis allée au théâtre hier soir*. Since the past participles of nearly all these verbs end in a vowel you cannot hear the agreement. The exception is *mourir*:

   (iv) *Colette, la romancière, est morte en 1954*

2 All the other verbs agree if there is a direct object and it comes before the verb. This is easy to spot if the direct object is a pronoun since it will come just before the verb anyway:

   (i)   *Ta sœur? Oui, je l'ai vue tout à l'heure*
   (ii) *Je les ai trouvées délicieuses, les pêches de son jardin*

But the agreement can be more easily overlooked if the direct object is a noun further away from the following verb:

   (iii) *Les pêches que j'ai achetées ce matin sont très bonnes*
   (iv) *Quels copains a-t-il vus là-bas?*
   (v)   *Voici les cartes postales que Jean et Marie m'ont envoyées*

If you still have difficulty in deciding what the object is and whether it is direct or indirect try the following formula: ask yourself 'who' or 'what' after the verb. So in the last two sentences for example: 'Saw who?' — 'friends' . 'Sent what?' — 'Postcards'. Conversely asking yourself 'who' or 'what' before the verb will give you the subject.

3 Direct or indirect? The simplest explanation is to say that an indirect object has a preposition (nearly always 'to') in front of it in English. So you would ask yourself 'to whom?' or 'to what?' after the verb to get the indirect object. There is no agreement with an indirect object so *lui* 'to him/her' and *leur* 'to them' do not agree:

   (i)   *Ta mère? Oui, je lui ai déjà parlé*

4 Reflexive verbs follow the rule already given. The past participle will agree if the reflexive pronoun is a direct object.

   (i)   *Elle s'est levée* – She got who up? Herself. *Se* is a preceding direct object.
   (ii)   *Ils se sont habillés* – They dressed who? Themselves. *Se* is again a preceding direct object
          The following cases need special care with agreements however:
   (iii) *Elle s'est coupée* – She cut **herself**
          Se is a preceding direct object so the past participle agrees but...
   (iv)   *Elle s'est coupé la jambe* – She cut her leg
          Cut what? Her leg. The direct object follows the verb in this case. The word *se* here means literally 'to herself' so is indirect.
   (v)   *Nous nous sommes écrit tous les jours* – We wrote to each other every day
   (vi)   *Elles se sont parlé souvent* – They often spoke to one another
          In both these examples there is no agreement since the reflexive pronouns are indirect objects, the equivalent in English of 'to each other/one another'.
   (vii) *Elles se sont posé toutes sortes de questions* –
          They asked each other all sorts of questions
   (viii) *Elle s'est demandé pourquoi* – She wondered (asked herself) why
   (ix)   *Ils se sont montré leurs cadeaux* – They showed each other their presents

No agreement here because, in French, you pose questions 'to someone', 'ask to someone' and 'show to someone'. The reflexive pronouns are all indirect here and not like the English verb construction. Since you cannot, in most cases, hear a past participle agreement (except for the few verbs and their compounds that end in a consonant like *écrit, mis, conduit*) making this agreement is purely a written convention. The French have to learn the rules for doing this at school and it does cause them some difficulty. Only very careful speakers would say:

    (x)   *Les lettres que j'ai mises sur la table* – The letters that I put on the table

5   There is never any agreement with the pronoun *en* meaning 'some, 'any', or 'of them'.

    (i)   *Ses lettres? Oui, j'en ai gardé beaucoup* – His letters? Yes, I've kept many of them

6   The past participle of an impersonal verb never agrees (an impersonal verb is one introduced by *il* meaning not 'he', in this case, but 'it' or 'there' in English). Examples likely to occur are:

    (i)   *La chaleur qu'il a fait cet été* – The heatwave we have had this summer
    (ii)   *Les efforts qu'il m'a fallu* – The effort it cost me
    (iii)   *Les problèmes qu'il y a eu cette année* – The problems there have been this year

Exercices

1   Faites accorder le participe passé, s'il le faut:
    (a) Ils sont arrivé
    (b) Mes deux sœurs sont parti
    (c) Marie-Antoinette est mort en 1793
    (d) Ma montre, où est-ce que je l'ai laissé?
    (e) Je les ai trouvé sans difficulté
    (f) Les poires que j'ai acheté hier ne sont pas mûres
    (g) Elle s'est baigné dans la mer
    (h) Marie a couché son petit frère et puis elle s'est couché
    (i) Nous avons descendu nos bagages
    (j) Quelles valises avez-vous descendu?
    (k) Ils sont descendu, vos frères?
    (l) Elles se sont regardé un moment puis se sont embrassé
    (m) Elle s'est gratté la tête
    (n) Ils se sont donné rendez-vous pour le lendemain
    (o) Des escargots? Ah, j'en ai trouvé de beaux après la pluie

4 Word order of negatives and object pronouns with the perfect tense

Rules

The negatives: *ne... pas, ne... personne, ne... rien, ne... jamais*

The object pronouns:

me	le	lui	y	en
te	la	leur		
se	les			
nous				
vous				

These grammatical items are usually encountered before you start using the perfect tense. You then have the problem of knowing where to fit them in with the two parts of the perfect tense. The three rules you have probably learned about the position of the pronouns with the perfect tense are:

1   For *ne... pas, ne... rien, ne... jamais, avoir* or *être* go in between the two words:
    (i)   *J'ai regardé la télé* – I watched television
    (ii)   *Je n'ai pas regardé la télé* – I did not watch television
    Note that in *ne... personne* phrases, *personne* always comes after the past participle because of its length:
    (iii)   *Je n'ai vu personne* – I saw no one

2   Pronouns come before *avoir* or *être*.

3   If there are two pronouns they come in the same order as the above table. For example:
    (i)   *Je ne les lui ai pas donnés* – I did not give them to him

These rules work quite well when you are writing but are impossible to apply on the spot when speaking. A good way of helping to acquire mastery of these rules is to practise manipulating certain combinations of negatives and object pronouns with the perfect tense. Start with a basic question sentence in the perfect tense that you might actually want to ask:

(ii)   *Vous avez vu mes clefs?* – Have you seen my keys?

and answer yourself first in the positive, next in the negative:

(iii)   *Oui, je les ai vues and non, je ne les ai pas vues*

Exercices

1   Essayez les questions:

(a) Vous avez trouvé mon sac?

    (i)   Oui, je...   (ii)   Non, je...

(b) Vous lui avez donné l'adresse?

    (i)   Oui, je la lui ai donnée   (ii)   Non, je...

(c) Il vous a donné son adresse?

    (i)   Oui, il...   (ii)   Non, il...

(d) Ces pêches, vous les avez achetées hier?

    (i)   Oui, je...   (ii)   Non, je...

(e) Je ne... achetées, on me... données

(f) J'ai écrit deux fois à ma correspondante

    Je lui ai écrit deux fois

    (i)   Je... envoyé une longue lettre

    (ii)   Je ne... envoyé de carte postale

5   Imperfect tense – *L'imparfait*

Use

1   'Imperfect' means unfinished, so this tense is used to describe an action that was continuous in the past. Its nearest equivalent in English is 'was' or 'were' doing something. The use of the imperfect tense for continuous action in the past is, in many ways, in direct contrast to the perfect tense (used for completed action). You often find them used together in the same sentence:

(i)   *Je prenais une douche quand mon voisin m'a téléphoné* –
    I was taking a shower when my neighbour rang me

(ii)   *J'ai trouvé la clef sous une chaise quand je nettoyais le salon* –
    I found the key under a chair when I was cleaning the lounge

You will often find that you have to decide between a perfect and an imperfect, particularly when translating from English into French or when answering questions on a passage in French.

2   The imperfect is also used for something that happened frequently or habitually in the past:

(i)   *Tous les soirs il buvait un grand verre de cognac avant de se coucher*

English conveys this idea by 'used to' or 'would drink'. The simple past tense might also be used in English 'every evening he drank'. In sentences like this, there is usually an adverbial expression like *toujours, souvent, tous les soirs* or *quelquefois* that makes the habitual meaning clear.

3   The third use of the imperfect is closely connected with **1** above. It is used for description or to convey the idea of the state of something in the past:

(i)   *Sa maison se trouvait à mi-hauteur sur la montagne* –
    His house was/stood half-way up the mountain

(ii)   *De ses fenêtres on avait une vue splendide sur tout le paysage* –
    From his windows you had a superb view over the whole countryside

The description of the world at the beginning of the book of Genesis illustrates this descriptive use very well.

(iii)   *'La terre **était** comme un grand vide, l'obscurité **couvrait** l'océan primitif et le souffle de Dieu **agitait** la surface de l'eau...'*

4   You have to be careful when translating 'was' and 'were' into French to distinguish between an imperfect and a perfect sense to the action:

(i)   *J'ai été triste quand il m'a téléphoné – Son coup de téléphone m'a rendu triste*

(ii)   *J'étais triste quand il m'a téléphoné – J'étais déjà d'une humeur triste au moment où il a téléphoné*

This 'was/were' problem also occurs with *il y a*. Compare the following:

(iii)   *Il y avait souvent des accidents à cet endroit mais hier matin il y a eu un accident fatal*

Thus, 'was' and 'were' are not always translated by the imperfect tense. (*See also* the passive, page 50.) Compare also the following:

(iv)   *J'avais une idée de son nom mais je ne pouvais pas me le rappeler*

(v)   *J'ai eu l'idée de le chercher dans l'annuaire*

In the first sentence, the idea **was present in the mind for some time** but in the second **it came suddenly**. To sum up then, the imperfect is used:

(a)   To say what was happening.

(b)   What used to happen.

(c)   Describe how things were or appeared to be in the past.

(d)   You need to distinguish between a completed and a continuous action in the past. Care is needed when dealing with 'was' and 'were'.

Formation

Go to the first person plural present tense and remove the *'-ons'* ending. Add the following endings for the imperfect tense:

-ais	*-ions*
-ais	*-iez*
-ait	*-aient*

Ralentir – to slow down (*nous ralentissons*)

Je ralentissais	*Nous ralentissions*
Tu ralentissais	*Vous ralentissiez*
il ralentissait	*Ils ralentissaient*

This works for nearly all verbs, regular or irregular.

Note

(a)   The imperfect of *être* is:

J'étais	*Nous étions*
Tu étais	*Vous étiez*
Il était	*Ils étaient*

(b)   Verbs ending in *'-ger'* and *'-cer'* need an *'e'* before the *'g'* and a cedilla under the *'c'* if the following vowel would otherwise make them soft (*see* present tense, page 27). Examples:

Je commençais	*Nous commencions*	*J'arrangeais*	*Nous arrangions*
Tu commençais	*Vous commenciez*	*Tu arrangeais*	*Vous arrangiez*
Il commençait	*Ils commençaient*	*Il arrangeait*	*Ils arrangeaient*

You will notice that in two cases, the first and second persons plural, the *'i'* always makes the respective consonant soft. (*See also* appendix 1, page 203.)

(c)   The imperfect endings *'-ais'*, *'-ait'* and *'-aient'* all sound the same. French primary-school children do lots of dictation practice to get this point home!

Exercices

1   Comblez les blancs dans le texte suivant:

Dimanche à 10 heures j'ét__ dans ma chambre avec mon frère. Mon père et notre voisin ét__ dans le garage. Ils essay__ de réparer notre voiture qui ét__ en panne. Maman ét__ dans le salon. Elle tricot__. Mon frère et moi jou__ aux échecs.

2   Répondez à ces questions en disant la vérité:

(a)   Que faisiez-vous dimanche dernier à 9 heures?

(b)   Et à 11 heures?

(c)   Que faisiez-vous hier soir à 8 heures?

(d)   Où habitiez-vous quand vous aviez cinq ans?

(e)   Est-ce qu'il pleuvait ce matin quand vous êtes sorti?

Sinon, quel temps faisait-il?

(f)   Hier, vous portiez un chemisier blanc, un tricot vert et une jupe grise?

Sinon, qu'est-ce que vous portiez?

3 Traduisez en français:
  (a) She usually woke at 6.00 and stayed in bed till 7.00
  (b) This morning however she got up at 7.30 and left the house at 8.00
  (c) While we were watching television last night someone stole my bike
  (d) I dreamt about a strange school where all the teachers wore blue-jeans and smoked in class. There were no lessons in the afternoon. We all played games and went home at 4.00
  (e) When my father went fishing he usually got up very early and came back late without any fish. Last Sunday though he came back with a large trout
  (f) 'I caught it myself' he said. We didn't believe him!
  (g) I was having a shower when you rang
  (h) When I was young I listened to the radio a lot
  (i) When my grandfather was young there was no television
  (j) What did people do in the evenings in those days?

4 Le récit suivant est tiré du Nouveau Testament où il est intitulé 'Jésus apaise les eaux'. Connaissez-vous son titre en anglais? Pour combler les blancs, trouvez le verbe qui convient le mieux dans la liste en bas.

Notez

Dans la version originale le passé simple (voyez plus loin) est utilisé au lieu du passé composé.

> Le soir de ce même jour, Jésus __ à ses disciples 'Passons de l'autre côté du lac'. Ils ont quitté la foule; les disciples __ Jésus dans la barque où il __. D'autres barques encore __ près de lui. Et voilà qu'un vent violent __ à souffler, les vagues __ dans la barque de sorte que, déjà , elle __ d'eau. Jésus __ à l'arrière du bateau et __ la tête appuyée sur un coussin. Ses disciples l'__ alors et lui __, 'Maître, nous allons mourir. Cela ne te fait-il rien?' Jésus __, il __ sévèrement au vent et __ à l'eau du lac: Silence! Calme-toi! Alors le vent __ et __ un grand calme. Puis Jésus __ aux disciples, 'Pourquoi avez-vous peur? N'avez-vous pas encore de foi?'
> Mais ils __ très effrayés et ils __ les uns aux autres:
> 'Qui est donc cet homme, pour que même le vent et l'eau du lac lui obéissent?'

dormait – était – a dit – il y a eu – ont emmené – se sont dit – étaient – s'est mis – est tombé – s'est réveillé – ont dit – a dit – a parlé – se remplissait – se trouvait –se jetaient – ont réveillé – étaient – a dit

6 Past historic tense – *Le passé simple*

This tense is not used in spoken French. You will meet it in works of fiction and non-fiction and in articles in newspapers and magazines. Because it is not acquired naturally, it has to be learned in school by native speakers of French. You need to be able to recognize it as a past tense.

You may be required to use it when translating into French passages written in a literary style or possibly in other kinds of writing. You should check with your teacher what is required by your particular Examining Board.

Use

The past historic is the direct equivalent in use of the perfect tense except for the fact that it is never spoken. In writing, choice between the two tenses depends on the literary style. The past historic is becoming less popular at the moment with some French writers. You cannot mix the two tenses in the same piece of writing. However, since the past historic is never spoken, when direct speech is given in a piece of writing — what someone actually said — the perfect tense must be used. Here is an example from an imaginary story:

> Bernard **entra** dans le salon et **s'assit** en face de Thérèse.
> 'Qu'est-ce que **tu as fait** hier soir? **Tu es sortie** sans manger et **tu es revenue** vers 6 heures ce matin.'
> Elle ne **répondit** rien et **continua** à regarder fixement le feu.

This tense is called *le passé simple* in French because it doesn't need another verb like *avoir* or *être* to form it. The verb itself changes. You can compare it in this respect to the simple past of some verbs in English: 'she sings' becomes 'she sang'; 'I see' becomes 'I saw'.

The English term 'past historic' is to do with the fact that this tense is used principally to relate the events in a story: *une histoire*.

Formation

1 '-*er*' verbs

All verbs ending in '-*er*' in the infinitive form the past historic in the same way. Remove the '-*er*' and add the following endings:

-ai	*-âmes*
-as	*-âtes*
-a	*-èrent*

J'allai	*Nous allâmes*
Tu allas	*Vous allâtes*
Il alla	*Ils allèrent*

2   Regular '*-ir*' and '*-re*' verbs (e.g. *ralentir*, *faiblir*, *descendre* and *rendre*) have the following endings:

-is	*-îmes*
-is	*-îtes*
-it	*-irent*

Je faiblis	*Nous faiblîmes*
Tu faiblis	*Vous faiblîtes*
Il faiblit	*Ils faiblirent*

3   Many verbs in '*-oir*', but not all of them, have the following endings:

-us	*-ûmes*
-us	*-ûtes*
-ut	*-urent*

Je voulus	*Nous voulûmes*
Tu voulus	*Vous voulûtes*
Il voulut	*Ils voulurent*

But this time you don't always just add the endings instead of the '*-oir*':

savoir – Je sus; boire – Je bus; pouvoir; Je pus; avoir – J'eus

Do you notice a similarity between the past participle and the past historic? In fact, the past participle is a good guide to the past historic of many, **but not all**, irregular verbs. One common verb you can't do this with is *voir*:

Je vis	*Nous vîmes*
Tu vis	*Vous vîtes*
Il vit	*Ils virent*

and also of course *revoir* and *prévoir*!

Note

(a)   The final '*-ent*' is not pronounced if you have to read a passage aloud.

(b)   There is always a circumflex accent over the '*-a*', '*-i*' or '*-u*' of the first and second persons plural.

4   There are a number of exceptions to rules **2** and **3** above. Sometimes the past participle is a guide; sometimes it is not. Note the following:

(a)   *écrire*, *décrire* (to describe), *s'inscrire* (to sign up, get enrolled) and others, add an extra syllable:

  (i)   *Il écrivit   Ils écrivirent*

Similarly *conduire* (and also *séduire* – seduce, *réduire* – reduce, *traduire* – translate and others) add another syllable too.

  (ii)   *Il conduisit   Ils réduisirent*

(b)   There is a group of verbs in '*-eindre*' and '*-aindre*' (e.g. *craindre* – fear, *peindre* – paint, *éteindre* – extinguish, put out). These all have a '*-gn*' in the past historic:

Il éteignit	*Ils peignirent*
Il craignit	*Ils craignirent*

(c)   Some verbs just have to be learned:

Etre	*Il fut*	*Nous fûmes* (nothing to do with *fumer* – to smoke!)
Faire	*Il fit*	*Nous fîmes*
Naître	*Il naquit*	*Nous naquîmes*

Note also *venir* and *tenir*:

Je vins	*Nous vînmes*
Tu vins	*Vous vîntes*
Il vint	*Ils vinrent*

Je tins	*Nous tînmes*
Tu tins	*Vous tîntes*
Il tint	*Ils tinrent*

Don't forget *retenir* – retain, *se souvenir* – remember, *maintenir* – maintain, *convenir* – agree, and others.

Note also the following which may be a puzzle when you first meet them:

Mettre	*– Je mis*
Prendre	*– Je pris*
Mourir	*– Il mourut*
Vivre	*– Il vécut*
Lire	*– Il lut*
Se taire	*– Il se tut* (not from *tuer* – to kill!)

Exercice

1   Trouvez l'infinitif et la signification des phrases suivantes:

les pompiers éteignirent le feu – ils purent le comprendre – nous fûmes bientôt dehors – il dut payer une amende – il produisit ses papiers – ils s'inscrivirent aux cours du soir – la grippe le retint au lit – les résultats surprirent le prof – ils revinrent au week-end – il but le verre d'un trait – à ce moment il sut la vérité – il fallut attendre un peu – le matin il plut – il maintint longtemps sa situation – son raisonnement me convainquit – il se tut un instant puis il rit – ils nous dirent bonjour – nous fumâmes deux cigarettes avant de nous coucher

7   Pluperfect tense – *Le plus que parfait*

The perfect tense is used to say what has happened in the past; the pluperfect goes one step further back and says what **had** happened (before something else). For example:

(i)   *Elle dit* (present) *qu'elle m'a souvent vu* (past) *au supermarché*

(ii)   *Elle a dit* (past) *qu'elle m'avait souvent vu* (further back in past) *au supermarché*

(iii)   *Je ne l'ai pas vue. Elle était déjà sortie*

You can reverse the order of these two statements:

(iv)   *Elle était déjà sortie. Je ne l'ai pas vue*

Due to the tenses it is still clear which event came first.

Use

1   The most frequent use of the pluperfect is in reported speech (i.e. when relating something someone said, did or saw etc.). For example:

(i)   **Actual statement** *Je ne suis pas sorti hier soir. J'ai regardé la télé jusqu'à 11 heures. J'ai bu un verre de lait et puis je me suis couché à 11h15.*

(ii)   **Reported statement** *Il a dit qu'il n'était pas sorti hier soir, qu'il avait regardé la télé jusqu'à 11 heures, qu'il avait bu un verre de lait et qu'il s'était couché à 11h15.*

The use of 'had' in English usually signals a pluperfect in French. However, English is not so particular and 'had' can often be left out: 'he asked me what time I arrived'.
In French this would have to be:

(iii)   *Il m'a demandé à quelle heure **j'étais** arrivé*

Similarly:

(iv)   *Elle m'a montré l'endroit où l'accident **s'était** produit –*
She showed me the spot where the accident happened (or had happened)

If you rely on thinking in English, you could miss the need for the pluperfect in such cases.
Note The phrase 'had been doing' in English, as a continuous **unfinished** action in the past, is translated by an imperfect tense. (*see* page 33)

Formation

Like the perfect tense, the pluperfect is made up of two parts: *avoir* or *être* + the past participle. However, this time you need the **imperfect** of *avoir* or *être*.

J'avais vu	*Nous avions vu*
Tu avais vu	*Vous aviez vu*

Il avait vu	*Ils avaient vu*
Elle avait vu	*Elles avaient vu*

J'étais sorti(e)	*Nous étions sorti(e)s*
Tu étais sorti(e)	*Vous étiez sorti(e)(s)*
Il était sorti	*Ils étaient sortis*
Elle était sortie	*Elles étaient sorties*

Je m'étais levé(e)	*Nous nous étions levé(e)s*
Tu t'étais levé(e)	*Vous vous étiez levé(e)(s)*
Il s'était levé	*Ils s'étaient levés*
Elle s'était levée	*Elles s'étaient levées*

Note

(a) The choice of *avoir* or *être* depends on the same rules as for the 16 verbs and reflexive verbs (*see* above)

(b) The past participle agrees if necesssary (*see* above)

(c) The negatives, *ne... pas*, *ne... rien* etc., go in exactly the same positions as with the perfect tense

Exercices

1   (a) Voici la déclaration de M. XX. Mettez les verbes au plus que parfait.

Je suis descendu à l'hôtel Splendide. J'y suis arrivé vers 7 heures. J'ai mangé à l'hôtel. Après je suis sorti me promener. J'ai marché pendant une heure. Puis je suis revenu à l'hôtel. Dans le bar j'ai rencontré un ancien collègue. Nous avons bu quelques verres ensemble. Je me suis couché vers 11h45.

(b) Même exercice, mais commencez avec 'Il a dit que...':

2   Traduisez (des verbes avec être):
   (a) I had arrived late so I went to bed early
   (b) When the bus stopped he got out
   (c) She had left early in order not to miss the train
   (d) They had presented themselves at the police station
   (e) I didn't know that she had got married

3   Traduisez (pronoms + expressions négatives):
   (a) I hadn't seen her since Saturday
   (b) He had said nothing to me
   (c) They hadn't found anyone there
   (d) Had he already talked to you about it?
   (e) My sisters had never visited Paris

4   Traduisez:
   (a) He says that he has never travelled by plane
   (b) He said that he had never travelled by plane
   (c) I found I hadn't understood what he said
   (d) She said she telephoned last week
   (e) I am sure the letter has arrived
   (f) I was sure the letter had arrived
   (g) 'I have never seen this man,' she said
   (h) He remembered he saw Fifi at the bank
   (i) He said he had never seen the man
   (j) I couldn't find the letter he sent me

5   Read the following 'fait divers':

INCENDIAIRE
Luneville: Un mineur de 13 ans a été interpelé samedi par les policiers de Luneville (Meurthe et Moselle) et a reconnu être l'auteur d'incendies, au cours de la semaine passée, dans des immeubles HLM de la ville. L'adolescent avait mis le feu à des poubelles. Quatre personnes, dont un bébé, avaient été légèrement intoxiquées au cours de ces incendies. Remis à ses parents, il sera présenté au juge des enfants.

Six incidents are referred to:
  (i)   Four people and baby affected by fumes
 (ii)   Confessed to being responsible
(iii)   Minor questioned by police
 (iv)   He will appear in court
  (v)   Returned to parents
 (vi)   Set fire to dustbins

(a) Number these in the order in which they occured.
(b) At what point in time does the report start?
(c) Explain why some verbs are in the pluperfect.

6   Lisez le fait divers suivant. Soulignez et marquez les verbes au passé composé et au plus que parfait. Quatre événements sont mentionnés, deux sont récents, deux datent du 18e siècle. Savez-vous les distinguer?

> **SUR LES TRACES DE DE SAUSSURE. GENEVE – MONT BLANC EN MOINS DE 24 HEURES**
> *Chamonix:* Il y a quelques jours, deux Haut-Savoyards – Pierre Cusin et Thierry Gazin – ont battu le record Chamonix: Mont Blanc et retour en moins de 8 heures. Ces deux spécialistes de cross en montagne avaient voulu saluer ainsi à leur manière le bicentenaire de l'ascension du Mont Blanc. Devant cette brillante réussite, ils ont décidé de ne pas en rester là. Avec Christophe Gotti du CAF* d'Annecy, ils ont décidé de refaire l'itinéraire du savant genevois, Horace Benedict De Saussure. Celui-ci bien avant avait réussi la conquête du Mont Blanc dont il fut l'instigateur. Il était allé de Genève à Chamonix à pied, puis bien plus tard, en 1787, avait gravi le Mont Blanc, avec Jacques Balmont, dans des conditions que l'on imagine il y a 199 ans.
> Le trio sportif est donc parti pour Genève hier soir pour remonter toute la vallée de l'Arve en courant.
> * Club Alpin Français

Anecdote

Si vous croyez que le plus que parfait est difficile pour les Anglais, les Français ont quelquefois des problèmes avec le '*had had*' dans notre langue. Par exemple:
  Had he had time he would have come – S'il avait eu le temps il serait venu
Mais considérez le cas en anglais du prof qui en corrigeant la composition de John, souligne son '*had*' et écrit au dessus '*had had*':
  The teacher, where John had had 'had', had 'had had'!

8   Past anterior tense

This tense is only found in books written in formal style. It is never used in spoken French. You don't need to learn how to use it, but you may need to recognize it for translation and understanding purposes.

Use

Virtually the only use is after the following conjunctions, when one action immediately follows another. The other verb in the sentence is then always in the past historic: *dès que, aussitôt que, du moment que, à peine que, quand, lorsque*.
For example:
  (i)   *Dès que son ami fut revenu il lui apprit la nouvelle* –
        As soon as his friend had returned he told him the news
 (ii)   *A peine eut-il terminé son discours qu'il tomba mort* –
        Scarcely had he finished his speech when he dropped dead

Formation

The past historic of *avoir* or *être* + past participle of the verb.

9   Future tense – *Le futur simple*

There are two ways of indicating future time in French: using the verb *aller* followed by the infinitive of the verb:
  (i)   *Qu'est-ce que nous allons faire ce soir?* – What are we going to do this evening?
Using the future tense of the verb:
 (ii)   *Est-ce qu'il fera beau demain?* – Will it be fine tomorrow?

There is a slight difference in implication between these two uses. The future with *aller* implies partly the immediate future but also a relationship between the present moment and a future event:

(iii)   *Qu'est-ce que nous allons faire ce soir? Et qu'est-ce que nous ferons demain?*

The implication is that the present situation has got something to do with this evening's plans but that tomorrow stands on its own as it were. If this sounds a bit complex don't worry too much. *Aller* + infinitive will serve in most circumstances where you can't remember the correct future tense.

Use

The future tense is used in much the same way in French as it is in English: to refer to future time. The main difference is that English doesn't always use a future when future time is implied.

 (i)   *Quand il **arrivera** dites-lui d'attendre* – When he **arrives** tell him to wait

 (ii)   *Je serai là aussitôt que je **serai** prêt* – I'll be there as soon as I **am** ready

You will see that English uses a **present** but French uses a **future** tense.

The one major exception to this is after *si* meaning 'if' in French:

(iii)   *S'il arrive, dites-lui d'attendre* – If he comes, tell him to wait

(iv)   *Je viendrai si je suis prêt* – I'll come if I'm ready

The most straightforward rule that works with *si* is the following: after *si* always use the same tense that is used in English. In the above examples, it is the present tense but the rule should also work for the other tenses considered below.

Formation

1   Regular verbs

Add the following endings to the infinitive (with '-re' verbs, remove the final '-e' first)

-ai	*-ons*
-as	*-ez*
-a	*-ont*

Réussir	*Je réussirai*	*Nous réussirons*
	Tu réussiras	*Vous réussirez*
	Il réussira	*Ils réussiront*

Apprendre	*J''apprendrai*	*Nous apprendrons*
	Tu apprendras	*Vous apprendrez*
	Il apprendra	*Ils apprendront*

Retourner	*Je retournerai*	*Nous retournerons*
	Tu retourneras	*Vous retournerez*
	Il retournera	*Ils retourneront*

2   Irregular verbs

The endings are the same but the inside part of the verb changes, sometimes substantially. These verbs have to be learned separately. They are nearly all commonly used verbs.

Voir	*Je verrai*	*Nous verrons*
	Tu verras	*Vous verrez*
	Il verra	*Ils verront*

Faire	*Je ferai*	*Nous ferons*
	Tu feras	*Vous ferez*
	Il fera	*Ils feront*

Aller	*J'irai*	*Nous irons*
	Tu iras	*Vous irez*
	Il ira	*Ils iront*

Look up the future tense of the following if you are not sure of them:

   être – avoir – envoyer – venir/tenir – pouvoir – savoir – vouloir – courir – mourir – devoir – recevoir – falloir – pleuvoir

Note the '*r*' sound just before the ending is the signal of a future tense being used when you hear spoken French.

10 Conditional tense – *Le conditionnel*

This tense may not have been pointed out to you during your preparation for GCSE. You would have used it without knowing it in such phrases as *je voudrais, j'aimerais* – I would like/love, and *Est-ce que je pourrais?* – Could I?

Use

The conditional is used in two ways:

1 To express a condition attached to a statement:
  (i) *J'irais la voir si j'avais le temps* – I would go and see her if I had the time

2 To put the future in the past (not so daft as it sounds!):
  (i) *Il dit qu'il arrivera tard* – He says he will arrive late (said now)
  (ii) *Il a dit qu'il arriverait tard* – He said he would arrive late (reporting what he said)

  Note Be careful to distinguish between 'would' in English that means 'used to' and needs an imperfect tense in French, and the 'would' that has a condition attached to it or is simply 'will' in the past.

3 The conditional is also used to express an allegation or an unsubstantiated fact:
  (i) *D'après les journaux, il y aurait des centaines de morts* –
    The newspapers claim that hundreds are dead
  (ii) *Selon certains observateurs on serait au bord d'une guerre* –
    Some observers think we are on the brink of war

  This use is **very common** today in newspapers and broadcasts.

4 Another use, closely connected to the last one, is to express a possibility or a supposition:
  (i) *Serait-il malade?* – Might he possibly be ill?
  (ii) *Y aurait-il quelque explication rationnelle de ce phénomène?* –
    Could there be some rational explanation for this phenomenon?

Formation

The imperfect endings are put on to the future stem (i.e. instead of the future endings you use the imperfect ones):

-ais	*-ions*
-ais	*-iez*
-ait	*-aient*

Venir	*Je viendrais*	*Nous viendrions*
	Tu viendrais	*Vous viendriez*
	Il viendrait	*Ils viendraient*

Arriver	*J'arriverais*	*Nous arriverions*
	Tu arriverais	*Vous arriveriez*
	Il arriverait	*Ils arriveraient*

Note
(a) The first person singular is pronounced almost exactly like the first person of the future tense.
(b) As with the imperfect tense '*-ais*', '*-ait*', and '*-aient*' all sound the same.

11 Future perfect and conditional perfect tenses – *Le futur antérieur et le conditionnel passé*

These two tenses need to be included in this group of 'future-type' tenses. As well as saying what someone 'will do' you can say what they 'will have' done; as well what they 'would do', what they 'would have' done

Future perfect: Use

It is used in the same way as English 'will have':
  (i) *Il aura déjà reçu ma lettre* – He will have already received my letter
  (ii) *A 6 heures elles seront arrivées là-bas* – By six they will have arrived there
Note English does not always use 'will have' when a future is implied:

(iii) *Téléphone-moi dès que tu auras reçu sa lettre* – Phone me as soon as you have received his letter

Compare this with the future tense example given above. You will find this use particularly after *quand, dès que* and *aussitôt que*.

Future perfect: Formation

The future perfect is formed from the future of *avoir* or *être* + the past participle.

Recevoir	*J'aurai reçu*	*Nous aurons reçu*
	Tu auras reçu	*Vous aurez reçu*
	Il aura reçu	*Ils auront reçu*

Arriver	*Je serai arrivé(e)*	*Nous serons arrivé(e)s*
	Tu seras arrivé(e)	*Vous serez arrivé(e)(s)*
	Il sera arrivé	*Ils seront arrivés*
	Elle sera arrivée	*Elles seront arrivées*

Conditional perfect: Use

It is used in the same way as the English 'would have':
  (i) *Il m'aurait entendu si j'avais crié un peu plus fort* –
       He would have heard me if I had shouted a bit louder
  (ii) *Je ne serais pas parti si tôt si j'avais su que le train aurait du retard* –
       I wouldn't have left so early if I had known that the train would be late

You will note that, in the examples for both these tenses, the future perfect is followed by a perfect tense and the conditional perfect by a pluperfect. This is a common combination of the tenses.

Note The conditional perfect is also used to express an allegation or a statement that cannot be vouched for, just like the conditional above.
  (iii) *Le voleur aurait pénétré dans le bâtiment par une fenêtre laissée ouverte* –
       It is thought that the thief got into the building through a window left open
  (iv) *Vous auriez donc vu, de vos yeux vu, le rhinocéros se promener en flânant dans les rues de la ville?* – You are supposed to have seen then, with your own eyes, the rhinoceros strolling through streets of the town?

Conditional perfect: Formation

The conditional perfect is formed from the conditional of *avoir* or *être* + the past participle:

Trouver	*J'aurais trouvé*	*Nous aurions trouvé*
	Tu aurais trouvé	*Vous auriez trouvé*
	Il aurait trouvé	*Ils auraient trouvé*

Partir	*Je serais parti(e)*	*Nous serions parti(e)s*
	Tu serais parti(e)	*Vous seriez parti(e)(s)*
	Il serait parti	*Ils seraient partis*
	Elle serait partie	*Elles seraient parties*

Tenses after *si*

It has already been noted that when the future is implied in French a future or a future perfect tense must be used, except after *si* where it means 'if'. *Si* can also mean 'if/whether':
  (i) *Je ne sais pas si je le verrai ce soir* – I don't know if/whether I will see him tonight
A future type tense is used after *si* that can mean 'whether'. As already pointed out, the simplest rule to follow after *si* is to use the same tense that is used in English.
  (ii) *S'il arrive, dites-lui d'attendre* – If he comes, tell him to wait
A present tense is used in English so a present tense is used in French. However, in these examples:
  (iii) *Je me demande s'il viendra* – I wonder if he will come
(Future tense in English after 'if', so same in French.)
  (iv) *Je lui ai demandé si elle aimerait sortir avec moi* –
       I asked her if she would like to go out with me
(Conditional in English so the same in French.)
     This rule with *si* can usually be relied upon.

Note The simple past in English is translated by the **imperfect** in French:
  (v) *Si je **savais** son adresse je lui écrirais* – If I **knew** his address I would write to him

Exercices

1 Traduisez en Français:
   (a) He will find the letter
   (b) He would have found the letter (if he had looked in the cupboard)
   (c) He will have found the letter
   (d) He would find the letter (if he looked in the cupboard)
   (e) Shall I go out with him tonight?
   (f) I would have gone out with him tonight
   (g) I would go out with her (if I had some money)
   (h) He will already have gone out

2 Les verbes suivants sont au futur. Trouvez:
   (a) L'infinitif de chaque verbe
   (b) Le conditionnel (à la même personne)
   (c) Le futur antérieur
   (d) Le conditionnel passé
   Exemple, *il retiendra:*
   (a) retenir
   (b) il retiendrait
   (c) il aura retenu
   (d) il aurait retenu
   ils feront – ils seront – je verrai – nous aurons – il pourra – il aura – il pleuvra – nous enverrons – il mourra – il faudra – ils jetteront – il vaudra

3 Traduisez en français:
   (a) When you see him give him this
   (b) If you see him give him this
   (c) As soon as I have finished I'll telephone you
   (d) If I had enough money I would like to travel
   (e) What are we going to do this evening?
   (f) What would we do without television?
   (g) I am sure he would have told you that
   (h) If we had been there we would have seen him
   (i) I asked her whether she would like to come with me to Greece
   (j) I don't know if she would come

4 (a) Traduisez en anglais.
   (b) Transposez au passé en commençant par 'C'était la veille du grand départ...'

   C'est la veille du grand départ. Bientôt Marie-Claude va faire ses valises car elle va partir demain matin à 5 heures. Demain soir elle sera à Cannes. Elle aura passé dix heures dans le train et aussitôt qu'elle aura mangé elle ira se coucher à l'hôtel. On lui a dit que, de sa fenêtre, elle pourra voir la mer dès qu'il fera jour.

5 Traduisez en français:
   (a) If I see him, I'll give him this. If he asks me who gave it to me, I'll tell him the truth.
   (b) When I see him, I'll give him this. When he asks who gave it to me I'll tell him the truth.

6 Traduisez en anglais:

   Deux cents militants kurdes ont manifesté hier à Paris et ont occupé le premier étage de la Tour Eiffel. Selon leurs responsables, deux d'entre leurs compatriotes seraient récemment morts à cause des suites de mauvais traitements dans les prisons turques, et plusieurs autres seraient actuellement dans un état critique.

7 Dans l'extrait suivant quels détails sont établis et lesquels sont supposés?

   Hier matin, sur un parking à Chateaudun, un homme a reçu plusieurs coups de couteau d'une jeune fille mineure, apparemment son amie. Ce serait un témoin qui aurait alerté la police. La victime dont l'identité n'est pas encore connue, a été transportée dans un état grave à l'hôpital. Il aurait notamment le poumon perforé. Quant à la jeune fille, elle se serait constituée prisonnière vers 4h 15 à la gendarmerie de Poulains.

12 Subjunctive mood

Use

The subjunctive is a mood of the verb. There are three moods:

(a) **indicative**, used most of the time for stating facts where there is no uncertainty in the mind of the speaker

(b) **subjunctive**, for stating ideas, possibilities and wishes which might not necessarily happen

(c) **imperative**, for giving orders and commands

The subjunctive has virtually disappeared from English. For example, do you say, 'If I **were** you I wouldn't do that' or 'If I **was** you I wouldn't do that'? The '**were**' here is used to state a possibility. You would still probably say 'May he **succeed** in his plans' but you might say instead 'I hope he **succeeds** in his plans'. 'I were' and 'he succeed' are both remnants of the subjunctive in English.

In French, the subjunctive in the present tense (and to some extent the perfect tense) is very much alive and used in the spoken language. The imperfect and the pluperfect subjunctives are confined to the written language and then most often to the third person singular.

You will need to be able to use the present and perfect subjunctives in essays and translations into French and to recognize the other two tenses when you meet them in texts.

Formation

1 Present tense

Regular verbs

Take the third person plural present tense, remove the '-*ent*' and add the endings:

-e	*-ions*
-es	*-iez*
-e	*-ent*

*ils finiss**ent***	*Que je finiss**e***	*Que nous finiss**ions***
	*Que tu finiss**es***	*Que vous finiss**iez***
	*Qu'il finiss**e***	*Qu'ils finiss**ent***
*ils chang**ent***	*Que je chang**e***	*Que nous chang**ions***
	*Que tu chang**es***	*Que vous chang**iez***
	*Qu'il chang**e***	*Qu'ils chang**ent***
*Ils entend**ent***	*Que j'entend**e***	*Que nous entend**ions***
	*Que tu entend**es***	*Que vous entend**iez***
	*Qu'il entend**e***	*Qu'ils entend**ent***

Note Since the subjunctive always has *que* before it it is a good idea to learn it in this way. French schoolchildren learn it like this.

Irregular verbs

The following verbs have almost the same endings as above but the inside part changes. They are all very commonly used and should be learned:

Que je sois	*Que nous soyons*
Que tu sois	*Que vous soyez*
Qu'il soit	*Qu'ils soient*
Que j'aie	*Que nous ayons*
Que tu aies	*Que vous ayez*
Qu'il ait	*Qu'ils aient*
Que je fasse	*Que nous fassions*
Que tu fasses	*Que vous fassiez*
Qu'il fasse	*Qu'ils fassent*
Que j'aille	*Que nous allions*
Que tu ailles	*Que vous alliez*
Qu'il aille	*Qu'ils aillent*
Que je puisse	*Que nous puissions*
Que tu puisses	*Que vous puissiez*
Qu'il puisse	*Qu'ils puissent*

Que je sache	*Que nous sachions*
Que tu saches	*Que vous sachiez*
Qu'il sache	*Qu'ils sachent*

Que je veuille	*Que nous voulions*
Que tu veuilles	*Que vous vouliez*
Qu'il veuille	*Qu'ils veuillent*

You should be able to tell which verbs these come from.

2 Perfect subjunctive

This is the present subjunctive of *être* or *avoir* + the past participle:

Que j'aie fini	*Que nous ayons fini*
Que tu aies fini	*Que vous ayez fini*
Qu'il ait fini	*Qu'ils aient fini*

Que je sois resté(e)	*Que nous soyons resté(e)s*
Que tu sois resté(e)	*Que vous soyez resté(e)(s)*
Qu'il soit resté	*Qu'ils soient restés*
Qu'elle soit restée	*Qu'elles soient restées*

3 Imperfect subjunctive

You will only meet this tense in written French where it is confined, almost entirely, to the third person singular. In everyday spoken French, when a past subjunctive is needed, the perfect subjunctive is used instead. The third person singular of the imperfect subjunctive bears a close resemblance to the past historic.

Note Even though the imperfect subjunctive is hardly used any more in speech (in casual conversation) it does give the speaker an unusual importance; people would stop to listen. Here are some examples:

il fut (past historic)	*il arriva* (past historic)	*il attendit* (past historic)
qu'il fût (imperfect subjunctive)	*qu'il arrivât* (imperfect subjunctive)	*qu'il attendît* (imperfect subjunctive)

The endings are as follows:

-sse	**-ssions**
-sses	**-ssiez**
-ût	**-ssent**

Que je fusse	*Que nous fussions*
Que tu fusses	*Que vous fussiez*
Qu'il fût	*Qu'ils fussent*

All you have to remember is to put the vowel from the past historic '*-a*', '*-u*' or '*-i*' before the double '*-ss*' and to put a circumflex before the '*-t*' of the third person singular. The imperfect subjunctive translates just like an ordinary past tense. French children have to learn about this tense in school.

4 The pluperfect subjunctive

This is formed from the imperfect subjunctive of *avoir* or *être* + the past participle.

(i) *Bien qu'il ne fût jamais allé en France il parlait très bien le français –*
Although he had never been to France he spoke French very well

It is used in the subjunctive clause when the meaning is clearly 'had'. It only occurs in 'literary-style' written French. You are unlikely to need to use it. The following special uses of it however, could be confusing in a translation:

Used instead of a conditional perfect:

(i) *Il eût mieux fait de rester chez lui – il aurait mieux fait de rester chez lui –*
It would have been better for him to stay at home

(ii) *Il aimait rester au lit le matin, ne fût-ce que pour dix minutes –*
He liked staying in bed in the morning, even if it were only for 10 minutes

If you are studying seventeenth or eighteenth century texts you will come across lots of examples of the above uses.

Using the pluperfect subjunctive as though it were a conditional perfect (see (i) above) is also fairly common today in 'literary-style' French.

Basic rules

A: After certain conjunctions:

1 Saying **'although'**– *quoique, bien que*:
   (i)   *Bien que ce ne soit pas toujours le cas* – Although it isn't always the case

2 Saying **'so that, in order that'** – *pour que, afin que*:
   Parlez plus haut pour qu'il puisse vous entendre – Speak louder so that he can hear you

3 Saying **'before, until'**, **'without'** – *avant que, jusqu'à ce que, sans que*:
   (i)   *Il nous faut attendre jusqu'à ce qu'elle soit prête* – We must wait until she is ready
   (ii) *Dites-le-lui avant qu'il ne le sache par ma lettre* –
         Tell him it before he finds out from my letter
   (iii) *Je suis entré dans la chambre sans qu'elle m'ait entendu* –
         I entered the room without her hearing me

Note
(a) An infinitive construction is preferred when the subject of both clauses is the same:
    Il est parti avant de lire ma lettre – **He** left and **he** didn't read my letter
(b) The phrase *après que*, referring to events that have already taken place does not need a subjunctive.
    Can you explain why?
(c) Also *avant de* is sometimes easier to use than *jusqu'à ce que*:
    Je vais travailler avant d'aller à l'université – I am going to work until I go to university

4 Saying **'provided that'**, **'on condition that'** – *pourvu que, à condition que*:
   Je le ferai à condition qu'elle ne me le reproche pas –
   I'll do it provided that she doesn't reproach me for it

5 Saying **'unless'** – *à moins que*:
   (i)   *A moins qu'on ne prenne vite des mesures importantes l'atmosphère de notre planète sera
         complètement dégradée* – Unless serious measures are taken quickly the atmosphere of our
         planet will be totally ruined

6 Saying **'so that'**, **'in such a way that'**– when intention rather than result is implied:
   (i)   *Il faut imposer des amendes très sévères de sorte que les industriels soient obligés d'arrêter
         la pollution* – Severe fines must be imposed so that industrialists are forced to stop pollution
   But
   (ii) *La loi a été si vigoureusement appliquée que personne n'ose plus l'enfreindre* –
         The law has been so rigorously applied that no one dares break it any more

7 Saying **'whoever'**, **'however'**, **'wherever'**, **'whatever'**, **'whether'**. These are best learned in
   phrases that could be used or adapted for essays:
   (i)   *Qui qu'il soit je ne le laisserai pas entrer* – Whoever he is I shan't let him in
   (ii) *Quelque désagréable que soit la tâche, il faut la faire* –
         However disagreeable the task is, it must be done
   (iii) *Où (quelque part) qu'on aille dans notre pays, on voit les mêmes problèmes* –
         Wherever you go in our country, you see the same problems
   (iv) *Quoi qu'il arrive, il faut continuer la lutte* –
         Whatever happens, we must continue the struggle
   Note Take care not to confuse *quoique* 'although' with *quoi que* 'whatever':
   (v)   *Que ce soit pendant ma vie ou pendant celle de mes enfants...* –
         Whether it's during my lifetime or that of my children...
   (vi) *Quels que soient vos vrais sentiments il vaut mieux ne pas les révéler tout de suite* –
         Whatever your real feelings are it's best not to show them straight away

8 **Giving a command**
   Que + subjunctive can be used as a command form in 'careful-style' French:
   (i)   *Qu'il parte tout de suite et qu'il ne revienne pas avant 6 heures* –
         Let him leave immediately and not return before six o'clock

B: After certain verbs

1   After verbs that, generally speaking, convey an emotional attitude:
Wishing; wanting; desiring; requesting; regretting; feeling sorry/pleased/surprised; demanding; commanding etc.

  (i)   *Je suis très content que tu sois venu* – I am very pleased that you have come
  (ii) *Il est surpris que j'aie accepté son invitation* – He is surprised that I accepted her invitation
  (iii) *Je veux que vous fassiez cela demain* – I want you to do that tomorrow
  (iv) *Nous regrettons qu'elle ne soit pas là* – We are sorry that she is not there
  (v)   *Il demande que j'y aille tout de suite* – He is asking that I go there immediately
  (vi) *Je m'étonne qu'il ait fait cela* – I am astonished that he did that

Note

These sentences are made up of two parts (clauses): a main clause and a subsidiary clause. The subjunctive always comes in the subsidiary clause and is always introduced by *que* (see the conjunctions above). If the tense in the subsidiary clause is a present tense in English, then a present subjunctive is needed in spoken French; if it's a past tense, then a perfect subjunctive is required. In 'careful-style' written French, an imperfect or pluperfect subjunctive might occur (see below). Most Examining Boards will accept a present subjunctive (in a translation or essay) where an imperfect is preferable.

2   After verbs expressing fear:
  (i)   *J'ai peur qu'il ne fasse quelque erreur* – I am afraid of him making some mistake
  (ii) *Nous craignons qu'il ne soit réélu comme Premier ministre* –
        We are afraid that he might get re-elected as Prime Minister
  (iii) *Vous avez peur qu'il ne soit pas réélu?* – You are afraid of him not being re-elected?

Note The *ne*, in the first two examples, occurs when **both** clauses are in the affirmative. When the subjunctive clause is in the negative *ne...pas* is used as normal. *A moins que* (see A5 on page 46) has a similar *ne* and behaves in the same way.

3   Verbs expressing personal opinion:
I think, believe, hope, am sure/am certain, say etc. A subjunctive is required after these verbs only when they are in the negative or used interrogatively. Here are some examples:

  (i)   *Je crois qu'il a parfaitement raison* – I think/believe he is quite right
  (ii) *Il est sûr qu'elle ne le fera pas* – He is sure that she will not do it

but:

  (iii) *Je ne crois pas qu'il ait parfaitement raison* – I don't think that he is quite right
  (iv) *Est-il sûr qu'elle ne le fasse pas?* – Is he sure that she won't do it?

Here are some other examples:

  (v)   *Je ne dis pas que cela soit vrai* – I don't say that that is true
  (vi) *Croyez-vous qu'ils disent toujours la vérité* – Do you think that they always tell the truth?
  (vii) *J'espère qu'elle reviendra* – I hope that she will come back

Note: the verb *espérer* (to hope), used affirmatively, expresses more certainty than 'hope' in English and only requires a subjunctive when used as a question or negatively (Compare with *probable* below.)

4   Impersonal verbs: most common examples
  (i)   *Il faut que* – It is necessary that
  (ii)   *Il se peut que* – It may be that
  (iii) *Il importe que* – It is important that
  (iv)   *Il est regrettable que* – It is regrettable that
  (v)   *Il est possible/impossible que* – it is possible/impossible that
  (vi)   *Il est improbable/peu probable que* – it is improbable/not very probable that
  (vii) *Il semble que* – It seems that
  (viii) *Il est douteux que* – it is doubtful that

Note

  (ix)   *Il est probable que vous comprenez*
  (x)   *Il est certain que vous comprenez*
  (xi)   *Il me semble que vous comprenez*

They all express a degree of certainty that does not require a subjunctive.

5   Subjunctive versus indicative:

The use of a subjunctive can depend on whether the statement or idea expressed is a personal opinion or an established fact:

(i)   *C'est la plus grande carotte qu'on ait jamais vue* (in the opinion of the speaker)

(ii) *C'est la plus grande carotte qu'on a jamais récoltée*
       (this one is in the Guinness book of records)

(iii) *L'Antarctique est la dernière région du monde où l'homme n'a pas détruit la nature*
       (speaker is sure and wants to convince his audience)

(iv) *L'Antarctique est la dernière région du monde où l'homme n'ait pas détruit la nature*
       (speaker gives this as his own opinion)

(v)   *Je cherche un petit coin à la campagne où je puisse vivre tranquillement* (a wish unfulfilled)

(vi) *J'ai trouvé un petit coin à la campagne où je peux vivre tranquillement* (a wish fulfilled)

You can also say, avoiding the subjunctive:

(vii) *Je cherche un coin pour vivre tranquillement*

Exercices

1   Traduisez les bouts de phrases suivants:

(a) So that he understands
(b) Although we know
(c) Unless he comes
(d) You must go there (*il faut*)
(e) Provided he does it
(f) Before he leaves
(g) Let him leave and not come back!
(h) Whatever he says
(i) Whatever your reasons are
(j) It may be that the government is right
(k) Without him knowing
(l) Until they learn
(m) Although they do not understand
(n) Although they have understood
(o) Provided that she has finished

2   Traduisez:

(a) I think you are right
(b) Do you think they are right?
(c) I am afraid that it is too late
(d) It is possible that the situation is too serious
(e) It is probable that he is taking the necessary measures
(f) It is not likely that he is taking the necessary measures
(g) I am sorry that you do not agree with me
(h) I am surprised that they have done that
(i) Do you think the government is following the right policy?
(j) I hope this information is correct
(k) I am pleased that he did that
(l) Do you think that is true?
(m) I do not think that is possible
(n) It is regrettable that he took this decision
(o) I am afraid that I might make a mistake

3   Traduisez:

(a) Vous eussiez mieux fait de venir me voir tout de suite
(b) Quelles que soient vos raisons je ne peux pas approuver cette action
(c) Quoi que vous fassiez, n'écoutez pas ses excuses
(d) Je cherche quelqu'un qui puisse m'aider aujourd'hui
(e) J'ai déjà trouvé quelqu'un qui pourra m'aider demain
(f) Quelque difficile que vous trouviez ce travail, il faut que vous fassiez de votre mieux
(g) Je vais voyager avant de commencer mes études à l'université
(h) Que vous trouviez ou non quelqu'un pour faire ce travail, cela m'est égal
(i) J'ai peur qu'elle ne soit déjà partie
(j) Il faut que vous vous reposiez un peu, ne fût-ce que quinze minutes

13 Modal verbs

May, must, might, ought, could, should, would

These modal verbs are best learned in an example together with the meaning:

  (i) *Pouvons-nous entrer?* – May we come in?

 (ii) *Il se peut que cela soit vrai* ⎫ – That may be true
      Il est possible que cela soit vrai ⎭

(iii) *Cela pourrait être vrai* – That could/might be true

 (iv) *Vous pourriez le faire ce soir* – You could do it this evening

  (v) *Vous auriez pu le faire sans moi* – You could have done it without me

 (vi) *Je dois le faire ce soir* ⎫ – I must/have to do it this evening
      Il faut que je le fasse ce soir ⎭

(vii) *J'ai dû le faire hier soir* – I had to do it last night

(viii) *Mon parapluie? J'ai dû le laisser chez moi* – I must have left it at home

 (ix) *Elle devait venir à 6 heures* – She was to come at six

  (x) *Vous ne devriez pas l'aider à faire ses devoirs* – You shouldn't help him with his homework

 (xi) *Vous devriez vous reposer un peu* – You ought to/should rest a little

(xii) *Vous n'auriez pas dû le faire sans moi* – You shouldn't have done it without me

(xiii) *Il ne voulait pas le faire sans moi* – He wouldn't do it without me (he was unwilling)*

(xiv) *Je voudrais vous aider* – I would like to help you

Note also:

(a) *Vous risquez de vous rompre le cou* – You **might** break your neck

(b) *'would' needs special care when translating. Distinguish between: (i) 'would' (a conditional, 'he would do it' if he could); (ii) 'would' (willing to); (iii) 'would' (used to, imperfect tense).

Can you?

  (i) *Vous savez jouer du piano?* – Can you play the piano? (have you learned?)

 (ii) *Vous savez nager?* – Can you swim? (do you know how to?)

(iii) *Pouvez-vous nager? (habillé de ce manteau)* – Are you capable of swimming? (with that coat on)

Knowing people/places/facts

(a) Being **acquainted** with people or places is expressed by *connaître*.

(b) Knowing **facts, having knowledge** is expressed by *savoir* (savvy).

   (i) *Vous savez où se trouve Apt? Oui, dans le Midi. C'est une ville que je connais très bien.*

Exercice

1 Traduisez:

   (a) I must have left it at home
   (b) You shouldn't be afraid
   (c) You ought not to have paid
   (d) Could you lend me 10 francs?
   (e) I must work harder
   (f) Will you come this evening?
   (g) Will she be there?
   (h) Do you know what the capital of Estonia is?
   (i) Before the war I knew Tallin very well
   (j) Can you do it before this evening?

14 The passive voice

Having dealt with the **mood** of the verb (*see* page 44) one further aspect needs to be considered: the **voice.** There are two main voices: **active** and **passive.** Consider the two following statements:

  (i) *Fifi m'embrasse* – Fifi kisses me

 (ii) *Je suis embrassé par Fifi* – I am kissed by Fifi

The first uses the verb actively; the subject 'Fifi' is doing the action to the object 'me'. The second uses the verb passively so that the object receives the action and comes first in the sentence while 'the doer' (or agent) comes last. Note that the passive in French is a direct translation of the English 'I am kissed', *je suis embrassé,* and the agent is indicated by *par.* You should now be able to work out what the following would be in French (cover up the right-hand column before checking your answer):

(i)	Fifi is kissed by me	*Fifi est embrassée par moi*
(ii)	I shall be kissed by Fifi	*Je serai embrassé par Fifi*
(iii)	I have been kissed by Fifi	*J'ai été embrassé par Fifi*
(iv)	I was kissed by Fifi (once)	*J'ai été embrassé par Fifi*
(v)	I was kissed by Fifi (all the time)	*J'étais embrassé par Fifi*
(vi)	I had been kissed by Fifi	*J'avais été embrassé par Fifi*
(vii)	I would be kissed by Fifi (if she liked me)	*Je serais embrassé par Fifi*
(viii)	I would have been kissed by Fifi	*J'aurais été embrassé par Fifi*
(ix)	Fifi would have been kissed by me	*Fifi aurait été embrassée par moi*
(x)	Fifi had been kissed by me	*Fifi avait été embrassée par moi*

Note The past participle in the passive always agrees with the subject. All the tenses of the active voice are possible in the passive and usually follow the English model word for word. Care has to be taken though with 'was'. Does it mean a single action or a repeated or habitual one? (*See also* imperfect tense, pages 33–34.)

Now try using the verb actively in the above sentences. The first one is done for you. Cover up the the section below which gives the answers.

- (i) *Fifi est embrassée par moi – J'embrasse Fifi*
- (ii) *Fifi m'embrassera*
- (iii) *Fifi m'a embrassé*
- (iv) *Fifi m'a embrassé*
- (v) *Fifi m'embrassait*
- (vi) *Fifi m'avait embrassé*
- (vii) *Fifi m'embrasserait*
- (viii) *Fifi m'aurait embrassé*
- (ix) *J'aurais embrassé Fifi*
- (x) *J'avais embrassé Fifi*

In theory any French verb that is transitive (takes a direct object) can be used in the passive voice. In practice however the passive is more often than not avoided. There are three ways of doing this:

1 By using *on* (as a subject)
2 By using a reflexive verb
3 By using the verb actively (if possible)

You have to avoid the passive with intransitive verbs in French (those that take an indirect object).

1 **Using *on* as a subject** You can say in English 'I was told to wait'. But in French you tell 'to' someone – *dire à quelqu'un,* so you would have to say something like 'to me was told to wait'. To avoid this difficulty you say instead:

- (i) *On m'a dit d'attendre* – I was told to wait (literally 'one told me to wait')
- (ii) *On m'a montré un siège* – I was shown a seat
- (iii) *On leur a demandé de s'asseoir* – They were asked to sit down
- (iv) *On m'a donné un programme* – I was given a programme

2 **Using a reflexive verb** You could in theory say:

- (i) *Je suis beaucoup intéressé par les films japonais* – I am very interested in Japanese films

In practice you would say:

- (ii) *Je m'intéresse beaucoup aux films japonais*

Here are some other examples:

- (iii) *Le français se parle beaucoup dans les pays africains* – French is spoken a lot in African countries
- (iv) *Cela se fait rarement ici* – That is done rarely here
- (v) *Il s'est fait beaucoup de mal en exprimant cette opinion* – He has done himself a lot of harm in expressing that opinion
- (vi) *Cela se trouve partout en Europe* – It is found everywhere in Europe
- (vii) *Cet appareil photo se vend maintenant dans tous les magasins* (or *Cet appareil photo est en vente dans tous les magasins*) – This camera is being sold now in all the shops

3 **Using the verb actively** Try the sentence 'I was given this idea by my sister' (if you start with *j'ai été donné* it starts to mean you were given *away*). So *Ma sœur m'a donné cette idée.* Here are some other examples:

- (i) *Mon prof m'a dit de ne pas travailler si dur* – I was told by my teacher not to work so hard
- (ii) *Son refus m'a surpris* – I was surprised by his refusal

In the latter example you could say *J'ai été surpris par son refus* but the active form gives a livelier style.

The past participles of some verbs can behave more like adjectives than active parts of verbs. Here are some examples:

   (i)   *Le magasin est ouvert de 8 à 18 heures*
   (ii) *J'étais embarrassé par ses visites*
  (iii) *Mon ami était respecté par tout le monde*
  (iv) *Vous serez accompagné d'un policier*
   (v) *La pièce était éclairée par une seule ampoule*

In these cases the passive (more like verb 'to be' + adjective) is more appropriate.

In the present tense some verbs differ in meaning according to whether they are used actively or passively. Compare:

   (i)   *la porte est ouverte* and *la porte s'ouvre*
   (ii) *les pêches sont vendues au marché* and *les pêches se vendent 2F le kilo*
  (iii) *elle est habillée* and *elle s'habille*

Exercices

1   Traduisez en utilisant le passif:
   (a) He was invited by a friend
   (b) You will be noticed by the police
   (c) The thief was arrested by a fireman
   (d) A solution had been found
   (e) The secrets were revealed
   (f) The theory of relativity was proposed by Einstein
   (g) He is known by everyone
   (h) This model is sold everywhere
   (i) My plans will be accomplished one day
   (j) The general would have been run over (*écraser*) by a tank

2   Même exercice en évitant le passif.

3   Traduisez:
   (a) He will not be re-elected (*réélu*) next time
   (b) I was ordered not to move (*ne pas bouger*)
   (c) We were not told the truth
   (d) We were asked not to wait
   (e) The advert is seen everywhere
   (f) He is thought to be very clever
   (g) That is not done here
   (h) I was forgiven by my sister
   (i) The face of the earth has been changed by man
   (j) The skin is burned by too much sun
   (k) The door opens slowly, a hand is seen in the opening (*dans l'embrasure*), a strange cry is heard!
   (l) The doors of the TGV open when the train stops
  (m) The doors are not open before the train stops

15 Present participle

Use

The present participle in French is used in the following ways:

1   **Like a verb ending in '-ing' (in English):**
   (i)   *Criant et gesticulant, la foule d'ouvriers s'est avancée vers le palais* –
       Shouting and waving their arms the crowd of workers advanced towards the palace
   (ii) *Rentrant chez moi très tard et réfléchissant à tous ces problèmes je me sentais triste* –
       Returning home late and reflecting upon all these problems I felt sad

Note The participle in '-ing' is used fairly loosely in English. In French it **always** implies an action(s) going on at the same time as the main verb. For example:

  (iii) *Assis derrière son bureau il avait l'air très important* –
       Sitting behind his desk he looked very important

If you started with *'S'asseyant à son pupitre'* this would mean 'as he was sitting down he looked important'. Similarly:

(iv)   *Caché derrière la porte il pouvait tout voir* –
       Hiding behind the door he could see everything

(v)   *Couché sur son lit* – Lying on his bed

(vi)   *Agenouillé devant le feu* – Kneeling in front of the fire

2   Like an adjective

(i)   *un livre intéressant* – an interesting book

(ii)   *une histoire émouvante* – a touching story

(iii) *une dame charmante* – a charming lady

(iv)   *un visage souriant* – a smiling face

Note Unlike the verbal use above, the participle agrees here just like an adjective.

3   After the preposition *'en'* to mean one of three things:

(a) 'By doing something'

(i)   *En écoutant tous les matins France-Inter, j'ai appris à comprendre le français quand on le parle vite* – By listening to France-Inter every morning, I learned to understand French spoken quickly

(ii)   *Le voleur a réussi à casser la fenêtre en se servant de son coude* –
       By using his elbow the thief managed to break the window

Note After verbs expressing the idea of beginning and finishing (*commencer, finir, débuter, terminer, achever*), 'by doing something' is expressed by *par* + infinitive:

(iii) *Il a commencé par m'expliquer la vraie situation* –
       He began by explaining the real situation

(iv)   *Il a fini par nier ce qu'il avait dit* – He finished by denying what he had said

In all other cases 'by doing something' will be rendered by *en* + present participle

(b) 'While doing something'

(i)   *Je préfère travailler en écoutant la musique* – I prefer to work while listening to music

(ii)   *En revenant de la banque j'ai vu un accident* –
       While on my way back from the bank I saw an accident

(c) 'Upon/on doing something'

(i)   *En entrant dans la pièce j'ai vu que tout était en désordre* –
       Upon entering the room I found that everything was in disarray

(ii)   *En le voyant sortir un revolver j'ai su qu'il allait peut-être me tuer* –
       On seeing him draw a gun I realized that he was perhaps going to kill me

Note The present participle is used in many cases in English where it is not used in French.

(iii) before leaving – *avant de partir*

(iv)   without saying goodbye – *sans dire au-revoir*

(v)   after seeing him – *après l'avoir vu*

(vi)   instead of working – *au lieu de travailler*

The golden rule with these examples is that **after a preposition you need an infinitive**.

(d) 'Having done something' followed by a consequence:

(i)   *Ayant reçu sa lettre, je savais ce qu'il comptait faire* –
       Having received his letter I knew what he expected to do

(ii)   *Son amie n'étant pas revenue il est parti sans elle* –
       His girl friend not having returned he set off without her

Note *avoir* or *être* is required according to the verb.

(e) 'After having done something', what happened next:

(i)   *Après avoir essayé de lui téléphoner plusieurs fois j'ai enfin réussi à le joindre* –
       After having tried several times...

(ii)   *Après m'être couché de bonne heure j'ai été réveillé par un grand bruit* –
       After having gone to bed early...

(iii) *Après être resté deux jours là-bas il m'a fallu revenir chez moi* –
       After having stayed there two days...

Note You could also say in English 'Having tried...', 'Having gone to bed...' or 'After trying...' etc.

Formation

This is formed by removing *'-ons'* from the first plural present tense and adding *'-ant'* which is phonetically similar. '-*ant*' is the equivalent in English of '-ing'. There are three present participles that cannot be obtained in this way: *ayant*, 'having'; *étant*, 'being'; *sachant*, 'knowing'.

Exercices

1   Traduisez:
   (a)   By working at weekends and by saving money (*faire des économies*) they were eventually able to buy a house
   (b)   I did it while watching television
   (c)   She was sitting in front of the fire with the cat lying on her lap (*sur les genoux*)
   (d)   Having arrived late I missed the first act
   (e)   After locking and bolting (*verrouiller*) the door I went to bed
   (f)   Before leaving check (*vérifiez*) that you have closed all the windows
   (g)   He found on arriving that the other guests had already started the meal
   (h)   Begin by learning the irregular verbs
   (i)   You can't get rid of (*se débarrasser de*) your rubbish by dumping it in the street.
   (j)   Waving her hands and motioning to me she managed to attract my attention
   (k)   A charming lady with a smiling face
   (l)   I like playing the guitar, watching football on television and going out with my mates

2   Traduisez. Dans ces exemples vous trouverez que l'emploi de '-*ing*' en anglais ne correspond pas avec le '-*ant*' en français:
   (a)   Il aime beaucoup la pêche et la chasse et il adore faire de la voile
   (b)   Voir c'est croire
   (c)   Toute la maison a besoin d'être nettoyée
   (d)   Je vous remercie de me l'avoir rappelé
   (e)   Les femmes ont la réputation d'être de bonnes conductrices
   (f)   Dans *l'Avare* de Molière, Maître Jacques est puni pour avoir dit la vérité
   (g)   Une machine à coudre; une salle à manger; une leçon d'équitation; une leçon de conduite; une auto-école
   (h)   Oui, je le vois qui s'approche. Il court très vite, il fait des signes de la main et il crie

16 Getting things done – *Faire* and the infinitive

Consider the difference between the following:
   J'ai réparé mon vélo and *J'ai fait réparer mon vélo au magasin*
In the first example you did the work yourself; in the second you got it repaired (had it repaired) by someone else. '*Faire* + infinitive' is used to convey this idea in French. This combination is used a great deal to express a variety of ideas where English often uses a different verb.
   Can you work out what the following mean?
   (i)   *Le ministre des transports a fait construire une route de contournement pour notre ville*
   (ii)   *Le prof essaie de faire travailler ses élèves*
   (iii)   *Maman m'a fait manger tout ce qui restait sur mon assiette*
   (iv)   *Je n'aime pas tellement ce pull, mes parents me l'ont fait acheter*
   (v)   *S'il conduit aussi vite que ça, il se tuera ou il se fera arrêter par la police*
   (vi)   *Servez-vous je vous en prie; je fais servir Jean d'abord parce qu'il est le plus petit*
   (vii)   *Faites entrer ces messieurs; faites venir le médecin*
   (viii)   *Vous portez cette lettre à la poste? Faites-la porter par un de vos élèves**
   (ix)   *Il a fait sécher ses vêtements devant le feu***
   (x)   *Faites taire ces élèves, ils font trop de bruit***
Note *Get one of your pupils to take it: you have to say in French *par un de vos élèves* to make it clear which is the direct and which the indirect object.
** If pronouns are used with *faire* + infinitive the pronoun goes before *faire*. So, in (ix) and (x) above *Je les ai fait sécher devant le feu* and *Je les ai fait taire* but the past participle does not agree.

You can say in English 'I boiled some water' but in French you have to say *J'ai **fait** bouillir de l'eau* since you don't really do the boiling yourself! This also applies to other cooking processes:
   (i)   *Faites cuire dans de l'eau bouillante pendant trois minutes*
   (ii)   *Faites griller le pain des deux côtés*
   (iii)   *Faites fondre du beurre dans une casserole*
   (iv)   *Faites frire dans du beurre*
   (v)   *Faites rôtir ce poulet pendant deux heures*
The verbs *voir*, *entendre*, *sentir* and *laisser* are also often combined with another verb in the infinitive in a similar way. For example:

(vi)   *Je le vois venir* – I can see him coming

(vii) *Je l'entends sonner* – I can hear him ringing

(viii) *Je sentais mes cheveux se hérisser* – I felt my hair standing on end

(ix)   *Laissez-les se battre* – Let them fight

(x)   *Laissez passer cette dame* – Let the lady through

(xi)   *Je l'ai entendu dire cela à son ami* – I heard him tell his friend that

(xii) *J'ai été triste de la voir nous quitter si tôt* –
       I was sad to see her leave us so early

Exercice

1   Traduisez:

   (a) Send for his father

   (b) Don't leave him waiting on the doorstep, show him in

   (c) Grill for ten minutes

   (d) I've had a house built in the country

   (e) Get him to eat something

   (f) He got some cakes brought from the pâtisserie

   (g) Let him speak

   (h) Keep those dogs quiet!

   (i) The thief got caught the next day

   (j) I got my sister to do this homework

17 Verbs taking prepositions

Some verbs do not need a preposition to link with the following verb. For example:

(i)   *Savez-vous nager?*

(ii) *J'aime faire du ski*

(iii) *Voulez-vous sortir ce soir?*

(iv) *J'espère aller à l'université l'année prochaine*

(v)   *Il n'ose pas prendre une décision*

(vi) *Il faut faire quelque chose*

Many verbs do need a preposition however. The main choice is nearly always between *à* or *de*. The following essential ones have to be learned, preferably in a meaningful combination with a following verb or noun.

1 Verb + *à*

(i)   *aider à faire ses devoirs*

(ii)   *s'attendre à réussir*

(iii) *consentir à venir*

(iv)   *se décider à partir*

(v)   *forcer à le faire*

(vi)   *inviter à venir*

(vii) *obliger à payer*

(viii) *réussir à le persuader*

(ix)   *apprendre à parler*

(x)   *commencer à pleuvoir*

(xi)   *continuer à écrire*

(xii) *encourager à continuer*

(xiii) *hésiter à prendre une décision*

(xiv) *se mettre à discuter*

(xv)   *persister à se plaindre*

2 Verb + *de*

(i)   *je suis chargé de lui parler* (have the job of)

(ii)   *cesser de pleuvoir*

(iii) *défendre de traverser la rue*

(iv)   *essayer de le persuader*

(v)   *faire semblant de consentir*

(vi)   *finir de faire des excuses*

(vii) *offrir de payer*

(viii) *oublier de le faire*

(ix)   *décider de lui parler*

(x)   *refuser d'accepter*

(xi)   *remercier de son offre*
(xii) *demander de le faire*
(xiii) *empêcher de faire quelque chose*
(xiv) *je vous félicite de votre succès*
(xv)   *menacer de dire la vérité*
(xvi) *ordonner de venir*
(xvii) *permettre de l'accompagner*
(xviii) *regretter de ne pas pouvoir venir*
(xix) *je vous excuse d'être en retard*

Many verbs require the preposition *à* before an indirect object. In the following examples make a note of the preposition used in English. It is not always 'to'. For example: *Il a acheté un vélo à mon frère.*

(i)   *J'ai conseillé à mon ami de dire la vérité*
(ii)   *Emprunter de l'argent à votre oncle*
(iii)   *Est-ce qu'on peut se fier à cette personne?*
(iv)   *Il faut obéir à ses parents*
(v)   *Ordonner aux soldats de tirer*
(vi)   *Il plaît beaucoup à cette fille*
(vii)   *Prêter ce roman à mon frère*
(viii) *Raconter des histoires à sa grand-mère*
(ix)   *J'ai réfléchi à ce que j'ai fait*
(x)   *Il volait aux riches pour donner...*
(xi)   *Il a ri de moi* (he laughed at me)
(xii)   *Il a dissimulé sa faute à son père*
(xiii) *Il a donné le secret à sa sœur*
(xiv)   *Envoyer une carte à ses parents*
(xv)   *Montrez ça au prof*
(xvi)   *Offrir sa place à une vieille dame*
(xvii) *Je pense souvent à elle*
(xviii) *Prendre l'argent aux riches pour le donner...*
(xix)   *Promettre au prof de le faire*
(xx)   *Répondre tout de suite à sa lettre*
(xxi)   *Il ressemble beaucoup à James Dean*
(xxii) *Enseigner le russe à sa grand-mère* (teach one's grandmother Russian)

Some other words, mainly adjectives and nouns, also require prepositions before a following infinitive. Here are some examples:

1 *à*

(i)   *Je suis prêt à vous aider* – I am ready to help you
(ii)   *J'ai beaucoup à faire* – I have a lot to do
(iii) *Le dernier à arriver* – The last to arrive
(iv)   *Le premier à parler* – The first to speak
(v)   *Je n'ai rien à dire* – I have nothing to say
(vi)   *J'ai quelque chose à dire* – I have something to say
(vii) *Maison à vendre* – House for sale

2 *de*

(i)   *Je suis heureux/triste/étonné/surpris/content de vous voir* –
       I am happy/sad/astonished/surprised/content to see you
(ii)   *Je suis obligé de lui parler* – I am obliged to talk to him
(iii) *J'ai la permission de lui parler* – I have permission to speak to him
(iv)   *J'ai l'occasion de lui parler* – I have the chance to speak to him
(v)   *Je n'ai pas le droit de lui parler* – I haven't the right to speak to him

Note

(a) A few verbs have *de* before an object
      (i)   *Il s'est approché de moi* – He came up to me
      (ii)   *Cela dépend des circonstances* –That depends on the circumstances
      (iii) *Je vous remercie de votre lettre* – I thank you for your letter
      (iv)   *Il ne faut pas se moquer du Premier ministre* –
             You mustn't make fun of the Prime Minister

     (v) *Je ne me souviens pas de son nom* – I don't remember his name

     (vi) *Il jouit* (from *jouir*) *d'une grande réputation* – He enjoys a great reputation

     (vii) *Il sait jouer de la guitare* – He can play the guitar

     (viii) *Se servir d'un tourne-vis pour ouvrir la boîte* –
To use a screwdriver to open the tin

(b) The following verbs have a preposition in English but none in French:

     (i) *J'ai payé les verres cassés* – I paid **for** the broken glasses

     (ii) *J'ai sonné et j'ai demandé Marianne* – I rang and asked **for** Marianne

     (iii) *J'ai regardé ma montre* – I looked **at** my watch

     (iv) *J'attends mon ami* – I'm waiting **for** my friend

     (v) *Je cherche mes clefs* – I'm looking **for** my keys

(c) Notice the *à* and *de* construction with the following:

     (i) *Il a demandé **à** Jean **de** le faire*

     (ii) *Il a promis **à** Jean **de** le faire*

     (iii) *Il a permis **à** Jean **de** le faire*

     (iv) *Il a dit **à** Jean **de** le faire*

     (v) *Il a ordonné **à** Jean **de** le faire*

(d) Take care with the following phrases which can cause difficulty:

     (i) *En vouloir à quelqu'un à cause de quelque chose* – To hold something against someone

     (ii) *Il m'en veut à cause de mon succès* – He bears me a grudge because of my success

     (iii) *Ne m'en voulez pas, hein* – Don't hold it against me, eh

     (iv) *Il tient beaucoup à réussir dans ce projet* (*tenir à faire quelque chose*) –
He's very keen on succeeding in this plan

     (v) *Il tient de son père* (*tenir de*) – He takes after his father

     (vi) *se passer de quelque chose* – To do without something

     (vii) *On peut se passer de nourriture pendant deux semaines, mais on ne peut pas se passer d'eau* – You can do without food for two weeks but you can't do without water

Se douter de quelque chose – to suspect something

     (viii) *Il est marié? Je ne m'en suis jamais douté* – He's married? I never guessed/suspected it

     (ix) *C'est lui qui a fait le coup? Ah, je m'en doutais!* –
He was the one responsible? I thought as much!

Douter de – to doubt something

     (x) *Je doute que ce soit lui qui ait fait cela.* – I doubt if it was him that did that (*see* subjunctive, page 47)

Se tromper de quelque chose – to make a mistake about something

     (xi) *Je me suis trompé d'appartement* – I got the wrong flat

Servir *à* + verb

     (xii) *Ce torchon sert à nettoyer le tableau* – This cloth is used to clean the board

Servir de +noun

     (xiii) *Son mouchoir lui sert de torchon* – His handkerchief serves as a rag

Se servir de

     (xiv) *Je me suis servi de mon mouchoir pour nettoyer mes souliers* –
I used my handkerchief to clean my shoes

Penser *à* 'think about' and **penser de** 'think of' are frequently confused

     (xv) *Que pensez-vous de sa nouvelle petite amie?* – What do you think of his new girlfriend?

     (xvi) *Elle pense souvent à son amie tuée pendant la guerre* –
She often thinks of her friend killed in the war

     (xvii) *Il a manqué son train* – He missed his train

     (xviii) *Il me manque deux cents francs* – I'm missing 200 francs (200 francs short)

     (xix) *Ses amis lui manquent* – He misses his friends

     (xx) *Il manque de respect* – He lacks (does not show) respect

(e) The following examples of unexpected use of pronouns are often pointed out:

     (i) *Quelqu'un a bu **dans** ce verre* – Someone has been drinking **out of** this glass

     (ii) *Elle a pris un verre **dans** le placard* – She took a glass **from out of** the cupboard

(iii) *Il a pris les bijoux **sur** le comptoir* – He took the jewels from (off) the counter

(iv) *Il nous faudra tous boire à la même bouteille* – We'll all have to drink **from** the same bottle

Exercices

1 Traduisez:

(a) He agreed to come and see me
(b) I hesitated to say anything
(c) I invited him to visit me
(d) I congratulated her on her success
(e) I forgot to write
(f) He refused to accept
(g) I refused to accept
(h) I tried to persuade them
(i) They offered to pay
(j) He bought the car from my father
(k) He borrowed the money from his sister
(l) Can you trust politicians?
(m) You must laugh at their behaviour
(n) I must rob a bank to pay for my holiday
(o) I am always the last to know

2 Traduisez:

(a) You have nothing to say?
(b) Everything depends on his decision
(c) You must pay for the damage
(d) Who are you waiting for?
(e) Tell your cousin to bring his sister
(f) I rang the wrong number
(g) I haven't had a chance to talk to her
(h) He was using his sleeve to clean the board
(i) I promised my teacher to work harder next year
(j) I was forbidden to use my handkerchief to clean my shoes with
(k) What do you think of him?
(l) Do you often think about her?
(m) Are you short of anything?
(n) I miss France!
(o) Can you play the piano?

3 Traduisez en anglais:

(a) On pourrait bien se passer de télévision
(b) Il est toujours en prison? Je m'en doutais
(c) Je tiens beaucoup à visiter la Corse cette année
(d) Il m'en voulait de ce que je lui avais fait
(e) A quoi ça sert?
(f) Nous n'allons pas tous boire dans le même verre, j'espère

18 Articles

Note Almost as many mistakes are made in exam papers with the articles in French as with the verbs.

1 The definite article: le, la and les

(*See also* gender, pages 19–24)

(a) The definite article is used in much the same way in French as in English to particularize a noun. Here are some examples:

(i) *Vous voyez **le** garçon là-bas?* – You see **the** boy over there?
(ii) *Fermez **les** fenêtres* – Close **the** windows

(b) It is also used to **generalize** a noun where, in English, this is done by **leaving out** the article:

(i) *Vous préférez **le** thé ou **le** café?* Do you prefer tea or coffee?
(ii) ***Les** chats sont plus intelligents que **les** chiens* – Cats are more intelligent than dogs

(c) The article is also used in French before countries, provinces, continents and languages where often it is left out in English:

- (i)   *La Lituanie, l'Estonie et la Lettonie ont gagné leur indépendance de la Russie* –
Lithuania, Estonia and Latvia won their independence from Russia
- (ii)   *La Bretagne se trouve à l'ouest de la France* – Brittany is in the west of France
- (iii) *Elle parle bien le français, l'espagnol et le portugais* –
She speaks French, Spanish and Portugese well

Note also the following:

- (iv) *le soir, l'après–midi, le matin* – in the evening(s), in the afternoon(s) etc.
- (v)   *lundi* – on Monday but *le lundi, le mardi* – on Mondays, Tuesdays
- (vi) *La semaine dernière, l'année prochaine* – last week, next year

(d) *De* combines with *le, la* and *les* to form the partitive articles *du, de la, des* and *de l'*, having the meanings in English of 'some' and 'any'. Here are some examples:

- (i)   *Vous avez du vin blanc? Non mais j'ai du cidre* –
Have you any white wine? No, but I've got some cider

Often no article at all is needed in English. For example:

- (ii)   *Qu'est-ce qu'il vous faut? De l'argent? Des provisions? De l'eau?* –
What do you need ? Money? Provisions? Water?

Note After *ne... pas* the partitives *du, de la, de l'* and *des* all change to *de*. Here are some examples:

- (iii) *J'ai de l'argent mais je n'ai pas de provisions et je n'ai pas d'eau*
- (iv)   *Vous n'avez pas de pêches blanches aujourd'hui? Non, mais j'ai des jaunes*
- (v)   *Vous avez du temps? Non, je n'ai pas de temps*

(e) Partitives *de l'* and *des* are replaced by prepositional *d'* before *autre(s)*. It is best to just learn likely combinations such as:

- (i)   *Vous avez d'autres amis?* – Do you have other friends?
- (ii)   *Vous avez d'autres idées?* – Do you have other ideas?
- (iii) *D'autres personnes vous diront le contraire* – Other people will say the opposite
- (iv)   *Certains prétendront que notre climat n'est pas en train de changer, d'autres maintiendront le contraire* – Some claim that our climate is not changing, others maintain the opposite

(f) *De l'* and *des* are possible however when the meaning is clearly **'of the'**. Here is an example:

- (i)   *Je n'ai pas visité la maison des autres garçons de ma classe* –
I haven't visited the houses **of the** other boys of my class.

(g) *De* should be used instead of partitive *des* with an adjective before a plural noun, as below

- (i)   *de grands enfants* but *des enfants indisciplinés*
- (ii)   *ce sont de petites erreurs* but *ce sont des erreurs considérables*
- (iii) *de jeunes adolescents* but *des adolescents maltraités*

There are some exceptions to this rule however; some combinations of adjective and noun are felt to be so common that they go naturally together with *des* in front of them. These include:

- (v)   *des petits pois*
- (vi)   *des jeunes filles*
- (vii) *des grands groupes*
- (viii) *des jeunes gens*
- (ix)   *des grands-pères*

(h) *De* is used after expressions of quantity. Here are some examples:

- (i)   *beaucoup de problèmes*
- (ii)   *trop de travail*
- (iii) *combien d'argent?*
- (iv)   *un verre de vin*
- (v)   *peu de gens*
- (vi)   *un plein d'essence* (a full tank)
- (vii) *une bouteille d'eau*
- (viii) *une semaine de pluie*
- (ix)   *rempli de vin* (filled with wine)
- (x)   *un bon nombre de personnes*

Note

Again, where the real meaning is 'of the', *du, de la, de l'* and *des* are possible. For example:

- (xi)   *Beaucoup des enfants ici sont malheureux* – A lot **of the** children here are unhappy
- (xii) *Donnez-moi un verre du vin que vous m'avez offert hier* –
Give me a glass **of the** wine that you offered me yesterday

In the latter phrase, you could also say: *...de ce vin que vous m'avez offert hier.*

(i) After *la plupart* and *bien* as expressions of quantity *du, de la, de l'* and *des* are required. For example:

    (i) *La plupart des invités n'étaient pas venus* – Most of the guests had not come

    (ii) *J'ai couru bien des risques* – I ran a lot of risks

    Note 'many of them' is *beaucoup d'entre eux.*

(j) *De* is needed in French after *quelqu'un, quelque chose, personne, rien, quoi* where there is nothing in English. For example:

    (i) *rien d'intéressant* – nothing interesting

    (ii) *quelqu'un d'important* – someone important

    (iii) *Personne de blessé?* – Anyone injured?

    (iv) *Il n'y a eu personne de blessé* – There was no one injured

    (v) *Quoi de neuf?* – What's new?

2   The indefinite article: un, une and des

There are fewer things to point out about the indefinite article. It is used in much the same way in French as in English with a few phrases which need to be learned:

Note the following:

    (i) *J'ai mal à la gorge* – I have **a** sore throat

    (ii) *Quelle grande maison!* – What **a** big house!

    (iii) *10F la livre* – 10 francs **a** pound

    (iv) *Mon père est dentiste, ma mère est médecin* – My father is a dentist, my mother is a doctor

In the last example, the definite article is usually left out when stating someone's profession. If you add an adjective to the statement however, the article reappears:

    (v) *Sartre était **un** philosophe célèbre*

Exercice

1   Traduisez:

    (a) I like football, swimming and basketball

    (b) Pass me the salt please

    (c) Whales (*baleines*) are still hunted by the Japanese

    (d) Elephants will soon be an endangered species (*une espèce en voie de disparition*)

    (e) Garlic is an important ingredient in Provençal cooking

    (f) I would like a bottle of water, a kilo of peaches and a tin of the beans that you recommended

    (g) My brother wants to become a doctor – he's full of strange ideas

    (h) Many doctors believe that jogging is dangerous for health

    (i) Most of the people that I have met don't go to church on Sundays

    (j) On Saturday nights I do the cooking

    (k) Many people had arrived late, others hadn't bothered to come

    (l) Last week; next year; in the evening; on Mondays

    (m) There was no wind but plenty of rain

    (n) We haven't got any bananas or peaches

    (o) France is nearly two and a half times bigger than England

    (p) What do we need for the picnic – ham, bread. butter, lettuce, wine or orange juice, peaches and cheese.

19 Object pronouns

me	*le*	*lui*	*y*	*en*
te	*la*	*leur*		
se	*les*			
nous				
vous				

The object pronouns are best remembered in this form. They always go in this order **in front of** the verb.

Note

(a) The **first** column pronouns are **direct** or **indirect** and have the following meanings:

    'me ' or 'to me'; 'you' or 'to you' ; 'himself, herself, oneself' or 'to himself, to herself, to oneself'; 'us' or 'to us'; and 'you' or 'to you'.

(b) The **second** column ones are **direct only** and mean:

    'it' (masculine), 'him'; 'her', 'it' (feminine); 'them' (people or things).

(c) The **third** column are **indirect only** and mean:

    'to him'; 'to her'; and 'to them' (people).

(d) *Y* means 'there' or 'to it'

(e) *En* means 'some', 'any' and 'of it'

Rules

To get the pronouns right make sure that

1   They go before the verb, or the auxiliary verb (*avoir* or *être*)

2   ...in the above order

3   You know whether a pronoun is direct or indirect, 'to' might not be used in English

(i) *Je **lui** ai envoyé la lettre hier* – I sent **him** the letter yesterday

Take special care with verbs that take an indirect object in French but a direct one in English. For example

(ii)   *Je lui réponds* – I answer him

(iii) *Je lui dis* – I tell her

(iv)   *Je lui demande* – I ask him

(v)   *Il lui promet* – He promises her

(vi)   *Elle lui téléphone* – She telephones him

Note

(a) Pronouns replace nouns: *y* replaces *à* + noun. Here are some examples:

(i)   *Vous allez souvent **à Biarritz**? Oui, j'y vais tous les ans*

(ii) *Vous pensez souvent **à votre** vie ensemble? Non, je n'y pense pas souvent*

(iii) *Je réfléchis **à cette question**, oui, j'y réfléchis beaucoup!*

(b) *En* replaces *de* + noun. For example:

(i)   *Vous avez **des croissants**? J'en ai quelques-uns. Il vous **en** faut combien?*

(ii) *J'ai besoin **d'argent**. J'en ai plus besoin que vous*

(iii) *Il se moque **de cette idée**, oui, il s'en moque*

(c) With a negative imperative (telling someone not to do something) the pronouns follow all the above rules. For example:

(i)   *Ne le lui donnez pas* – Don't give it to him

(ii) *Ne lui répondez pas* – Don't answer her/him

(iii) *N'y allez pas!* – Don't go there!

(iv) *Ne vous couchez pas par terre* – Don't lie on the ground

With a **positive imperative** they come **after** the verb, **direct before indirect** joined by hyphens.

(d) *Me* and *te* change to *moi* and *toi* if they come in final position.

For example, from the above phrases:

(i)   *Donnez-le-lui!*

(ii) *Répondez-lui!*

(iii) *Allez-y!*

(iv) *Couchez-vous par terre!*

(v)   *Assieds-toi!*

(vi) *Envoyez-le-moi* but *Donnez-m'en une douzaine*

General note You must learn the basic rules of position and meaning of the pronouns with the tenses of verbs. You are less likely to need to use them with imperatives however unless you are writing dialogue or direct speech.

The object pronouns are best practised in their different combinations with verbs so that order and position become fixed in your mind (*see* perfect tense, pages 32–33).

Exercices

1   (a)   Suivez le modèle:

Me le donnez-vous? Oui, je vous le donne

Me les donnez-vous? Oui, je...

Me les prêtez-vous? Oui, je...

Allez-vous me les envoyer? Oui, je vais...

Allez-vous m'en envoyer? Oui,

Allez-vous le lui présenter? Oui,

(b)   Refaites les mêmes exemples en commençant la réponse par 'non':

2   (a)   Suivez le modèle:

Est-ce que vous allez souvent en France? Oui, j'y vais souvent.

Est-ce que vous allez maintenant au café? Oui, ...tout de suite

Est-ce qu'il s'intéresse beaucoup à la mécanique? Oui,

Est-ce que vous réfléchissez beaucoup à ce problème? Oui,

Est-ce que vous pensez souvent à ce temps-là? Oui,

(b) Refaites le même exercice en répondant 'non':

3 (a) Suivez le modèle:

Avez-vous des places? Oui, j'en ai quelques-unes

Est-ce qu'il reste des places? Oui, il...

Avez-vous besoin de ces brochures? Oui,

Vous a-t-il parlé de son accident? Oui, il

Des pêches? Combien... voulez-vous?/Il... faut combien?

(b) Refaites en répondant 'non':

4 A frequent criticism by examiners is that, when writing French, candidates tend to repeat nouns instead of using pronouns in their place. In the following exercises, replace nouns by object (or subject) pronouns wherever possible:

(a) Les brochures? J'ai envoyé les brochures à mon ami la semaine dernière.

(b) Mon rapport? J'ai déjà présenté mon rapport au comité.

(c) Mon télex à M. Dupont? J'ai déjà envoyé le télex à M. Dupont ce matin. Quoi, M. Dupont n'a pas encore reçu mon télex? M. Dupont aurait dû recevoir mon télex.

(d) Téléphonez à M. Dupont et dites à M.Dupont que j'ai bien envoyé un télex à M. Dupont et que M.Dupont devrait recevoir bientôt ce télex.

(e) 'Mon projet? Vous voulez que je vous explique mon projet? Bon, je vais vous expliquer mon projet.'

'M. Dupont?'

'Ah, oui, j'ai déjà expliqué à M. Dupont mon projet. M. Dupont était très content de mon projet.'

5 Traduisez:

(a) I have already sent them to him

(b) Send him it. He needs it straight away

(c) Telephone her and tell her that I will talk to her about it later

(d) Possibilities? Yes, there are several of them. Let's examine them

(e) He sent you them last week

(f) He didn't send you them last week?

(g) I am sure I told him to send you them.

6 The imperatives are best practised in set phrases, both positive and negative. Give the contrary command in each case. For example: Donnez-le-moi – ne me le donnez pas.

(a) (i) Donnez-les-moi!

(ii) Envoyez-les-lui!

(iii) Expliquez-les-nous!

(iv) Répondez-lui tout de suite!

(v) Parlez-lui-en!

(b) (i) Ne le lui dites pas!

(ii) Ne me l'envoyez pas!

(iii) Ne lui en parlez pas!

(iv) Ne m'en donnez pas beaucoup!

(v) Ne vous asseyez pas là! (la peinture y est fraîche)

20 Emphatic pronouns

moi	*nous*
toi	*vous*
lui	*eux*
elle	*elles*

Use

1 To stress the subject in a sentence or phrase.

(i) *Toi, tu es bête* – **You** are stupid

(ii) *Lui, il ne comprend rien* – **He** doesn't understand a thing

(iii) *Elles, qu'est-ce qu'elles en savent?* – What do **they** know about it?

Spoken English stresses the subject in these examples by emphasizing the word 'you'. This cannot be done in French.

Note that *lui* as an emphatic pronoun means 'him' or 'he'.

2 After prepositions

   (i)   *avec moi*
  (ii) *à côté d'elle*
 (iii) *derrière nous*
  (iv) *sans eux*
   (v) *venez avec elle*
  (vi) *c'est mon idée à moi* (its **my** idea)

3 With a preposition after the verb

Where there is no *le, la* or *les* as an object in front of the verb.
You can say:

   (i) *Je vous la présenterai* – I'll introduce her to you

But you cannot say;

  (ii) *Je vous lui présenterai* – I'll introduce you to her (or is it **her** to **you**?)

To avoid this ambiguity, you say:

 (iii) *Je vous présenterai à elle* (you to her)

Here are some other examples:

  (iv*)* *Je pense à elle tout le temps*
   (v) *Il a besoin d'elle*
  (vi) *Il est content de moi*
 (vii) *Elle est fière de lui* – She is proud of him
(viii) *Je ne me fie pas à lui* – I don't trust him
  (ix) *Il se moque de moi* – He's poking fun at me

4 After *c'est* and *c'était*

   (i) *C'est lui qui a tort*
  (ii) *C'était moi le gagnant* – I was the winner
 (iii) *Qui est là? C'est elle*

5 After *ni... ni*

   (i) *Ni lui ni elle ne savaient la vérité* – Neither he nor she knew the truth
  (ii) *Ni moi ni lui ne nous attendions à une telle réponse* –
      Neither he nor I were expecting such a reply

6 With *-même(s)*

   (i) *moi-même* – myself
  (ii) *lui-même* – himself
 (iii) *eux-mêmes* – themselves

Exercice

1 Traduisez:
   (a) Repeat after me
   (b) In front of her; behind him; with us
   (c) **They** don't understand
   (d) What does **he** think about it?
   (e) Neither she nor I knew the answer
   (f) I need him
   (g) They are afraid of her
   (h) I made it myself
   (i) What does he think of us?
   (j) I am ashamed of you

21 Relative pronouns

1 Qui

This means 'who', 'which' or 'that' as **subject** to the verb and is usually found joining two clauses together. For example, on page 63:

    (i)   *C'est un mot qui n'est pas français* – It's a word that/which is not French

    (ii) *Vous voyez l'homme qui porte un chapeau?* – You see the man (who is) wearing a hat?

2 Que or qu'

These mean 'whom', 'who', 'which' or 'that' as **object** to the verb. For example:

    (i)   *Voici le pull que j'ai acheté* – Here is the jumper (that/which) I bought

    (ii) *La propriété que j'ai achetée en France* – The property (that/which) I bought in France

    (iii) *Une fille que j'ai recontrée pendant les vacances* – A girl (that/who/whom) I met in the holidays.

You will see from the brackets used above that in English you can leave out the relative pronoun. You **cannot** do this in French.

Note

(a) *Qui* never loses its final vowel before a word beginning with a vowel.

    If you are not sure about subject and object, the simplest rule of thumb (to decide whether *qui* or *que* is needed) is to use *que* when the verb already has a subject, and *qui* when there is no subject. Between *que/qu'* and the verb there will be a subject pronoun (*il, elle, nous, vous* etc.) or a noun. Between *qui* and the verb there will be either an object pronoun or nothing at all. For example:

    (i)   *Le vélo **que** j'ai acheté*

    (ii) *Le vélo **que** mes parents ont acheté*

    (iii) *Le vélo **qui** est dans le garage*

    (iv) *Le vélo **qui** se trouve dans le garage*

(b) The subject can sometimes come after the verb in French so that the above rule won't work. For example: *L'instrument que mon frère utilisait, était un vieux trombone* is more easily expressed as

    (i)   *L'instrument qu'utilisait mon frère était un vieux trombone*

This avoids the two verbs of each clause coming together.

3   Ce qui and ce que/ce qu'

Where 'which' means 'that which', translate it by *ce qui* or *ce qu(e)*. *Ce qui* and *ce que* refer to ideas already mentioned (or about to be stated). The choice of *qui* or *que* depends on the subject/object relationship as above. Here are some examples:

    (i)   *Je ne comprends jamais ce qu'il dit* – I never understand what he is saying

    (ii) *Il n'a pas expliqué ce qui était arrivé* – He didn't explain what had happened

    (iii) *Ce que je ne comprends pas c'est pourquoi il a fait cela* –
            What I don't understand is why he did that

    (iv) *Ce qui m'intéresse dans cette affaire c'est le rôle du Premier ministre* –
            What interests me in this affair is the part played by the Prime Minister

Another way of looking at *ce qui* and *ce que* is to regard them as the end bit of the interrogative phrases *qu'est-ce que* and *qu'est-ce qui*:

    (v) *Qu'est **ce qu'**il a dit? Je n'ai pas entendu **ce qu'**il a dit* – I didn't hear what he said

    (vi) *Qu'est-**ce qui** l'intéresse? Je ne sais pas **ce qui** l'intéresse* – I don't know what interests him

Note

(a) The form *tout ce que/qui* means 'everything that' or 'all that':

    (i)   *Tout ce que je peux vous dire c'est que...* – All I can tell you is that...

    (ii) *On aurait pu prédire tout ce qui était arrivé* –
            You could have predicted everything that had happened

(b) *Ce dont* means literally 'that of which' and is found in a clause depending on a verb that takes the preposition *de*:

    (i)   *Je ne me rappelle pas ce dont il a parlé* – I don't remember what he talked about

4   Lequel, laquelle, lesquels and lesquelles

These mean 'which' and only refer to things. They are used in the following ways:

1 To ask a question

    (i)   *J'ai un vin blanc sec et un demi-sec. Lequel préférez-vous?* – Which (one) do you prefer?

    (ii) *J'ai des pêches blanches et des jaunes. Lesquelles prenez-vous?* – Which (ones) are you having?

Note *Lequel* is the pronoun to the adjective *quel*. For example:

    (iii) *Quel vin préférez-vous?*

2 With a preposition:

    (i)   *L'église devant laquelle se trouve une petite place* – The church in front of which is a little square

    (ii) *Le train dans lequel il avait voyagé* – The train in which he had travelled

    (iii) *La compagnie pour laquelle je travaille* – The company for which I work

Note That in the last two examples you can also say in English:

'The train he had travelled in' and 'The company I work for'.

Qui is used when referring to people in similar phrases except after parmi (among, amongst) and *entre* (between):

(iv) *L'ami avec qui j'ai voyagé* – The friend I travelled with

(v) *L'homme pour qui je travaille* – The man I work for

(vi) *Les spectateurs parmi lesquels était un inspecteur de police* –
The spectators amongst whom was a police inspector

De combines with *lequel* etc. to give the following:
duquel, de laquelle, desquels and *desquelles*.

Similarly, *à* combines with *lequel* to give:
auquel, à laquelle, auxquels and *auxquelles*.

They have the meanings respectively of 'of which' and 'to which' and agree with the noun to which they refer. Although you can say *L'école à laquelle je vais* it is preferable to say *L'école où je vais* and *Le village où j'habite* instead of *Le village dans lequel j'habite*.

Dont means 'of which', 'of whom', 'whose' and can refer to people as well as things. It always refers back to the noun immediately before it. *Duquel* and *de qui* also have the same meanings, but *dont* is always used instead unless there is any ambiguity:

(vii) *Le livre dont je parle est français* – The book I am talking about is French

(viii) *Ce monsieur dont j'ai oublié le nom* – The man whose name I have forgotten

(ix) *Il m'a montré la voiture dont deux des vitres étaient cassées* –
He showed me the car of which two of the windows were broken

But

(x) *Ce monsieur avec les deux chiens dont je vous ai parlé* (you talked about the dogs)

(xi) *Ce monsieur avec les deux chiens de qui je vous ai parlé* (you talked about the man)

Note *Dont* cannot be used to ask a question. Other forms are used instead:

(xii) *De qui parlez-vous?* – Who are you talking about?

(xiii) *De quels chiens parlez-vous?* – Which dogs are you talking about?

(xiv) *A qui est ce livre?* – Whose book is this?

22 Interrogatives

1 'What' as a question

1 *Qu'est-ce que* or *Que* begin the question **'what'.** For example:

(i) *Qu'est-ce qu'il a répondu?/Qu'a-t-il répondu?* – What answer did he give?

(ii) *Qu'est-ce qu'on joue/Que joue-t-on ce soir au théâtre?* –
What's on at the theatre this evening?

Note If you start with *que* you turn subject and verb the other way round.

Qu'est-ce qui also means **'what'** but as **subject** to the verb. For example:

(i) *Qu'est-ce qui se passe/ Qu'est-ce qui arrive ?* – What's happening?

These can also be expressed as *Que se passe-t-il?* and *Qu'arrive-t-il?*

2 *Quoi* is used in **'what'** question phrases like 'with what?', 'in what?' etc.

(i) *Avec quoi est-ce qu'il a ouvert la porte? Il n'avait pas de clé* –
What did he open the door with?

(ii) *A quoi pense-t-il?* – What is he thinking of (*see* penser à/de, page 56)

(iii) *Dans quoi allons-nous mettre nos achats?* – What are we going to put our shopping in?

Note The preposition in English is often detached from the word 'what':

(iv) *Je vais à Londres demain. Pour quoi faire?* –
I'm going to London tomorrow. To do what?

2 'Who' as a question

Qui, qui est-ce qui, qui est-ce que all ask the question 'who?'. Here are some examples:

(i) *Qui est venu? Qui est-ce qui est venu?* – Who has come?

(ii) *Qui cherchez-vous? Qui est-ce que vous cherchez?* – Who are you looking for?

Exercices

1 Traduisez:

(a) I know she is right

(b) I think he will arrive late

(c) I don't know what he is going to say

(d) What will you tell him?

(e) Which of these two wines do you prefer?

(f) There's the house I talked to you about

(g) There's the tree under which we sat and on which we carved our names

(h) What I don't understand is that he never has any money

(i) Which politician are you talking about?

(j) You don't know the difficulties we have had

(k) What is interestng is the fact that he has denied all responsibility

(l) Among these problems which is the most serious?

(m) Who left the door open?

(n) It's a programme that starts tonight and that you mustn't miss

(o) Whose shoes are these?

2 Dans l'extrait suivant remplacez les blancs par le relatif qui manque:

LES MAUVAIS EFFETS DU SOLEIL

Chaque année, les services d'urgence récupèrent des touristes inconscients, _____ se sont laissé aller sous notre soleil sans penser_____ il n'avait rien à voir avec celui du bord des plages anglaises. On ignore le fait _____ le sable réfléchit 20% des radiations et l'eau 10% et_____ la quantité d'UVB est maximale entre 11 heures et 14 heures. _____ on ignore surtout, c'est _____ les effets du soleil sont cumulatifs. Voici _____ m'a expliqué un chef de service de dermatologie, 'Tout s'additionne. Je vois parfois des patients_____ me disent_____ depuis deux ou trois ans, ils ont nettement diminué leurs expositions au soleil. Mais tout_____ ils ont emmagasiné il y a 10 ou 20 ans est enregistré'.

23 Demonstrative adjectives and pronouns

Demonstrative adjectives

Ce, cet, cette and ces

These are the equivalent of 'this' or 'that' in English. (*Cet* is only used before masculine singular nouns beginning with a vowel or an *'h'* not pronounced. e.g. cet homme, cet hôtel, cet incident)

The suffixes *'-ci'* or *'-là'* can be added to the noun following *ce, cet, cette* or *ces* to mean specifically 'this' or 'that' but it then becomes emphatic so you only use it when stressing something. For example:

(i) *Que voulez-vous que je lise? Cet article-ci ou cet article-là?*

Demonstrative pronouns

1 Celui, celle, ceux and celles

These look a bit like the adjective *ce* + a combination of the strong form pronouns (*see* page 61). Three things can be added to *celui, celle, ceux* and *celles*.

(a) *'-ci'* or *'-là'*

(i) *celui-ci, celle-ci, ceux-ci, celles-ci*

(ii) *celui-là, celle-là', ceux-là', celles-là'*

These have the meanings 'this one', 'this', 'these ones', 'these' and 'that one', 'that', 'those ones' and 'those'. Here are some examples:

(iii) *J'hésite entre ces deux tricots, celui-ci est très joli mais celui-là en cachemire est plus chic* – I can't decide between these two jumpers, this one is very pretty but this one is made of cashmere and is smarter

(iv) *Quelles pêches préférez-vous? Celles-ci ou celles-là –* Which peaches do you prefer? These or those

(b) *De*

De indicates belonging to someone and is the equivalent of 's and s' in English:

(i) *Voici notre système pour les brosses à dent, pour ne pas se tromper: celle de ma mère est bleue, celle de mon père est rouge, celle de mon petit frère est verte –* ...my mother's is blue, my father's is red and my little brother's is green

(c) *Que, qu' and qui*

These mean: 'the one that/which' 'those that/which' and 'the ones that/which' respectively. Here are some examples:

(i) *Donnez-moi encore de ces pêches blanches. Celles que j'ai achetées hier étaient délicieuses* – Give some more of those white peaches. The ones I bought yesterday were delicious

(ii) *Ceux qui arriveront en retard ne seront pas admis* – Those arriving late will not be admitted

(d) The pronoun can exist by itself in a sentence:
(i) *Tous ceux ayant le même âge* – All those of the same age
(ii) *Cette marque est celle recommandée à la télévision* –
This brand is the one recommended on television

(e) The pronoun can also be followed by *dont*, like *ce* above:
(i) *Tu vois cette fille aux cheveux blonds là-bas? C'est celle dont je t'ai parlé* –
She's the one I told you about

Note This is a common use in written French:
(ii) *Mes filles, Marie-Claire et Sandrine, sont très différentes de caractère: celle-ci est bavarde et oisive et celle-là est taciturne et travailleuse* –
My daughters Marie-Claire and Sandrine have very different characters: the latter is quiet and hard-working the former is lazy and a chatterbox

Can you work out why *celle-là* should mean 'the former' and *celle-ci* 'the latter'?

2 *Cela, (ça), ceci*

These mean 'that' and 'this' respectively and are **indefinite** demonstrative pronouns. *Ça* is the abbreviated form of *cela* and is much used in colloquial French:
(i) *C'est formidable, ça!* – That's wonderful!
(ii) *Ça, où l'as-tu acheté?* –Where did you buy that?
(iii) *Ça alors!* – You don't say!
(iv) *Ça, je ne le crois pas* – I don't think so at all

It should be replaced by cela when you write French except when you are writing colloquial dialogue. *Ça* and *ceci* refer to facts or statements previously mentioned or about to be, and also to things. They have no gender. Here are some examples:
(i) *Faire le trajet en moins de six heures? Ça, c'est pas possible* –
Do the journey in less than six hours? That's not possible
(ii) *Est-ce que ça vous gêne si je fume?* – Does it bother you if I smoke?
(iii) *Deux comme ça (en indiquant des gâteaux)* – Two like that
(iv) *Retenez bien ceci: l'argent ne fait pas le bonheur* –
Always remember this: money doesn't bring happiness.

Ça can also be added to single words to give a bit more weight to them:
(v) *Je ne suis pas sorti samedi soir. Tiens, pourquoi ça?* –
I didn't go out on Saturday night. Really, why was that?

You will also find: *Où ça? Quand ça? Comment ça?*

Exercice

1 Traduisez:
(a) Which jumper would you like? This one is pretty but that one will be warmer
(b) Cotton ones are easier to wash but woollen ones don't crease (*se froisser*)
(c) This summer; this year; this time; this weather; these mosquitoes (*moustiques*)!
(d) That's really annoying that is!
(e) My car's broken down. I've borrowed my brother's
(f) Which peaches would you like ? These are 6F a kilo and those are 8,50F
(g) Natural resources must be conserved. That is very important
(h) Which box do you want? The one on the kitchen table
(i) These solutions are difficult to apply (*appliquer, mettre en œuvre*). Let's examine the ones proposed by M. Dupont
(j) That's the last straw (*le comble*)! **Those** ideas are ridiculous

Other common indefinite adjectives and pronouns

On

This subject pronoun is much more widely used in French than its English equivalent 'one'. Always singular, it can mean: 'we'; 'you'; 'they'; or 'people'. What meanings would you give to 'on' in the following?
(i) *On a bien mangé dans ce restaurant*
(ii) *On ne fait pas ça ici!*
(iii) *On vous a dit d'attendre*
(iv) *On'dit que la maison est hantée*
(v) *On était plus honnête quand j'étais jeune*
(vi) *On ne me fait pas comme ça, hein!*

(see also passive, page 50)

Quelque(s)

The adjective *quelque(s)* means 'a few' or 'some'. For example:
  (i) *J'ai eu quelque difficulté à resoudre ce problème* –
     I had a little difficulty in resolving this problem
  (ii) *Quelques centaines de personnes ont été blessées* – A few hundred people were hurt
  (iii) *J'ai quelques idées* – I have a few ideas

Quelqu'un

A pronoun meaning 'some one' or 'somebody'. For example:
  (i) *Quelqu'un a volé mon argent* – Some one has stolen my money
  (ii) *Je connais quelqu'un qui aurait pu le faire* – I know somebody who could have done it
Note These phrases are also important:
  (iii) *N'importe qui* – anyone (no matter who)
  (iv) *N'importe qui aurait pu le faire* – Anyone could have done it

Quelques-uns, quelques-unes

Pronouns having the meanings 'some' and 'a few' and refer back to nouns. For example:
  (i) *Quelles belles pêches! Achetons-en quelques-unes* – Let's buy a few
  (ii) *Quelques-uns de mes amis ont déjà leur permis de conduire* –
     Some of my friends have already passed their driving test
  (iii) *Quelques-unes de ses amies sont belges* – Some of his/her friends are Belgian

Quelque chose and autre chose

These mean 'something' and 'something else' respectively. Here are some examples:
  (i) *Vous connaissez quelque chose au sujet de cette affaire?* –
     Do you know something about this business
  (ii) *Non, pas grand-chose* – No, not much
  (iii) *Vous n'avez pas autre chose à faire?* – Haven't you got something else to do?

Plusieurs and certains

These mean 'several' and 'certain' respectively. The adjective *plusieurs* is often confused with the adjective *quelques* (*see* above):
  (i) *Il y a **plusieurs** années* – **Several** years ago
  (ii) *Il y a **quelques** années* – A **few** years ago
Note also Some other phrases:
  (iii) *plusieurs fois* – several times
  (iv) *quelquefois* – sometimes
Plusieurs can also work as a pronoun:
  (v) *Il était là. Plusieurs l'ont vu* – He was there. Several people saw him
Compare this with:
  (vi) *Certains affirment qu'ils l'ont vu* – Certain/some people are sure they saw him.

Chaque, chacun

These mean 'each' and 'each one' respectively. *Chaque* is the adjective and is always followed by a noun:
  (i) *Chaque personne avait apporté son déjeuner* – Each person had brought their lunch
  (ii) *Tous mes amis sont venus. Chacun m'a apporté un cadeau* – All my friends came. Each one brought me a present

Tout, toute, tous and toutes

This is the **adjective** meaning 'all', 'every' 'the whole'. For example:
  (i) *tous les jours* – every day
  (ii) *tous mes amis* – all my friends
  (iii) *toute la ville* – the whole town
Note The masculine plural form *tous*.
Tout is also a pronoun meaning 'everything' and 'all':
  (iii) ***Tout** n'est pas perdu* – All is not lost
  (iv) *Je crois tout ce qu'il m'a dit* – I believe everything he has told me.
Tous is also a pronoun meaning 'everyone' (the 's' is pronounced):

(v)   *Ils étaient tous là* – They were all there
(vi) *Tous étaient venus* – They had all come

(If 'they' are all feminine, you would of course say – *Elles étaient toutes venues.*)

Note *Tout* occurs in numerous expressions like:

(vii) *tout de suite* – immediately
(viii) *tout à coup* – suddenly
(ix)   *tout de même* – all the same
(x)   *tout à fait* – completely

It never has an '*e*' on the end in these cases.

Tel, telle, tels and telles

These are mainly used as adjectives:

(i)   *Une telle réponse est inacceptable* – Such a reply is unacceptable
(ii) *Un tel homme mérite d'être puni* – Such a man deserves to be punished

Note The order of words in French is different. For example, *pareil/pareille* can often be substituted for *tel*:

(i)   *Avez-vous jamais entendu une pareille idée?* – Have you ever heard of such an idea?

You can also use the adverb *tellement* where *si* doesn't fit, in phrases like:

(iii) *J'étais tellement en colère* – I was so angry
(iv) *Il avait tellement besoin de cet argent* – He needed the money so much
(v)   *Il aime tellement cette fille* – He loves that girl so much

Exercice (suite de la page 66)

2   Traduisez:
   (a) People say that money doesn't bring happiness. I can't accept such an idea
   (b) I spent the evening with a few friends
   (c) Some of his best friends had come to say good-bye
   (d) That happened some years ago
   (e) I have some idea of what you mean
   (f) Did you do anything interesting at Bognor? Not much
   (g) Each time I saw him he looked different
   (h) In Ionesco's play, each character eventually turns into a rhinoceros
   (i) There were several girls in the photo. Each one was wearing a white dress
   (j) All the efforts I have made are useless
   (k) They had all arrived too early
   (l) Everything is possible if you feel that people have confidence in you

24 C'est and Il est

Rules

The following guidelines should help to decide which to use.

1   *Il* (or *elle*) is always used when 'it' refers back to a particular noun or person:
   (i)   *Faites attention à **mon chien**, **il** est méchant*
   (ii) *Tu as vu **sa sœur**? **Elle** est chouette, hein?*
   (iii) ***Mon verre**, où est-ce que je l'ai mis? **Il** est là*

2   *Il est* introduces an idea not made clear until the end of the statement. It is often found in the following type of phrase: *il est* + adjective + *de* + infinitive. Here are some examples:
   (i)   *Il est difficile de trouver quelqu'un qui parle russe*
   (ii) *Il est dangereux de s'aventurer dans le lit de cette rivière*
   (iii) *Il est impossible de tout savoir*
   (iv) *Il est facile de trouver un bon restaurant en France*

   Note In spoken French, *c'est* tends to be used instead of *il est* in the above construction. You should keep to *il est* in written French.

3   *C'est* is used to refer to an idea already made clear. For example, in the above sentences another speaker would add, if he or she agreed:
   (i)   *Oui, c'est difficile*
   (ii) *Oui, c'est dangereux*
   (iii) *Oui, c'est impossible*
   (iv) *Oui, c'est facile*

Other examples are:
- (v) *Il viendra? Oui, c'est probable* ('it' here means 'the fact that he will come')
- (vi) *J'ai couru 10 kilomètres sans être fatigué. Vraiment, c'est formidable ça.*

4 *Il* (or *elle*) *est* is used, when saying what someone is like or does:
- (i) *Vous voyez mon frère sur la photo? Oui, il est grand*
- (ii) *Je vous présente mon ami Jean-Paul. Il est ingénieur. Et sa femme Colette, elle est dentiste.*

However if you qualify the individual by adding an adjective, *c'est* is used:
- (iii) *C'est un grand garçon votre frère!*
- (iv) *Je vous présente M. Moulin, c'est notre dentiste*
- (v) *Vous connaissez M. Rodez? Il paraît que c'est un scientifique distingué*

A rule sometimes given for the last example is: use *il est* when an adjective or noun follows; *c'est* when adjective as well as noun follows.

5 **Emphasis** *C'est* is used to lay particular emphasis on a part of a sentence or phrase. For example, take the sentence:

Marie m'a prêté sa jupe. Various parts could be emphasized as follows:
- (i) *C'est Marie qui m'a prêté cette jupe (Marie et pas une autre)*
- (ii) *Cette jupe, c'est qu' elle me l'a prêtée (pas donnée)*
- (iii) *C'est à moi que Marie a prêté la jupe (pas à ma sœur)*
- (iv) *C'est cette jupe que Marie m'a prêtée (et pas une autre jupe)*
- (v) *C'est une jupe que Marie m'a prêté (et pas une robe)*

Note In these examples the tonic accent would also fall on the word being emphasized. How would the same parts of the sentence be stressed in English: (i) in speech (ii) in print?

Exercices:

Comblez les blancs dans les phrases suivantes avec *il est, c'est, elle est, ils sont, elles sont.*
- (a) Qui a fait ça? _____ mon père
- (b) Je vous présente ma tante_____ institutrice
- (c) _____ formidable l'Angleterre a gagné au Parc des Princes!
- (d) On peut maintenant traverser la Manche par le tunnel. _____ incroyable! Mais _____ impossible de faire cela dans sa voiture.
- (e) Ma sœur? _____ au Brésil
- (f) Mes deux sœurs rient et bavardent tout le temps. _____ bêtes
- (g) _____ inspecteur de police. _____ un inspecteur bien connu en France.
- (h) Les croissants? _____ sur la table dans la cuisine, n'est-ce pas?

25 Possessive adjectives and pronouns

Possessive adjectives should be familiar to you as the following:

mon, ma, mes – my	*ton, ta, tes* – your (singular)	*son, sa, ses* – his or her
notre, notre, nos – our	*votre, votre, vos* – your (plural)	*leur, leur, leurs* – their

They must agree with the noun they refer to. The commonest mistake is to assume that *sa* means 'her', *son* means 'his' and *ses* means 'their'. But:
- (i) *son père* – his or her father
- (ii) *sa mère* – his or her mother
- (iii) *ses parents* – his or her parents (or relations)
- (iv) *leur père* – their father
- (v) *leurs parents* – their parents

Possessive pronouns are as follows:

le mien	*le tien*	*le sien*	*le nôtre*	*le vôtre*	*le leur*
la mienne	*la tienne*	*la sienne*	*la nôtre*	*la vôtre*	*la leur*
les miens	*les tiens*	*les siens*	*les nôtres*	*les vôtres*	*les leurs*
les miennes	*les tiennes*	*les siennes*	*les nôtres*	*les vôtres*	*les leurs*
mine	yours	his or hers	ours	yours	theirs

They have to agree with the noun they refer to:
- (i) *Cette valise, c'est la vôtre? Oui, c'est la mienne.*
- (ii) *Cette voiture, c'est la sienne?* (Its/his/hers)

You can also indicate possession by using the strong form pronouns (*moi, toi, elle, lui* etc.) with *c'est.*
For example:
- (iv) *Cette valise, c'est à vous? Oui, c'est à moi*

(v) *Cette voiture, c'est à elle?*

Note In the last example, it is possible in this way to make it clear whom you are referring to.

Exercice

1 Traduisez:
(a) Her son, his sister, his mother, his (female) cousin, their parents
(b) Is this book his? No, it's hers
(c) She arrived with their friends and he came with his
(d) Which book is his?
(e) Whose is this?
(f) Mine (socks) are grey, his are blue
(g) It's not mine (car), it's theirs

26 Adjectives

Adjectives agree with the nouns they describe in the following ways:

1 Add an '*-e*' for the feminine singular, '*-es*' for feminine plural and '*-s*' for masculine plural. For example:
(i) *Une petite ville*
(ii) *Un petit village*
(iii) *Des petites villes*
(iv) *Des petits villages*

The effect of adding '*-e*' to an adjective ending in a consonant is to make the final consonant sounded where before it was silent. It is important when reading and speaking to observe this sound change.

2 Adjectives already ending in '*-e*' stay the same:
(i) *Un jeune garçon*
(ii) *Une jeune fille*

3 Many adjectives in common use behave in slightly different ways. The following patterns need to be learned:
(a) **Masculine plurals –**
(i) Adjectives ending in '*-al*' have '*-aux*' in the masculine plural:
les routes nationales but les plans nationaux
(ii) A few adjectives in '*-eau*' have '*-eaux*' in the masculine plural:
les nouvelles publications but *les nouveaux journaux*
(iii) Adjectives already ending in '*-s*' or '*-x*' in the masculine singular stay the same:
les jours les plus **heureux** *de la vie*
(b) **Feminine singulars –**

		masculine singular	feminine singular
(i)	**'-el'/'-elle'**	*un parc naturel*	*une ressource naturelle*
(ii)	**'-eil'/'-eille'**	*un exemple pareil*	*une idée pareille*
(iii)	**'-er'/'-ère'**	*le Premier ministre*	*la première séance*
(iv)	**'-eur'/'-euse'**	*un homme menteur*	*une fille menteuse*
(v)	**'-f'/'-ive'**	*un marché actif*	*la vie active (working life)*
(vi)	**'-ien'/'-ienne'**	*un vin italien*	*la cuisine italienne*
(vii)	**'-x'/'-euse'**	*un ami heureux*	*une vie heureuse*

The following don't have a regular pattern and they are best remembered in an example:

adjective	masculine singular	feminine singular
bas/basse	*un ton trop bas*	*la marée basse*
blanc/blanche	*un vin blanc*	*faire nuit blanche* (not to sleep a wink)
bon /bonne	*un bon exemple*	*une bonne idée*
bref/brève	*un bref discours*	*une brève explication*
complet/complète	*un dossier complet*	*une collection complète*
doux/douce	*un temps doux*	*une voix douce*
faux/fausse	*un faux billet*	*une fausse idée*
favori/favorite	*mon sport favori*	*ma matière favorite*
frais/fraîche	*un matin frais*	*une boisson fraîche* (cool)
gentil/gentille	*il est gentil*	*elle est gentille*
long/longue	*un long voyage*	*une longue journée*

meilleur/meilleure	*mon meilleur ami*	*une meilleure solution*
public/publique	*l'ordre public*	*une nouvelle publique*
		(common knowledge)
sec/sèche	*un temps sec*	*une serviette sèche*

Position of adjectives

The general rule is that most adjectives come after the noun. However, the following commonly used ones usually come before:

autre	*grand*	*meilleur*	*bon*
*beau**	*gros* (feminine *grosse*)		*nouveau**
chaque	*jeune*	*plusieurs*	*petit*
court	*joli*	*quelque*	
*fou** (feminine *folle*)		*mauvais*	*vieux** (feminine *vieille*)
gentil	*méchant*	*vilain* (ugly, nasty)	

* These adjectives have an additional masculine singular form that is only used before a noun beginning with a vowel or a silent '*h*'. (Compare *ce, cet*, page 65.) For example:

   (i)   *un bel endroit*
  (ii) *un vieil ami*
 (iii) *un nouvel hôtel*
 (iv) *un adolescent français*
  (v) *un jeune adolescent*
 (vi) *un adolescent heureux*
(vii) *un adolescent travailleur*
(viii) *une fille française*
(xix) *une jeune fille*
  (x) *une fille heureuse*
 (xi) *une fille travailleuse*

Note *Des* in front of an adjective before a plural noun usually changes to *de*. For example:
(xii) *de jeunes adolescents* (*see* partitive, page 58)
(b) Adjectives can also be combined:
      (i)   *les jeunes adolescents français*
     (ii)   *les jeunes filles heureuses*
(c) Two adjectives following a noun are always joined with *et*.
      (i)   *un jeune adolescent travailleur et heureux*

Exercices

1 Traduisez:
  (a) Natural resources
  (b) A good idea
  (c) Low tide
  (d) A cool morning
  (e) A mild winter
  (f) A soft voice
  (g) A long day
  (h) A new solution
  (i) An untruthful girl
  (j) A complete collection
  (k) A false idea
  (l) There were several pretty young French girls at the party
  (m) The working population
  (n) Some old friends; an old friend (male)
  (o) Parisian life
  (p) A few new French publications
  (q) Small Italian towns
  (r) A brief explanation
  (s) A public place
  (t) A public square

2 Some adjectives change their meaning according to whether they precede or follow the noun. Here are some of the most frequently used ones. Check their meanings with the help of a dictionary.
  (a) De Gaulle était un grand homme; c'était aussi un homme grand

(b) Ce millionnaire est un pauvre homme, mais il n'est pas un homme pauvre
(c) Mon ancienne école est une école ancienne
(d) L'année dernière c'était 1990 mais 1999 sera la dernière année du siècle.
(e) Ma propre maison; j'aime habiter une maison propre
(f) Un certain homme; trouvez un homme certain
(g) Ma chère femme a acheté un manteau cher
(h) Je suis né le même jour que vous; il est tombé malade le jour même de son arrivée
(i) Il a une nouvelle voiture. C'est un modèle nouveau?
(j) Le seul Chinois que je connaisse; les Chinois seuls savent le faire
(k) Encore un verre? Je t'apporte un nouveau verre? Voilà un nouveau verre tout neuf
(l) Je le lui dirai la prochaine fois que je le verrai, ce sera peut-être la semaine prochaine

27 Adverbs

1 Most adverbs are formed by adding '*-ment*' to the feminine of the adjective. For example:
   (i) *lent, lente, lentement* – slowly
   (ii) *heureux, heureuse, heureusement* – happily, fortunately

2 A small group of adjectives in '*-ent*' and '*-ant*' (**not** *lent* above) form their adverbs in '*-emment*' and '*-amment*' respectively. The most frequently met with are:
   (i) *abondant, abondamment*
   (ii) *constant, constamment*
   (iii) *courant, couramment*
   (iv) *évident, évidemment*
   (v) *récent, récemment*
   (vi) *violent, violemment*
Note '*-emment*' is always pronounced '*-amment*'.

3 Here are some adverbs which may cause difficulty:
   (i) *profond, profondément*
   (ii) *énorme, énormément*
   (iii) *précis, précisément*
   (iv) *aveugle, aveuglément*
   (v) *bref, brièvement*
   (vi) *gentil, gentiment*

4 The following adjectives having irregular adverbs:
   (i) *bon, meilleur*
   (ii) *mauvais, pire*
   (iii) *petit, peu*
   (iv) *bien, mieux*
   (v) *mal, pis*
Make sure you can distinguish an adjectival use from an adverbial one: adjectives describe or refer to nouns, objects or things; adverbs describe how the verb is carried out. For example:
   (vi) *Ecrivez en bon français* – Write in good French (*bon* describes the kind of French)
   (vii) *Il parle bien le français* – He speaks French well (*bien* describes how the speaking is done)
Similarly:
   (viii) *Il a peu mangé* and *il a pris un petit repas*
The words *meilleur* (adjective) and *mieux* (adverb, both with the meanings 'better' and 'best' are frequently confused. Also, *mauvais* (adjective) meaning bad, and *mal* (adverb) meaning badly, can cause problems:
   (ix) *Mon meilleur ami* – My best friend
   (x) *Ce dictionnaire est meilleur que celui-là* – This dictionary is better than that one
   (xi) *Il parle mieux le français que moi* – He speaks French better than I do
   (xii) *Faites de votre mieux* – Do your best
   (xiii) *J'ai mal dormi; j'ai fait un mauvais rêve* – I slept badly; I had a bad dream

28 Comparisons

Both adjectives and adverbs can be used in comparisons. Here are some examples:
   (i) *Brigitte est plus jolie que Sylvie mais Sylvie est plus intelligente que Brigitte* (adjective)
   (ii) *Sylvie parle mieux le français que Brigitte* (adverb)

2 Note also the following comparative phrases:
   (i) *Il travaille **autant** que moi* – He works **as much as** I do

    (ii)   *Il se sentait **de plus en plus** fatigué* – He was becoming **more and more** tired
    (iii) ***Plus** on travaille **plus** on se sent fatigué* – **The more** you work **the more** tired you become
    (iv) *J'ai **de moins en moins** envie de travailler* – I feel **less and less** like working
    (v)   ***Moins** on travaille, **moins** on a envie de travailler* –
        The less you work **the less** you feel like working

Exercice

1 Traduisez:
    (a) A former colleague
    (b) She alone can do it
    (c) Evidently he can speak Russian as well as you
    (d) He has bought another house. Is it a new one?
    (e) The very day that he arrived
    (f) These letters arrived on the same day
    (g) I was deeply moved (*ému*)
    (h) The last time I saw her she was wearing brand new shoes
    (i) Would you like another cup? (two possibilities)
    (j) I met him recently
    (k) Put some clean socks on
    (l) The more he explained the less I understood
    (m) She can draw better than me
    (n) It's not a bad car but the engine is running badly at the moment
    (o) They don't go out very much, just a little walk now and again
    (p) Are you feeling better?
    (q) It's getting more and more difficult to find a good programme on television
    (r) Which programme do you like watching best?
    (s) They all believe blindly in progress
    (t) Britain is not the least polluted country in the world

2 Answers to grammar exercises

1 Present tense

1 (a) Est-ce que vous regardez (tu regardes) la télévision tous les soirs?
    (b) Est-ce que vous faites (tu fais) tes devoirs en regardant la télé/pendant que vous regardez (tu regardes) la télé?
    (c) Est-ce que vous attendez (tu attends) le train de six heures?
    (d) Non. J'attends mon ami.
    (e) Il travaille à Londres?/Est-ce qu'il travaille à Londres?
    (f) Je pense à elle pendant que j'écris cette lettre.
    (g) Il va venir avec nous/Il vient avec nous?
    (h) Est-ce qu'il parle russe?
    (i) Je vous écris pour vous (te) remercier pour le (du) cadeau.
    (j) Qu'est-ce que vous faites (tu fais) ce soir?

2 (a) How long has he been living in Brussels?
    (b) For two weeks I've been getting strange telephone calls.
    (c) We have been writing to each other for two years.
    (d) How long has he known her?
    (e) I've been waiting for a letter for two months

3 (a) Depuis combien de temps est-ce que vous m'attendez?/ tu m'attends?
    (b) Je suis ici depuis 6 heures.

    (c) Voici/Il y a des années qu'ils s'écrivent?/ Ils s'écrivent depuis des années.

    (d) Elle est en Angleterre depuis des années/ Ça fait des années qu'elle est ici en Angleterre.

    (e) Ça fait cinq ans que je vous (te) connais.

2   *Perfect tense*

1   16 être verbs

A	A	D	D	E	M	M	N	P	R	R	R	S	T	V
R	L	E	E	N	O	O	A	A	E	E	E	O	O	E
R	L	S	V	T	N	U	I	R	T	S	N	R	M	N
I	E	C	E	R	T	R	T	T	O	T	T	T	B	I
V	R	E	N	E	E	I	R	I	U	E	R	I	E	R
E		N	I	R	R	R	E	R	R	R	E	R	R	
R		D	R						N		R			
		R							E					
		E							R					

2   Alors maman est montée dans sa chambre et papa est descendu dans la cave. Ma sœur Alice n'est pas encore rentrée. Sandrine est allée à la discothèque. Mon frère Albert est sorti ce matin et il n'est pas encore revenu. Claudette est sortie avec ses amis. Marie-Claude est rentrée à 6 heures, elle est restée 5 minutes puis elle est repartie. La chatte est tombée de la fenêtre, elle est morte, je crois!

3   (a) Est-il parti?

    (b) Il est resté longtemps?

    (c) Il est monté dans sa chambre.

    (d) Il n'est pas sorti.

    (e) Il est arrivé à l'heure?

    (f) Je suis rentré(e)/ retourné(e)/ revenu(e) tard.

    (g) Il est tombé devant le café.

    (h) J'ai rendu les livres.

    (i) Mes amis sont revenus/rentrés.

    (j) J'ai descendu vos bagages.

    (k) Il a sorti un stylo.

    (l) Je suis né(e) en Ecosse.

4   **Role-play**

M. Camembert: Eh bien, je me suis levé à six heures, je suis descendu, j'ai pris un café et puis je suis sorti de la maison. Je suis entré dans le tabac du coin. Je suis arrivé à la gare et j'ai pris le train de 7h15. Je suis descendu à la gare St Lazare. Je suis arrivé à mon bureau et je suis monté au 5ème étage. J'y suis resté toute la journée.

L'agent: Vous ne vous êtes pas lavé? Vous ne vous êtes pas habillé? Vous n'avez rien mangé? A quelle heure êtes-vous sorti? Au tabac, qu'est-ce que vous avez acheté? Qui vous a vu entrer dans l'immeuble où se trouve votre bureau? Qu'est-ce que vous avez fait pendant le déjeuner? Vous n'êtes pas sorti pendant la journée?

5   (i) réduit, séduit, introduit, produit, déduit, construit

      (ii) traduit, détruit, bien cuit (verbe 'cuire')

3   *Past participle agreement*

1   (a) Ils sont arrivés.

    (b) Mes deux sœurs sont parties.

    (c) Marie-Antoinette est morte en 1793.

    (d) Ma montre, où est-ce que je l'ai laissée?

    (e) Je les ai trouvé(e)s sans difficulté.

    (f) Les poires que j'ai achetées hier ne sont pas mûres.

    (g) Elle s'est baignée dans la mer.

    (h) Marie a couché son petit frère, puis elle s'est couchée.

    (i) Nous avons descendu nos bagages.

    (j) Quelles valises avez-vous descendues?

    (k) Ils sont descendus, vos frères?

    (l) Elles se sont regardées un moment puis se sont embrassées.

(m) Elle s'est gratté la tête.

(n) Ils se sont donné rendez-vous pour le lendemain.

(o) Des escargots? Ah, j'en ai trouvé de beaux après la pluie.

4 Word order of negatives and object pronouns with the perfect tense

1 (a) Oui, je l'ai trouvé/ Non, je ne l'ai pas trouvé.

(b) Non, je ne la lui ai pas donnée.

(c) Oui, il me l'a donnée/ Non, il ne me l'a pas donnée.

(d) Oui, je les ai achetées hier/ Non, je ne les ai pas achetées hier.

(e) Je ne les ai pas achetées, on me les a données.

(f) Je lui ai envoyé une longue lettre. Je ne lui ai pas envoyé de carte postale.

5 Imperfect tense

1 Dimanche à 10 heures j'étais dans ma chambre avec mon frère. Mon frère et notre voisin étaient dans le garage. Ils essayaient de réparer notre voiture qui était en panne. Maman était dans le salon. Elle tricotait. Mon frère et moi jouions aux échecs.

2 (a) J'étais au lit. Je lisais.

(b) Je faisais mes devoirs.

(c) Je regardais la télé.

(d) J'habitais Walsall.

(e) Il ne pleuvait pas. Il neigeait et il faisait du vent.

(f) Non, je portais un pantalon gris, une chemise bleue et un tricot bleu.

3 (a) Elle se réveillait d'habitude à 6 heures et elle restait au lit jusqu'à 7 heures.

(b) Pourtant ce matin elle s'est levée à 7h30 et elle a quitté (elle est sortie de la maison) à 8 heures..

(c) Pendant que nous regardions/qu'on regardait la télévision hier soir quelqu'un a volé mon vélo.

(d) J'ai rêvé d'une drôle d'école où tous les profs portaient des blue-jeans et fumaient en classe. Il n'y avait pas de leçons l'après-midi. Tout le monde faisait du sport et rentrait à la maison à 4 heures.

(e) Quand mon père allait à la pêche, il se levait normalement très tôt le matin et rentrait tard le soir bredouille (sans poissons). Cependant dimanche dernier, il est revenu avec une grande truite.

(f) 'Je l'ai attrapée moi-même', a-t-il déclaré. Nous ne l'avons pas cru.

(g) J'étais sous la douche/je me douchais quand vous avez téléphoné.

(h) Quand j'étais jeune j'écoutais beaucoup la radio.

(i) Quand mon grand père était jeune, il n'y avait pas de télévision.

(j) Qu'est-ce que les gens faisaient le soir à cette époque-là?

4 The calming of the waters

Le soir de ce même jour, Jésus a dit à ses disciples, 'Passons de l'autre côté du lac'.

Ils ont quitté la foule; les disciples ont emmené Jésus dans la barque où il se trouvait. D'autres barques encore étaient près de lui. Et voilà qu'un vent violent s'est mis à souffler, les vagues se jetaient dans la barque, de sorte que, déjà, elle se remplissait d'eau. Jésus était à l'arrière du bateau et dormait, la tête appuyée contre un coussin. Ses disciples l'ont réveillé et lui ont dit,

'Maître, nous allons mourir. Cela ne te fait-il rien?'

Jésus s'est réveillé, il a parlé sévèrement au vent et a dit à l'eau du lac,

'Silence! Calme-toi!'

Alors le vent est tombé et il y a eu un grand calme. Puis Jésus a dit aux disciples,

'Pourquoi avez-vous peur? N'avez-vous pas encore de foi?'

Mais ils étaient très effrayés et ils se sont dit les uns aux autres,

'Qui est donc cet homme, pour que même le vent et l'eau du lac lui obéissent?'

Marc 4,5 (Traduction de *l'Alliance Biblique Universelle*, 1988)

6 Past historic tense

1 *éteindre* – The firemen put out the fire.

pouvoir – They could/were able to understand.

être – We were soon outside.

devoir – He had to pay a fine.

produire – He produced his papers.

s'inscrire – They signed on for evening classes.

retenir – The flu kept him in bed.

surprendre – The results surprised the teacher.

revenir –They came back at the weekend.

boire – He emptied/drank the glass in one go.

savoir – At that moment he knew the truth.

falloir – It was necessary to wait for a bit.

pleuvoir – In the morning it rained.

maintenir – He kept his job for a long time.

convaincre – His explanation/reasoning convinced me.

se taire, rire – He remained silent/said nothing for a moment then burst out laughing.

fumer – We smoked two cigarettes before going to bed.

7 Pluperfect tense

1 La déclaration de M. XX:

(a) J'étais descendu à l'hôtel Splendide. J'y étais arrivé vers 7 heures. J'avais mangé à l'hôtel. Après j'étais sorti me promener. J'avais marché pendant une heure. Puis j'étais revenu à l'hôtel. Dans le bar j'avais rencontré un ancien collègue. Nous avions bu quelques verres ensemble. Je m'étais couché vers 11h45.

(b) Il a dit qu'il était descendu à l'hôtel Splendide, qu'il y était arrivé vers 7 heures et qu'il avait mangé à l'hôtel; il a ajouté qu'après il était sorti se promener et qu'il avait marché pendant une heure; ensuite qu'il était revenu à l'hôtel et que, dans le bar, il avait rencontré un ancien collègue. Puis, il a déclaré qu'ils avaient bu quelques verres ensemble. Enfin, il a affirmé qu'il s'était couché vers 11h45.

2 (a) J'étais arrivé tard donc je me suis couché tôt.

(b) Quand le bus s'est arrêté il est descendu.

(c) Elle était partie de bonne heure pour ne pas manquer le train.

(d) Ils s'étaient présentés au commissariat.

(e) Je ne savais pas qu'elle s'était mariée.

3 (a) Je ne l'avais pas vue depuis samedi.

(b) Il ne m'avait rien dit.

(c) Ils n'y avaient trouvé personne.

(d) Il vous en avait déjà parlé?

(e) Mes sœurs n'avaient jamais visité Paris.

4 (a) Il dit qu'il n'a jamais voyagé en avion.

(b) Il a dit qu'il n'avait jamais voyagé en avion.

(c) J'ai trouvé que je n'avais pas compris ce qu'il avait dit.

(d) Elle a dit qu'elle avait téléphoné la semaine dernière.

(e) Je suis sûr que la lettre est arrivée.

(f) J'étais sûr que la lettre était arrivée.

(g) 'Je n'ai jamais vu cet homme' a-t-elle dit.

(h) Il s'est rappelé qu'il a vu Fifi à la banque.

(i) Il a dit qu'il n'avait jamais vu cet homme.

(j) Je ne pouvais pas trouver la lettre qu'il m'avait envoyée.

5 (a) Incendiaire: (vi), (i), (iii), (ii), (v), (iv)

(b) Following being questioned by police.

(c) At this point in the account we go back to the events before this.

6 **Sur les traces de De Saussure**

Chamonix: Il y a quelques jours, deux Haut-Savoyards — Pierre Cusin et Thierry Gazin — ont battu(pc) le record Chamonix–Mont-Blanc et retour en moins de 8 heures. Ces deux spécialistes des cross en montagne avaient voulu(pp) saluer ainsi à leur manière le bicentenaire de l'ascension du Mont-Blanc. Devant cette brillante réussite ils ont décidé(pc) de ne pas en rester là. Avec Christophe Gotti du CAF d'Annecy ils ont décidé(pc) de refaire l'itinéraire du savant genevois, Horace Benedict De Saussure. Celui-ci bien avant avait réussi (pp) la conquête du Mont-Blanc dont il fut l'instigateur. Il était allé(pp) de Genève à Chamonix à pied, puis bien plus tard, en 1787, avait gravi(pp) le Mont-Blanc avec Jacques Balmont dans des conditions que l'on imagine il y a 199 ans. Le trio sportif est donc parti pour Genève hier soir pour remonter toute la vallée de l'Arve en courant. Les quatre événements sont:

(i)   Trajet à pied Genève-Chamonix par De Saussure.
(ii)   Même trajet, en courant, par P Cusin, T Gazin et C Gotti.
(iii) Ascension du Mont-Blanc par De Saussure en 1787.
(iv)   Ascension du Mont-Blanc par P Cusin et T Gazin, aller et retour en courant en moins de huit heures.

9, 10 and 11 Future tenses

1 (a) Il trouvera la lettre.
(b) Il aurait trouvé la lettre (s'il avait jeté un coup d'œil dans le placard).
(c) Il aura trouvé là lettre.
(d) Il trouverait la lettre (s'il jetait un coup d'œil dans le placard).
(e) Est-ce que je sortirai avec lui ce soir?
(f) Je serais sortie avec lui ce soir.
(g) Je sortirais avec elle(si j'avais de l'argent)
(h) Il sera déjà sorti.

2 (a) (i) faire (ii) ils feraient (iii) ils auront fait (iv) ils auraient fait
(b) (i) être (ii) ils seraient (iii) ils auront été (iv) ils auraient été
(c) (i) voir (ii) je verrais (iii) j' aurai vu (iv) j' aurais vu
(d) (i) avoir (ii) nous aurions (iii) nous aurons eu (iv) nous aurions eu
(e) (i) pouvoir (ii) il pourrait (iii) il aura pu (iv) il aurait pu
(f) (i) avoir (ii) il aurait (iii) il aura eu (iv) il aurait eu
(g) (i) pleuvoir (ii) il pleuvrait (iii) il aura plu (iv) il aurait plu
(h) (i) envoyer (ii) nous enverrions (iii) nous aurons envoyé (iv) nous aurions envoyé
(i) (i) mourir (ii) il mourrait (iii) il sera mort (iv) il serait mort
(j) (i) falloir (ii) il faudrait (iii) il aura fallu (iv) il aurait fallu
(k) (i) jeter (ii) ils jetteraient (iii) ils auront jeté (iv) ils auraient jeté
(l) (i) valoir (ii) il vaudrait (iii) il aura valu (iv) il aurait valu

3 (a) Quand vous le verrez donnez-lui ceci.
(b) Si vous le voyez donnez-lui ceci.
(c) Aussitôt que j'aurai fini je vous téléphonerai.
(d) Si j'avais suffisamment d'argent j'aimerais voyager.
(e) Qu'est-ce que nous allons faire ce soir?
(f) Que ferions-nous sans la télé?
(g) Je suis sûr qu'il vous aurait dit cela.
(h) Si nous avions été là nous l'aurions vu.
(i) Je lui ai demandé si elle voudrait venir avec moi en Grèce.
(j) Je ne sais pas si elle voudrait venir (be willing to come).

4 (a) It's the day before the big day when she sets off. Soon Marie-Claude will be packing her cases because she is setting off tomorrow morning at 5.00. Tomorrow evening she will be in Cannes. She will have spent ten hours in the train and, as soon as she has eaten, she will go to bed at the hotel. She has been told that, from her window, she will be able to see the sea as soon as it gets light.
(b) C'était la veille du grand départ. Bientôt Marie-Claude allait faire ses valises car elle allait partir demain matin à 5 heures. Demain soir elle serait à Cannes. Elle aurait passé dix heures dans le train et aussitôt qu'elle aurait mangé elle irait se coucher à l'hôtel. On lui avait dit que de sa fenêtre elle pourrait voir la mer dès qu'il ferait jour.

5 (a) Si je le vois, je lui donnerai ceci. S'il me demande qui me l'a donné, je lui dirai la vérité.
(b) Quand je le verrai je lui donnerai ceci. Quand il me demandera qui me l'a donné, je lui dirai la vérité.

6 Two hundred militant Kurds demonstrated yesterday in Paris and occupied the first floor of the Eiffel Tower. According to their leaders, two of their fellow countrymen have allegedly died recently after being badly treated in Turkish prisons and several others are said to be in a critical condition.

7 **Established facts:** man received several stab wounds; his identity not known; taken to hospital in serious condition.
Alleged events: a witness to the crime alerted the police; suffering from perforated lung; the young girl gave herself up.

12 Subjunctive

1 (a) Pour qu'il comprenne.
   (b) Quoique nous sachions.
   (c) A moins qu'il ne vienne.
   (d) Il faut que tu y ailles/vous y alliez.
   (e) Pourvu qu'il le fasse.
   (f) Avant qu'il ne parte (avant son départ).
   (g) Qu'il parte et qu'il ne revienne pas!
   (h) Quoi qu'il dise.
   (i) Quelles que soient vos raisons.
   (j) Il se peut que le gouvernement ait raison.
   (k) Sans qu'il le sache.
   (l) Jusqu'à ce qu'ils apprennent.
   (m) Bien qu'ils ne comprennent pas.
   (n) Bien qu'ils aient compris.
   (o) Pourvu qu'elle ait fini.

2 (a) Je pense que vous avez raison.
   (b) Pensez-vous qu'ils aient raison?
   (c) J'ai peur qu'il ne soit trop tard.
   (d) Il est possible que la situation soit trop préoccupante.
   (e) Il est probable qu'il prend les mesures nécessaires.
   (f) Il est peu probable qu'il prenne les mesures nécessaires.
   (g) Je regrette que vous ne soyez pas de mon avis/d'accord avec moi/que vous ne partagiez pas mon opinion.
   (h) Je suis surpris qu'ils aient fait cela.
   (i) Pensez-vous que le gouvernement suive la bonne politique.
   (j) J'espère que ces renseignements sont corrects.
   (k) Je suis content qu'il ait fait cela.
   (l) Pensez-vous que cela soit vrai?
   (m) Je ne crois pas que cela soit possible.
   (n) Il est regrettable qu'il ait pris cette décision.
   (o) J'ai peur que je ne fasse quelque erreur/de faire une erreur.

3 (a) You would have done better to have come and seen me straight away.
   (b) Whatever your reasons might be I cannot approve this action.
   (c) Whatever you do, do not listen to his excuses.
   (d) I am looking for someone to help me today.
   (e) I have already found someone who can help me tomorrow.
   (f) However difficult you find this work you must do your best.
   (g) I am going to travel before beginning my studies at university.
   (h) Whether you find someone or not to do this work, it's all the same to me.
   (i) I am afraid that she may have already left.
   (j) You must take a little rest even if it's only for fifteen minutes.

13 Modal verbs

   (a) J'ai dû le laisser à la maison.
   (b) Vous ne devriez pas/Tu ne devrais pas avoir peur.
   (c) Vous n'auriez pas /Tu n'aurais pas dû payer.
   (d) Pourriez-vous/pourrais-tu me prêter 10 francs/balles?
   (e) Je dois travailler plus dur.
   (f) Voulez-vous venir ce soir?
   (g) Est-ce qu'elle sera là?
   (h) Savez-vous quelle est la capitale de l'Estonie?
   (i) Avant la guerre je connaissais très bien Tallin (la capitale de l'Estonie).
   (j) Est-ce que vous pouvez/tu peux le faire avant ce soir?

14 Passive

1 (a) Il a été invité par un ami.
   (b) Vous serez remarqué par la police.

    (c) Le voleur a été arrêté par un pompier.
    (d) Une solution a été trouvée.
    (e) Les secrets ont été révélés.
    (f) La théorie de la relativité a été proposée par Einstein.
    (g) Il est connu de tout le monde.
    (h) Ce modèle est vendu partout.
    (i) Un jour, mes projets seront réalisés.
    (j) Le général aurait été écrasé par un tank.*

2   (a) Un ami m'a invité.
    (b) La police vous remarquera.
    (c) Un pompier a arrêté le voleur.
    (d) On a trouvé une solution.
    (e) Les secrets se sont révélés (on a révélé) les secrets.
    (f) Einstein a proposé la théorie de la relativité.
    (g) Tout le monde le connaît.
    (h) Ce modèle se vend partout/ on vend ce modèle partout.
    (i) Je réaliserai, un jour, mes projets.
    (j) Un tank aurait écrasé le général.*
    *Both these sentences could also mean – *is supposed /alleged to have been run over by a tank*
    (*See* conditional, page 41)

3   (a) Il ne sera pas réélu la prochaine fois.
    (b) On m'a ordonné de ne pas bouger.
    (c) On ne nous a pas dit la vérité.
    (d) On nous a demandé de ne pas attendre.
    (e) Cette réclame se voit partout.
    (f) On pense qu'il est très intelligent/on le croit très intelligent.
    (g) Cela ne se fait pas ici/On ne fait pas ça ici.
    (h) Ma sœur m'a pardonné.
    (i) La face du monde a été changée par l'homme/ L'homme a changé la face du monde.
    (j) Trop de soleil brûle la peau./ La peau est brûlée par trop de soleil.
    (k) La porte s'ouvre lentement, une main apparaît dans l'embrasure, un cri bizarre se fait entendre on voit la porte s'ouvrir lentement, on voit une main dans l'embrasure, on entend un cri bizarre.
    (l) Les portes du TGV s'ouvrent quand le train s'arrête
    (m) Les portes ne sont pas ouvertes quand le train s'arrête.

15 *Present participle*

1   (a) En travaillant pendant le week-end et en faisant des économies ils ont finalement réussi à acheter une maison.
    (b) Je l'ai fait en regardant la télévision.
    (c) Elle était assise devant le feu, le chat sur les genoux.
    (d) Etant arrivé en retard, j'ai manqué le premier acte.
    (e) Après avoir fermé la porte à clef et mis le verrou je me suis couché.
    (f) Avant de partir vérifiez que vous ayez(si vous avez) fermé toutes les fenêtres.
    (g) En arrivant il a constaté que les autres invités avaient déjà commencé le repas.
    (h) Commencez par apprendre les verbes irréguliers.
    (i) On ne peut pas se débarrasser de ses ordures en les laissant dans la rue.
    (j) En gesticulant et en me faisant des signes elle a réussi à attirer mon attention.
    (k) Une dame charmante au visage souriant.
    (l) J'aime jouer de la guitare, regarder les matchs de football à la télévision et sortir avec mes copains.

2   (a) He likes fishing and hunting a lot and he loves sailing.
    (b) Seeing is believing.
    (c) The whole house needs cleaning.
    (d) Thank you for reminding me about it.
    (e) Women are reputed to be good drivers.
    (f) In Molière's *L'Avare,* Maître Jacques is punished for telling the truth.
    (g) A sowing machine; a dining room; a riding lesson; a driving lesson; a driving school.
    (h) Yes, I can see him coming. He is running very fast, he is waving and shouting.

16 Getting things done: Faire and the infinitive
1 (a) Faites venir son père.
   (b) Ne le faites pas attendre sur le seuil, faites-le entrer.
   (c) Faites griller pendant dix minutes.
   (d) J'ai fait construire une maison à la campagne.
   (e) Faites-lui manger quelque chose.
   (f) Il a fait apporter des gâteaux de la pâtisserie.
   (g) Laissez-le parler.
   (h) Faites taire ces chiens!
   (i) Le voleur s'est fait arrêter/attraper le lendemain.
   (j) J'ai fait faire ces devoirs par ma sœur.

17 Verbs taking prepositions
1 (a) Il a accepté de venir me voir.
   (b) J'ai hésité à dire quoi que ce soit.
   (c) Je l'ai invité à me rendre visite.
   (d) Je l'ai félicitée de son succès.
   (e) J'ai oublié d'écrire.
   (f) Il a refusé d'accepter.
   (g) J'ai refusé d'accepter.
   (h) J'ai essayé de les persuader.
   (i) Ils ont proposé de payer.
   (j) Il a acheté la voiture à mon père.
   (k) Il a emprunté l'argent à sa sœur.
   (l) Est-ce qu'on peut se fier aux hommes politiques?
   (m) Il faut rire de leur conduite.
   (n) Il me faut voler une banque pour payer mes vacances.
   (o) Je suis toujours le dernier à savoir.

2 (a) Vous n'avez rien à dire?
   (b) Tout dépend de sa décision.
   (c) Vous devez payer les dégâts.
   (d) Qui attendez-vous?
   (e) Dites à votre cousin d'amener sa sœur.
   (f) Je me suis trompé de numéro/ j'ai fait le mauvais numéro.
   (g) Je n'ai pas eu l'occasion de lui parler.
   (h) Il s'est servi de sa manche pour nettoyer le tableau.
   (i) J'ai promis à mon prof de travailler plus dur l'année prochaine.
   (j) On m'a défendu de me servir de mon mouchoir pour nettoyer mes souliers.
   (k) Que pensez-vous de lui?
   (l) Vous pensez souvent à elle?
   (m) Il vous manque quelque chose?
   (n) La France me manque!
   (o) Savez-vous jouer du piano?

3 (a) You could easily do without television.
   (b) He is still in prison? I thought as much.
   (c) I am very keen on visiting Corsica this year.
   (d) He bore me a grudge for what I did to him.
   (e) What is it used for/ what use is it?
   (f) We are not all going to drink out of the same glass, I hope.

18 The articles
1 (a) J'aime le football, la natation et le basket.
   (b) Voulez-vous me passer le sel s'il vous plaît.
   (c) Les Japonais chassent toujours les baleines.
   (d) L'éléphant sera bientôt une espèce en voie de disparition.
   (e) L'ail est un ingrédient important de la cuisine provençale.
   (f) Je voudrais une bouteille d'eau, un kilo de pêches et une boîte des (de ces) haricots que vous avez recommandés.
   (g) Mon frère veut devenir médecin — il est plein d'idées bizarres.

(h) Beaucoup de docteurs croient que le jogging est mauvais pour la santé.

(i) La plupart des gens que j'ai rencontrés ne vont pas à l'église le dimanche.

(j) Le samedi soir c'est moi qui fait la cuisine.

(k) Beaucoup de gens étaient arrivés en retard, d'autres n'avaient pas pris la peine de venir.

(l) La semaine dernière; l'année prochaine; le soir; le lundi.

(m) Il n'y avait pas de vent mais beaucoup de pluie.

(n) Nous n'avons ni bananes ni de pêches.

(o) La France est presque deux fois et demie plus grande que l'Angleterre.

(p) Qu'est-ce qu'il nous faut pour le pique-nique – du jambon, du pain, de la salade, du vin ou du jus d'orange, des pêches et du fromage.

19 Object pronouns

1 (a) Oui, je vous les donne.
Oui, je vous les prête.
Oui, je vais vous les envoyer.
Oui, je vais vous en envoyer.
Oui, je vais le lui présenter.

(b) Non, je ne vous les donne pas.
Non, je ne vous les prête pas.
Non, je ne vais pas vous les envoyer.
Non, je ne vais pas vous en envoyer.
Non, je ne vais pas le lui présenter.

2 (a) Oui, j'y vais tout de suite.
Oui, il s'y intéresse beaucoup.
Oui, j'y réfléchis beaucoup.
Oui, j'y pense souvent.

(b) Non, je n'y vais pas tout de suite.
Non, il ne s'y intéresse pas beaucoup.
Non, je n'y réfléchis pas beaucoup.
Non, je n'y pense pas souvent.

3 (a) Oui, il en reste.
Oui, j'en ai besoin.
Oui, il m'en a parlé.
Combien en voulez-vous?
Il vous en faut combien?

(b) Non, il n'en reste pas.
Non, je n'en ai pas besoin.
Non, il ne m'en a pas parlé
Je n'en veux pas/Il ne m'en faut pas.

4 (a) Les brochures? Je les lui ai envoyées la semaine dernière.

(b) Mon rapport? Je le leur ai déjà présenté.

(c) Mon télex à M. Dupont? Je le lui ai déjà envoyé ce matin. Quoi, il ne l'a pas encore reçu? Il aurait dû le recevoir.

(d) Téléphonez-lui et dites-lui que je le lui ai bien envoyé et qu'il devrait bientôt le recevoir.

(e) Mon projet? Vous voulez que je vous l'explique? Bon, je vais vous l'expliquer. M. Dupont? Je le lui ai déjà expliqué. Il en était très content.

5 (a) Je les lui ai déjà envoyé(e)s.

(b) Envoyez-le-lui. Il en a besoin tout de suite.

(c) Téléphonez-lui et dites-lui que je lui en parlerai plus tard.

(d) Des possibilités? Oui, il y en a plusieurs. Examinons-les.

(e) Il vous les a envoyé(e)s la semaine dernière.

(f) Il ne vous les a pas envoyé(e)s la semaine dernière?

(g) Je suis sûr que je lui ai dit de vous les envoyer.

6 (a) (i) Ne me les donnez pas.
(ii) Ne les lui envoyez pas.
(iii) Ne nous les expliquez pas.
(iv) Ne lui répondez pas tout de suite.
(v) Ne lui en parlez pas.

(b) (i)   Dites-le-lui.
     (ii) Envoyez-le-moi.
     (iii) Parlez-lui-en.
     (iv) Donnez-m'en beaucoup.
     (v)   Asseyez-vous là, la peinture y est fraîche!

20 Emphatic pronouns

1 (a) Répétez après moi.
   (b) Devant elle; derrière lui; avec nous.
   (c) Eux, ils ne comprennent pas.
   (d) Lui, qu'est-ce qu'il en pense?
   (e) Ni elle ni moi savions la réponse.
   (f) J'ai besoin de lui.
   (g) Ils ont peur d'elle.
   (h) Je l'ai fait moi-même.
   (i) Que pense-t-il de nous?
   (j) J'ai honte de vous.

21 and 22 Relative and interrogative pronouns

1 (a) Je sais qu'elle a raison.
   (b) Je pense qu'il arrivera tard.
   (c) Je ne sais pas ce qu'il va dire.
   (d) Qu'est-ce que vous lui direz?
   (e) Lequel de ces deux vins préférez-vous?
   (f) Voilà la maison dont je vous ai parlé.
   (g) Voilà l'arbre sous lequel nous nous sommes assis et sur lequel nous avons gravé nos noms.
   (h) Ce que je ne comprends pas c'est qu'il n'a jamais d'argent.
   (i) De quel homme politique est-ce que vous parlez?
   (j) Vous ne savez pas les difficultés que nous avons eues.
   (k) Ce qui est intéressant, c'est qu'il a nié toute responsabilité.
   (l) Parmi ces problèmes lequel est le plus préoccupant?
   (m) Qui a laissé la porte ouverte?
   (n) C'est un programme qui commence ce soir et que vous ne devez pas manquer.
   (o) Elles sont à qui ces chaussures?

2 **Les mauvais effets du soleil**
   Chaque année, les services d'urgence récupèrent des touristes inconscients, **qui** se sont laissé aller sous notre soleil sans penser **qu'**il n'avait rien à voir avec celui du bord des plages anglaises. On ignore le fait **que** le sable réfléchit 20% des radiations et l'eau 10% et **que** la quantité d'UVB est maximale entre 11 heures et 14 heures. **Ce qu'**on ignore surtout, c'est **que** les effets du soleil sont cumulatifs. Voici **ce que** m'a expliqué un chef de service de dermatologie: 'Tout s'additionne. Je vois parfois des patients **qui** me disent **que** depuis deux ou trois ans, ils ont nettement diminué leurs expositions au soleil. Mais tout **ce qu'**ils ont emmagasiné il y a 10 ou 20 ans est enregistré.'

23 Demonstrative adjectives and pronouns

1 (a) Quel tricot préférez-vous? Celui-ci est joli mais celui-là sera plus chaud.
   (b) Ceux en coton sont plus faciles à laver mais ceux en laine ne se froissent pas.
   (c) Cet été; cette année; cette fois; ce temps; ces moustiques.
   (d) Ça, c'est vraiment embêtant.
   (e) Ma voiture est en panne. J'ai emprunté celle de mon frère.
   (f) Quelles pêches préférez-vous? Celles-ci sont à 6F le kilo, et celles-là sont à 8F,50.
   (g) Il faut conserver nos ressources naturelles; cela est très important.
   (h) Quelle boîte voulez-vous? Celle qui est sur la table de la cuisine.
   (i) Ces solutions sont difficiles à mettre en œuvre. Examinons celles proposées par Dupont.
   (j) Ça, c'est le comble! Ces idées-là sont ridicules.

Other indefinite pronouns

2 (a) On dit que l'argent ne fait pas le bonheur. Je ne peux pas accepter une telle idée.
   (b) J'ai passé la soirée avec quelques amis.
   (c) Quelques-uns de ses meilleurs amis étaient venus lui dire au-revoir.

    (d)   Cela s'est passé il y a plusieurs années.

    (e)   Je vois/comprends ce que vous voulez dire.

    (f)   Vous avez fait quelque chose d'intéressant à Bognor? Pas grand-chose.

    (g)   Chaque fois que je le voyais il avait l'air différent.

    (h)   Dans la pièce de Ionesco tous les personnages, sauf le héro Bérenger, se changent finalement en rhinocéros.

    (i)   Il y avait plusieurs jeunes filles sur la photo. Chacune portait une robe blanche.

    (j)   Tous les efforts que j'ai faits sont inutiles.

    (k)   Ils étaient tous arrivés trop tôt.

    (l)   Tout est possible si vous croyez que les gens ont confiance en vous.

24 *C'est and il est*

(a)   Qui a fait ça? **C'est** mon père.

(b)   Je vous présente ma tante. **Elle est** institutrice.

(c)   **C'est** formidable, l'Angleterre a gagné au Parc des Princes!

(d)   On peut maintenant traverser la Manche par le tunnel. **C'est** incroyable! Mais **il est** impossible de faire cela dans sa voiture.

(e)   Ma sœur? **Elle est** au Brésil.

(f)   Mes deux sœurs rient et bavardent tout le temps. **Elles sont** bêtes.

(g)   **Il est** inspecteur de police. **C'est** un inspecteur bien connu en France.

(h)   Les croissants? **Ils sont** sur la table dans la cuisine, n'est-ce pas?

25 *Possessive adjectives and pronouns*

1   (a)   Son fils, sa sœur, sa mère, sa cousine, leurs parents.

    (b)   Ce livre, est-il à lui?/C'est à lui, ce livre? Non, c'est le sien/à elle.

    (c)   Elle est arrivée avec leurs amis et il est venu avec les siens/avec ses amis à lui.

    (d)   Quel livre est à lui/est le sien?

    (e)   C'est à qui ceci?

    (f)   Les miennes sont grises et les siennes sont bleues.

    (g)   Elle n'est pas à moi, elle est à eux/ ce n'est pas la mienne, c'est la leur.

26 *Adjectives*

1   (a)   Des ressources naturelles.

    (b)   Une bonne idée.

    (c)   La marée basse.

    (d)   Un matin frais.

    (e)   Un hiver doux.

    (f)   Une voix douce.

    (g)   Une longue journée.

    (h)   Une nouvelle solution.

    (i)   Une fille menteuse.

    (j)   Une collection complète.

    (k)   Une fausse idée.

    (l)   Il y avait plusieurs jolies filles françaises à la boum.

    (m)   La population ouvrière.

    (n)   De vieux amis; Un vieil ami.

    (o)   La vie parisienne.

    (p)   Quelques nouvelles publications françaises.

    (q)   De petites villes italiennes.

    (r)   Une explication brève.

    (s)   Un lieu public.

    (t)   Une place publique.

2   Change of meaning tasks

(a) De Gaulle was a great man; he was also a tall man.

(b) You feel sorry for that millionaire but he is not poor.

(c) The school I used to go to is a very old one.

(d) Last year was 1990 but 1999 will be the last year of the century.

(e) My own house; I like to live in a clean house.

(f) A certain man; find me a man I can rely on.

(g) My dear wife has bought an expensive coat.

(h) I was born on the same day as you; he fell ill the very day he arrived.

(i) He has another car. It's a new model.

(j) The only Chinese man that I know; only the Chinese know how to do it.

(k) Another glass (to drink)? I'll bring you a fresh glass. Here's one that has never been used.

(l) I'll tell him the next time I see him, perhaps that will be next week.

27 and 28 Position of adjectives, adverbs and comparisons

(a) Un ancien collègue.

(b) Elle est la seule qui puisse le faire.

(c) Evidemment il parle le russe aussi bien que vous.

(d) Il a encore acheté une maison. C'est une maison neuve?

(e) Le jour même de son arrivée.

(f) Ces lettres sont arrivées le même jour.

(g) J'ai été profondément ému.

(h) La dernière fois que je l'ai vue elle portait des chaussures neuves.

(i) Vous voulez encore une tasse (another drink)? Vous voulez une autre tasse (another cup – this one is cracked)?

(j) Je l'ai rencontré récemment.

(k) Mettez des chaussettes propres.

(l) Plus il a expliqué, moins j'ai compris.

(m) Elle sait dessiner mieux que moi.

(n) Ce n'est pas une mauvaise voiture mais le moteur ne marche pas bien/marche mal à présent.

(o) Ils ne sortent pas souvent, une petite promenade de temps en temps.

(p) Vous vous sentez mieux?

(q) Il devient de plus en plus difficile de trouver un bon programme à la télévision.

(r) Quel programme aimez-vous le mieux regarder?

(s) Ils croient tous aveuglément au progrès.

(t) La Grande Bretagne n'est pas le pays le moins pollué du monde.

Part III French language

1 Writing

Contents

Writing in French will be required for a significant part of the A-Level examination and this section usually carries between a fifth and a quarter of the total marks. For AS Level, however, writing in French is required by only a few of the Boards (*see* table, pages xii–xiii). For A Level, some (or all) of the literature/topic questions may be set, and require an answer, in French. Coursework done over the two years and sent for moderation is always in French. You might also be required to write in French in response to the reading or listening test.

Almost every Board has a section of one of its papers devoted to a continuous piece of writing (of 250-300 words) called 'essay' (or 'composition') or to a report, dialogue or letter of about 200 words. It is worth remembering that in this section marks are awarded for:

(a) **Content** – the quality, relevance and overall structuring of the ideas

(b) **Range** of vocabulary, structures and idioms used

(c) **Accuracy** of language

The last factor is not the overriding one and often has fewer marks awarded than the first two elements. It is important therefore to carefully plan the layout of your piece of writing and to be adventurous with words and expressions.

1 Letters

You will be familiar with this task from your experience at GCSE. The following points about general structure however need to be observed:

(a) The introduction

Check to whom the letter is to be written. If it is a formal or an official letter start with the following if addressing a company:

(i) *Mademoiselle/Madame/Monsieur* or *Messieurs*.

These titles are never abbreviated at the beginning of a letter.

If you know the title of the person to whom you are writing this should be given in the following form:

(ii) *Madame la Directrice*

(iii) *Monsieur le Président*

(iv) *Monsieur le Maire*

(v) *Madame l'Attachée Culturelle*

If it is implied or stated in the instructions for the letter that you know the person quite well you may begin:

(vii) *Chère Madame* or *Cher Monsieur*

Do **not** use the form *Mon cher Monsieur* or *Ma chère Madame*.

When writing to a friend you may use *Cher* or *Chère* followed by first name or *Cher Monsieur__* and *Chère Madame__*. If you want to include a whole family or group you can start *Chers amis*.

(b) Openings

It is not possible to include here examples of all the possible beginnings for a letter since much depends on the specific instructions given. There are some general guidelines on page 86.

Formal or official letters

The style of such letters in French often sounds a bit pompous to English speakers but this level of formality is the norm and continues to be used.

- Thanks for a letter or services already received:
    - (i) *J'ai l'honneur d'accuser réception de votre lettre du...*
    - (ii) *J'ai l'honneur de vous remercier...*
        J'ai le plaisir de vous remercier pour...
- Asking for a service or a favour:
    - (iii) *Je vous serais très reconnaissant(e) de bien vouloir...*
    - (iv) *Je vous serais très obligé(e) de me faire savoir...*
    - (v) *Je sollicite votre bienveillance pour me fournir des renseignements...*
- Following up:
    - (vi) *Ayant lu votre annonce parue dans le Figaro, ...*
    - (vii) *En réponse à votre annonce parue...*
    - (viii) *En réponse à votre lettre du...*
    - (ix) *Comme suite à votre demande téléphonique...*
        Faisant suite à notre conversation téléphonique...
- Opening a subject for correspondence:
    - (x) *Je me permets de vous écrire pour/au sujet de...*
    - (xi) *J'ai le plaisir/l'honneur de...*

Personal letters

Distinguish between writing to a friend (or friends) of your own age and to perhaps a family you stayed with or worked for. You would probably use *'tu'* (or *'vous'* if there is more than one friend), in the first case, but *'vous'* when addressing a family. The following are some possibilities for openings:

- (i) *Je vous/te remercie de/pour votre/ta lettre*
    (or if writing in more familiar style)
- (ii) *Merci de ta lettre*
- (iii) *Votre/Ta lettre m'a fait grand plaisir*
- (iv) *Quelques mots pour vous/te remercier de...*
    (Or if in apology)
- (v) *Je tarde quelque peu à répondre à votre/ta lettre*

(c) Main part of letter

Advice on this depends very much on the brief you are given in the examination instructions and the purpose of the letter. It is important to have a **clear plan** and careful paragraphing (i.e. one idea — or subject — per paragraph). Make sure that what you write is relevant to the brief given. Do not be tempted to 'pad' your letter with, say, remarks about the weather.

(d) The ending

Formal style

Just before signing off the following might be appropriate:

- (i) *Dans l'attente d'une réponse favorable...*
- (ii) *Avec mes remerciements anticipés...*
- (iii) *Dans l'attente de votre réponse...*

The possibilities for the actual signing off are more formal and varied than the English 'Yours faithfully' (which normally should follow a 'Dear Sir' beginning). The following diagram gives you a basic pattern.

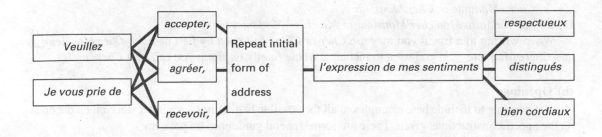

For example:
Veuillez agréer, Monsieur le Président, l'expression de mes sentiments distingués

Personal style

The following will suffice for most occasions:

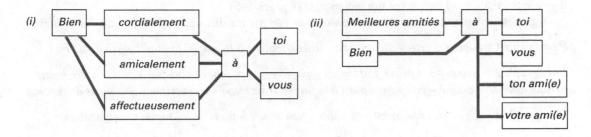

Expressions such as:
  (iii) *Je t'embrasse affectueusment*
  (iv) *Bons baisers* (to children)
   (v) *Grosses bises*
are only used between people who usually kiss each other when saying hello or goodbye.

The above framework belongs to what are known as *'les convenances épistolaires'* (the conventions of letter writing). You will find the following 'epistolary' terms useful in many cases too:
  (vi) *Veuillez trouver ci-joint* – Please find enclosed
 (vii) *Par retour de courrier* – By return of post
(viii) *Enveloppe timbrée à mes nom et adresse* – Stamped addressed envelope
  (ix) *dès que possible* – as soon as possible
   (x) *dans les delais les plus brefs* – as soon as possible
  (xi) *expédier/expéditeur* – to send or post/sender
 (xii) *un colis* – postal packet or parcel
(xiii) *l'emballage* – wrapping or packing
 (xiv) *au déballage* – when we/I unpacked it
  (xv) *Je suis au regret de vous informer que* – I regret to inform you that
 (xvi) *Il faut constater que* – It must be noted that
(xvii) *Je dois vous signaler que* – I must point out to you
Note *'Signaler'* and *'constater'* are both useful words to replace *'dire'*
(*see* page 3)

Model answer: English stimulus

1 In the Easter holidays you worked for the Legrand family in Lyon for three weeks. They agreed to pay you 450 francs per week pocket money in return for certain duties. They paid you for the first week, but then they suffered a bereavement, everyone was upset and when you left at the end of three weeks they still owed you for the second and third weeks. They promised to send the money on but have not yet done so. You have written once but received no reply.

Now write a letter of about 200 words to the French agency who arranged the job for you explaining the position and asking them to take action.

London AS-Level, June 1989

This type of stimulus just gives a general description of the type of letter you are required to write. You are allowed to use a dictionary with this Board. You have one hour for planning and writing. Give yourself: about 15 minutes to read the instructions, plan the letter and consult a dictionary if need be; 30 minutes to write the letter; and 15 minutes to check through what you have written. Always write on alternate lines, it makes inserting corrections easier later.

(a) Answer plan

You will need three paragraphs:
   (i) to say who you are
  (ii) to explain the situation
 (iii) to make the request and sign off.

Next plan the detail. Do not be tempted to translate from the beginning of the instructions. If you begin with 'Pendant les vacances de Pâques' you will miss out the first part of your plan. When you read through the brief for the letter French words may come to your mind, write these down before they float out again. Don't panic at phrases like 'suffered a bereavement', find another way of saying it in English (i.e. 'someone died', then say who and write the French 'la grande-mère est morte'. It is a good idea to jot down French phrases for the detail of the plan. It is also helpful if you concentrate on the verbs since they are the main working part of the sentence. (*See* pages 1–5)

A possible plan, with a few alternative words as you use the dictionary, might be the following:

Paragraph 1 *trouvé/obtenu – votre agence – trois semaines à Pâques – famille Legrand – Lyon*

Paragraph 2 *convenu – me payer 450 francs – payé/reçu – première semaine –grande-mère morte – famille désolée – oublié – pas payé – parti à la fin des trois semaines – écrit une fois – pas de réponse*

Paragraph 3 *obligé / reconnaissant – m'aider – leur écrire – prendre les mesures nécessaires*

If you concentrate on the verbs, and their tenses you should find that your outline reads like an abbreviated message that you can fill out.

(b) Possible answer

The final letter, with a few comments in bold might be as follows:
Messieurs, (**sounds business-like**)

Je vous écris (**but better**) Je suis obligé de vous écrire (**a more forceful phrase here**) au sujet d(e) (**another useful phrase, equivalent of about, concerning**) de l'emploi que votre agence m'a obtenu pour les vacances de Pâques.

J'ai travaillé au pair pour la famille Legrand à Lyon pendant trois semaines. M. Legrand avait convenu de me payer 350 francs par semaine comme argent de poche. J'ai reçu cette somme pour la première semaine mais au milieu de mon séjour, la grande-mère qui habitait avec la famille est morte subitement. Tout le monde était si bouleversé qu'on a oublié de me payer. Quand je suis reparti après les trois semaines, ils ont promis de m'envoyer l'argent. J'ai écrit une fois mais je n'ai pas reçu de réponse.

Je vous serais très obligé si vous pouviez prendre les mesures nécessaires pour obtenir la somme qu'ils me doivent.

Dans l'attente de votre réponse veuillez agréer, Messieurs, l'expression de mes sentiments distingués.

(c) Checking your work

You will need to have a system for checking what you have written for mistakes. The following method can be applied to any piece of French you have written:

(i)   Verb
- Does the subject (singular or plural) fit the ending? Have I spelt the ending correctly?
- Is the tense the right one? Is it an *'avoir'* or an *'être'* verb, if it's a compound tense?
- Is it an irregular verb? (e.g. the past participle may not end in *é*.)

(ii) Nouns and adjectives
- Check that *'s'* is there if required
- Check the gender of the noun and the adjective ending, if it needs to agree.

(iii) Object pronouns
- Check that they are the right ones.
- Check that they are direct or indirect as required (e.g. *le la les* or *lui leur*).
- Check that object pronouns are in their right place, before the verb if it's not in the imperative, and that they are in the right order.

Model answer: French stimulus

The stimulus provided is usually a letter to be answered, an advertisement for a job or an article in a newspaper. The letter might be formal (e.g. a job application, a letter to a newspaper) or written to a friend, describing something that happened to you which you have to imagine using the material provided. Sometimes the article (or report) has already been part of a comprehension question.

Having a stimulus in French does have advantages. You should be able to 'lift' some of the phrases used and 'manipulate' some of the structures to fit into your letter. On the other hand you will not just be able to copy out bits of the text hoping this will do the trick!

You still need of course a clear framework to your letter, a beginning, a middle and an end. Here is a typical example of this kind of letter question:

1   **L'ORDONNANCE ANTISTRESS**

Un hiver à couper au brise-glace et un printemps plutôt frisquet: il est temps de se refaire une santé en vacances.

Les vacances doivent tout changer: effacer les symptômes du stress, liquider la vie harassante. Un Français sur deux part en congés d'été pour une durée moyenne de vingt-cinq jours. De quoi, normalement, transformer le citoyen moyen, maussade, épuisé et blafard en un surhomme bronzé, assuré et dispos. Mais gare aux pièges! D'innombrables estivants reviendront comme ils sont partis. Voire plus mal. Car ils commettent bien des bévues. Ils se bousculent par milliers au volant de leur voiture le même jour. Ils veulent se reposer, mais s'éclatent dans les boîtes de nuit jusqu'au petit matin. Ils désirent se donner bonne mine, et s'affalent des heures durant en plein soleil, au risque d'y 'laisser leur peau'. Ils s'occupent de leur corps, mais s'épuisent en activités physiques auxquelles rien ne les a préparés. Profiter des vacances, c'est presque un art.

On se baigne et on bronze, on drague et on se défonce sur les courts de tennis. Le soleil est un excellent médicament contre la déprime. Et puis, bronzé on se sent beau, plus sûr de soi, bref, mieux dans sa peau. Mais gare aux excès, car comme tout changement dans le rythme de vie, les vacances occasionnent un stress.

Préparez donc votre départ, ne faites pas vos achats à la dernière minute. Cette constrainte s'ajouterait à la fatigue d'une année de travail. Prenez plutôt un temps de répit à la maison pour vous détendre, et vous éviterez également l'énervement des embouteillages sur les routes.

Si vous choisissez malgré tout de partir, dès le premier jour de vos congés, au volant de votre voiture, faites de nombreuses pauses et des mouvements de relaxation. Soyez positif! Comptez les kilomètres que vous avez parcourus et non la distance qui vous reste à parcourir.

Ne cédez pas à la tentation d'une alimentation trop riche. La 'bonne bouffe' conviviale fait plaisir. Quotidienne, elle stresse l'organisme. Redressez au contraire les égarements de l'année, mangez plus de fruits et de légumes.

Vous venez de commettre quelques-unes des erreurs dont on a fait mention dans le texte ci-dessus. Dans une lettre à un(e) ami(e) vous racontez ces vacances malheureuses et leurs conséquences. (300 mots environ)

JMB A-Level, June 1989

This kind of question expects you to use your imagination since you will need to elaborate and expand on the mistakes referred to in the text. It also gives you the opportunity to write in conversational-style French.

It's a good idea to begin by underlining the parts of the text that you might be able to manipulate or work into your letter. The text is written in the present tense. Decide which tense you need. Since you will be telling someone what happened to you, you will be writing in the past tense, using the perfect tense for events and the imperfect for describing how things were. Remember that, if you refer to an event that happened before another one in the past, you need a pluperfect, signalled by the word 'had' in English (e.g. 'I found that I had forgotten' – *Je me suis rendu compte que j'avais oublié*).

Answer plan

1 *Bonjour à votre ami*
2 *Les désagréments des vacances, avec exemples en paragraphes*
3 *Ne fais pas comme moi! au revoir*
      It would be helpful to jot down some notes about the errors made, together with any other words that come into your mind, so that a plan gradually forms as you work:
4 *Départ immédiat – routes encombrées – conduire sans pause – fatigué, énervé*
5 *Achats au dernier moment – oublié quelque chose*
6 *Trop de soleil – rester en plein soleil – insolation*
7 *activités sportives – centre sportif – possibilités de faire de nouveaux sports – résultat*
8 *Boîtes de nuit – dormir pendant la journée – rythme de vie changé*
Write your letter on every other line and leave at least ten minutes at the end for checking.

Possible answer

Cher Jean-Paul,

Comment se sont passées tes vacances? J'espère que tout le monde est rentré bronzé et en pleine forme. Pour nous c'est le contraire. Nos vacances ont été un désastre. Je vais te raconter comment cela s'est passé.

Papa a voulu partir dès le premier jour de ses congés, le samedi matin, très tôt pour éviter les embouteillages. Mais il était si fatigué qu'il n'a pas entendu le réveil-matin. Résultat — départ vers

9 heures sur des routes déjà encombrées. Papa a pris l'autoroute et, malgré toutes nos protestations, il a insisté pour conduire sans pause pendant cinq heures. Par conséquent, il était tout à fait épuisé et nous nous étions énervés quand nous sommes enfin arrivés à notre hôtel.

C'est en arrivant, et en défaisant ma valise, que j'ai découvert que j'avais oublié un maillot et un nouveau pull, tous les deux achetés au dernier moment.

Le lendemain sur la plage on était si fatigué qu'on a dormi en plein soleil. Conséquence — maman et ma petite sœur ont pris un mauvais coup de soleil. Elles ont dû garder la chambre pendant deux jours.

Quant à moi, je me suis lancé dans toutes les activités proposées par l'hôtel dans son centre sportif. Je n'avais jamais fait de squash, ni d'escrime. Plus tard, j'y ai ajouté le mountain-bike et la planche à voile. Tous ces sports demandent une activité physique extraordinaire. Je n'y étais pas préparé!

Mes deux frères aînés ont passé leur temps à draguer dans les boîtes de nuit, et rentraient à l'hôtel au petit matin. Vers la fin des vacances, ils dormaient pendant la journée et se réveillaient seulement le soir. Ils avaient réussi à changer complèment leur rythme de vie.

Et tes vacances? J'espère que tu n'as pas commis les mêmes erreurs que nous.
Ton ami...

Here are more examples of examination questions requiring a letter:

2   Vous êtes un homme d'affaires et vous avez manqué un rendez-vous important à cause d'une grève. Vous écrivez une lettre à un journal national pour exprimer vos sentiments. (250–300 mots)

Oxford and Cambridge A-Level, June 1990

3   Voici une petite annonce que vous avez vue dans un journal français:
Ecrivez une demande d'emploi en expliquant pourquoi vous êtes la personne qu'il leur faut et en demandant des renseignements supplémentaires. (150 mots)

WJEC, June 1990

Nous cherchons:
SERVEUSES/SERVEURS

pour juillet août

Ecrire ou se présenter

au

Café-Restaurant du Palais

06000 Nice

Clientèle internationale

Note: The convention for setting out this letter would be with the French address at the top **right**-hand side with the name of **your** town and the date, but your full address on the **left**-hand side as follows:

J. Lindsay	Café-Restaurant du Palais
3, Castle Street,	06000
Kilmarnock	Nice
Strathclyde	France
Scotland	

Kilmarnock, 16 juin 1991

Monsieur,

4 Des ami(e)s français(es) vous ont dit qu'ils espèrent vous voir au cours d'un voyage que vous vous proposez de faire pendant les vacances. Ecrivez une lettre pour leur expliquer que vous ne passerez pas par la région qu'ils habitent. (150 mots)

WJEC, June 1989

2 Dialogue

You may be asked to write the dialogue for a job interview, an interview to find something out, or a conversation on a particular topic. Read the instructions carefully. You are often asked to include several points in the dialogue. Decide who will take the initiative in the dialogue and work out part of what they may ask or say first. Answers to questions will then come much more naturally. For example, in an interview for a job, the interviewer will be much more dominant at the beginning. Don't fall into the trap of starting with a list of your hobbies and interests. You don't have to tell the truth so you can invent things about yourself, provided they are relevant. The style will be conversational and should therefore follow more naturally from what you did at GCSE. Some of the dialogue will be in the present tense but the perfect and future tenses are likely to be needed. You can give the piece a brief title or make the subject clear from the opening question. Try to achieve a balance between questions and answers (i.e. not too much of one or the other). Make sure you make a neat concluding remark to an interview or a conversation.

Model answer

1 Vous vous présentez à une entrevue pour obtenir un poste. Ecrivez le dialogue qui a lieu entre vous et le chef d'entreprise (écrivez 300 mots environ)

JMB A-Level, June 1989

Possible answer

(In this case you have to invent the job!)

M. Duteuil Bonjour mademoiselle, très heureux de faire votre connaissance. Je m'excuse de vous avoir fait attendre. Alors, vous vous présentez comme candidate pour le poste de responsable d'animation dans notre village vacances.

Mlle Smith Enchantée monsieur. Oui, c'est exact, j'ai vu l'annonce dans le journal et cela m'a beaucoup intéressée.

M. D Je vois que vous parlez couramment le français. Avez-vous déjà quelque expérience dans ce genre de travail?

Mlle S Oui, le samedi je travaille dans un club des jeunes et, l'été dernier, j'étais employée comme organisatrice dans un village vacances à Skegness en Angleterre.

M. D Ah, bon. Vous pouvez me décrire un peu ce que vous faites dans le club.

Mlle S Eh bien, en hiver je surveille les jeux et activités comme le tennis de table et le billiard et, en été, j'organise des randonnées et des manifestations sportives.

M. D Et vous faites cela toute seule?

Mlle S Non, non, nous sommes trois ou quatre et on fait cela à tour de rôle; chacun a des responsabilités particulières.

M. D Racontez-moi ce que vous avez fait l'été dernier dans le village vacances.

Mlle S Là-bas, il était plutôt question de surveiller des enfants et d'organiser leurs activités.

M. D Vous n'avez aucune expérience avec les adultes?

Mlle S Oui, c'est vrai. Mais, à Skegness, j'ai eu l'occasion d'observer ce qu'on faisait et le genre d'activité qui plaisait le plus.

M. D Quel aspect du travail d'une animatrice vous semble le plus difficile?

Mlle S Pour les jeunes, il faut avoir quelques activités en réserve et il faut garder quelques surprises. Le plus difficile c'est quand il pleut toute la journée!

M. D Vous n'aurez pas ce problème chez nous! Qu'est-ce que vous avez comme diplômes?

Mlle S J'ai mes certificats de GCSE en huit matières et j'ai suivi des cours de secourisme. J'ai aussi l'intention de faire un stage pour animateurs qui aura lieu bientôt dans mon collège.

M. D Et qu'est-ce que vous faites pendant vos loisirs?

Mlle S J'aime la lecture, je fais un peu de cuisine et je joue au tennis.

M. D Vous avez des frères ou des sœurs?

Mlle S Oui, j'ai deux frères, plus jeunes que moi.

M. D Vous vous en occupez beaucoup?

Mlle S Oui, la plupart du temps, surtout depuis que mes parents sont divorcés.

M. D Je comprends. Eh bien mademoiselle je suis très heureux d'avoir fait votre connaissance. On se mettra bientôt en contact avec vous.

Mlle S Merci monsieur.

Note

(a) This example, about 350 words, is rather longer than is normally required. About 40-50 extra words are likely to be ignored as far as accuracy is concerned but will probably be taken into account for content, style and range of vocabulary. More than 50 and you are likely to be penalized!

(b) If you are a girl, be careful of adjective and verb agreements.

(c) Miss Smith hasn't had the opportunity to ask any questions. The following might have been appropriate:

Pouvez-vous me donner des informations plus précises sur le travail?

Quelles seraient mes responsabilités?

Quelles sont les heures de travail?

Le logement et les repas sont-ils gratuits?

J'aurais du temps libre?

Quelles activités sont disponibles pour les jeunes et pour les enfants?

Quel équipement et quel matériel sont disponibles?

Qui est-ce qui décide du programme du jour ou de la semaine?

3 Narrative, imaginative and descriptive writing

Here are some examples of questions:

1 Si une fée promettait de vous accorder un vœu, qu'est-ce que vous souhaiteriez? Expliquez votre réponse.   *Cambridge A Level, June 1989*

2 Est-ce que vous croyez aux expériences surnaturelles? Décrivez ou imaginez une telle expérience.   *Cambridge A Level, June 1989*

3 Une nuit dans un rêve vous êtes transporté(e) à une autre époque. Racontez ce que vous avez vu et dites quels étaient vos sentiments à votre réveil.   *JMB A Level, June 1989*

4 Le bonheur des week-ends.   *London A Level, June 1990*

5 Quelle a été pour vous la journée la plus longue?   *London A-Level, June 1990*

6 'Quand l'ascenseur s'est arrêté, je suis sorti(e). Je n'oublierai jamais ce qui s'est passé ensuite. Racontez la suite de cette histoire.   *JMB A-Level, June 1990*

These kinds of titles allow full range of your imagination within the bounds of the subject. You are free to enlarge on (or embellish) something that happened to you, or to invent it entirely. Keep to the format of a beginning, a middle and an end. Take care with tenses.

Question 1 for example, will require some use of the conditional tense.

Question 2 requires an opening sentence or two in the present tense, about your personal beliefs, but will then be in the past; with the perfect tense for events and the imperfect for how things were or seemed.

Question 3 is in two parts and requires perfect and imperfect with perhaps the pluperfect in the last part (e.g. *Quand j'ai réfléchi à ce qui m'**était arrivé***).

If doing **question 5**, it is tempting to start *'la journée la plus longue de ma vie c'était quand...'* but this almost tells the story before you have started. Better to have a beginning like: *Une heure du matin. Rien ne bougeait dans la maison. J'attendais. Est-ce qu'il allait téléphoner?* – thus adding a certain amount of suspense.

Model answer: Question 2

Possible answer

Si vous m'aviez demandé il y a une semaine si je croyais aux expériences surnaturelles je vous aurais répondu non. Mais depuis samedi dernier j'ai révisé mon opinion.

Vers onze heures du soir, je suis sorti comme d'habitude pour promener le chien. Il faisait très froid. La rue où j'habite est sans réverbères et normalement à cette heure il fait très noir. Mais ce soir-là il y avait un clair de lune spectaculaire. La lumière était si intense que les arbres jetaient des ombres sur la chaussée. Comme il n'y a presque pas de circulation sur cette route, je laisse normalement le chien en liberté et il marche devant moi.

On avait fait quelques centaines de mètres et on était arrivé près d'une vieille maison inhabitée depuis des années. Soudain, mon chien s'est arrêté tout net et a refusé de bouger. Il poussait des petits cris plaintifs et le poil de son échine était tout raide. Alors, je l'ai ramassé pour poursuivre notre route parce qu'il faisait trop froid pour s'attarder. Je croyais qu'il avait peut-être vu notre voisin le renard. En le tenant dans mes bras j'ai remarqué qu'il grelottait. Nous avons poursuivi notre route, lui, tenu en laisse.

Cette route est sans issue et il nous a fallu revenir sur nos pas. Je me demandais si mon chien aurait la même réaction en repassant devant la maison abandonnée. On était à 100 mètres de là quand j'ai aperçu deux formes sortir de la maison. Quelqu'un ou bien quelque chose promenait un chien! Mais le plus remarquable c'était que, malgré le clair de lune, ils ne jetaient absolument pas d'ombre. Je me suis arrêté et les deux formes ont fait halte aussi. La personne s'est retournée pour me regarder tout en ramassant le chien comme pour continuer son chemin. Tous deux semblaient devenir plus pâles et se dissoudre dans la clarté de la lune.

Voilà pourquoi j'ai changé d'avis sur l'existence du surnaturel! (320)

Note The perfect tense is used for the narrative part of the story and the imperfect for the descriptive. Also, where the sense would clearly be 'had' in English, a pluperfect is used.

Here are further examples of the above kinds of writing:

7   Ecrivez une lettre à un(e) ami(e) lui décrivant les sources de pollution dans votre région et les problèmes qui en résultent. *JMB A Level, June 1990*

8   Décrivez les effets du tourisme dans votre région ou dans une région que vous connaissez. *WJEC A Level, June 1990*

9   Vous êtes témoin d'un accident. Rédigez pour la police un rapport dans lequel vous offrez une description de la scène juste avant l'accident aussi bien que les détails de l'événement et de ses conséquences. *JMB A Level, June 1990*

Questions **7** and **8** require mainly descriptive use of language and probably mainly the present tense. Question **9** will need description but also some narration of events in the past tense.

Model answer: Question 9

Possible answer

A possible version of the latter might be the following:

EXPLOSION DANS UN HYPERMARCHÉ

Je me trouvais dans l'hypermarché Mammouth vendredi soir vers 18 heures. L'établissement était bondé parce que tout le monde faisait ses courses pour le week-end. Il y avait aussi pas mal de visiteurs étrangers à cause du grand match qui allait avoir lieu au stade dimanche.

J'avais presque terminé mes achats mais je me suis rappelé, soudain, qu'il me fallait des cartouches de gaz pour la lampe. Donc, je me suis dirigé vers le rayon de camping qui se trouvait au fond du bâtiment. Soudain, j'ai été bousculé par deux garçons qui se précipitaient en courant vers les caisses. J'ai poursuivi mon chemin mais j'ai entendu des cris et des exclamations venant du fond de l'hypermarché et puis j'ai senti une odeur désagréable.

'Ça doit être ces garçons qui ont laissé tomber des boules puantes', me suis-je dit.

Et à ce moment, il y a eu comme un grand éclair suivi d'une détonation assourdissante. Puis le silence; ensuite des gens criaient et pleuraient. Je me suis précipité dans la direction de l'explosion. Tout le rayon de camping était démoli, il y avait des débris partout et trois personnes étaient couchées par terre. Je me suis dépêché pour porter secours au premier, une fillette. Elle était sans connaissance et elle saignait beaucoup. Puis d'autres personnes se sont occupées des deux autres blessés qui avaient aussi l'air d'être vivants. Il y avait un tohu-bohu incroyable à l'intérieur du magasin. Je crois que la plupart des gens essayaient de fuir l'endroit mais n'arrivaient pas à passer les caisses. Puis j'ai entendu les sirènes des ambulances et peu de temps après, les services du SAMU sont arrivés sur les lieux. Voilà à peu près ce que j'ai vu et entendu. (300 mots environ)

4 Discursive writing

This kind of writing is usually required when you are asked to write an essay or composition which presents two sides of an argument. The ability to do this has many applications as a life-skill as well as being useful when answering questions on literary or topic-work texts. Marks are given for:

(a) content and organization of ideas
(b) quality of French in terms of structures, vocabulary and authenticity
(c) accuracy (spelling and grammar)

Most marks are given for (a) and (b). Therefore, it is important to have a clear plan for your essay (to make sure that the material is arranged logically) and to use vocabulary and expressions that have a genuine French ring to them rather than sounding like English translated into French and to be generally more adventurous with vocabulary and structures. You are asked to write from between 200 to 400 words, depending on the Examining Board. Presenting a series of convincing 'for and against' arguments, in so few words, is more difficult than if you had more space in practice. It is important therefore to plan your essay carefully and assemble your ideas before starting to write.

Planning the structure of your essay

Structure

The simplest and most effective structure consists of:

(a) an introduction
(b) arguments for and arguments against (the main body of the essay)
(c) conclusion.

First plan out the 'for and against' arguments. The introduction and the conclusion will both be easier to write when you have done this. Start by writing the main idea or cause for debate (not necessarily the title) at the top of the page. Leave a gap and draw a line down the middle of the page. Label each side *'pour* and *contre'* or *'avantages* and *inconvénients/désavantages'*. Leave another gap for your conclusion.

Some people prefer the spider's web or bubble form of patterning for ideas. Others like to write down phrases or words that come to mind as they work through the arguments. If you choose this method leave yourself plenty of space so that you can circle phrases and link them with a pencil line. When you have finished your outline it is a good plan to number your ideas in the order you want to present them. Remember that your best ideas and strongest points are most effective when they are put last in a paragraph or list. You should therefore keep your own point of view for the second half of the essay and end with your main point. This will lead you more naturally into your conclusion.

Here is a topic for debate on an environmental issue, showing how facts and ideas might be assembled.

Model answer

La dégradation de notre planète est un processus continuel: on peut le ralentir mais on ne peut l'arrêter.

Two columns

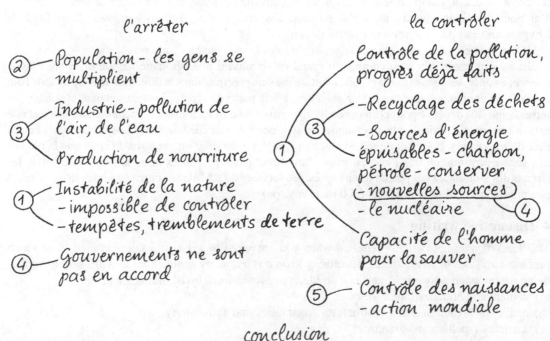

Dégradation de la terre

introduction

l'arrêter

② — Population - les gens se multiplient

③ ⟨ Industrie - pollution de l'air, de l'eau
    Production de nourriture

① ⟨ Instabilité de la nature
    - impossible de contrôler
    - tempêtes, tremblements de terre

④ — Gouvernements ne sont pas en accord

la contrôler

Contrôle de la pollution, progrès déjà faits

③ ⟨ - Recyclage des déchets
    - Sources d'énergie épuisables - charbon, pétrole - conserver
    (- nouvelles sources)
    - le nucléaire ④

① Capacité de l'homme pour la sauver

⑤ — Contrôle des naissances - action mondiale

conclusion

Spider's web or balloon-linking

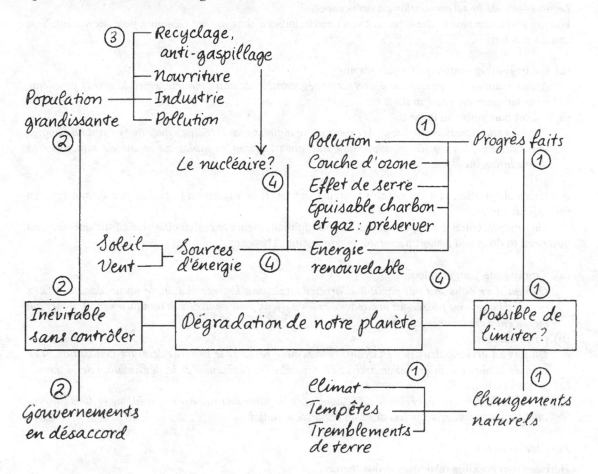

You will see that both ways of assembling ideas rely on writing down words or phrases **in French** so that you get an overview of your thinking and put some order into the ideas for and those against.

Avoid making notes in English and trying to translate them into French. This nearly always leads to anglicized French. If you have read a number of articles, and discussed the topics of essays in class, you should find that phrases stick in your mind. It helps if you make a habit of writing down useful words and phrases on various themes and if you read through these at regular intervals, including the period before the exam.

Having made your plan, and decided which side of the argument you support, you need to write an introduction. The purpose of the introduction is to present the theme which you are going to debate. It can often take the form of a restatement of the title and be expressed as a question to be answered. So taking the title of this essay you could begin:

Est-ce que nous sommes condamnés à accepter la dégradation de notre planète comme inévitable ou pouvons-nous jouer un rôle préventif en limitant autant que possible les effets de la pollution?

You could also make use of a general statement linked to the topicality of the theme:

Les médias ne cessent de nous signaler presque tous les jours de nouveaux exemples de la destruction de notre environnement

and follow this by a question:

Cette dégradation, est-elle inévitable ou pouvons-nous la limiter ou même la contrôler?

Having written the introduction, begin with the side you do not support. Present your ideas in their most effective order, keeping to one idea per paragraph. It makes a better impression if you avoid plunging in with subjective statements like: *je crois; je pense; je suis convaincu;* or *à mon avis.* Keep your personal convictions for the conclusion. You can present facts or opinions more objectively by:

(a) using an impersonal verb form
   Il est impossible d'ignorer les problèmes posés par la surpopulation

(b) using the 1st person plural of the verb
   Considérons un problème difficile à ignorer: la surpopulation

(c) using the *on* form
   On ne peut pas ignorer les problèmes posés par la surpopulation

It is better not to overwork these forms though. It is more succinct and just as impersonal to write:
Le problème de la surpopulation est préoccupant.
Having given one side of the argument you need to indicate that you are changing your viewpoint. You can do this by:

(a) the beginning sentence of a paragraph
   Ayant examiné l'impossibilité d'arrêter la dégradation de notre planète, considérons le problème sous un autre aspect/ l'antithèse.
(b) a short paragraph on its own
   Face à cette situation que faire? Accepter notre impuissance à réaliser quoi que ce soit ou adopter une attitude plus sensée en supposant que nous sommes capables au moins de minimiser la dégradation du globe.

A rhetorical question is a very useful bridging device. It is a question to which you do not give an immediate answer.

   Having presented the opposing, and in your opinion, the more convincing side of the question, all you need to do is add a short paragraph in conclusion. This can:

(a) simply state your standpoint
   Quoiqu'il ne nous soit pas possible d'arrêter totalement la dégradation de notre planète, je suis persuadé que nous possédons la capacité et les moyens pour contrôler et minimiser les dangers qui menacent l'environnement
(b) point a lesson
   Un pas en arrière, deux pas en avant: cela semble résumer le progrès de notre civilisation et ce sera de la même manière qu'on arrivera à résoudre les problèmes de la dégradation de la terre
(c) express a hope
   Je préfère vivre dans la certitude que l'homme est capable de résoudre ce problème et dans l'espoir que des mesures seront prises dans un contexte mondial

Possible answers

Here are two possible responses to this theme:

1   La dégradation de notre planète est devenue un sujet de débat impossible à ignorer à notre époque. Les médias ne cessent de nous signaler de nouveaux exemples de destruction de notre environnement et de nous avertir des terribles dangers qui pèsent sur nous comme des épées de Damoclès. Faut-il accepter comme inévitable la dégradation de notre globe ou pouvons-nous jouer un rôle préventif?

   L'histoire de notre planète nous fait constater que depuis sa naissance elle se trouve dans un état d'évolution perpétuelle. L'éruption des volcans, les tremblements de terre et les extrêmes climatiques nous montrent que la terre, et son atmosphère, ne restent jamais calmes. Bien avant l'arrivée de l'homme, des périodes glaciaires et des périodes de réchauffement se sont succédées à plusieurs reprises et ont apporté de profonds changements à la surface de la terre.

   On ne peut pas nier le fait pourtant que c'est l'homme qui a changé et marqué le plus profondément la terre où il a fait son apparition il y a un million d'années. Notons, entre parenthèses, que la présence de l'homme est relativement récente par rapport à l'âge de la planète qui a environ cinq milliards d'années.

   Depuis son arrivée il n'a cessé de se multiplier. En 1900 il y avait déjà un milliard d'êtres humains. Aujourd'hui, on en compte cinq milliards. Ce chiffre va doubler avant 2025. Pour subvenir à ses besoins, il a rasé des forêts et fait disparaître de nombreuses espèces animales et végétales: selon certains chercheurs, 75% auraient disparu. A cause des activités industrielles, il a pollué les rivières, la mer et la terre. Un bon nombre de scientifiques pensent que la dégradation de l'atmosphère a conduit le monde au bord d'une catastrophe climatique.

   Le rythme de tous ces changements est d'autant plus alarmant que les gouvernements du monde ne sont pas tombés d'accord sur un plan capable de sauver notre planète.

   Face à cette situation, que faire? Faut-il contempler ce scénario en spectateur impuissant ou adopter une attitude plus sensée; si l'on ne s'avère pas capable d'arrêter cette destruction il reste néanmoins la possibilité de la minimiser.

   La même capacité, qui a permis à l'homme de créer et de perfectionner ses moyens de production, peut être mise en place pour résoudre les problèmes de la pollution. Des progrès dans ce domaine ont déjà porté leurs fruits.

   Le recyclage des déchets s'est montré rentable et efficace; les organismes qui s'y consacrent ne manquent pas. Une attitude anti-gaspillage se manifeste dans la population mais pour tirer le maximum de résultats de tout ceci il faudrait inclure les idées anti-gaspillage plus fermement dans les programmes scolaires, surtout au niveau de l'école primaire.

Les sources d'énergie épuisables (comme le charbon, le gaz et le pétrole) doivent être contrôlées et utilisées avec prudence. En même temps, il ne fait aucun doute que les scientifiques perfectionneront les sources d'énergie non-polluantes et renouvelables en utilisant l'action du soleil, du vent ou des marées.

Dans le domaine de l'énergie nucléaire des progrès restent à faire. C'est sans doute par un hasard ironique que l'homme a d'abord fait la découverte de la fission nucléaire au lieu de trouver les secrets de la fusion. Une fois découvert, ce deuxième procédé nous fournira une énergie propre, sans les inconvénients de la radioactivité.

Le problème d'une population mondiale toujours croissante se montre très préoccupant. Des moyens existent pourtant pour limiter le nombre des naissances, que ce soit par des méthodes obligatoires ou volontaires. Mais ce sera surtout par des voies économiques que l'on trouvera une solution car les statistiques prouvent que c'est dans les pays développés que le nombre de naissances se stabilise. Donc pour établir un équilibre de la population mondiale il faudrait améliorer le niveau de vie des pays sous-développés.

Apporter tous ces remèdes s'avèrera inutile si l'homme n'accepte pas de le faire dans un contexte mondial où chaque nation assumera sa responsabilité. Bien qu'il nous semble souvent que l'humanité fasse un pas en arrière et puis deux en avant, force est de constater que finalement nous avançons. Si nous sommes encore incapables d'arrêter totalement la destruction de notre globe, la capacité et les moyens existent pour en contrôler et en minimiser les effets.

2   La dégradation de notre planète se montre le problème le plus préoccupant de notre époque. Est-ce que l'homme possède la capacité d'arrêter ce phénomène ou faut-il se contenter seulement d'en minimiser les plus mauvais effets?

La nature est instable par elle-même. Depuis sa naissance, le monde a vécu des changements fondamentaux. C'est pourtant l'arrivée de l'homme sur la terre, et son intervention, qui l'a marqué de la manière la plus profonde.

La population mondiale ne cesse de s'accroître et elle va doubler d'ici 35 ans. Par un étrange paradoxe, c'est la réussite de l'homme à se nourrir, à se protéger et à prolonger sa vie qui a amené une surpopulation impossible à contrôler.

La pollution qui résulte de presque chaque activité humaine ne cesse également d'augmenter au point que l'environnement devient inhabitable et le climat subit des changements importants. Les gouvernements ne réagissent que trop lentement devant cette situation.

Que devons-nous faire? Pratiquer la politique de l'autruche ou examiner l'horizon des possibilités.

L'intelligence humaine et la créativité peuvent être mises à contribution pour se tirer d'affaire. Non seulement faut-il économiser les sources d'énergie non-renouvelables mais aussi faudrait-il poursuivre la recherche de sources d'énergie non-polluantes.

Il est nécessaire de s'adapter à un nouveau mode de vie sur notre globe où on vivra en harmonie avec la terre. Le recyclage et l'anti-gaspillage feront partie de cette nouvelle attitude.

Des progrès dans le domaine de la prévention de la pollution ont déjà été constatés et l'on prend conscience à l'échelle mondiale de la fragilité de l'espèce humaine.

Si l'homme reste incapable d'arrêter le processus naturel de vieillissement de la terre, il possède néanmoins la capacité à contrôler et à limiter les plus mauvais effets de sa présence.

Essay phrases and vocabulary

It would be an enormous task to give a definitive list of vocabulary and phrases that could be used in any argumentative essay. The following list is based on what students have found useful in giving structure to a piece of writing. It provides only a series of signposts or markers which you will have to fill out with your own ideas and facts. You will find that these marker or structure words sometimes bring you to a halt when trying to put your ideas into order. This is because 'thinking in French' (for the purposes of writing) is often a mixture of thinking in two languages, unless you are totally immersed in them both simultaneously. So, having remembered an authentic phrase like *tous les jours la situation devient de plus en plus préoccupante*, you come to a dead stop with 'according to certain scientists' because you can't think of 'according to' (*selon certains scientifiques* or *de l'avis de certains scientifiques*) or the word for scientists does not come immediately to mind.

The following words and phrases are given with an English equivalent and sometimes given a context:

(a) *Introductory paragraph*

(i)   *Nous vivons dans un monde où la violence est devenue une norme –*
     We live in a world where violence has become a norm

    (ii)   *Chaque année le nombre d'actes terroristes augmente* –
             Every year the number of acts of terrorism is increasing

    (iii)   *Il n'est guère possible d'ouvrir le journal sans y découvrir un nouvel exemple de l'inhumanité de l'homme* – You can scarcely open a newspaper without finding a fresh example of man's inhumanity

    (iv)   *La violence lors des matchs de football est désormais un problème courant* –
             Violence at football matches is a very common problem nowadays

(b) How to refer to the title as a whole if necessary

    (i)   *Cette affirmation/Cette déclaration/Cette proposition mérite d'être examinée de plus près* –
             This statement deserves to be looked at more closely

(c) Paragraph openings

    (i)   *Examinons d'abord/en premier lieu/l'aspect négatif de la question* –
             Let's look first of all at the negative side

    (ii)   *Abordons ce problème par une étude de la situation actuelle* –
             Let's tackle this problem by looking at the present situation

    (iii)   *Prenons le cas du chômage de longue durée* – Take the case of long-term unemployment

    (iv)   *Citons l'exemple de ceux qui ont été condamnés à tort pour un crime* –
             Take the example of those wrongly accused of a crime

    (v)   *On peut invoquer plusieurs raisons pour que ce problème demeure* –
             We can think of several reasons why this problem will continue

(d) Structure words within the paragraph

    (i)   *Plusieurs facteurs ont contribué à la densité de la circulation en ville: **d'abord** les transports urbains ne sont pas suffisants; **ensuite** la voiture est plus confortable que l'autobus, et **enfin** le prix des carburants reste relativement modéré* – Several factors have contributed to the density of traffic in towns: **in the first place** urban transport is not adequate; **next** cars are more comfortable than buses and **lastly** the price of fuel is relatively low

    (ii)   *d'une part... d'autre part...* – on the one hand... on the other hand...
             D'une part nous ne comprenons pas encore tous les mécanismes de notre climat mais d'autre part certaines tendances comme les sécheresses prolongées sont bien évidentes

    (iii)   *cependant; pourtant; néanmoins; tout de même* – (all have the approximate meaning of) however; yet; nevertheless; all the same
             bref; en un mot – in a word; in short

    (iv)   *Bref, quelle autre solution peut-on envisager?* –
             In a word what other solution can be imagined?

    (v)   *quant à - en ce qui concerne_____* – as far as _____ is concerned

    (vi)   *dans ce domaine* – in this field, area (of thought, activity)
             Je n'ose guère m' aventurer dans le domaine de la physique nucléaire –
             I scarcely dare venture into the field of nuclear physics

    (vii) *à cet égard* – in this respect

    (viii) *par conséquent/en conséquence* (**Not** *par conséquence*) – in consequence

    (ix)   *étant donné que...* – given that...

    (x)   *d'une façon ou d'une autre* – one way or another

    (xi)   *après tout* – after all

    (xii) *en réalité; en effet* – in fact; in reality

    (xiii) *Malgré toutes les prédictions des écologistes* – Despite all the ecologists' forecasts

    (xiv) *Grâce aux actions des Amis de la Terre* – Thanks to the action of Friends of the Earth

(e) Impersonal statement introduced by 'il'

    (i)   *Il est évident/possible/probable/certain/clair que cette politique a échoué* –
             It is possible/probable/certain/clear that this policy has failed

Note The construction here is *il est* + adjective + *que* + noun (*see also* subjunctive, page 47)
There are other examples where the construction is *il est* + adjective + *de* + infinitive:

    (ii)   *Il est dangereux de fermer les yeux devant cette situation*

    (iii)   *Il est impossible d'ignorer ces problèmes*

    (iv)   *Il est facile de ne rien faire*

    (v)   *Il est important de considérer toutes les possibilités*

Here are some other vital phrases:

    (vi)   *Il faut* – It is necessary
    (vii)   *Il nous faut* – We must
   (viii) *Il faudrait* – We should
    (ix)   *Il nous faudrait* – We ought to
    (x)   *Il reste peu de temps* – There's not much time left
    (xi)   *Il manque des ressources* – Resources are lacking/There is a lack of....
         or *Il y a un manque de ressources*
   (xii)   *Il s'agit/Il est question de valeurs personnelles* – It's a question of personal values
  (xiii) *Il suffit d'un sourire pour faire confiance aux gens* –
         All that's needed is a smile to inspire confidence

(f) Increases/decreases

    (i)   *Le nombre d'accidents de la route augmente/s'accroît* –
        The number of road accidents is rising
    (ii)   *Le taux des naissances diminue* – The birth rate is falling/dropping
   (iii) *Une augmentation des salaires* – An increase in wages
   (iv) *Une baisse sur les marchés internationaux* – A fall on foreign markets
    (v)   *Une hausse des niveaux de la mer* – A rise in sea levels
   (vi)   *Le coût de la vie est en hausse* – The cost of living is up

(g) Numbers of people or things

    (i)   *La plupart des gens/bien des gens* – Many people
    (ii)   *Beaucoup de gens ont refusé de payer leur impôt* –
        Many people have refused to pay their tax
   (iii) *Certains prétendent que l'impôt est injuste, d'autres affirment le contraire*
        Some claim the tax is unfair, others say the opposite
   (iv) *Comme nous l'avons déjà dit/signalé/fait remarquer/indiqué/affirmé/constaté/souligné* –
        As already stated/indicated/pointed out/shown/noted/stressed

(h) Perhaps/may be

    (i)   *Nos scientifiques ont peut-être tort*
    (ii)   *Peut-être nos scientifiques ont-ils tort*
   (iii) *Peut-être qu'ils ont tort, nos scientifiques*

Inversion is needed if you begin with *peut-être*. Similarly with *sans doute*:

   (iv) *Sans doute ces opinions sont-elles mal fondées* –
        Doubtless these opinions are not well-founded

Note (v)   *Il se peut que* – It may be that
   (vi)   *Il se peut que nous ayons tous tort* – It may be that we are all wrong

(i) Times and periods

    (i)   *de nos jours/ à l'époque actuelle/ à l'époque où nous vivons* –
        at the present time, nowadays etc.
    (ii)   *à l'avenir* – in the future
   (iii) *les générations futures* – future generations
   (iv) *autrefois* – formerly
    (v)   *jadis* – in times past
   (vi)   *du temps de mon grand-père* – in my grandfather's day
   (vii) *à l'âge de pierre* – in the stone age
  (viii) *à l'époque médiévale/victorienne* – in medieval/victorian times
   (ix) *au début de ce siècle* – at the beginning of the century
    (x)   *dans les années 90* – in the nineties
   (xi)   *pendant longtemps* – for a long time
   (xii) *en moins d'un siècle* – in less than a century

(j) Giving examples/quoting opinion

    (i)   *citons en exemple/à titre d'exemple* – (as titles above – **note** spelling of *exemple*)
    (ii)   *prenons l'exemple de/le cas de* – let's take the example/case of
   (iii) *selon certains chercheurs* – according to some researchers
   (iv) *à en croire les experts* – if the experts are to be believed
    (v)   *l'un des exemples les plus frappants* – one of the most striking examples

(k) Comparisons

(i)   *certains disent que... d'autres prétendent que...* – some say that... others claim that...

(ii) *Comparées à nos autoroutes, celles de France sont mieux entretenues et aménagées* –
      Compared to our motorways, the French ones are better maintained and have more facilities

(iii) *faisons une comparaison entre/avec* – let's make a comparison between/with

(iv) *si l'on compare notre époque à celle d'avant-guerre* –
      if you compare our times with those before the war

(v)   *en contraste/par rapport à la situation actuelle* – compared with the situation today

(vi) *Le professeur français est mieux payé que son homologue britannique* –
      The French school teacher is better paid than his British counterpart

(l) Conclusions

(i)   *tout bien considéré* – taking everything into consideration

(ii) *en fin de compte* – when all said and done

(iii) *il faut conclure que* – we must conclude that

(iv) *en conclusion affirmons que* – in conclusion let us say that

(v)   *Au lieu de sombrer dans le désespoir je préfère adopter une attitude optimiste* –
      Instead of wallowing in despair I prefer to take an optimistic attitude

Further reading

R Hares and G Elliot, (1984), *Compo! French Literature Essay Writing*, Hodder & Stoughton

2 Reading

Contents

1 Questions and answers in English

One of the ways of testing understanding of a text is to ask questions about it in English. This is the method used by most Examining Boards. Questions are normally in the same sequence as the points in the text. The place in the text is indicated by some of the Boards as is the number of marks to be scored (by each question). The latter can be a useful guide to the relative difficulty of the question but, more importantly, a rough indication of the number of points or details that you are expected to include in your answer. Questions are normally phrased in such a way that they cannot be answered by straight translation of a piece of the text. It is of little use translating a likely bit of the text in the hope that this will be acceptable!

Many questions will be what are called **inference** questions. This means that you will have to search for the information required in different parts of the text. Often, details will be implied rather than stated so that you will have to do some deduction (and checking that your deduction is correct).

Another possibility is the **interpretive** question. In this case you are expected to be able to interpret the question using your general knowledge or common sense.

Some questions could be **evaluative**. This means you are expected to be able to make your own assessment (or judgement) about the intentions (or attitude) of the author that are revealed in the way he has written. (*See below* for examples of these.)

You should read the text through at least three times before looking at the questions. Try to get an overall impression of what it is about; only then turn your attention to the questions. Read these carefully and pay attention to every word. Try to 'stand back' from the text when working out your answer. Review the information given in the sentence before (as well as the one following) the place you are looking at, rather than keep on reading over the same phrase or group of words. Also, when working out your answer, have a glance at the next question. You may find that you are jumping ahead with details needed for that question rather than the one you are doing.

'What', 'how' and 'why' questions usually predominate, followed in frequency by the instructions 'describe', 'explain' and 'list'. If you are not required to write in full sentences don't waste time by repeating part of the question in the answer. Marks are given for particular elements from the text required for that question. You have to show that you have understood the text and include all **relevant** details. Extra material is not usually penalized but you risk taxing the patience of the marker if they have to plough through many words to find the relevant bit. To summarize: be brief wherever possible.

Model answers

1   Read the following passage carefully. Do not translate. Then answer the questions in English, basing your answers only on the material given in the text. Answers should be concise but include all relevant information.

Je suis dans le commissariat d'un quartier chic de Paris à la recherche de renseignements sur une nouvelle variété de petites mouches qui sèment la panique dans le métro. Les Parisiens les connaissent bien. Elles sévissent depuis quelques années, fondent sur leurs proies en formations serrées, bruissent, virevoltent et s'égaillent après avoir piqué. Piqué les portefeuilles, bien sûr, car
5   il s'agit en fait de gamines dont le passetemps est le vol à la tire.

Leurs lieux de prédilection sont les stations de métro où les touristes égarés cherchent nez au vent la sortie. 'Elles adorent les Japonais, m'indique un gardien de la paix. Ils sont doux et transportent tour leur argent en liquide.' Leur scénario est parfaitement au point. Armées parfois d'un morceau de carton ou d'un journal, par petits groupes de cinq ou six, elles effectuent une sorte
10   de ballet tout autour de la victime choisie en un clin d'œil, lui exhibent le carton sous le nez pour faire diversion et utilisent le journal pour protéger une petite main agile. Le temps pour la victime de réaliser qu'elle n'assiste pas à une innocente danse enfantine, les gamines ont disparu dans toutes les directions, et bien malin qui aura pu suivre la trace du portefeuille dérobé. Il est passé de main en main aussi vite que les cartes des joueurs de bonneteau.
15   Le phénomène a pris depuis quelques mois des allures d'institution, à tel point que lorsque des petites gitanes mettent leurs pieds nus à l'intérieur d'une rame de métro, le conducteur n'hésite pas à prévenir les passagers. Sa voix, qui semble tomber du ciel, les informe de l'entrée dans leur moyen de transport habituel de voleurs à la tire et leur conseille de surveiller leurs sacs. Les travailleurs endormis dressent l'oreille et les femmes serrent leur sac contre leur poitrine. Il ne s'agit pourtant
20   que d'une bande d'enfants âgés de sept à treize ou quatorze ans environ: nous sommes loin des gangsters de cinéma qui terrorisent le métro new-yorkais. Les bruits étranges qui courent sur ces enfants nous ont poussés à tenter de cerner la vérité. On parle de trafic d'enfants achetés ou loués en Yougoslavie et amenés en France par convoi. Ils seraient dressés à voler dans des écoles spéciales. Les hommes, dit-on, les déposent le matin avec leurs somptueuses voitures aux stations
25   de métro, pour venir récupérer l'argent le soir. Bref, une vie d'enfants esclaves.

Dans un commissariat d'un arrondissement de Paris où ils sévissent régulièrement, j'attends la réponse à toutes ces questions. 'D'abord, il ne faut pas dire que la police ne fait rien, affirme l'officier D., vexé. Mes hommes les arrêtent, mais que voulez-vous qu'on en fasse? Demandez au gardien les problèmes qu'il rencontre.' Le gardien en question raconte son calvaire: 'D'abord ces
30   gosses font semblant de ne pas parler un seul mot de français. Tout ce qu'ils savent dire c'est 'Moi pas voler'. Lorsqu'on leur demande leur adresse ils annoncent: 'Caravane nationale 5'. C'est pratique! Ils sont totalement dépourvus de papiers et donnent tous le même nom de famille. Dans la plupart des cas il s'agit de fillettes que je n'ai pas le droit de fouiller. Seules les femmes policiers ont le droit de fouiller les femmes et ici il n'y a que des hommes. Je ne regrette pas d'ailleurs, elles sont pleines de poux.'

(a) What is the writer of this article investigating and why do you think she is doing her research in a 'quartier chic' (lines *1–5*) [4].
Answer *The growing numbers of gangs of young pickpockets operating in the metro. Fashionable districts are the most profitable.*
(The first part is an inference question: the word pickpocket is not used in the text and you have to 'infer' what these children are up to. The second part is an interpretive question – you have to judge yourself about the *quartier chic.)*

(b) The author begins by comparing these gangs to flies (line 2) why does this comparison seem very apt? [4]
Answer *Because like flies they come in swarms, are agile and fast-moving. Theft of valuables is their 'sting'.*
(This is more of an evaluative question since you are invited to assess the appropriateness of the author's comparison)

(c) Why do gangs prefer to operate in the metro? (lines *6–7*) [3]
Answer *Because tourists unfamiliar with the underground have their attention distracted while they are looking for the way out.*

(This is a mixture of inference and interpretation. The phrase *nez au vent* should create a visual image of a tourist looking up at signs and not paying attention to anything else.)

It is not really important to decide in each case which kind of question you are dealing with. It is important though to be aware that a wide range of reading and thinking skills are usually called for in reading comprehension at A Level.

(d) Who are their most popular victims and why? (lines *7–8*) [3]

Answer *Japanese tourists because they are mild-mannered and carry all their money in cash.*

(e) Describe how they mount their attacks. (lines *8–11*) [5]

Answer *They work in groups of 5 or 6 children who dance around their chosen victim and thrust a piece of card or a newspaper in his face so that nimble fingers can work unseen.*

(f) What might the unsuspecting victim think he is watching, and why can't he see where his wallet has gone? (lines *11–14*) [3]

Answer *He might think he is watching some kind of childish dance. They all run off in different directions so it is hard to trace who has taken his wallet.*

(g) Explain what the author means by saying that the process which has been described '*a pris des allures d'institution* ' (line *15*) [3]

Answer *Theft of this kind has become a standard feature of life in Paris.*

(h) What action do metro drivers now take and why does the voice of the driver seem to descend from heaven? (lines *15–18*) [4]

Answer *When he sees barefoot children getting into the train he warns passengers. His voice sounds like the voice of God coming through the p.a. system, above the heads of the passengers.*

(i) What differences are there between the Paris gangs and those of New York? (lines *19–21*) [2]

Answer *In Paris they are young children 7–14 years old, not grown-up gangsters as in New York.*

(j) What was the motive of the author in pursuing this matter? (lines *21–22*) [2]

Answer *Strange rumours circulating about these gangs of children — where they come from, how they are trained.*

(k) Why, according to the stories told, might these children be called slave children? (lines *22–25*) [5]

Answer *They have been hired or bought in Yugoslavia, trained to steal and brought to the metro and collected at night by men in cars who pocket what they have stolen.*

(l) Why do you think '*officier D*' is described as '*vexé*'? (line *28*) [2]

Answer *because of the accusation that the police are not doing anything about these gangs.*

(m) What are the problems of the police in interrogating the children (lines 29-32)

Answer *They pretend to speak only a few words of French; they give their address as a caravan number; have no papers; all give the same family name.*

(n) What particular problem is there at this police station in dealing with the girls, and what is the officer's personal reaction to this? (lines *32–34*) [5]

Answer *The male police have no authority to search them and at this police station there are only policemen; he is grateful because they are covered in lice.*

Cambridge A Level, June 1989

2 Read the following passage carefully, and then answer **in English** the questions printed below the passage. As much **relevant** detail as possible should be given in your answers, but this need not be in the form of complete sentences.

Danger: attention aux rayons invisibles!

Il est de plus en plus nécessaire et urgent d'examiner sérieusement les dangers que peuvent représenter pour la santé les radiations qui sont devenues à la fois un bienfait et un fléau de la société moderne. Elles sont un bienfait parce que l'emploi d'appareils émettant des ondes electromagnétiques favorise le progrès scientifique, accroît la productivité dans l'industrie, facilite les communications et, dans les traitements médicaux, aide à sauver des vies humaines. Mais elles sont un fléau parce que ces mêmes appareils, de plus en plus nombreux, ont envahi les lieux de travail et que les radiations qu'ils émettent peuvent avoir un effet nuisible, en particulier sur la peau, les yeux, et dans certains cas, sur le système nerveux central des travailleurs. Ces risques sont particulièrement importants si le personnel utilisant ce genre d'appareils est composé en majorité de femmes en âge de procréer; il y a des effets sur le foetus de l'exposition à la pollution par radiation qui restent à être précisés.

La technologie des micro-ondes et des fréquences radio-électriques est appliquée principalement dans les communications et la radiodiffusion. Les grands postes émetteurs de radio et de télévision peuvent menacer la santé des équipes qui s'occupent de l'entretien du matériel sur les pylônes alors que ces émetteurs sont en marche. Dans les imprimeries et les autres établissements pratiquant les arts graphiques, les lampes à arc sont utilisées pour faire des négatifs et des plaques de photo-offset. Les grands appareils de prise de vue devraient être situés à l'écart des zones de travail et de passage. Il faudrait faire appel à la prudence des travailleurs en leur demandant d'éviter de regarder directement les lampes exposées. Ces dernières années ont vu une croissance phénoménale de l'application des lasers dans de nombreuses industries. Les lasers sont maintenant utilisés dans les domaines aussi divers que les communications par satellite, la chirurgie, le matériel employé dans les coulisses des théâtres et les systèmes de contrôle automatiques dans les supermarchés. Le dommage causé à l'œil par des radiations du laser est souvent irréversible.

Dans les ménages, l'exposition personnelle aux radiations émises par les fours à micro-ondes est normalement faible, car la densité de puissance décroît rapidement avec l'augmentation de la distance par rapport à la source. Mais l'exposition à des ondes émises par des fours à micro-ondes industriels, qui sont plus puissants, devrait être réduite dans la plus grande mesure possible, afin de protéger les travailleurs contre les fuites excessives de radiations qui pourraient causer des dommages oculaires. Comme de nombreux appareils électroniques, dont les récepteurs de télévision, certains terminaux de visualisation génèrent des radiations électromagnétiques qui sont plus fortes au voisinage de l'écran et s'affaiblissent rapidement avec la distance. A une distance de 20 à 30 centimètres, l'émission potentiellement nuisible n'est pas décelable ou, au pire, atteint des niveaux bien inférieurs aux seuils d'exposition fixés de la façon la plus rigoureuse.

Les travailleurs devraient être sensibilisés aux dangers potentiels et la description des précautions à prendre devrait être affichée pour rappeler constamment que le danger existe. Une coopération internationale est nécessaire aussi pour fixer de nouvelles normes et harmoniser celles qui existent déjà.

(a) Say very briefly how the writer tries to avoid presenting a biased argument in the opening paragraph. [3]

Answer *He points out that electronic equipment has numerous benefits (for example, in providing jobs, helping research, improving productivity and even saving lives) but that this has in turn led to a proliferation of such equipment in places where it can have a harmful effect on the work force.*
(This question requires the skill of summary.)

(b) According to the writer, which group of women may be particularly at risk and why? [6]

Answer *Women of child-bearing age. Radiation has effects on unborn children that are not yet fully understood .*
(Dictionaries are not allowed with this Board. You should however be able to guess that *procréer* has something to do with 'procreate',' give birth to'.)

(c) In what circumstances are radio and television transmitters considered dangerous and who would be affected? [4]

Answer *They are dangerous to maintenance engineers working on them while they are transmitting.*
(The verb *émettre* means 'to emit' or 'transmit'; knowing your compound verbs should help here! What does *en marche* mean? *équipe* and *entretien* are the key words for the second part. Which of the following do you think fits best: 'teams of repairers'; 'service men'; or 'maintenance engineers'?)

(d) What advice does the writer give about cameras in printing works? [4]

Answer *They should be situated well away from where people work and move about.*
(You should know the word *appareil* from GCSE. Don't forget to include the *de passage* bit.)

(e) What safety precautions are workers in this industry urged to take? [3]

Answer *Avoid looking directly at the arc lights.*

(f) What information is given about microwave ovens used in the home? [5]

Answer *Risks from radiation are small because the latter decreases rapidly away from the source.*

(*décroît* is a key word here. *de-* as a prefix often gives a verb an opposite meaning. *croître* – to grow, therefore *décroître* 'to diminish, lessen'. You should have learned this one in a pair of opposites. (*see* vocabulary, page 3))

(g) As far as safety is concerned, how do microwave ovens used in industry compare with the domestic variety? (6)

Answer *They are much more powerful and therefore more dangerous, particularly to the eyes of workers over-exposed to them.*

(Don't forget the word *oculaire*. Did you guess that it has to do with 'eyes'?)

(h) How safe are the screens of television sets and other display units? [8]

Answer *Radiation is strongest very near the screen. It decreases rapidly away from the screen and at 20 to 30 centimetres away harmful levels are either scarcely detectable or at worst well below the most stringent danger limits.*

(Include all the relevant details you can here since there are 8 marks awarded.)

(i) In the last paragraph the writer recommends measures which should be taken in places of work. What are they? [7]

Answer *Workers should be made constantly... by means of posters, of the ever present dangers of radiation and the precautions that they must take.*

(There are 7 marks here so don't leave anything out. What is a good word for *sensibilisés*?)

(j) In your own words, explain clearly why international cooperation is considered necessary. [4]

Answer *It is necessary in order to establish new norms for danger levels and to coordinate those that are already operational.*

(You need to find ways of explaining *nouvelles normes* and *harmoniser*.)

London A-Level Syllabus A, January 1991

2 Questions and answers in French

A few Examining Boards test reading comprehension, partly or wholly, by asking questions about a text in French. Most of the remarks about answering questions in English also apply here. Read the passage through several times before you start writing. You will not necessarily have to understand every word fully in order to answer the questions. You will not be able to copy down a likely looking bit of the text as an answer. You may however be able to use some of the original words, provided that you make appropriate grammatical changes. Marks are usually given for conveying the details rather than for the accuracy of the French. It helps to remember this when you are trying to find your own words in French. Inference and interpretive questions might also be used.

Model answers

1   Lisez attentivement le texte suivant, puis répondez aux questions. Nous vous recommandons de passer au moins cinq minutes à la lecture du texte. Nous vous conseillons de ne pas recopier mot à mot des section entières du texte.

La Société Protex et les pouvoirs publics mis en cause

RAPPORT ACCABLANT SUR LA POLLUTION DE LA LOIRE EN JUIN DERNIER

Il y a déjà trente ans que la Protex, installée sur la rivière la Brenne, à trente kilomètres de Tours, avait attiré l'attention de ses voisins. Les élus, les associations de pêcheurs et les groupes de défense de l'environnement n'avaient cessé de s'inquiéter des inconvénients et des risques présentés par l'usine chimique.

5   De 1963 à 1987, cinquante-six cas de pollution avaient été dûment constatés, dont seize avaient donné lieu à d'importantes destructions de poissons. Quelques plaintes seulement avaient été suivies de poursuites et une seule s'était soldée, après d'interminables procédures, par une condamnation à 2000F d'amende. Loin de s'en émouvoir, les dirigeants de l'usine – qui faisaient d'excellentes affaires – ne cessaient de demander des autorisations d'extension... et de les obtenir.

10   Les visites des inspecteurs des établissements classés étaient traitées avec désinvolture. Le flux de pollution liquide émis en permanence par l'enterprise était quatre fois plus élevé que les normes

15 autorisées. L'usine ne disposait pas de bassin de sécurité. Les déchets étaient stockés sans
précaution et le personnel d'encadrement était toujours notoirement insuffisant malgré les
promesses de la direction. Tous ces éléments expliquent pourquoi un accident qui aurait dû rester
très limité – une explosion dans un réacteur chimique – a pris des allures catastrophiques.

20 Le rapport d'évaluation dresse le bilan des dégâts: non seulement l'usine a été partiellement
détruite, mais il a fallu hospitaliser trois blessés, dont un dans un état très grave, et une quinzaine
d'intoxiqués parmi les sauveteurs. En outre, deux cents personnes du voisinage one été évacuées
à la hâte. L'écoulement de produits toxiques a stérilisé 53 kilomètres de cours d'eau, tuant de quinze
à vingt tonnes de poissons et empoisonnant les oiseaux d'eau, les petits mammifères et les végétaux.
Plus de 150,000 habitants du département ont été privés d'eau potable durant une semaine, et
l'ensemble de l'économie locale en a souffert, y compris le tourisme. Dans l'usine même, fermée
pour trois mois et qui n'a reçu depuis qu'une autorisation de réouverture provisoire, 120 personnes
se sont trouvées en chômage.

(a) Pourquoi les pêcheurs et les autres groupes se sont-ils inquiétés de la conduite de la compagnie?

[1]

Answer *Ils craignaient les risques de pollution présentés par une compagnie chimique située sur le bord même de la rivière.*

(b) Dans quelle mesure a-t-on réussi à empêcher ou à limiter la pollution causée par cette compagnie? Expliquez votre réponse.   [2]

Answer *Ce n'est qu'après plusieurs cas de pollution que quelques plaintes ont donné lieu à des poursuites judiciaires et une fois seulement, la compagnie a dû payer 2000F d'amende; donc la réussite n'a été que partielle.*

(c) Qu'est-ce qui montre que les autorités ont continué à traiter la compagnie avec beaucoup d'indulgence?   [1]

Answer *On lui accordait sans difficulté des autorisations d'extension.*

(d) En vous référant à la dernière phrase, citez deux façons dont la compagnie elle-même a souffert de cet accident.   [2]

Answer *Elle est restée fermée pendant trois mois et n'a reçu qu'une autorisation d'ouverture provisoire.*

(e) Laquelle des conséquences du désastre est la plus importante à votre avis? Expliquez pourquoi. Ecrivez environ 50 mots.

Answer *La conséquence la plus sérieuse est l'empoisonnement des poissons, des oiseaux d'eau et des végétaux sur une grande longueur de la rivière, 53 kilomètres. Il faudra beaucoup de temps pour réparer tous ces dégâts causés à l'environnement et on comprend mal les conséquences à long terme de cette espèce de pollution chimique. (54 mots)*

JMB A Level, June 1990

Study techniques

1 Try every week to read part of a French magazine or newspaper. Pick out an article which interests you and make up ten questions on it. Write your answers to the questions. Then, if possible, get a friend to answer your questions. Compare your answers and help each other to produce the best possible answers.
2 Use passages from your set texts to do the same kind of exercise. This should give you the opportunity to invent and practise 'evaluation' and 'interpretation' questions.
3 Get from your library copies of past papers from the Board for whose exams you are preparing. Work through these. Try to find another student (or your teacher) to look at and comment on your work.

3 Questions in French on a passage in English

This task, used by some of the Boards, puts you in the situation of having to explain details of an article to a French person who cannot fully understand the article themselves. The task is very like the reporting one in some oral examinations except that specific questions are usually asked and these might include a résumé of part of the passage. The number of marks awarded for each answer is also given. Marks are given for: (a) content and language; or (b) accurate transmission of information, depending on the Board. The second requirement does not exclude completely considerations of language however, since you are still faced with the problem of getting the meaning across in French.

Model answers

1   (a) You read the article below in an English newspaper and sent it to a French friend who is a
        secretary in Paris, and who you knew would find it interesting. However, her English was not
        good enough to follow the whole text and she has sent you the following list of questions. Write
        answers to her questions in French.

LIFE IN THE FRENCH OFFICE

In France, the role played in the office can easily be kept distinct from the person occupying it,
thanks to a battery of props.

    To start with, physical distance is consciously maintained. Individuals are quite literally 'stand-
offish' and there are few spontaneous violations of personal space of the back-slapping or hand-
on-the-shoulder variety.

    On the other hand, there is a particularly ritualized form of contact – namely, the handshake.
It is usual for colleagues to shake hands on meeting and parting and failure to do so will give offence.
Etiquette demands that the superior instigate the gesture. Paradoxically then, while the handshake
reduces physical distance between individuals, it reinforces the organizational distance between
them. The distinct set of rules that govern the salutation leave those concerned in no doubt as to
who is boss, particularly since touch is traditionally related to dominance, whether between the
sexes, generations or classes.

    This physiological manifestation of inequality is compounded linguistically by the *tu/vous*
distinction. The polite *vous* form of address is *de rigueur* in French offices. Individuals of the same
rank who empathize may use the familiar *tu*, but between grades it is rare.

    Like the handshake it is subject to a number of rules – the basic one being that it is up to the
superior to determine the form of address since this defines the relationship. The resilience of this
norm can be gauged by the mortified reaction of a secretary to my suggestion that she employs the
familiar form with her boss. She confessed that even with his blessing, she could not 'bring herself'
to do so. And he was equally adamant that he would not address her as *tu* since it might make
subsequent censure awkward.

    Psychological distance is further guaranteed by the limited use of first names and the outward
respect for titles (the chairman is addressed as *monsieur le président*). It is noteworthy that even in
the more homely environment of a small firm (*une dimension humaine*), the boss still insists his
staff call him *monsieur*.

    The combination of these signals leaves the participants under no misapprehension as to which
of them is the senior. Thus the French are less reliant on personal qualities as a basis for asserting
their authority. They have at their disposal the means of conveying authority without having to
invest their personality – simply by parading the trappings of authority. A familiar relationship is

deemed to leave the individual 'vulnerable' because people are apt to take advantage of it – and use it as a lever for favours. The French believe that friendship obliges, exposes the 'friend' to manipulation and makes him or her dependent. In other words they regard informality in the workplace as something of a Trojan horse – outwardly appealing but inherently dangerous. This may also provide an explanation for the fact that the French rarely indulge in joking in the office. Basically there is a profound apprehension that a relationship will degenerate if one reveals too much of oneself – and since humour exposes one's personality, it tends to be repressed.

   Apparently, in the French context, the desire to avoid conflict and to be protected from manipulation are more important than the immediate gratification derived from social contact. Distance and independence require a certain ritualization, which protects the individual from personal involvement.

(b) Répondez *en français* aux questions suivantes.

   (a) Comment le geste amical de se serrer la main peut-il souligner et même renforcer la distance hiérarchique entre les gens? [4]

   (b) Pourquoi le patron ne voudrait-il pas tutoyer sa secrétaire? [4]

   (c) Pourquoi, selon l'auteur, les Français comptent-ils si peu sur leurs qualités personnelles pour affirmer leur autorité? [4]

   (d) Expliquez comment, selon les Français, une relation trop amicale entre patron et employé peut rendre 'vulnérable'? [4]

   [Total 16 marks]

(c) Résumez les différents comportements adoptés par les Français dans leurs relations au bureau. Est-ce que vous trouvez, comme les Français, qu'un code de comportement plus formel au bureau présente des avantages pour l'individu? Ou, au contraire, est-ce qu'un contact amical et personnel vous semble souhaitable? Expliquez votre point de vue. Ecrivez 100–120 mots *français*.

Cambridge AO and A Level, June 1990

Possible answers

(b) (i) Ce geste renforce la distance hiérarchique parce que c'est toujours la personne supérieure qui offre sa main à l'autre.

   (ii) Il ne voudrait pas le faire parce qu'il deviendrait alors plus difficile pour lui de la critiquer.

   (iii) Ces qualités comptent peu parce que les Français peuvent se servir de leur supériorité de rang ou de cadre pour imposer leur autorité.

   (iv) Une relation trop amicale peut être exploitée par l'autre personne.

(c) La distance physique entre individus est rigoureusement maintenue: on ne touche pas les autres sauf pour leur serrer la main. C'est toujours le cadre supérieur qui offre d'abord sa main à l'autre. On ne tutoie pas son supérieur. La forme *'vous'* est de rigueur dans les bureaux. On ne s'adresse pas aux personnes par leur prénom. On emploie la forme *'monsieur'* ou son titre. On évite les relations amicales de peur que cette amitié soit exploitée. On ne fait pas non plus de plaisanteries au bureau parce que cela pourrait révéler sa personnalité.

   Je pense qu'un comportement formel au bureau présente certains avantages. Tout le monde est conscient de son rang. On est poli et on respecte les autres personnes. On n'est pas obligé d'être amical quand peut-être on ne voudrait pas l'être. Tout ceci contribue au bon fonctionnement du bureau.

Ou

Je pense que le système français présente certaines difficultés. On est obligé d'être tout le temps poli, ce qui est quelquefois un peu difficile. Je crois que je préférerais travailler dans une ambiance plus décontractée. Les gens travaillent mieux dans ces conditions. Il faut pouvoir rire de temps en temps, de soi-même et des autres.

(130 words approximately)

Note

(a) The Cambridge Board's report on this examination contained the following comment on how this part of the paper was done:

Question 1(b) This question sometimes led to rather lengthy answers, where only short answers were envisaged. Since marks are allocated partly for language and partly for content, a lengthy answer is likely to lead to more errors, and thus to lose marks. In general, there were few problems with content, but quite a few difficulties in rendering the content into adequate French.

Question 1(c) Marks here were awarded equally for language and content. Again, candidates are advised to pay careful attention to the **number of words** required and to the formulation of the task. If a résumé is requested as part of the **task**, it should not be omitted. Candidates clearly understood the original text; and the problem lay, therefore, in finding adequate French expressions for their opinions and for the résumé. Opinions of this subject were often strongly held, and the passage seemed successful in eliciting a variety of genuine personal responses. The best answers contained all the necessary factual information as well as personal opinions. The task differentiated well, with work varying from the very impressive to the weak.

(b) Advice on the length of answer seems sound provided no important information is omitted. The main problem lies with adequate French and this is related to skills already mentioned: being used to finding more than one way of saying things; thinking of an alternative word in English that might suggest a suitable French one (e.g. 'instigate the gesture' – offers his/her hand – *offre sa main*; 'subsequent censure' – criticize on another occasion – *critiquer à une autre occasion*.)

Don't forget to use words from the questions if appropriate (e.g. *serrer la main* and *tutoyer*). You will also note that the skill of summary comes into play here.

Study skill

Make a collection of short articles in English about France. Useful sources are books on French background and the more serious newspapers. *The European* newspaper is a good source of material. Practise by reading and underlining the main points and then finding words to convey the information. It is better if you can practise brief summaries for a French person (e.g. a pen-friend).

2 Read the following passage and then answer in French the questions which follow. Ensure that you have given all the required information. Marks will be awarded for the accurate transmission of information.

THE DUCHESS ON THE ILE SAINT LOUIS
by Caroline Ross

This year marks the two hundredth anniversary of the French Revolution and lavish celebrations have been laid on to mark the event. The new Opera house at Bastille will open its doors, specially commissioned plays will be performed at the Comédie Française, there will be fireworks and dancing on the streets of Paris.

It seems like a good enough excuse for a national bash, but not all the natives are friendly to the idea. There are still six thousand *familles nobles* in France (proof, if you like, that revolutions don't work) and two hundred years have failed to dull their enormous sense of injury.

But whatever the feelings of the French aristocracy, they won't be taking their protest to the streets. History has taught them that keeping their heads down is the best way to avoid getting it in the neck, and in public they seem quietly resigned to republicanism. In private, however, it's as if Marie Antoinette (together with thousands of friends and relations) went to the guillotine yesterday. And bicentinary 'celebrations' are, to put it mildly, in the worst possible taste.

'It's appalling to have this hanging over us,' one very elevated Duchess told me when we met for lunch on the Ile Saint Louis. She and the Duc relived the horrors of the Reign of Terror. It was a catalogue of suffering and humiliation, spiced with gory detail.

Later, I was in the company of a Countess at her sixteenth-arrondissement home. 'The Revolution was murder,' the Countess said. I nodded meekly and ate my gâteau. 'The only thing to do in the face of these ghastly festivities is to stay inside and pray for the souls of the poor innocent victims.' To the Countess, to the Duchess, to all of them it was as if it had happened yesterday.

'In France, there's noble and there's noble,' Monsieur le Duc explained. First division aristos, he said, between twenty and thirty families, date their titles back to the twelfth century. Later ennoblements (or purchases of titles) are not so highly regarded, and status decreases in chronological order. Thus a Mortemart (very *chic,* very *ancien régime*) can look down on a Magenta (not so *chic,* rather Napoléon III). Lower down still come the BCBG (*bon chic, bon genre*), the equivalent perhaps of the English Sloanes, the *haute bourgeoisie* anyway.

Such divisions occur in Britain too, but there are significant differences. The French spend less time in gumboots, for one. A circumstance that dates back to the days of Louis XIV. He permanently changed the environs of the French nobility when he opened the gates of Versailles and invited them all over for a bite to eat and a spot of Racine afterwards. This turned out to be rather a long evening, lasting the whole reign through, and it caused the aristocracy to remove their home bases from the country to Paris, to be near the fun. Here they've remained ever since – city people who occasionally visit rural châteaux, the reverse of their British counterparts, who are countryfolk with places in town.

Since the Revolution, French inheritance law has decreed that estates must be divided equally amongst the children. This has progressively eroded noble legacies, and effectively sent the aristocracy out to work to save their châteaux. In England, inheritance law ensures that huge fortunes still exist, and Gloucestershire girls continue to dance in stately homes comfortingly full of priceless possessions.

So now, more and more, you have châteaux for sale. During the past three or four years a huge number of country homes have been sold, often to English buyers. 'And not to anyone of very good family either,' said the Countess. The Countess knew. She was bemoaning the loss of her château, in the family since the 1300s.

Spare a thought, then, for the poor French nobility, as the skies of Paris light up to celebrate the birth of the guillotine.

Source: Punch

(a) Quelle est la signification de l'année 1989?   [3]
(b) Que fera-t-on pour célébrer cet événement?   [5]
(c) Décrivez l'attitude et les réactions des aristocrates français   [10]
(d) Quelles catégories sociales le Duc a-t-il distinguées?   [5]
(e) Traduisez en français à partir de 'So now, more and more,' jusqu'à la fin   [17]

AEB A Level, June 1990

Possible answers:

(a) C'est le bicentenaire de la Révolution française.

(b) On va ouvrir un nouveau opéra à la Bastille; on va jouer à la Comédie Française, des pièces de théâtre spécialement écrites pour le bicentenaire; il y aura des feux d'artifice et on va danser dans la rue.

(c) Pour eux, la Révolution ne devrait pas être célébrée mais ils ne vont pas protester en public. En privé, ils disent qu'ils ont beaucoup souffert et ont été humiliés pendant la Terreur. Ils préfèrent maintenant prier pour ceux qui ont été tués pendant la Révolution et ne pas prendre part aux festivités.

(d) Il y a d'abord les vrais nobles, les plus anciens; puis ceux qui ont acheté leur titre; ensuite il y a la haute bourgeoisie, qui n'est pas vraiment noble.

(e) Les aristocrates français vivent en ville, surtout à Paris, mais à la campagne, ils sont plus pauvres et ne possèdent pas de grands châteaux, ni de grandes fortunes comme les aristocrates anglais.

(f) Et maintenant donc, de plus en plus, il y a des châteaux à vendre. Ces trois ou quatre dernières années, un grand nombre de propriétés ont été vendues, souvent à des Anglais. 'Et pas à des personnes de bonne famille' a dit la comtesse. Elle, elle le savait. Elle se lamentait sur la perte de son château, qui avait appartenu à sa famille depuis le 14 ème siècle

Donc, n'oubliez pas la pauvre aristocratie française quand le ciel au-dessus de Paris sera illuminé pour célébrer la naissance de la guillotine.

Note

Many of the previous comments apply here again. The number of marks given is a good guide to the amount of content. The skill of summary is important. There is an element of translation into French. Finding alternative words in English can be helpful here and provide access to possible French words: *'bemoaning'* – lamenting, *'spare a thought'* – don't forget.

3 Translation

Contents

1 Translation into English

You may have to translate a whole text into English, or extracts from a text, as part of a group of language tasks. There are two aspects to this:
(a) understanding what the text means
(b) giving a version of it that sounds and reads like English.
The usual pitfalls are:

1   Not understanding or knowing what words mean (when a dictionary is not allowed).
2   Making a mistake with a word because it looks like another one or like an English word (e.g. *volant* – steering wheel confused with *voleur* – thief or *des milliers de personnes* – thousands (not millions) of people); or because it is a *faux ami*, exactly like an English word but with a different meaning in French (e.g. *sensible* means 'sensitive' not 'sensible' which is *sensé*).
3   Not understanding because of grammar or syntax (e.g. *selon les informations il y aurait deux morts* – according to the news two people are supposed to have died, not 'would be dead'; *les touristes que m'envoyait le bureau* not 'the tourists that sent me the office' but 'the tourists that the office sent me' — subjects often follow the verb like this in French).
4   Giving a word for word translation, based closely on the word order of the French. The result is something that sounds more like French than English:

A partir de ce soir, 20 heures, les usagers de la SNCF connaîtront trois jours bien difficiles –
At leaving of this evening the users of the SNCF will know three days very difficult.

The latter kind of pitfall usually disappears fairly quickly with practice. You do need to read through your translation, aloud if possible and to someone else, to test whether it sounds like English. Numbers **1** to **3** are remedied by lots of practice and getting to know your *bons amis* and your *faux amis*.

Read through a sentence several times before attempting a translation and try to keep all the bits of meaning together in your mind before assembling them. With long sentences, it helps to read them through several times quickly in your mind, pausing at commas or semi-colons. Try to sort the sentence into natural blocks of meaning. If you get stuck on this find the main verbs and try to establish what their subjects and objects are. Remember too that there is often more than one way of translating tenses into English. The present and perfect tenses, for example, could each have three possibilities (*see* pages 26 and 28). You might find it is necessary to rearrange the order of the sentence to make it sound like good English. Another tip: English verbs, unlike French ones, are rich in their use of prepositions. Bear this in mind when reading your translation out aloud. You can often give it a more English flavour by the change or insertion of a preposition (*see* exercise 9, page 18.)

When you are reading through your version check that all the meaning of the original is there. Sometimes the meaning of quite small words have been confused (e.g. the definite or indefinite articles, the demonstrative adjective *ce, cette* etc. or pronouns and adjectives).

It is also worth remembering that more than one version is usually possible. The perfect translation is said not to exist although the following has been cited as near perfect:

Est-ce que la vie vaut la peine d'être vécue? Question de foi(e) –
Is life worth living? It depends on the liver

Exercices

1   Try correcting the English of the following publicity brochure:

Open all
the days

MONSTRE CALAIS

The
most
up to date
**HYPERMARKET
IN FRANCE OFFERS YOU**

- A staff who speaks english
- The possibility to pay in
  sterlings at the cashier
- The biggest wine
  cellar in the area
- Stores where you will find
  the french spécialities

Cheese

Bread made and baked
in front of you

Cristal

Le Creuset Pans

Clothing and so on

**Monstre is in side the CALAIS ouest
shopping centre – real place of leisure
where you can purchase all your presents.**

*P.S. Don't throw this guide. Give it to your
friends they will be thankfull to you.*

2 (a) Complete the same exercise as for question 1 but this time you also have the original French:

HOW TO VISIT THE EIFFEL TOWER

The most beautiful view over Paris is from the second floor. From the 1st floor, Paris seems run-over as one finds one's self at the level of the highest roofs. From the 3rd floor, everything seems too small and one cannot distinguish many of its monuments, but when the weather is clear, one has a magnificent view of the country surrounding Paris.

Forty per cent of the visitors ascend to the 3rd floor. The price of the ascent and the waits for the lifts discourage many as, in the best season, the wait to take the lift from the 2nd to the 3rd floor is often from 30 to 40 minutes.

I advise going first to the 2nd floor and making a tour of it. Then mount to the 3rd floor, tour it, and write postal cards which bear a special 'top of the Tower' stamp, and then go down to the 1st floor (you will find restaurants there suited to every pocket book)

COMMENT VISITER LA TOUR EIFFEL

La plus belle vue sur Paris est depuis la deuxième plate-forme. Au premier étage, Paris semble un peu écrasé car on se trouve au niveau des toits les plus hauts. Au troisième, tout semble trop petit, on ne distingue plus bien les monuments; en revanche, par temps clair, on a une très belle vue sur les environs de Paris.

40% des visiteurs montent au troisième étage. Le prix de la montée et l'attente aux ascenseurs en découragent beaucoup: en effet à la belle saison, l'attente au deuxième étage pour prendre l'ascenseur du troisième est souvent de 30 à 45 minutes.

Je conseille d'abord d'aller au deuxième, en faire le tour. Puis monter au troisième, bien le visiter, y écrire des cartes postales qui recevront une oblitération spéciale du sommet de la tour, puis s'arrêter au premier en redescendant et y faire un repas (restaurants à tous les prix: luxe et brasserie)

(b) How many marks out of ten would you give the original translation for:
 (i) accuracy (are any parts totally wrong?)
 (ii) style (how 'English' it sounds)

(c) Have any important bits of meaning been left out?

3 Here is part of an article singing the praises of butter:

QU'EST-CE QUI EST TENDRE, PUR, DOUX, FRAIS ET QUI SENT LA NOISETTE? C'EST LE BEURRE BIEN SÛR — QUI DIT MIEUX? PERSONNE CAR RIEN N'ÉGALE LE BEURRE, CE SEIGNEUR DES BONNES TABLES DONT LE NOM ÉVOCATEUR RIME AVEC SAVEUR.

L'atout du beurre est d'être riche en vitamine A. Cette précieuse vitamine a une action polyvalente sur l'organisme. Indispensable à la croissance, elle joue un rôle fondamental dans la vision et aide l'organisme à résister contre les infections. Vitamine-beauté, elle favorise l'éclat des cheveux et la santé de la peau.

Grossir

Consommé en quantités raisonnables, sans apport d'autres corps gras, le beurre ne fait pas grossir. C'est surtout le déséquilibre alimentaire qui en est responsable, l'absorption incontrôlée de ce que l'on nomme 'les graisses cachées': charcuterie, fritures, pâtisseries, etc. consommées souvent au cours du même repas. Nous devons être vigilants afin d'utiliser les lipides dits 'visibles': corps gras d'assaisonnements (beurre)...

Quelle dose peut-on consommer?

Tout dépend de notre activité physique. Plus on est actif, plus on a besoin d'énergie: la ration quotidienne d'un athlète est estimée à 3500 kcal, dont 120g de graisses, y compris 35g de beurre environ. La suppression totale du beurre s'avère seulement nécessaire dans les cas de maladie de surcharge lipidique. Un adulte sans problème peut en consommer 30g par jour. Il s'agit évidemment de beurre cru ou fondu.

(a) Corrigez la traduction suivante de la première partie, qui a été faite par une personne sans grande connaissance de l'anglais.
What is tender, pure, mild, fresh and smells the nuts? It is butter very sure — who says better? No person, for nothing equals butter, this lord of the table of whom the evoking name rhymes with savour.

(b) The translations of part of the second paragraph on page 113 both have their merits.
Think about these and compose the definitive version:

(i) *Consumed in reasonable quantities without being added to with other fatty substances butter does not make you fatter. It is an unbalanced diet that is mainly responsible for this: the uncontrolled consumption of what are called disguised fats: cold meats, fried foods, cakes etc. which are eaten during the course of one meal.*

(ii) *Eaten in moderation without the addition of other fats, butter does not make you put on weight. It is especially eating in an unbalanced way that causes this: the unregulated consumption of hidden fats so called: delicatessen, fried things, pastries etc. often eaten during a single meal*

(c) 'saveur' veut dire ici *taste, flavour*. Avec l'aide d'un dictionnaire précisez la signification des mots suivants et utilisez-les dans une phrase: odeur; senteur; parfum; odorat.

(d) 'ça sent la noisette' – *it smells of hazelnuts, so how would you express*:
It smells of onions | fish | feet | cooking | garlic

2 Retranslation

Retranslation is a task required by some Examining Boards as part of the written paper. It consists of a short passage of English for translation based on a text already used for other language tasks. Retranslation is a useful task because it makes you re-use words and expressions that you have met already, thus helping memorization and fluency in thinking and writing in French. Usually, about a quarter to a third of words from the French text can be re-used in the English translation. You will not however be able to just copy down chunks of the original. Tenses may have to be changed, as well as adjectives and the person of the verb. You will also have to find words from your own store to fill in the bits in between.

Before tackling the translation, read carefully through the French text again. Read the English and then the French once more, this time underlining words or expressions that seem as if they could be wholly or partly re-used. Then start the translation, paying particular attention to tenses and subjects of verbs and other words you may need.

Model answers

1   **UN MORT, DIX-HUIT BLESSÉS DANS UN CAMPING DE LA NIÈVRE, DIMANCHE SOIR: CES DÉCHAÎNEMENTS BRUTAUX DU TEMPS FRAPPENT N'IMPORTE OÙ PENDANT L'ÉTÉ**

Un mort, deux blessés graves, seize personnes plus légèrement atteintes, d'énormes dégâts matériels ... La météo ayant prévu une accalmie après les orages de lundi, on n'attendait pas la tornade qui s'est abattue sur la ville de La Charité sur Loire (Nièvre) ravageant en quelques minutes une zone de deux kilomètres de long sur 200 mètres de large et détruisant tout sur son passage. La jeune femme, Viviane Lepage, trente et un ans, qui a trouvé la mort dans la catastrophe, ainsi que la plupart des blessés séjournaient sur un terrain de camping qui a été totalement détruit par les rafales de pluie, de vent et de grêle.

Entre la zone industrielle et la vieille ville, la tornade a gravement endommagé les immeubles, arraché le toit des maisons, jeté à bas une usine et plusieurs bâtiments, déraciné tous les arbres. 'On aurait dit un bombardement, a déclaré le sénateur maire de La Charité-sur-Loire, Robert Guillaume. On marchait sur les débris de toitures, les poutres, les panneaux, tout était par terre, c'était absolument dantesque.'

Le président François Mitterrand s'est rendu hier après-midi en hélicoptère dans la ville sinistrée. Après avoir constaté l'étendue des dégâts, il devait s'entretenir avec les campeurs hébergés dans la salle des fêtes et les habitants dont les appartements ont été dévastés.

Hier, vers 15 heures, un orage de grêle d'une violence exceptionnelle s'est abattu sur la petite ville de Bourg-Saint-Andéol, dans le sud de l'Ardèche, provoquant là encore d'importants dégâts matériels, mais sans heureusement faire de victimes. Août est décidément le mois des terribles orages et il y a à cela des raisons très connues.

Translate into French:

A tornado occurs in very hot weather when masses of hot and cold air meet. Although it is possible to tell when it is likely to strike, you never know where, or what path it will follow. As the energy created by a single tornado is the same as that of the atomic bomb which exploded on Hiroshima, it can cause a great deal of devastation. Trees may be ripped up and cars and other vehicles overturned. The tornado which recently caused damage over such a large area near La Charité-sur-Loire blew down numerous old buildings and lifted caravans into the air.   [20]

London A-Level (syllabus A), June 1989

Possible answers: French version

Une tornade se produit par grande chaleur lorsque des masses d'air froid et chaud se rencontrent. Bien qu'il soit possible de prédire quand une tornade va frapper, on ne sait jamais où elle se produira ni quel chemin elle suivra. Puisque l'énergie dissipée par une seule tornade est équivalente à celle de la bombe atomique qui a éclaté sur Hiroshima, elle peut provoquer d'importants dégâts. Les arbres peuvent être déracinés, les voitures et d'autres véhicules renversés. La tornade qui a récemment causé des dégâts sur une si importante zone près de La Charité-sur–Loire a abattu plusieurs vieux bâtiments et soulevé des caravanes.

Note

(a) More than one word from the text could sometimes have been used (e.g. 'overturn' could be *abattre* or *jeter bas* and 'ripped up' could be *déraciner* or *arracher*).

(b) There is a tense change in the last sentence of the English.

(c) It is important to have in your memory store structure words like *bien que* and *puisque* as well as common ideas like 'happen' and 'it is possible'.

2 Read this passage carefully and carry out the instructions which follow it.

Chaque année, un peu plus de 200 jeunes encadrent 280 000 enfants venus s'oxygéner dans les nombreux centres de vacances et de loisirs répartis sur le territoire. Leur fonction: animateur ou animatrice. Un job idyllique mais exigeant, car les journées commencent avec l'aurore pour se terminer bien après la nuit. Dans l'intervalle, il aura fallu surveiller et occuper un bon nombre d'enfants. Une tâche intéressante mais éprouvante, surtout si on est seul face à une trentaine de petits indisciplinés.

Accueillant des enfants et des adolescents de 4 à 18 ans, les centres présentent des caractéristiques très différentes selon l'âge des participants.

Les centres de vacances maternels sont réservés aux animateurs/animatrices les plus dévoués et les plus patients. Comme leur nom l'indique, ils accueillent des enfants de 4 à 6 ans. Les centres de vacances pour 6–12 ans sont plus connus sous le nom de 'colonies de vacances'. Dans les camps d'adolescents, on a coutume de distinguer les préados (12–14 ans) des véritables détenteurs du titre (15-17 ans). Janine, 18 ans, a travaillé comme animatrice dans une colonie de vacances organisée par l'EDF (Electricité de France):

'J'avais fait une variété de petits emplois pendant les vacances d'été: pompiste, baby-sitter, serveuse, mais j'ai trouvé ce job vraiment intéressant surtout au niveau des contacts avec les enfants. L'animatrice doit savoir écouter, comprendre et aimer les enfants, souvent défavorisés. Les relations entre animateurs sont plutôt sympas. En fait, je suis très contente de cette expérience qui m'a permis de passer un mois de semi-vacances au bord de la mer. Ce que j'ai aimé sont les contacts avec les enfants. Vraiment, j'ai eu l'impression de leur apporter quelque chose, de me sentir utile. Ils sont formidables.'

Translate into French:

More than 100 underprivileged children will be able to go on holiday this summer thanks to the generosity of a French bank, the Crédit Lyonnais. It has just set up a new holiday centre near St Raphaël to take children from the Paris region. They will be looked after by twenty or so students from Nice.

Keeping young adolescents busy all day is a very demanding task but it will enable the students to spend a month in the sun. Moreover, they feel that this kind of holiday job has particularly interesting features, for they are all intending to become teachers when they have finished their studies.

[20]

London A-Level (Syllabus A), June 1990

Possible answer: French version

Plus de 100 enfants défavorisés pourront aller en vacances cet été grâce à la générosité d'une banque française, le Crédit Lyonnais. Celui-ci vient d'installer un nouveau centre de vacances près de St Raphaël pour accueillir des enfants de Paris et de la région parisienne. Ils seront surveillés par une vingtaine d'étudiants venus de Nice.

Occuper toute la journée des jeunes adolescents est une tâche exigeante mais cela permettra aux étudiants de passer un mois au soleil. De plus, ils ont l'impression que ce genre d'emploi de vacances leur apportera quelque chose de particulièrement utile car ils ont tous l'intention de devenir enseignants lorsqu'ils auront fini leurs études.

Note:

(a) There are perhaps fewer re-usable words here.

(b) Certain grammar points are being tested (e.g. 'has just' –*vient de* – 'keeping busy' *occuper* (an infinitive) and *lorsqu'ils auront fini leurs études* (a future perfect tense).

Exercices

The best way of practising this language task is to do lots of examples. The passages that follow have three stages of practice:

(a) phrase spotting

(b) easy retranslation

(c) more demanding retranslation

1 HOLD-UP A 14 ANS

Une adolescente de 14 ans a commis un hold-up avant-hier dans une caisse d'épargne de Hambourg, emportant un butin de 10 000DM (35 000F). La police a arrêté la jeune braqueuse peu après les faits, ainsi qu'un homme de 22 ans, qui l'attendait sur une moto, mais qui avait pris la fuite seul.

Armée d'un revolver d'alarme et coiffée d'un casque de moto, la jeune fille a fait irruption dans la caisse d'épargne et a présenté au caissier un papier sur lequel était écrit,' Ceci est un hold-up, mettez tout l'argent dans le sac et que personne ne bouge. Vite!'

En sortant de la banque, la jeune fille a été suivie par un employé qui a pu indiquer à la police une cour où elle s'était cachée.

(a) **Phrase spotting** Find the following words and phrases from the text:
Savings bank – arrested – nobody move – a haul – an alarm - pistol – day before yesterday – wearing a crash helmet – burst into – this is a hold-up – a piece of paper – had fled on his own – armed with – shortly after the incident – carried out a hold-up

(b) Now translate this paragraph into French:
Armed with an alarm-pistol, a young girl of 14 burst into a Hamburg savings bank yesterday and showed the cashier a piece of paper on which was written, 'This is a hold-up'. A young man was waiting for her outside on a motorbike but he made off on his own. The girl was followed by an employee when she left the bank. He was able to show the police the block of flats where she had hidden.

(c) Now translate this paragraph into French:
Two teenage girls of 14 and 15 burst into a Paris bank yesterday and got out with a haul of 100 000F. The two young gangsters had shown the cashier a card on which was written, 'This is a hold-up. Nobody move!' They were armed with alarm-pistols and were wearing crash-helmets. Outside the bank two young men were waiting for them in a car but they fled at the last moment. The police were able to arrest the girls later thanks to an employee who had followed them to a block of flats.

2 LE SIDA – FLÉAU DES ANNÉES 90

Personne n'en doute aujourd'hui: le SIDA constitue le fléau des années 90. Dans les pays en voie de développement, il frappe aveuglément, décimant hommes et femmes laissant derrière lui des cohortes d'orphelins. En Europe, aux Etats Unis, la contamination hétérosexuelle s'étend. Les femmes à leur tour paient leur tribut au virus HIV. Il y a sept ans qu'il a été découvert par une équipe de l'Institut Pasteur. Depuis sept ans, les scientifiques imaginent des parades à la maladie et à l'épidémie. Les campagnes d'information et la prévention restent indispensables. Cependant, seule la recherche apportera une arme décisive, traitement ou vaccin.

Mais chercher coûte cher. Et les scientifiques européens manquent cruellement de moyens. D'où l'idée du Pr. Luc Montagnier de faire appel à la générosité du public par le biais de la Fondation Européenne de Recherche sur le SIDA, pour donner à l'Europe des atouts supplémentaires dans cette bataille dont dépend la vie de milliers d'êtres humains.

(a) **Phrase spotting**
is spreading – seven years ago – indiscriminately – effective weapon – information campaign – developing countries – research on its own – on which depends the life – appeal to – killing thousands – scientists – pay their price to the virus – hordes of children – an extra advantage – was discovered – the scourge of the 90s

(b) Translate the following paragraph into French:
AIDS continues to spread in the developing countries causing the deaths of thousands of men and women and leaving great numbers of orphaned children. In Europe and the United States, AIDS is spreading amongst heterosexuals and the number of women with the HIV virus is growing. Only research can provide an effective weapon against this disease. Researchers in Europe however are desperately short of funds. The European Foundation for Research into AIDS is appealing to the generosity of the public in order to gain the upper hand in this battle for the lives of thousands.

(c) Now translate this paragraph into French:

Since the discovery of AIDS seven years ago by the Pasteur Institute the disease has continued to spread in Europe, in the United States and the developing countries. AIDS has become the scourge of our times. Contrary to the predictions of certain doctors it has also spread amongst the heterosexual population. Scientists fear an epidemic. A sad effect of the disease is to create hordes of orphan children who nobody wants to look after. Information and prevention campaigns are only partly an answer. What is needed is to discover either a treatment that is effective or a vaccine.

3 Read the following advertisement carefully, then complete the tasks based on it.

I ❤ ENGLISH

DÈS 12 ANS UN COPAIN ANGLAIS

I LOVE ENGLISH,
QUAND ON AIME, ON COMPREND TOUT!

Un très grand succès dès son premier numéro en janvier 87! Ceci s'explique par l'alliance unique d'intelligence et d'humour de ce magazine **totalement nouveau**, qui parle en version originale à ses lecteurs des sujets qu'ils aiment. Que de bons moments vos enfants vont pouvoir passer avec *I Love English*, tout en progressant rapidement en anglais.

Mensuel, *I Love English* apporte des aventures à suivre, en bande dessinée, qui constituent autant d'albums à collectionner. Des jeux, des tests pour **vérifier et mémoriser des connaissances nouvelles**. Des histoires vraies, comme la véritable origine du blue-jeans, la création d'Apple par deux jeunes Américains, ...

Vos enfants se familiariseront vite avec le monde anglo-saxon, grâce **aux fiches de documentation** à découper, très pratiques, et aux articles consacrés à tous les aspects de la vie quotidienne. De célèbres personnages contemporains sont interviewés (Steven Spielberg par exemple), les grandes villes de Grande-Bretagne et des Etats-Unis sont décrites, de bonnes adresses sont données.

Conçu et mis en forme par deux professeurs d'anglais et des anglophones, *I Love English* facilite l'accès direct aux textes. Un 'mini dico' donne tout de suite, page par page, le sens des mots et expressions courantes les plus difficiles, sans recourir au dictionnaire.

I Love English, c'est le moyen astucieux de faire des progrès rapides en anglais, d'acquérir un vocabulaire précis, de se trouver à l'aise dans l'ambiance anglo-saxonne. **Un atout de première force pour les études et la préparation à l'avenir pour vos enfants.**

Un grand coup de cœur pour l'anglais, dès la 5è

(a) A French friend has sent you this advertisement for *I Love English* and asks your opinion of it. Write a letter of about 150 words in French in reply. You should select some of the points made in the advertisement, and write about them at greater length, indicating to your friend how useful you think they would be for language learning. [40]

(b) Translate into French:

Most[1] English people still[2] think that learning[3] a foreign language is unnecessary. Some [4] have no intention of getting to know about life in another country. Others, however, <u>make</u> remarkable <u>progress</u>, having found[5] that there are <u>ways</u> in which[6] their efforts <u>can be made easier</u>. It is possible[7] that <u>English speakers</u> will <u>feel at home</u> in a Spanish or French[8] <u>atmosphere</u> if they have studied some of[9] the <u>magazines</u> and books which have been <u>designed</u> by well-known[10] <u>teachers</u>. By collecting[11] these <u>documents</u> they will have a <u>practical means</u> of[12] <u>acquiring</u> a <u>knowledge</u> of the <u>everyday</u> vocabulary and of the <u>inhabitants</u> concerned.[13]   [20]

London A-Level, Syllabus A, June 1991

Note This text contains a number of words that you can re-use. Find a French word for the ones underlined in the text. Sometimes there might be more than one way of re-using them. Use the notes to help you do a faultless version of the passage. You may find it helpful to refer to the grammar section.

1 Is it *la plupart des* or *beaucoup de* ?
2 Position of adverbs!
3 Don't be tempted to use a present participle (*see* page 53, exercise 2(b))
4 *certains... d'autres*
5 *ayant...*
6 *pour* + infinitive, using a suitable expression from the text
7 *il est possible que* — Do you need a subjunctive?
8 Position of adjectives?
9 e.g. 'some ones of the magazines...'
10 *bien connus* — Position of adjectival expression?
11 'by doing something', *en* + present participle
12 After a preposition you need an infinitive
13 *dont il est question*

Study techniques: practising translation and retranslation

You can practise these skills by using any sort of bilingual texts; sets of instructions for the use of equipment, lists of contents of food or beauty products and labels are now often produced in more than one language. When in France you can often obtain tourist brochures in English. You might be surprised at the English in some of these, so look at them carefully! (*see* the example on page 111) You could offer your services and do a good translation for the organization concerned. At trade fairs, brochures and publicity material are often available in several languages. When you obtain any material, like the above, read both versions and then try translating the French one into English and vice versa, glancing only occasionally at the original. You could also use translations of your set texts for this exercise, provided the French is not too complex or literary in style. Texts suitable for this purpose are: Pagnol's autobiographical novels, (*La gloire de mon père*, *Le château de ma mère*, *Le temps des secrets*); Camus's *L'Etranger*; many of Prévert's poems; *Les petits enfants du siècle* by Rochefort; and plays by Beckett or Ionesco. Other bilingual texts already mentioned are: the Press-Pocket series of English novels and the publication *La vie Outre-Manche* (*see* page 210).

Look for suitable journalistic material. Any articles you come across in French newspapers, about aspects of life in England, can be useful because you are already familiar with the context. You could also buy English and French newspapers on the same day and compare articles on the same themes. You might sometimes find it profitable to work from French into English first.

Exercices (suite)

4 (a) In the following extract see if you can pick out the phrases that stand for the following:

family allowances – home owners – mortgages – local authorities – council homes – above their means – social security – young unemployed – hundreds of thousands – cheap housing market – for each child – the homeless – dole mentality – evictions – repayments – interest rates – taken on – its aim was – frozen – low-income families – shrunk – according to inflation

TROIS MILLE SANS-ABRI — CONTRE 250 EN 1975 — DORMENT DANS LES RUES DE LONDRES ET LE PAYS COMPTERAIT NEUF MILLIONS DE PAUVRES

Les allocations familiales sont gelées depuis trois ans au même niveau et leur valeur réelle diminue donc en raison de l'inflation. Elles sont de 288F par mois par enfant.

La principale réforme de l'aide sociale a eu lieu en 1988. Elle avait pour but de concentrer les ressources sur les familles les plus démunies et les personnes âgées, tout en cherchant à éviter la création d'une 'mentalité d'assistés' chez les plus jeunes. Les allocations aux jeunes chômeurs ont ainsi été nettement réduites.

Le gouvernement s'efforce depuis onze ans de rendre les Britanniques propriétaires de leurs maisons. Des centaines de milliers de logements sociaux construits par les municipalités, surtout depuis la guerre, ont été vendus. Le parc locatif à bon marché a donc considérablement diminué.

On a assisté aussi depuis quelques mois à la multiplication des expulsions. Des familles très modestes ont contracté des prêts hypothécaires dont le remboursement se révèle au-dessus de leurs moyens: les traites varient en effet proportionnellement aux taux d'intérêt, maintenus très hauts pour combattre l'inflation.

(b) Now translate the following:

(i)   Many low-income families have taken on mortgages that are beyond their means
(ii) Many council homes have been sold since the war
(iii) Mortgage repayments vary according to the rate of inflation
(iv) Family allowances are too modest for deprived families
(v)   Payments to young unemployed people have been reduced
(vi) The interest rate has dropped
(vii) We have seen more evictions during the last few months
(viii) The government has been trying to control inflation since 1988
(ix) The aim of many people is to own their own home
(x)   This reform was aimed at helping the homeless

Note The above passage illustrates the importance of being familiar with the context or subject matter of what you are translating. You should look through past papers from your Examining Board to see what kinds of subject matter they use. The latter may be of a documentary nature covering such things as: social and political issues; education; trade union; and environmental problems. Or they may be of a more literary nature. It is important therefore to make a habit of reading widely so that you increase your general knowledge. Pick a short article or news item, each week, about a different subject and make a list, as you read, of key words or phrases. You will sometimes find words or expressions pertaining to current matters that cannot be found easily in a dictionary!

4 Summary

Contents

The skill of being able to pick out the main points of a speech or written report and to summarize these in brief form, has many practical applications in both work and study. This skill is tested by several of the Examining Boards at A and AS Level, in the reading and writing sections of their papers. It is also tested to some extent in the listening part of the examination. Depending on the Board, you may be asked to write a summary (in English or in French) of: (a) a whole text; or (b) part of one.

Whether the end result is in English or French, you need to start by using your reading skills. If the text has a title, or subheadings, these will give you the general idea of the whole subject. A quick glance, at the first few lines and the last, will also give you clues to what it is about (i.e. the purpose of the piece of writing). Next skim read the passage by letting your eye run along each line without stopping at any difficult parts. You won't understand (or remember) all the words on this occasion. If you have difficulty in skimming, run your finger along a few lines below where you are reading. Now read through again, a little more slowly, marking any words or phrases that cause difficulty. Read through a third time and, if dictionaries are allowed, look up anything you think is essential to the meaning. Not every word will be. Some meanings you will be able to guess at because of the context. Leave these to last to look up and then only if they are still essential to the summary. Next, re-read a paragraph at a time, underlining the words that contain your choice of the main ideas. You may find pencil is better than a highlighter since you can erase it if necessary.

1 Summary in English

You might be required to reduce a French passage to about one-third of its original length and not to exceed a given number of words. There are two main considerations here:

(a) Picking out the essential information (as outlined on page 118)
(b) Writing economically in English

Both these skills are acquired through practice.

Having read the text at least four times, and having underlined the main points, begin writing your summary on alternate lines (paragraph by paragraph), using your underlinings as a guide but also trying to assess the whole value of each section. Do not be tempted to translate. About a third of the way through, count up the words used so far to make sure you are roughly on target. If you have used too many, you may have put in too much detail; so read through what is left to gauge the amount of information left to convey. Finish the summary and count up the number of words. If there are 3-5 too many it doesn't matter. If there are 10 or more, as usually happens, you might be at the point where you would lose marks because any ideas in the excess of words are not counted. You can reduce the number of words in two ways:

(a) Pruning the English — using one word instead of two or more, or by leaving words out, provided they don't remove important detail.
(b) Leaving out details that you can see are not essential to the overall meaning now that you have the whole before you.

Most texts will contain information that is either circumstantial or just an accessory to the main ideas. Sometimes lots of examples are quoted or the text simply repeats itself.

Model answer

1 In about 170 to 180 words, reducing the passage to approximately one-third of its length, write a summary **in English** of the extract, to show you have understood and to prepare yourself for the letter-writing. No extra marks will be gained by candidates who write more than 180 words. State the number of words you have used; there are 509 in the original passage.

[30]

– Du *Manuel du Routard*

La croyance selon laquelle le fait d'être pris ou non dépendrait essentiellement du conducteur est fausse, ou du moins inexacte: être pris, ou non, dépend en effet dans une large mesure de l'auto-stoppeur lui-même et de son habileté.

Il existe donc une technique, ou plutôt des techniques qui élèvent le stop au rang d'un art et qui font qu'il ne suffit pas de se tenir debout au bord d'une route pour que l'on puisse décemment appeler cela 'faire du stop'.

Attitude et tenue
Se tenir bien droit et non avachi comme certains(!). Paraître détendu, même si vous attendez depuis trois heures et surtout un léger sourire aux lèvres – sans exagération! Regardez l'automobiliste droit dans les yeux afin d'établir aussitôt un contact entre vous deux. C'est d'ailleurs pour cela qu'il ne faut jamais stopper avec des lunettes de soleil. Enfin, quand vous descendez, n'oubliez jamais de dire au revoir ou merci à votre conducteur dans sa propre langue. C'est le détail qui l'incitera à prendre systématiquement tous les autres stoppeurs par la suite.

Habillement
Une règle fondamentale est de porter une chemise de couleur claire, voire blanche. De plus, contrairement à ce que pensent bon nombre de stoppeurs, une certaine forme d'originalité dans l'habillement n'est pas à bannir. Bon nombre d'automobilistes aiment s'arrêter pour prendre des 'petits-rigolos-qui-ont-l'air-bien-sympathiques'. C'est sans doute par le couvre-chef que vous pourrez le mieux vous donner cette touche d'originalité (choisir un chapeau de cow-boy, un sombrero espagnol...).

On a déjà rencontré des petits astucieux qui n'hésitent pas à stopper en veste et cravate (le type qui a loupé son train) ... ça marche très bien. Si vous êtes amateur de déguisements carnavalesques, évitez de stopper en habit militaire, à moins que vous ne soyez sous les drapeaux. Les amendes sont très élevées et il y a risque de prison. A choisir, louez une soutane, c'est moins dangereux.

Un lecteur nous a écrit qu'il préférait se déguiser en footballeur avec les grosses chaussettes et tout. Résultat assuré. En gros, il faut donc jouer au stoppeur occasionnel. Faire celui qui est 'obligé' marche presque toujours.

Le stop sur les autoroutes

Il présente de grands avantages, notamment celui de faire de longues distances sans changer de véhicule. Le mieux est de stopper sur les bretelles de raccordement ou aux postes de péage ou mieux dans les stations d'essence en demandant directement. Mais attention, stopper sur l'autoroute même est non seulement interdit mais fort difficile. En conséquence, bien se faire préciser au préalable la destination de votre chauffeur afin de ne pas débarquer dans un endroit désert!

Il existe une carte Michelin (no. 400) traitant uniquement des autoroutes françaises, avec toutes les entrées, sorties, haltes, aires de repos, et surtout barrières de péages. Extrêmement pratique donc pour ne pas stopper sur un périphérique. Permet aussi de se faire déposer avant une sortie peu fréquentée. Chaque autoroute est notée avec toutes les villes et les villages situés à moins de quinze kilomètres de celle-ci. Pratique pour passer du train ou du car au stop.   (509 words)

Le Manuel du Routard, copyright Hachette 1982
Oxford and Cambridge AS-Level, June 1989

Possible answer

Getting a lift depends largely on a hitch-hiker's expertise and techniques. Stand up straight, smile, look the driver straight in the face and don't wear sunglasses. Thanking a driver afterwards in his own language will encourage him to take others.

It is important to wear light-coloured clothing. A certain originality, perhaps in headgear, can work to your advantage. Some wear collar and tie as if they had missed their train. If you like disguises avoid military uniform. It is illegal if it is not genuine. Try a surplice or football gear instead! Looking like a casual hitch-hiker usually works. Motorway hitch-hiking is good for long distances. Stand by slip roads, toll-gate areas or in the petrol stations. Waiting on the motorway is forbidden. Check the driver's destination first to avoid being dropped off in a remote place. The Michelin motorway guide is invaluable.   (140 words)

Practising summary

Summary is not needed at GCSE Level and is therefore a new skill to be acquired for A and AS Level. It is closely connected to reading skills (as already mentioned). You will get plenty of practice in reading literary and background texts. Make a habit, right from the start, of jotting down notes on what you are reading. Doing this **in French** will help you later in answering questions in French, if these are required by your Examining Board. Find out these requirements at the start of your course.

You will also need more specific practice. Start by reading short extracts from French newspapers using the *'faits divers'* or *'en bref'* sections. It helps if you can imagine you are explaining the news item not to yourself but to another person, who in this case understands very little French. Aim to give as faithful an account as possible.

Model answer

'Le titre de 'Chanson de l'année', créé à l'initiative de la Communauté des Radios Publiques de Langues Françaises (CRPLF) qui regroupe le RSR, la RTBF, Radio Canada et France Inter, a été décerné hier à la chanson 'Hélène', interprétée par le chanteur canadien Roch Voisine. Cette chanson a été choisie par les auditeurs des quatre radios francophones, à l'issue d'un référendum au cours de l'émission spéciale programmée sur France Inter, hier, de 17 à 19 heures, en multiplex avec la Belgique, le Canada et la Suisse. L'interprète de la chanson récompensée reçoit comme chaque année, un trophée original créé par le sculpteur Christian Renonciat.

This item is about a song of the year competition that took place yesterday on four French-speaking radio channels. It was won by the Canadian singer Roch Voisine with the song 'Helène'. It was chosen by listeners during a link-up broadcast. The winner got a specially sculptured trophy. This could be condensed to:

'The radio song of the year contest was won by a Canadian singer, Roch Voisine, for the song 'Hélène' chosen by listeners in four French-speaking countries during a radio-link broadcast yesterday on France-Inter.'

Deciding which bits of information to discard, and which to keep, depends partly on how short your summary needs to be and partly on how important certain details are. For example, in the above summary, the detail about the trophy has been left out.

Exercice

1 (a) Read the following news item and select the brief English summary which seems most accurate:

DEUX ÉLÈVES JAPONAIS ENTERRÉS VIVANTS

Deux élèves japonais, âgés de treize et de quatorze ans, ont été enterrés vivants sur une plage l'automne dernier par leurs enseignants qui entendaient les punir ainsi pour avoir racketté leurs camarades. Ils ont passé plus de vingt minutes enfouis dans le sable jusqu'au menton, la tête balayée par les vagues qui venaient s'échouer sur la plage de Fukuoka, une ville située dans le sud du Japon. 'Nous pensions que nous allions mourir' a déclaré l'un d'entre eux, en précisant que lorsqu'il avait essayé de s'extirper du sable, un enseignant était arrivé aussitôt pour l'en empêcher. Sept enseignants au total auraient participé à l'incident. Le directeur de l'école les a réprimandés d'avoir agi 'de façon excessive' mais aucune sanction n'a été prise par les autorités scolaires locales.

Summaries

 (i) Two Japanese schoolchildren narrowly escaped drowning after being buried alive in the sand on a beach by their teachers.

 (ii) Two Japanese schoolboys were punished by being buried alive by their teachers.

 (iii) A headmaster in Japan denied a charge of excessive cruelty when seven of his teachers buried two of their pupils in the sand.

 (iv) Two Japanese kids were buried up to their necks in sand by their teachers to teach them a lesson.

 (b) Are you satisfied completely with the summary you have chosen? If not write your own summary in not less than 25 words.

 (c) The original text had a single word title. Which of the following do you think it was?

SAUVÉS   ENTERRÉS   PUNITION

It helps when deciding this to think of cause and effect, in other words what action preceded what action or led to another one?

2 Read the following item:

INTERDICTION D'ARROSER

Le maire informe la population que suite à l'arrêté numéro 88-002 réglementant l'utilisation de l'eau potable pendant les mois de juillet et août, il est interdit d'arroser avec l'eau potable le samedi et le dimanche de 7 à 22 heures, l'alimentation des personnes en eau potable étant prioritaire sur l'arrosage des végétaux. Il est rappelé que les contrevenants seront poursuivis conformément à la loi.

 (a) Which is cause and effect among the following statements?

 (b) What is their most logical sequence?

Watering gardens is forbidden – You will be fined if you break the law – Providing drinking water is a priority – The Mayor has made an announcement

 (c) Write a one-sentence summary of the item.

3 **Background information**

You are planning to attend one-day symposium on environmental issues. The organizer, Jean Dupèbe, has written you a letter. Part of this letter and the text of a statement he refers to are given in the reading material for part A.

Instructions

Write the summary Jean asks for in his letter. Your summary must be written **in English** and should contain between 190–210 words. Do not write more than 210 words as no credit will be given for additional material. You must write in **continuous prose** not note form. State the number of words you have used; there are 405 words in the original passage.   [30]

Oxford and Cambridge AS Level, June 1991

Signe des temps: pour la seconde fois de son histoire, l'hebdomadaire américain *Time* n'a pas désigné une personne mais la planète Terre comme 'l'homme de l'année'. En la choisissant comme l'homme malade de notre monde, les Américains enfoncent le clou déjà planté par les Européens en 1987 avec la très discrète 'Année européenne de l'environnement'. Pour les Douze, il s'agissait d'un thème parmi d'autres, destiné à encourager ceux qui se battaient pour la sauvegarde de l'environnement en Europe. Mais l'hebdomadaire américain va plus loin: il tire la sonnette d'alarme pour l'avenir de la planète entière.

En France, ceux qui sonnent le tocsin à ce propos sont considérés comme de doux rêveurs, bref des 'écolos' qui prennent plaisir à tout bouleverser. Lorsque le commandant Cousteau dénonce les pollueurs de l'océan et demain, ceux qui veulent se partager l'exploitation du dernier continent vierge, l'Antarctique, on hausse les épaules en prétextant la fatalité de la chose.

Cependant, tous les grands voyageurs peuvent constater de leurs yeux à quel point la planète se transforme rapidement: au pillage des forêts tropicales et à la surexploitation des océans s'ajoute l'entassement humain dans les villes et particulièrement dans les mégapoles comme Mexico ou le Caire: tout cela fait peser une menace directe sur la survie — normale — de l'humanité.

On peut toujours se rassurer en se disant que l'homme a de la confiance dans la science et que de toute façon, elle trouvera la parade, même si elle est prise de court actuellement avec le SIDA. L'Europe a trouvé les moyens de se nourrir grâce aux engrais chimiques, mais elle risque, à terme, de ne plus pouvoir boire l'eau du robinet tant il y aura de nitrates dans la nappe phréatique. Les sociétés industrielles débordent d'énergie grâce notamment à l'exploitation du pétrole et de l'atome, mais on en connaît les limites. Sans parler des marées noires qui maculent régulièrement le littoral, il faut admettre que les réserves pétrolières ne sont pas illimitées. Quant à l'atome, il est redoutable en cas d'accident (Tchernobyl), mais aussi problématique pour l'avenir, dans la mesure où on ne sait pas trop quoi faire du combustible irradié, c'est-à-dire des déchets nucléaires.

Parmi tous ces dangers, ces menaces, ces inquiétudes pour l'avenir, quel est le pire à redouter? Instruits par l'histoire, nous redoutons toujours la guerre et nous avons raison: c'est le pire. Mais la dégradation de l'environnement peut être considérée comme notre première ennemie en temps de paix.

Note

Before you begin Try following the advice given at the beginning of this section. Read through several times finally making your underlinings of the text. Write your own summary and compare it with the one underneath (Summary A). This one contains too many words (260). See what you can prune or change, keeping what is necessary to reduce it to the target of 210 words. Then compare your result with the next summary (B) which is within the limit. Are you happy with it? Can you reduce it still further to reach the bottom target of 190 words?

Possible answers

Summary A

The American magazine *Time* has chosen Planet Earth for their 'sick' man of the year award, thus following the example set by the EC countries in 1987. This was only one of the themes in the 'European Year of the Environment'. The 12 wanted to give encouragement to European environmentalists but the Americans have stressed the dangers involved for the whole world.

Environmentalists who sound the alarm in France are regarded as dreamers, bent on causing trouble. When exploiters pose a fresh threat to the environment, people accept it as inevitable (e.g. the Antarctic, the last virgin continent).

World-wide travellers will tell you how rapidly the world is changing. Forests and oceans are being over-exploited. Over-population of large cities poses a direct threat to normal human survival — take Cairo and Mexico city as examples.

Can we just trust that science will eventually find a solution when it has solved the problem of AIDS? In Europe, adequate food production relies on chemical fertilizers whose nitrate run-off is making tap water undrinkable. Oil and nuclear sources have provided industrial societies with a super-abundance of energy. Oil has left its mark on our beaches and supplies are not limitless. Nuclear power carries the threat of possible accidents and problems for the generations to come are caused by the accumulation of radioactive waste.

War remains the biggest threat to the future of mankind, as history shows us, but deterioration of our environment is just as serious a menace in peacetime, enemy number one in fact. (260)

Summary B

Time magazine has chosen Planet Earth for their 'sick' man of the year award, thus following the example set by the EC countries in 1987. The 12 wanted to give encouragement to European environmentalists but the Americans have stressed the dangers involved for the whole world.

In France, environmentalists are regarded as dreamers, bent on causing trouble. When exploiters pose a fresh threat to the environment, the Antarctic for example, people accept it as inevitable.

World-wide travellers will tell you how rapidly the world is changing. Forests and oceans are being over-exploited. Over-population of large cities poses a direct threat to normal human survival.

Can we just trust that science will eventually find a solution? In Europe, adequate food production relies on chemical fertilizers whose nitrate run-off is making tap water undrinkable. Oil and nuclear sources have provided industrial societies with a super-abundance of energy. Oil has left its mark on our beaches and supplies are not limitless. Nuclear power carries the threat of possible accident and problems for the future are caused by the accumulation of radioactive waste.

War remains the biggest threat to the future of mankind but deterioration of our environment is just as serious a menace in peacetime. (205)

2 Summary in French of an English text

This language task, required by some of the Examining Boards, is based on a practical life-skill. It puts you in the situation of a bilingual person, providing information for a French organization, or company, from an English source which you can cope with but they can't so easily. A similar situation is used as part of the oral test by some groups where you have to pass on information in French taken from a document in English.

You should have no difficulty in understanding the text. However, read it carefully at least four times. The same comments about selecting the main ideas still apply. Distinguish between main or new points and examples or minor details. Is there any repetition? Are any comparisons being made? Does cause and effect play a part?

Having marked out your text, go back to the opening paragraph and its main idea. Do not be tempted to start translating. Pick a phrase (i.e. noun and adjective, subject and verb) and think of the French for them. You may have already been thinking of some French words when you were underlining; these should be jotted down as you go along. Again, it helps if you can imagine that you are doing this summary for someone else. You may want to work through the whole text in phrases or you may choose to start writing the summary a paragraph at a time, not necessarily following exactly the paragraphing of the original. Don't just translate all your underlined phrases. Try to think of the most appropriate French for the context.

The following is a typical example of summary in French from an English text. The ideas have been marked in second colour and jottings made in French:

Model answer

1   FRENCH DISPLAY TUNNEL VISION

THE FRENCH have achieved what seemed only a pipe-dream in Britain: they have turned a hole in the ground into a major tourist attraction

If the new Eurotunnel Exhibition Centre at the terminal now being built at Folkestone does as well as its counterpart at Sangatte, near Calais, a considerable amount of money will be made. Since the French end of the consortium opened its exhibition centre in October last year nearly

500 000 people have visited it, spending thousands of pounds on souvenirs and on meals in local restaurants. Sangatte is renowned as one of the most stupendously unattractive parts of the coastline around Calais.

The exhibition centre contrasts sharply with the Channel tunnel works at Dover which are based on a small outcrop of land at the foot of the 485 Shakespeare Cliff, making public viewing of the area awkward.

Parties of visiting VIPs need to be carefully controlled because of the danger. Only 10 at a time are allowed through the Tunnel entrance, and only five at a time are allowed to the chalk face.

A spokesman for Eurotunnel said: 'The situation in Dover is very different from that in Sangatte where there is much more room. The French have their exhibition centre close to the main works which are at the foot of a huge shaft making it safer for spectators. You really can't compare the two.'

The Portakabin museum and a raised platform at the French end of the tunnel offer views of Sangatte, a ribbon of uninteresting red-roofed houses running for two kilometres along the town's one road, a few metres from the sea.

A shaft 60 metres deep and 55 metres wide is seen to herald an era of *tourisme sans frontières* a vision clung to be local residents as the dust and dirt of construction envelop their town.

Wherever two or three Frenchmen are gathered together, one will eventually open a shop. The French were quick to grasp the possibilities for tourism around the tunnel entrance.

The discerning *tunneliste* leaves the exhibition centre equipped with a Eurotunnel brolly (£15), a watch (£19.50), a brooch (£3.50), and a pure silk scarf (£27.50).

Mlle Katie Taylor, whose grandfather came from Dublin, is a bilingual hostess at the exhibition centre and shop.

'We find young people especially are interested in the tunnel and also the old, although they don't really believe it will happen. For many, this is the third tunnel they have seen.'

The centre has attracted 40 coachloads of English schoolchildren. The French visit as well. During the Bastille holiday weekend the souvenir shop took £1700 in two days and this is despite the fact that the French end of the tunnel has advanced only 200 metres compared with 1500 metres in England.

All souvenirs and no action? 'Just a few difficulties with the subsoil,' explained M. Marcel Bernard, of the consortium's construction office in Sangatte.

(500 words approximately)

Eurotunnel – centre d'exposition – foule de visiteurs – dépensé des milliers de francs – contraste avec l'Angleterre – difficultés d'accès à Douvres – chantier de construction – Sangatte a bénéficié – on accueille des visiteurs – des jeunes, des vieux – groupes scolaires anglais – salle d'exposition – observer le travail de construction

WJEC A Level, June 1989

Here are two versions of a summary. You will notice that the jotted notes do not all appear in the final text. The number of words used is not so crucial as in an English-from-French summary.

Possible answers

Summary A

Les Français, en avance sur les Anglais, ont réussi à faire du chantier de construction de l'Eurotunnel, une attraction touristique majeure. Au fond du puits central a été aménagé un centre d'information, avec salle d'exposition et magasin de souvenirs. On a également la possibilité d'observer le travail des tunneliers. Sangatte, ville sans aucun intérêt autrefois pour le touriste, bénéficie d'un afflux de visiteurs. 500 000 touristes ont visité le centre et l'exposition depuis octobre dernier et y ont dépensé des milliers de francs.

Cette réussite en France contraste terriblement avec le chantier de construction en Angleterre qui est situé en bas d'une haute falaise difficile d'accès, où par conséquent le nombre de visiteurs doit être strictement limité. On ne peut qu'espérer que le centre d'exposition actuellement en construction à Folkestone connaîtra le même succès que son homologue français. Les constructeurs anglais sont pourtant en tête par la longueur de leur tunnel: 1500 mètres comparés aux 200 mètres du côté français.

Summary B

Les Français ont transformé un trou en une attraction touristique majeure. On espère que le centre d'exposition Eurotunnel en construction actuelle à Folkestone aura le même succès que son homologue français, qui depuis octobre dernier compte 500 000 visiteurs et un chiffre d'affaires de plusieurs milliers de francs.

Le chantier de construction à Douvres présente un aspect très différent. Placé au pied d'une haute falaise, il est dangereux et difficile d'accès, et de ce fait le nombre de visiteurs est strictement limité.

A Sangatte par contre, il y a beaucoup de place et le centre d'exposition se trouve à proximité du chantier de construction. Sangatte, ville sans grand intérêt, profite de l'afflux de touristes tout comme le magasin de souvenirs du centre d'exposition. Les jeunes et les vieux s'intéressent au tunnel et à sa construction qui, il faut le dire, avance plus rapidement à Douvres — 1500m – qu'à Sangatte: 500m seulement.

Examine, and/or discuss, the merits or defects of these two versions.

Study Techniques

1 Once a week, choose a newspaper article that interests you and write a summary of it in French. Check that your summary is interesting and that it contains all the important information. If possible, find a friend to read your summary and to tell you, in English, what they think the English original was about. It would also be useful, when selecting your article, to bear in mind the interests of the person helping you. If you choose something that they know a lot about, they are bound to ask you questions or want further explanations.

2 Most texts contain 'key sentences'. These often occur at the beginning of a paragraph. They carry the important information and the rest of the paragraph usually amplifies, re-states or gives examples. These key sentences are invaluable for the summary writer. Once a week, choose a text in English or French and underline the key sentences in it. Think what you would need to add, if anything, to make a good summary.

Exercices

1 Croyez-vous à la vie après la mort?

(a) Pour les Hindous, la vie s'écoule à travers plusieurs existences successives, en un flux de naissances, de morts et de renaissances qui élargit l'histoire d'un individu à des milliards d'années. Le lien entre toutes ces vies charnelles successives c'est 'le karma' d'un individu: c'est ce qu'il a fait de sa vie, la somme de chacun de ses actes, bons ou mauvais, de ses pensées, de ses courages et de ses faiblesses, c'est tout ce qui le rapproche ou l'éloigne de la sagesse divine. Tout Hindou espère qu'un jour, sa quête incessante de la connaissance élèvera son karma jusqu'à la fusion avec L'Absolu mettant fin ainsi au cycle de vies successives.

(b) Pour les Bouddhistes, le but des vies successives n'est pas d'élever son moi spirituel (son 'atman') jusqu'à la fusion en Dieu. Il est au contraire de se libérer de ce 'moi' considéré comme une illusion et comme la source de toutes nos souffrances, pour parvenir, par la méditation principalement, au 'nirvana'. Il s'agit d'un état de repos indescriptible, comparé à la lampe éteinte qui ne peut plus transmettre sa flamme car aucun désir, aucune action, aucune passion, ne viennent plus l'alimenter.

(c) Les Chrétiens affirment qu'il y a une vie après la mort: Jésus est mort et a été ressucité au matin de Pâques. De la même façon nous aussi, nous retrouverons la vie après la mort dans un corps spirituel. Nous serons réunis avec Dieu et entrerons dans une lumière ou une lucidité dans sa présence. Grâce à cette proximité avec Dieu, nous pourrons réinterpréter notre passé, positif ou négatif. Nous ne pourrons pas le changer mais nous le réassumerons pour arriver enfin à un état de lucidité amoureuse à la suite de cette opération de lucidité sur soi.

(d) La vie après la mort est au cœur de la foi musulmane et présente dans *le Coran* (livre sacré des musulmans, la parole d'Allah transmise à Mahomet par l'archange Gabriel).
   'Tu vois la terre désertique, mais dès que nous y faisons descendre l'eau, elle remue, elle gonfle, elle fait pousser toutes sortes de belles espèces de plantes. Il en est ainsi parce que Dieu est la vérité, qu'il est celui qui rend la vie aux morts, qu'il est puissant sur toutes choses…et parce que Dieu ressucitera ceux qui se trouvent dans les sépulcres... (*Coran*, sourate XXII, 5 à 7)

Les idées exprimées dans ces quatre résumés en quoi se ressemblent-elles et en quoi diffèrent-elles? Faites votre résumé en anglais ou en français.

3 Paraphrasing and explanation

There are two main skills involved here:

(a) Reworking sentences or phrases used in a text while keeping the same meaning
(b) Explaining in your own words something already stated in a succinct or figurative way.

You may be asked, for example, to rephrase sentences 'keeping the meaning as close as possible to the original'. Sometimes a key word is provided. For example:

(a) *Le gouvernement a d'abord **minimisé** l'affaire*
    *Le gouvernement a d'abord dit que l'affaire **n'était pas très importante***
(b) *Mon grand-père **me réservait** les enveloppes que lui adressaient ses clients*
    *Mon grand-père **me mettait de côté***

There are often other ways of doing the same thing:

Le gouvernement a d'abord dit/soutenu que l'affaire n'avait pas d'importance
Le gouvernement n'a d'abord pas voulu exagérer l'importance de cette affaire

In the second example you could have written:

Mon grand-père me gardait...

You can see that words are either manipulated (e.g. with adjectives becoming nouns) or alternative words/expressions are found. Knowing the opposite of a word can be helpful; the antonym as distinct from the synonym. A monolingual French dictionary is an invaluable aid when working with paraphrase. You will discover synonyms, antonyms and paraphrases in the form of definitions of meanings. Try to build up a repertoire of words whose definitions you can give in French. Go over these each week to make sure you still know them, then learn and add ten more.

Being able to manipulate language in this way is a useful skill that has an application in many of the writing tasks you need for A Level as well as in some of the speaking tasks which require you to do the explaining or persuading.

It is interesting to note that the word 'paraphrase' is defined in a French–French dictionary as *'explication ou commentaire diffus, verbeux, qui ne fait qu'allonger un texte sans l'enrichir'*. In other words, not to be encouraged if you want to develop a good style! *'Reformulez'*, *'transformez'* or *'trouvez un synonyme'* are closer to the English meaning. Which of the 'paraphrases' above are closer to the idea of 'reformulation'?

Being able to explain in your own words in French is like being able to think in French. It is a skill that becomes important when you try to explain to a French person some aspect of your way of life that is similar but not quite the same as theirs.

A good way into paraphrase, or explaining in French, occurs in class when words in a text you are studying are explained, in French, by the teacher rather than just translated. You can encourage this process by asking for meanings in French:

Je ne comprend pas le mot/l'expression ____
Qu'est-ce que cela veut dire?
Quelle est la signification du mot ...?

Encouraging the reverse process can also be helpful (i.e. getting you to explain simple meanings in French). Listening to someone else explaining and trying it yourself are the two processes involved. Using a monolingual dictionary is a good substitute for the first process. You will find ready-made definitions of words in rather terse and precise language. Nevertheless, by using a French–French dictionary either instead of, or in conjunction with, a bilingual one, you will greatly increase your vocabulary and ability to manipulate words.

Study skill

Work with a friend for a few minutes whenever you can. Take a short paragraph from a French newspaper and together see how many ways you can find of varying each sentence.

The following exercises are examples of other activities you and your friends can do together to help you to learn the kind of language you need for this sort of work. Using a monolingual French dictionary, you can make up many other similar puzzles for each other. You will learn equally from making up the puzzles and from doing them.

Exercices

1   Trouvez dans les propositions ci-après une définition qui correspond à un des mots (page 127).
    Attention! Il y a plus de mots que de définitions:

épicier – supermarché – pharmacien – self-service – pharmacie – hypermarché – lycée – instituteur – mineur – collège d' enseignement secondaire – marin – instituteur – école

(a) Grande surface qui vend des produits alimentaires en libre service
(b) Établissement scolaire pour les élèves de 15 à 18 ans
(c) Grande surface proposant une grande variété de produits en libre service
(d) Personne qui enseigne dans une école primaire
(e) Jeune personne qui n'a pas encore atteint l'âge de 18 ans
(f) Membre du personnel d'un navire
(g) Ouvrier qui travaille dans une mine

2 Trouvez un mot anglais et un mot français qui correspondent aux définitions suivantes:
(a) Personne qui tue un être humain avec préméditation
(b) Personne qui pénètre dans une maison pour voler
(c) Pièce de métal frappée et donnée souvent comme distinction honorifique
(d) Dire à quelqu'un des paroles injurieuses
(e) Répandre des matières toxiques dans la nature
(f) Opinion exprimée par chaque personne participant à une élection
(g) Esprit d'un mort qu'on suppose revenir d'un autre monde
(h) Manque presque total de produits alimentaires dans un pays
(i) Cercle imaginaire tracé autour de la terre à mi-distance des pôles
(j) Situation à laquelle on ne trouve pas d'issue

3 Expliquez en français la différence entre:
(a) Un professeur et un instituteur
(b) Un voleur et un meurtrier
(c) Un fleuve et une rivière
(e) Le football et le rugby
(f) Une église et une cathédrale
(g) Un dentiste et un médecin
(h) Un café et un restaurant
(i) Une librairie et une bibliothèque
(j) Une chemise et un chemisier
(k) La margarine et le beurre

4 Groupez chacun des mots suivants avec son opposé:
accepter – avouer – agréable – facile – privé – humide – nier – construire – parler – désagréable – se taire – refuser – détruire – difficile – trouver – libérer – public – emprisonner – augmenter – chuchoter – perdre – absence – artificiel – arriver – présence – diminuer – partir – naturel – sec – crier

5 Expliquez à une Française ou à un Français ce que veulent dire les expressions et sigles suivants:
(a) **MOT** (devant un garage)
(b) **PYO strawberries** (devant une ferme)
(c) **PLOUGHMAN'S — CHEDDAR or STILTON £2.20** (devant un pub)
(d) **UFO SEEN OVER SLOUGH** (dans un journal)
(e) **VAT** (sur une facture)
(f) **EARLY CLOSING WEDNESDAYS** (devant une boutique)
(g) **BEST-KEPT VILLAGE 1991** (à l'entrée d'un village)

6 Lisez le texte suivant:

DES LUMIÈRES MYSTÉRIEUSES AU-DESSUS DE LA MER

Hier soir vers 22 heures, de nombreux témoins ont observé pendant un bon quart d'heure des lumières mystérieuses qui sont apparues à la surface de la mer et se sont élevées dans l'air. Elles ont manœuvré comme pour faire plaisir aux spectateurs puis ont plané au-dessus de la plage. Parmi les témoins se trouvait René Poulain, pilote d'essai chez Aviex. Lui reste confondu. 'L'absence de tout bruit,' a-t-il déclaré à notre correspondant, 'me fait croire qu'il ne s'agit ni d'avions ni d'hélicoptères. Des ballons météorologiques ne pourraient pas faire des manœuvres aussi compliquées. Je ne trouve aucune explication à ce phénomène.' Monsieur Courtain, maire de Lacanuet, a ajouté, ' Ce n'est pas la première fois que l'on observe d'étranges lumières ou des soucoupes volantes dans cette région. Depuis des années, nous avons en moyenne un témoignage par mois en été et deux ou trois par mois en hiver. Personnellement je ne prends pas l'affaire trop au sérieux. Il doit y avoir une explication naturelle. Je ne vais pas me plaindre quand même, cela attire les touristes et notre petite ville devient célèbre.'

(a) Le sigle couramment employé pour ce genre de phénomène est OVNI. Que veut dire cette abbréviation?

(b) Trouvez dans le texte les expressions qui correspondent aux paraphrases suivantes. Elles ne sont pas dans le même ordre que dans le texte:

il reste perplexe – elles ont fait des mouvements – je n'arrive pas à expliquer – ça fait plusieurs années – il n'est pas question – ont flotté dans l'air – pour ma part – pour amuser ceux qui regardaient – c'est une attraction touristique – le silence absolu

7 Lisez le texte suivant:

LES DAMES DU CRIME

Agatha Christie aurait eu cent ans le mois prochain. La 'duchesse du crime' a fait école, découvrez avec nous les petites nouvelles. D'autant qu'il n'y a pas meilleur cocktail que vacances, soleil et roman policier.

Agatha Christie, Phyllis Dorothy James, Mary Higgins Clark, Laurence Oriol… ces dames ont choisi de faire bouillir la marmite en mijotant de bons petits crimes que nous vous invitons à dévorer.

Drôle de genre pour une femme, pouvait-on penser dans les années vingt, lorsque Agatha Christie publia son premier roman policier *La mystérieuse affaire des styles*. Mais depuis qu'Hercule Poirot et Miss Marple, ses détectives vedettes, mènent l'enquête pas mal de romanciers ont trempé dans le crime, lui offrant une dimension toute féminine, le policier intimiste. Le crime est commis entre gens de bonne compagnie, qui se révèlent, en trois chapitres, être sans exception des modèles d'hypocrisie. L'intérêt de ce huis-clos criminel c'est que le lecteur dispose des mêmes éléments que le détective pour démasquer le coupable.

(a) Ce passage contient plusieurs phrases ou expressions au sens figuratif. Voici un commentaire numéroté présenté sous forme d'explication. Relisez le texte avec l'aide de celle-ci plutôt que d'employer un dictionnaire.
  (i) *Les dames du crime* – les femmes, auteurs célèbres qui écrivent des romans policiers
  (ii) *aurait eu cent ans* – c'est parce qu'elle est déjà morte
  (iii) *duchesse du crime* – elle s'est fait une réputation comme femme qui écrit des romans policiers
  (iv) *elle a fait école* – plusieurs romancières ont suivi son exemple avec grand succès
  (v) *meilleur cocktail* – un mélange agréable de trois ingrédients: le temps libre, le soleil, et la lecture d'un roman policier
  (vi) *faire bouillir la marmite en mijotant de bons petits crimes – dévorer.*
      une métaphore tirée de l'art de la cuisine: un crime qui se révèle lentement dans un récit délicieux à savourer
  (vii) *Drôle de genre pour une femme* – un choix bizarre pour une femme écrivain
  (viii) *détectives vedettes* – détectives renommés qui figurent comme héros dans plusieurs romans
  (ix) *ont trempé dans le crime* – ont 'participé' au crime
  (x) *huis clos* – monde privé et caché de la criminalité (*un tribunal à huis clos* – où le public n'est pas admis)

(b) Dans l'exercice suivant trouvez la phrase anglaise dont le sens, à votre avis, correspond le mieux au français. Il ne s'agit pas nécessairement d'une traduction fidèle. Vous pouvez adapter ou changer les traductions si bon vous semble:
  (i) female crime writers – great lady crime writers – feminine writers of crime
  (ii) would be a hundred – could have been a hundred – would have been a hundred
  (iii) queen of crime – duchess of crime – grand old lady of crime
  (iv) created a reputation – started a new trend in writing – set a precedent for other women writers
  (v) (for the good reason that there is no better) mixture – combination – cocktail
  (vi) slow cooking of delicious crimes – delicious aroma of slowly cooked crimes – crime that bubbles slowly and deliciously away
  (vii) a funny occupation for a woman – funny kind of writing for a woman –an odd choice of subject for a woman writer
  (viii) star detectives – detective heros – hero detectives
  (ix) become involved in crime – got mixed up in crime – have become absorbed in crime
  (x) private criminal world – hidden society of the criminal – secret world of crime

4 Gap-filling tasks: cloze tests

These tasks are used by some Examining Boards as part of the written paper. They can take two forms:

(a) filling in gaps in a short text with no clues to the missing words
(b) filling in gaps using a list of possibilities, some of which are not appropriate
    (i.e. the number of words exceeds the number of gaps)

When we read a text, or listen to speech, we do not give full attention to every word printed or spoken. Instead, we take it for granted that certain words will occur in certain places. It's a bit like listening to football results when you can predict whether the second mentioned team has won, lost or drawn from the intonation of the announcer's voice. In a printed text, several things affect our expectation of what is coming next:

(a) the general content of the passage
(b) the meaning of what has come before
(c) the sense of what follows
(d) the grammatical rules governing words and their endings.

You should be able to guess many words missing from a French text. Try filling in the gaps in the following cloze tests:

Model answers

1   **L'AVENTURE EN AMÉRIQUE**

C'est Christophe Colomb qui a (i) ____ l'Amérique; depuis, beaucoup de gens y sont (ii) ____ pour chercher l'aventure. Le premier homme qui a (iii) ____ sur la lune (iv) ____ américain. En Amérique tout est tellement plus (v) ____ que chez nous! Même les champs (vi) ____ immenses et pour récolter le blé il (vii) ____ des douzaines de moissonneuses-batteuses*, les unes à côté des autres. Maman m'a (viii) ____ des photos. C' (ix)____impressionnant. C'est vraiment le pays de (x)____.

* de grandes machines qui coupent le blé, en détachent le grain et laissent derrière elles de grands paquets de paille.

Possible answers

  (i)   *découvert* – part of a compound tense is missing, so a past participle is needed
 (ii)   *allés* – fits here, though *partis* would also: same grammatical reason
(iii)   *marché* – fits the context but *mis le pied* would also fit: same reason
 (iv)   *était* – fits the sense: verb missing, a past tense required
  (v)   *grand*: – adjective is missing: meaning of the following sentence gives the best clue
 (vi)   *sont* – verb missing, subject is plural
(vii)   *faut* – ' are necessary', 'are needed' fits the sense: *il* doesn't refer to anything else in the sentence and so is impersonal
(viii) *montré* – fits the sense: perfect tense, so a past participle is missing
 (ix)   *est* – fits the sense: verb missing
  (x)   *l'aventure* – though other words could also make sense: more difficult, a noun (used as an adjective with *de*)

You will see from this exercise that two things are important:
1 Understanding the meaning of the words surrounding the missing ones
2 Reading the grammatical clues that tell you:
    (a) What part of speech is required (verb – pronoun – adjective – noun etc.)
    (b) The tense or the part of the verb needed
    (c) What the subject is to get the agreement right

2 Essayez maintenant le même exercice avec le passage suivant en vous servant de la liste ci-dessous. Attention! il y a plus de mots qu'il ne faut. Ce sont ici les verbes qui manquent.

LES SERVICES PUBLICS

Dans chaque ville des équipes (i) ____ du confort et de l'hygiène des habitants. Ils (ii) ____ partie des *Services publics*. Tous les jours nous (iii)____ — de leur travail. Par exemple, ce matin, c'est grâce aux PTT que j' (iv) ____ une carte postale de tante Marie qui (v) ____ en Afrique. J' (vi) ____ très content et j' (vii) ____ beaucoup le facteur. Tous les jours aussi j' (viii)____ les employés de la voirie qui (ix) ____ les rues et (xi) ____les poubelles. Sans eux la ville (xi) ____ dégoûtante.

*a reçu – s'occupe – font – bénéficient – fait – ai reçu – nettoyons –
êtes – est – ai remercié – avons remercié – aperçu – nettoient – ai été – a été – serait – s'occupent–
bénéficions – aperçois – vident*

It is a good plan to cross off the words as you find a place for them. But you may find that having narrowed down the field the words left don't fit very well. This usually means that you have crossed off wrong ones earlier, so you need to go back over them.

Possible answers

This text illustrates how grammatical points are tested in this language task:

(i)   This requires a third person plural. Match the ending **and** the meaning
(ii) This is same part of the verb; *fait* won't fit;
(iii) *nous* tells you that you need a verb ending in *-ons*. Find one where the meaning fits in with the following *de* (e.g. 'benefit **from** their work')
(iv) *j'* shows a first person singular verb but which tense is suggested by *ce matin?*
(v)   *Tante Marie* is the subject, and is third person singular
(vi) This is the first person singular, what is the tense?
(vii) The sense requires a perfect tense, which first person singular verb fits the sense?
(viii) This is in the first person singular. What is the tense?
(ix) This is the third person plural. Which of the remaining verbs would fit the sense?
(x)   This is also in the third person plural. Which of the remaining verbs would fit the sense?
(xi) Which word would fit the meaning in English? 'Without them the town ____'

Note

You can see from model answer 2 that the extra words are put in for drawing a logical and usually a **grammatical** conclusion. In multiple-choice tests these are called distractors. So, don't write down the first word that catches your eye and looks as though it fits. Ask yourself the following questions:

1 Do I need a verb, noun, adjective, pronoun, preposition in this gap? If you then look at the available words, you should be able to narrow down your search.
2 If a verb, is it an infinitive? (e.g. after a preposition or the second verb in the clause).
3 If not an infinitive what is the subject of the verb? (e.g. If it's *vous* you will need a word ending in *-ez*).
4 Next check the tense. Does it fit the other tenses in the sentence and the meaning needed?
5 Is a subjunctive needed? (e.g. following another verb like *il faut que* or after a conjunction like *bien que* or *quoique*).
6 If it's a noun, check on its meaning in the sentence. If there are a few nouns to choose from, try eliminating those that don't fit the meaning.
7 If it's an adjective, check that the ending and the meaning fit.
8 Take particular care with the relative pronouns *qui, que,* and *qu'.* because subject and verb are frequently reversed in French. For example: *Les lettres que mon père écrivait* can also be expressed as *Les lettres qu'écrivait mon père*. So a gapped phrase like: *Le programme ____ suivaient les enfants*, with a choice of *qui* or *que* in the list, must have *que* in the gap (*see also* grammar section, page 63).

By applying this system to the list of spare words for the gaps you can gradually eliminate the possibilities. If you tackle cloze tests systematically in this way they become like crossword puzzles!

3   For this question no words are given and only **one** word fits:

POUR UNE FRANCE PROPRE

A peine rentré des vacances, je ____ peux m'empêcher de vous faire parvenir ____ impressions sur le voyage que j'____ accompli en compagnie de mon oncle polonais ____ travers la France. De même l'____ dernier, nous nous étions rendus en compagnie ____ amis allemands sur l'île d'Oléron ____ nous avions visitée en détail. Le jugement ____ étrangers se résume à ceci: 'Ah ____ la France serait belle si elle ____ plus propre!' Eh oui, il faut ____ reconnaître: que l'on visite Paris, ____ capitale, et toutes les villes de la France, ____ arrive toujours à la même constatation: partout ____ les trottoirs on ne rencontre ____ des papiers. J'ai passé tout cet ____ à Nancy, j'ai constaté devant l'____ de bus de point central un amas ____ papiers de toutes sortes. ____ situation se retrouve partout en ____ .

Scottish Higher, specimen question paper, 1987

Answer plan

These are the points of grammar being tested in the passage:

(i)   Verbs: perfect tense, imperfect tense

(ii) Pronouns: object pronoun *le*, relative *que*, subject pronoun *on*
(iii) Prepositions: *à, sur*
(iv) Adjectives: possessive *mes*
(v) Negatives: *ne, ne que* – only
(vi) Articles: definite/gender, partitive *de, des*, exclamative *que!* (how...!)
(vii) Nouns: (four)

4
UN PORTAIT EXPRESS DE BILLY IDOL

Billy Idol est (i) ____ le 30 septembre 1957 (ii)____Angleterre. Son père, employé (iii)____ banque, voulut que son fils suive le (iv)____ chemin. Mais Billy Idol (v)____ pensait qu'à la (vi)____ et spécialement à la punk. Pour ne (vii)____ entrer en conflit avec sa famille, il quitte (viii)____parents et fonde avec trois (ix)____ le groupe *Generation X* qui (x)____ l'un des groupes punk les plus (xi)____ en Angleterre. En 1981, il quitte Londres (xii) ____ New York. Très (xiii)____, il se retrouve avec ses titres en tête (xiv)____ charts américains et se (xv)____ connaître grâce à ses shows vidéo. Mais ce n'est que plus (xvi)____ qu'on reconnaîtra son talent de musicien.

    (xvii)____ est surtout avec la tournée *Rebel Yell* (xviii)____Billy devient populaire. Aujourd'hui, Billy a décidé de s'établir définitivement (xix)____ Etats-Unis et vit à Greenwich Village, le (xx)____ des artistes de New York.

Scottish Higher (Revised) 1991

Answer plan

The above task requires understanding the text as well as grammatical skills. Here are some notes on each of the blanks:
   (i) 'born' must fit here
   (ii) 'in': which word comes before countries ending in an 'e'?
  (iii) How can you make a noun work like an adjective?
  (iv) 'wanted his son to follow the ____ path'
   (v) Which word goes with the *'qu'* before the verb?
  (vi) He only thought about one thing — which word fits?
 (vii) What goes with *'ne'* before an infinitive?
(viii) 'his' parents (plural!)
  (ix) With three what? Read the rest of the sentence
   (x) 'becomes'
  (xi) 'the most famous'
 (xii) 'for New York'
(xiii) 'quickly' fits the sense
 (xiv) 'of the'
  (xv) 'gets known' (e.g. 'makes himself known')
 (xvi) 'later'
(xvii) and (xviii) you need to consider both gaps here 'it is only that'
 (xix) 'in' before a masculine plural country?
  (xx) 'centre' fits

Exercices

1 (a)   Essayez de combler les blancs dans le passage suivant sans l'aide d'une liste de mots.

QUE FAIRE EN CAS D'INCENDIE

- **Si vous pouvez vous enfuir**
- **Coupez le gaz**
Dès que vous avez____ qu'un ____ se développe dans ____ où vous ____, fermez immédiatement le ____d'arrêt du ____ au compteur, ou ____ de la bouteille si vous n'avez pas le gaz de ville.

    En effet le____ est certainement une des ____ principales du développement et de la propagation des incendies urbains.

- **Fermez votre porte**
Avant de quitter votre ____, fermez-en soigneusement toute les ____ et les ____, y compris, bien sûr, la porte____, que vous verrouillerez* avec soin pour isoler le mieux possible votre logis.

    N'____ surtout pas de ____ sur vous les ____, car les sauveteurs pourraient en avoir besoin et vous les ____.

    Enfin, il est bon de rappeler ici que vous ne____ jamais, en aucun cas, regagner votre habitation sans la ____ expresse des ____, qui seuls peuvent apprécier le danger et les risques d'un réveil de l'incendie.

* Means literally bolt but it is always used to mean 'lock'; *mettre le verrou* means specifically 'to bolt'

(b) Le passage suivant a été pris dans une autre partie de l'article d'où est tiré le texte précédent. Sans recopier le texte faites une liste des mots qui manquent. Attention! Vous ne les utiliserez pas tous.

SI VOUS NE POUVEZ VOUS ENFUIR

● **Enfermez-vous**

(i) ____ que vous avez constaté que la sortie est (ii)____ et (iii)____vous ne pouvez fuir par (iv)____ issue, fermez votre porte et songez immédiatement à la (v)____. En effet, c'est (vi)____ et de sa résistance au feu (vii)____ dépend votre salut. Ne cherchez surtout pas à vous engager à tout prix: ce (viii)____ un véritable suicide. Agressé par les flammes, aveuglé et asphyxié par les fumées (ix) ____ et les gaz chauds, (x)____ peuvent également vous brûler les poumons, vous (xi)____ en quelques instants.

coupée – que – protéger – succomberiez – serait – aucune – qui – toxiques –que – dès – sera – de lui – sera – d'elle – succombez – coûtée – qui protège

2   Même exercice avec ce récit d'un hold-up à Bastia, en Corse:

HOLD-UP

Bastia Deux malfaiteurs, qui (i)____ de commettre un hold-up dans un hypermarché de Borgo, à une vingtaine de kilomètres au sud de Bastia, ont (ii) ____ à échapper samedi aux gendarmes qui les (iii) ____ en semant sur la chaussée des billets de banque qui ont (iv) ____ un important embouteillage. Vers 16 heures, deux individus armés de fusil à pompe et (v) ____ les visages étaient (vi) ____ sous des cagoules, ont (vii)____ irruption à l'intérieur de l'hypermarché 'Corsaire' de la RN 193, et se sont fait remettre une importante somme d'argent avant de (viii) ____la fuite sur une moto en direction du sud. Très rapidement (ix) ____ en chasse par une voiture de la gendarmerie, les malfaiteurs n'ont rien (x)____ de mieux pour (xi) ____ de leurs poursuivants que de répandre derrière eux une pluie de billets. De nombreux (xii) ____ garaient à la hâte leurs voitures pour faire main basse sur cette manne* inespérée et pris dans un important embouteillage, les gendarmes (xiii)____ abandonner leur poursuite.

* manne – la nourriture miraculeuse que Dieu a envoyée du ciel aux Israélites dans le désert.

provoqué – réussi – venaient – suivait –fit – réussir – dissimulés – prendre – trouvait –pris – trouvé – piétons – fallait – dissimulaient – poursuivaient – venait – fait – que – devaient – automobilistes – dont – se débarrasser – perdre

3   Faites cet exercice sans une liste de mots qui manquent:

ASSURANCES MOINS CHÈRES POUR LES FEMMES:

Elles ____plus prudentes au volant que les hommes, et ____ moins d'accidents — les chiffres le ____ . Le groupe Azur____ donc aux conductrices de moyennes cylindrées ____ont leur permis depuis plus de trois ans, des tarifs réduits (de 15 à 25% inférieurs aux tarifs habituels) Pour tout ____ et obtenir gratuitement un devis personnalisé,____ 01 23 49 35.

4   Attention! il y a plus de mots dans la liste que de blancs:
(a)

JEUNES

Selon l'INSEE, 90,3% des 15-19 ans ____chez leurs parents. 9,5% d'entre eux____dans leur propre appartement, et une infime minorité (seulement 0,2%) _____en couple. La majorité des jeunes gens ne____ le domicile familial avant 23 ans, âge qui ne ____ de reculer avec le temps. Les jeunes filles, quant à elles ____ leur envol vers 22 ans, plus tôt que les garçons.

finit – sortent – vit – habitent – commence – cesse – finissent – prend – habitent – prennent – vivent – quitte – quittent

(b)

SOS ANIMAUX

Plusieurs milliers de chiens et de chats ____ de leur maison chaque année. La Société protectrice des animaux____à les ____. Un ordinateur____ tous les renseignements concernant l'animal et ____de recouper les données ____par son maître. Même les animaux non-tatoués ____concernés par ce service. 70% des chiens____ auraient ainsi été____

retournent – aide – échappent – sont – enregistre – fournies – permet – permettent – récupérés – égarés – égaré – retrouver

5 Sans liste!

> **Correspondance** Minicom ____un nouveau service de France Telecom qui ____ de s'écrire comme on se ____. Par le 36, 12 vous ____envoyer un message de ____lignes ou de ____pages à un ou plusieurs____ Leur lecture ____ protégée par un ____ de passe confidentiel. Il est tout de même nécessaire de s'inscrire sur le Minicom, et le____ de l'envoi n'est____ de 0,98 F la minute.

Study techniques

1   Ask a friend or relation to choose an article at random from a French newspaper. Make two photocopies; on one copy remove every tenth word with correcting fluid. You then will have a text to work on and one to check your version. You could make it harder by having every ninth word removed! If more than every seventh word is taken out it is usually impossible — even for French people! You could also get someone to photocopy an article so that the last 2 or 3 letters on the end of each line are missing. This is not quite the same format as a cloze test but simulates what you sometimes have to do in reality.
2   Find someone to work with and make up cloze tests for each other, using newspaper and magazine articles which you think might interest each other.
3   You could also make up cloze tests with extracts from set texts. If you choose key passages, this will really help you to get to know them and you can kill two birds with one stone.
4   Word processors are very useful for producing cloze tests!

5   Reading and writing tasks

The following questions have been devised to practise many of the language tasks required by each Examining Board.

Exercices

1 Lisez et interprétez les gros titres ci-dessous:

Le meurtrier d'un pompiste arrêté: son meilleur ami

Valise diplomatique dans le Boeing détourné sur l'Iran

Les faux policiers cambriolaient les vieilles dames

A Lyon l'ex-religieuse est accusée d'avoir détourné 900 000 francs

Réclusion à perpétuité pour l'auto-stoppeur assassin

Afflux de lettres piégées à Dublin

Deux jeunes gens tués par la drogue à Nice

Le chantage à la bombe contre 'Buckingham Palace'

Hold-up à la poste

Un incendie de trop pour le pompier pyromane

Grenades lacrymogènes au consulat italien

Assassin de sa grande-mère, on l'arrête trois jours après son crime

Métro incendié: une bouteille de gaz retrouvée sur la voie près de la porte de Vincennes

Vol de voiture à main armée

Vingt-deux tableaux dérobés dans un magasin-exposition

Sabotage sur la voie ferrée près de Montpellier

(b) Trouvez la traduction du titre à la page 133

 (i) Two young people die from drugs in Nice
 (ii) Petrol pump murderer arrested: his best friend
 (iii) Fire in the Metro: bottle of gas found on line near the Porte de Vincennes
 (iv) Man arrested three days after murdering his grandmother
 (v) One fire too many for the fireman arsonist
 (vi) Former nun accused in Lyon of misappropriating 900 000F
 (vii) Armed theft of car
 (viii) Hold-up in post office
 (ix) Men dressed as police burgled old ladies
 (x) Tear grenades in the Italian Consulate.
 (xi) US diplomatic bag in Boeing hijacked over Iran
 (xii) Hitchhiker murderer gets life
 (xiii) Spate of booby-trap letters in Dublin.
 (xiv) Twenty-two paintings stolen from store exhibition
 (xv) Sabotage on rail-line near Montpellier
 (xvi) Bomb blackmail attempt on Buckingham Palace

(c) Après avoir fait ce travail, que veulent dire les mots et les phrases suivants:
 (i) un meurtrier
 (ii) cambrioler
 (iii) le chantage
 (iv) tués
 (v) une religieuse
 (vi) un vol
 (vii) un incendie
 (viii) la voie ferrée
 (ix) un piège
 (x) un pompier
 (xi) un pompiste
 (xii) détourner un avion
 (xiii) détourner de l'argent
 (xiv) réclusion à perpétuité
 (xv) arrêté
 (xvi) faux policiers

(d) Traduisez ces titres en anglais:
 (i) Hold-up à la poste par un pompier
 (ii) Il cambriolait son meilleur ami
 (iii) Avion détourné par une grande-mère
 (iv) Valise diplomatique volée par une religieuse
 (v) Policier tué par un pompiste
 (vi) Diplomate arrêté avec la drogue
 (vii) Grenades lacrymogènes saisies à la poste
 (viii) Vieilles dames pyromanes arrêtées avec des bouteilles de gaz devant le consulat
 (ix) Tué par une valise diplomatique tombée d'un avion
 (x) Chantage d'un pompier par une grande-mère

(e) Traduisez ces titres en français:
 (i) Killed by his best friend
 (ii) Air France plane hijacked over London
 (iii) Tear grenades seized after hold-up
 (iv) Robbery at the consulate
 (v) Life for murderer of petrol-pump attendant
 (vi) Fireman arrested with stolen tapestries
 (vii) Booby-trap briefcase in post office
 (viii) Former nun blackmails diplomat
 (ix) Man posing as policeman steals diplomatic bag
 (x) Grandmothers burgle fireman's house
 (xi) Former policeman misappropriates best friend's money
 (xii) Bogus nun holds up post office
 (xiii) Murdered by ex-policeman: his best friend

(f) Try making up your own headlines, say three in English and three in French, and pass them to a partner for translating.

2 Lisez trois ou quatre fois l'article ci-dessous avant d'aborder les exercices:

Michel Leclerc l'a annoncé hier:

Une crèche bilingue, dès septembre, à Coulogne...

On en avait déjà entendu parler... Mais pas encore sur le ton péremptoire dont usa, hier Michel Leclerc, le promoteur de l'opération: une crèche bilingue sera ouverte dès le mois de septembre, à Coulogne, par l'association Eurobaby.

La nouvelle s'accompagne de plusieurs indications. En premier lieu, la crèche coulonnoise ne sera pas unique en son genre puisque Michel Leclerc annonça cinq ouvertures pour le mois de septembre, à Nice (deux), à Bordeaux, dans la réserve animalière de Thoiry et bien entendu à Coulogne.

Ces cinq crèches pourront accueillir 300 jeunes enfants au total qui pourront commencer à apprendre l'anglais, l'italien, l'espagnol et l'allemand.

Chaque crèche de 60 enfants, répartis en quatre ou cinq classes comprendra cinq moniteurs français et cinq autres ne parlant que les langues en question. Par des jeux et diverses animations, ces derniers devront amener les enfants à s'exprimer dans l'une des quatre langues 'européennes', en plus du français.

Lancée par M. Leclerc, l'association Eurobaby envisage de mettre sur pied, d'ici 1995, dans l'ensemble de la France 1000 crèches de ce type pouvant recevoir 60 000 enfants de un à six ans et employant 10 000 moniteurs dont une moitié de français et l'autre d'étrangers. Ces crèches seront gérées directement par des particuliers ou des associations avec le soutien et sous la surveillance d'Eurobaby. M. Leclerc souhaite que '30% à 50% des Français soient bilingues d'ici vingt ans' et prévoit 'd'ajouter le chinois et le russe' aux langues étrangères déjà programmées pour ces crèches. La contribution des parents, compte tenu de leurs revenus, devrait être en moyenne de 1800 francs par mois

Une des premières crèches bilingues sera donc coulonnoise ... Ou plutôt serait. Personne encore, à Coulogne ne put nous confirmer cette décision. 'Nous l'avons apprise par les médias, nous dit M. Dubut, adjoint au maire, M. Béharelle, étant en vacances actuellement. Rien n'est entériné sur le plan municipal...'

Cela dit, les Coulonnois ne semblent pas se liguer contre une telle décision... 'Nous sommes ni pour ni contre, dit encore M. Dubut. Le tout est de savoir si c'est vraiment intéressant...'

Notez Coulogne se trouve dans la banlieue de Calais

(a) Questions en anglais:
    (i) What do we know from the article about M. Leclerc?
    (ii) What does the 'Eurobaby' organization hope to achieve by the end of September?
    (iii) What are its long-term ambitions?
    (iv) How will work in the five crèches be organized?
    (v) What do M. Beharelle and M. Dubut think of the project?
    (vi) Who will be responsible for running individual crèches?

(b) Explication en français –
    (i) Expliquez en vos propres termes en français:
        une crèche – être bilingue – sur un ton péremptoire – un moniteur – la crèche coulonnoise ne sera pas unique – un adjoint au maire
    (ii) Pourquoi dans l'avant-dernier paragraphe écrit-on '...**serait** coulonnoise'?

(c) Questions en français:
    (i) Comment les enfants vont-ils apprendre à parler les langues en question?
    (ii) Quels détails sont donnés sur le financement du projet?
    (iii) A votre avis, est-ce que les sommes mentionnées seront suffisantes pour rémunérer le personnel.
    (iv) Que veut dire, à votre avis, le mot 'intéressant' employé au dernier paragraphe par M. Dubut?
    (v) Quelles difficultés pourriez-vous envisager pour la mise en place de ces crèches et leur personnel?
    (vi) Un Français veut se renseigner sur les écoles maternelles en Angleterre. Quelles informations pourriez-vous lui donner?
    (vii) Mettez-vous à la place d'un parent français désirant envoyer son enfant à une de ces crèches et formulez cinq questions que vous voudriez poser à M. Leclerc.

(d) Vocabulaire –

(i) Trouvez dans le texte l'équivalent des phrases suivantes:
ne sera pas la seule – en somme – dont s'est servi – distribués – se faire comprendre – désire

(ii) Faites une liste de mots dans le texte se terminant en *'-tion'*. Trouvez dans votre tête encore une douzaine de mots avec cette terminaison.

(iii) Arrangez par ordre de mérite les phrases suivantes:
Elle parle couramment le français – Elle se fait comprendre en français – Elle se débrouille en français – Elle maîtrise le français – Elle a quelques connaissances en français

3 Dans le passage suivant, une mère décrit une période difficile dans la vie d'une d'entre ses filles, Alberte. Celle-ci a commencé à voler des sommes d'argent dans la maison. Françoise, la mère, tâche d'abord de faire voir à sa fille le mal qu'elle a fait, mais sans succès. Vous allez découvrir ce qui arrive à la fin.

Alberte a traversé une période difficile. Rétive, paresseuse, elle qui ne l'a jamais été, s'est mise à dérober de petites sommes, tantôt dans mes poches, tantôt dans celles de Dolorès, puis dans le sac d'une épisodique femme de ménage. Cela finit par prendre des proportions inquiétantes: des billets de mille francs disparaissent. En même temps nous apprenons qu'elle arrive régulièrement en retard à l'école, où elle se fait conduire par des agents de police qui lui servent d'alibi et auxquels elle soutient qu'elles s'est égarée. (Elle traverse Paris en tous sens sans jamais se perdre.)

Notre inquiétude grandit. Je raisonne la coupable.

'Voyons, essaie de comprendre; Christina, elle gagne cinq cents francs par heure, quand elle fait des ménages. Tu te rends compte que quand tu lui prends mille francs, tu lui voles deux heures de son travail!'

'Oui, mais tu l'a remboursée', dit-elle, butée.

'Je l'ai remboursée avec de l'argent qui représente mon travail à moi. Tu ne peux pas sortir de là.'

'Oui, mais c'est quand même plus juste...'

'Quoi?'

'Que tu me donnes ton travail à toi...'

'Que je te le donne, oui, que tu me le voles, non.'

'Est-ce que l'argent, c'est toujours du travail? Il y a des gens qui en ont et qui ne font rien.'

'Alors c'est ce qu'on appelle un capital, c'est l'argent qui travaille pour eux, quand il est placé. Mais c'est trop long à expliquer.'

'Oh! Je comprends bien!' dit-elle, le visage illuminé de malice. 'C'est ces gens-là qu'il faudrait voler, hein?'

Je ne trouve pas de réponse. Inculquer à un enfant le respect du capital ne me semble pas besogne exaltante; par ailleurs, transformer ma fille en un Mandarin en jupons.... J'en suis à demander s'il faut consulter un psychologue, un psychanalyste même, quand brusquement, le remords ayant fait son œuvre (de quelle façon mystérieuse?) Alberte manifeste tout à coup, un matin, après cinq semaines de cynisme, une violente contrition, 'Je ne volerai plus, je ne volerai plus jamais!' et dépose sur mes genoux le fruit de ses rapines. Un reste de monnaie, une quantité invraisemblable de paquets de bonbons à moitié vides, biscuits et chocolats à demi rongés, un papillon artificiel en plastique, des boucles d'oreilles également en plastique, un singe mécanique qui bat du tambour, une boîte d'aquarelle, une trousse d'école en faux crocodile, et j'en passe. Que faire d'autre que de la consoler, la féliciter, prononcer un petit discours moral sur la force de la conscience (Caïn!) qui me fait rougir un peu, mais qu'Alberte approuve gravement.

Françoise Mallet-Joris *La Maison de Papier*

Quelques expressions:

rétif /rétive – une personne rétive est quelqu'un difficile à persuader ou à diriger

un mandarin en jupons – une fille ou une femme qui fait le rôle d'un bandit en volant l'argent des autres

(a) Questions en anglais:

(i) Where did Alberte steal from?

(ii) Why did she get the police to take her to school?

(iii) Why is her mother amazed at her explanation?

(iv) How does the mother try to convince her daughter that stealing from Christina is wrong?

(v) What two kinds of money are referred to eventually and why is the mother lost for an answer?

    (vi)   Why does Alberte suddenly change her ways?

    (vii) Judging from the things bought by Alberte with the stolen money, what age do you think she is?

(b) **Expliquez en français** Expliquez en vos propres termes en français ce que veulent dire les expressions suivantes:

    (i)   une épisodique femme de ménage
    (ii)   qui lui servent d'alibi
    (iii)   le fruit de ses rapines
    (iv)   je raisonne la coupable
    (v)   inculquer à un enfant
    (vi)   tu ne peux pas sortir de là

(c) Questions en français:

    (i)   A votre avis, pourquoi est-ce qu' Alberte n'avait mangé que la moitié des chocolats et des biscuits qu'elle avait achetés?

    (ii)   Pourquoi la mère rougit-elle un peu en parlant à sa fille après sa confession?

    (iii)   Expliquez la référence à Caïn.

(d) Choisissez la traduction anglaise la plus convenable des phrases suivantes:

    (i)   *Alberte a traversé une période difficile*
        ● It has been a difficult time for Alberte
        ● Alberte has traversed a difficult period
        ● Alberte has been through a difficult time.

    (ii)   *Cela finit par prendre des proportions inquiétantes*
        ● It finished by taking on worrying proportions
        ● In the end it was getting out of hand
        ● Finally the thing started to get serious

    (iii)   *'Oh! je comprends bien!' dit-elle, le visage illuminé de malice*
        ● 'Oh, I understand well', she said, her face shining with malice
        ● 'I understand alright', she said, with a malicious look on her face
        ● 'I can see what you mean alright', she said her face glowing with mischief

    (iv)   *Alberte manifesta tout à coup, un matin après cinq semaines de cynisme, une violente contrition*
        ● Suddenly one morning, after five weeks of cynicism, Alberte had an attack of remorse
        ● Alberte suddenly one morning after five weeks of cynicism was overwhelmed by contrition
        ● After five weeks of cynicism, suddenly one morning Alberte was overcome by feelings of sorrow for what she had done

    (v)   Comment est-ce que vous traduiriez en anglais les mots et expressions suivants:
        butée – l'argent... quand il est placé – sur mes genoux – un singe mécanique – que faire d'autre que de la consoler

4   Dans le passage suivant, Françoise Mallet-Joris raconte les différentes étapes dans la vie de son fils aîné, Daniel, de 5 jusqu'à 18 ans:

A cinq ans il manifesta un précoce instinct de protection en criant dans le métro, d'une voix suraiguë, 'Laissez passer ma maman.' A huit ans il 'faisait ses courses' et 'son' dîner tout seul, quand il estimait que je rentrais trop tard le soir. Il me dépassait déjà complètement. A neuf ans, nous eûmes quelques conflits. Il refusa d'aller à l'école, de se laver et de manger du poisson. Un jour je le plongeai tout habillé dans une baignoire, un autre jour Jacques le porta sur son dos à l'école: il hurla tout le long du chemin. Ces essais éducatifs n'eurent aucun succès. Du reste, il se corrigea tout seul. Nous décidâmes de ne plus intervenir.

A dix ans, au lycée, ayant reçu pour sujet de rédaction, 'Un beau souvenir', il écrivit ingénuement: 'Le plus beau souvenir de ma vie, c'est le mariage de mes parents.'

A quinze ans il eut une période yé-yé. Nous collectionnâmes les 45 tours. A seize ans il manifesta un vif intérêt pour le beau sexe. De jeunes personnes dont j'ignorais toujours jusqu'au prénom s'engouffraient dans sa chambre, drapées dans d'immenses imperméables crasseux, comme des espions de la *Série noire*.

Il joua de la clarinette. Il but un peu.

A dix-sept ans il fut bouddhiste.

Il joua du tuba. Ses cheveux s'allongèrent.

A dix-huit ans il passa son bac. Un peu avant il avait été couvert de bijoux comme un prince hindou ou un figurant de cinéma, une bague à chaque doigt. J'attendais en silence, ébahie et intéressée, comme devant la pousse d'une plante, la mue d'une chenille.

Les bijoux disparurent. Il joua du saxophone, de la guitare. Il fit 4000 kilomètres en auto-stop, connu les tribus du désert en Mauritanie, vit un éléphant en liberté, voyagea couché à plat ventre sur un wagon, à demi asphixié par la poussière. Il constata que Dakar ressemble étonnamment à Knokke-le-Zoute (Belgique).

Il revint pratiquement sans chaussures, les siennes ayant fondu à la chaleur du désert, mais doté d'un immense prestige auprès de ses frères et sœurs. Il rasa ses cheveux et fit des sciences économiques. Voilà la saga de Daniel.

Dans tout cela, où est l'éducation? Si Daniel, qui va atteindre sa majorité cette année, est un bon fils, un beau garçon, doué d'humour et de sérieux, de fantaisie et de bon sens, y suis-je pour quelque chose? Ah! pour rien, pour rien, et pourtant pour quelque chose, une toute petite chose, la seule peut-être que je lui ai donnée, la seule, me dis-je parfois avec orgueil, qu'il était important de lui donner: la confiance.

Ce qui ne veut pas dire que tous les problèmes soient résolus. Daniel vient d'acheter un singe!

Françoise Mallet-Joris *La Maison de Papier*

Quelques explications

Jacques – c'est le mari de Françoise

la Série noire – des romans policiers dans le genre 'espionnage international'

la mue d'une chenille – une chenille c'est la larve d'un papillon

la mue – c'est le changement dans la peau de la chenille à mesure que celle-ci grandit

(a) Questions en anglais:
   (i)   Why exactly was Daniel's behaviour in the underground embarrassing?
   (ii) How were Daniel's problems at the age of nine overcome?
   (iii) What decision did his parents take at that time?
   (iv) Why might the opening line of his essay have been embarrassing to his parents?
   (v)   Explain what Françoise's reaction was when she wrote *j'attendais en silence, ébahie et intéressée comme devant la pousse d'une plante, la mue d'une chenille.* How apt is her use of these images?
   (vi) What countries did Daniel visit before going into higher education?
   (vii) What do you understand by the phrase *il constata que Dakar ressemble étonnammnent à Knokke-le-Zoute (Belgique)?*
   (viii) What is Daniel like at twenty, according to his mother?
   (ix) What part has she played in his education?
   (x)   What attitude do you think she shows in her closing remark about Daniel? Explain your reason.

(b) Travail en anglais et en français —
   (i)   Expliquez en anglais ce que vous entendez par les phrases ou les expressions suivantes:

   - *un précoce instinct de protection*
   - *il écrivit ingénuement*
   - *il eut une période yé-yé*
   - *nous collectionnâmes les quarante-cinq tours.*
   - *un espion*
   - *atteindre sa majorité*

   (ii) Lesquelles des expressions suivantes correspondent le mieux au sens de celles d'en haut:
   - *l'instinct féroce de protéger – un instinct prématuré de protection – un instinct de protection au delà de son âge*
   - *il écrivit naïvement – avec toute innocence – sincèrement*
   - *à un certain temps il aimait beaucoup la musique pop – chanter en s'accompagnant de la guitare – écouter la musique pop*
   - *nous faisions une collection des disques à 45 tours – des disques des années 45 – des photos des châteaux de la Loire*
   - *un agent provocateur – un agent secret – un agent de police*
   - *avoir le droit de voter – avoir 18 ans – avoir 21 ans*

(iii) **Traduction en anglais** Trouvez une phrase anglaise pour:
le beau sexe – un éléphant en liberté – couché à plat ventre – doué... de fantaisie et de bon sens – y suis-je pour quelque chose?

(iv) **Retranslation** Lisez le texte suivant puis relisez deux ou trois fois le passage en français. Essayez de faire la traduction sans trop regarder le français original.

> Françoise got married when she was 18. Daniel was born nine months later. Her son was a precocious child. When he was 5, he used to get his own dinner ready if he thought his mother was late in returning home. When he was 9, his parents had several battles with him. Once he refused to get washed so his mother dropped him fully clothed into the bath. On another occasion he didn't want to go to school so his father carried him there on his back. He once wrote in an essay 'The nicest thing I can remember is when my mum and dad got married'. At 16 he became very keen on girls. He went through a pop-music period. He became a buddhist and let his hair grow long. After sitting his bac exam, he hitch-hiked 4000 kilometres in Africa. When he returned home, he enjoyed great prestige with his brothers and sisters.
>
> Today, Daniel is a handsome boy with a sense of humour but also a serious side. His mother believes they were right not to interfere too much in his life. She is proud that she has played a small but significant part in his upbringing by giving him confidence.

5 Lisez trois ou quatre fois le passage en dessous:

> Clémentine était très adroite, mais elle trichait impudemment, et refusait d'admettre qu'elle avait perdu.
>
> De plus, elle mentait sans cesse, pour rien, pour le plaisir.
>
> Par exemple, venant à ma rencontre sur la pointe des pieds, elle m'annonçait à voix basse, avec des mines terrorisées, que M. le directeur était gravement malade, et que plusieurs médecins entouraient son lit. Cinq minutes plus tard, tandis que je songeais aux funérailles grandioses de ce puissant chef, M. le directeur lui-même traversait la cour, tout guilleret, et la canne à la main.
>
> Une autre fois, un superbe tirailleur sénégalais — un sergent — était venu, disait-elle, la demander en mariage à sa mère, 'parce que dans son pays les filles se marient à douze ans'. Naturellement, sa mère avait refusé, 'parce qu'en Afrique, il fait trop chaud, et puis là-bas, ce sont les femmes qui portent les paquets'.
>
> 'D'ailleurs', ajoutait-elle, 'je suis fiancée avec un prince américain. Il gagne tellement d'argent qu'il a de grandes caisses pour le mettre. Mais ça m'est défendu de vous dire son nom'.
>
> 'Qu'est-ce que tu as? Pourquoi ris-tu?'
>
> Mais au lieu de répondre, elle se levait d'un bond, courait prendre son balai, et elle dansait avec lui.
>
> Un jour, dans un élan d'amitié, je lui avais dit, 'Tu aurais de beaux yeux, s'ils étaient pareils.'
>
> Sur quoi, cette idiote avait fondu en larmes, avec des sanglots et des hoquets déchirants.
>
> Pour la calmer, je lui expliquai que c'était un compliment, et que je trouvais avantageux d'avoir deux œils au lieu de deux yeux. Avec la rapidité d'un chat, elle me griffa la joue sous l'oreille, à quoi je répondis par une gifle absolument réussie. Elle demeura un instant comme stupéfaite, puis elle courut au platane et, le front sur son avant-bras, elle se mit à ululer si fort qu'il me parut prudent de rentrer chez moi au pas de course.
>
> M Pagnol *Le temps des secrets*

Quelques explications
M. le directeur – est le chef d'une école primaire
un tirailleur – est un soldat de l'infanterie
guilleret – veut dire 'gai et vif'

(a) Questions en français:
   (i)   Expliquez ce que vous entendez par l'expression *elle trichait impudemment.*
   (ii) Pourquoi le garçon est-ce qu'il croit au premier mensonge de Clémentine?
   (iii) A votre avis où est-ce que Clémentine a trouvé les détails au sujet de la vie des femmes en Afrique?

(iv)   Quel détail des mensonges de Clémentine trouvez-vous le plus exagéré?

(v)   Qu'est-ce que le garçon voulait dire en racontant à Clémentine qu'elle avait *deux œils au lieu de deux yeux?*

(vi)   Comment expliquez-vous la réaction de la jeune fille?

(b) **Traduction en anglais** Choisissez la version la plus convenable ou si aucune version ne vous plaît, composez en une qui convient:

(i)   *Clémentine était très adroite, mais elle trichait impudemment, et refusait toujours d'admettre qu'elle avait perdu*

● Clementine was very clever but she cheated impudently and always refused to say she had lost

● Clementine was very smart but full of impudent tricks always refusing to admit that she had lost

● Clementine was very clever but cheated shamelessly never wanting to be wrong

(ii)   *elle m'annonçait à voix basse, avec des mines terrorisées, que M. le directeur était gravement malade, et que plusieurs médecins entouraient son lit.*

● she announced in a low voice that the Headmaster was seriously ill and that his bed was surrounded by several doctors

● she told me in a whisper that the Head was gravely ill and that several doctors were standing around his bed

● She announced in a whisper that the Head was seriously ill and that several doctors were grouped around his bed

(iii)   *la demander en mariage à sa mère*

● ask her mother for her in marriage

● ask for her hand in marriage

● ask the mother if he could marry her

(c) Comblez les blancs avec un mot ou une phrase choisis dans la liste ci-dessous:

Un soir, quand elle _____ des commissions, un homme énorme, avec une barbe _____, l'avait poursuivie dans la rue. Il _____ nuit, elle _____ couru de toute ses forces.

'S'il m'avait _____, je ne sais pas ce qu'il m'_____ fait'

Paul était d'avis qu'il voulait la faire _____ dans un cirque, ou peut-être la _____ à vendre des paniers dans un pays étranger, comme Toulouse ou Avignon.

Alors elle hôcha la tête plusieurs fois et ricana tout bas en me _____ de côté; puis elle dit, 'C'_____ un enfant! Il ne _____ pas!'

aura – faisait – grande – a – dansé – rattrapé – aurait – dansant – obliger – forcer – avait – rattrapée – a fait – noire – revenait – regarder – était – comprend – est – regardant – est revenue – comprends

(d) **Retranslation:**

When I was 10 I used to play with a girl called Clementine. I remember that she was very pretty and clever but that she had the bad habit of telling lies all the time. One day, for example, she came running up to me with tears in her eyes and told me that the Headmaster was seriously ill and that the doctors said he was going to die. Imagine my surprise half an hour later when I saw the Head walking across the playground accompanied by Clementine's mother!

One day for a joke I said to Clementine, 'You would have lovely hair if it was dark instead of blond.' She immediately burst into tears. I tried to console her by explaining that I really preferred girls with blond hair. With a speed that surprised me she turned round and scratched my face.

Part IV French literature

A study of a number of French literary texts (novels, plays or poetry) is required to a greater, or lesser degree, by all the Examining Boards. Students beginning an A-Level course find this one of the most demanding tasks. GCSE written texts are very different and usually consist of shorter pieces taken from newspapers, magazines and advertising (which aim mainly at practising understanding of factual details). Texts are usually unconnected with one another and the language used generally reflects everyday matters and events.

Above all, it is important to remember that novels and plays each have a story to tell with a beginning, a middle and an end. You are presented with a series of events that unfold as you read. One of the reasons for reading a novel (or seeing a play performed) is to find out what happens next and how things turn out in the end.

For stories to work you need people (the characters) whose collective, or individual, actions and decisions influence what happens. To some extent they are like people you know or have met. They behave in ways that you admire or, perhaps more often, in ways you disapprove of.

The third element to consider is that plays and novels take place against a certain background either carefully described or vaguely referred to. The background may be a particular place in a certain part of the country with a way of life that affects, to some extent, the people who live there. The background could also be influenced by a particular time in history with standards and values that were different. Some past event could also play a part (e.g. a war, a plague or a famine). Economic conditions could also influence how people behave. Moral considerations might also have their impact on background because expectations and conventions of behaviour can change according to time and place.

The other major literary genre, poetry, is also about life. As well as being in a recognizably different form from novels and plays, poetry presents life as chunks of concentrated and intense experience. Poems are often therefore shorter than novels and plays and the language used is different with changed values. Some poems are nevertheless stories with characters who think and speak.

Novels, plays and poems present us with other people's experience and interpretation of life. They espouse ideas, opinions and behaviour that are partly familiar but in many ways fresh. Reading a novel (or poem) or seeing a play performed becomes, therefore, a two-way exchange. The reader brings his or her experience into contact with that of the author. It important to bear in mind that reading is entertainment, even if it is a 'serious' hobby. It gives pleasure. Also that reading is finding out, not only of what happened next or in the end, but of how people are, how they behave and how they think. Because there is also the target of an examination, A-Level reading has the additional aim of reading to remember, so that you have a recollection of the whole story and can talk or write about the characters and ideas.

How can I understand the text?

This is the difficulty experienced by all students in the transition from GCSE to A Level and there is no short cut. You have to practise reading to get better at it! It does help though if you have an outline or an impression of the whole before you begin to read. In many ways it is easier to start with a play, if one is included in the syllabus, because the division into acts and scenes gives it a formal structure. You will also find at the beginning a list of the characters; sometimes even a description of them. The writer's stage directions can also help understanding. Some texts of plays have a synopsis of the action at the beginning.

With a novel, it is a good idea to look first at the contents list and the division into chapters or parts. Most nineteenth and twentieth century works don't have rubrics or titles at the beginning of chapters. Voltaire's short story *Candide*, written in the eighteenth century, is an example of a book with a brief résumé at the head of each chapter. It helps if you have some idea beforehand of the overall pattern of events in the novel. Your teacher should be able to give you this or you could look for a description (or synopsis) in a book of criticism. For example, it is useful to know if events are linear, (i.e. starting at one point in time and finishing later at another without interruption); or whether the story is told as a flashback (or a series of flashbacks) alternating with present time. It is difficult to make sense of the beginning of François Mauriac's *Thérèse Desqueyroux* unless you know that the action begins after the investigation and trial for attempted murder of Thérèse's husband and that the first part of the novel is a long flashback through the events leading up to this point.

Having got some idea of the overall pattern of the book, try reading the text straight through without pausing too much over parts that you don't understand or looking up too many words. With a play, it is important to remember that it was written to be acted rather than read. The words have only a face value. Their interpretation is revealed by tone of voice, gesture, movement and look of the performing actors.

Using translations

Texts should be read in French. If you really do find this too difficult, you could:

(a) try reading an English translation of the book first, making a chapter by chapter summary as you do so, and then read the original

(b) as you do the above, produce a summary of each chapter in French. You will find that the 'value' of words in English for you is different to their value in French

You will have a large range of associations, and shades of meaning, that you can attach to English words but a much more restricted one in French, as yet. If you rely too heavily on translations these values will never balance out.

Use the French text (rather than the translation) for reference, note-making and general work on the book, so that you know your way around it. Try to make your notes and comments about the book in French or, if you do jot down things in English, leave a space, look up the French later and add in the comment. Some Boards allow you to take the text into the examination. Check the requirements of your Board.

1 Methods of study

Contents

1 Novels and short stories

Structure

Make your own synopsis, or summary, of the action as you read the text a second time. You can do this according to the parts or chapters. It is also useful, in some cases, to give your own titles to chapters, indicating roughly what they are about. Create your own divisions in the text, if none exist already, as in Balzac's novels for instance. Is the story one continuous account, are there flashbacks, or are there events subsidiary to the main action? Do the events unfold in one place or is the reader whisked from one social setting to another?

Characters

Make a list of the characters. Divide them into main, secondary and minor characters. Where large families are concerned, make a family tree so that you have a visual impression of the people, their chronology and relationships. This is particularly helpful with some of Mauriac's or Zola's novels. Try to determine the function of the characters in the story. Some will be responsible for initiating and maintaining the course of events. Others may play a lesser role, in influencing the action, but may have a functional role in illuminating the personality or behaviour of the main characters. In Flaubert's *Madame Bovary*, for example, the guests that Emma meets at the Vaubyessard ball remain nameless but their behaviour and conversation have a profound effect on her romantic yearnings and tendencies.

It is also helpful to think of the main characters, in terms of their effect on each other, by asking yourself whether they clash or complement one another. Look for any ambiguity in behaviour and also for development. Do personalities change or evolve during the period described in the book? Is change brought about by events, by other people, or by the growth of a tendency within a character. Write your own brief character description of the main protagonists, illustrating your judgements with examples from the text of what people say, think and do. Take into account any details of physical appearance. Do the names of the characters have any significance?

Narration and viewpoint

Ask yourself who is the narrator of the story. It may be an anonymous person, exterior to the action, so that events are narrated in the third person singular (as in many novels by Balzac and Zola). The narration might be in the first person singular, by someone directly involved in events (as in Mauriac's *Le Nœud de Vipères* or Camus *L'Etranger*. Another possibility is first person narration, by someone close to the main characters but not of interest in themselves (as in Alain Fournier's *Le Grand Meaulnes*).

Manner of narration is closely related to the focus or viewpoint in the novel. If the narrator is an outsider, he or she may just describe what people say and do without giving the reader access to the thoughts of the characters. Such a point of view makes no judgements about people so the picture we derive is said to be more objective.

If the viewpoint is from inside the story, by somone taking part in the events, then their interpretation of what happens is limited and tends to be subjective. We see everything through their eyes.

A third possibility is the viewpoint of the omniscient (all-knowing) narrator who has full knowledge of the characters, their past and present history and what goes on in their minds. Such a viewpoint is often most noticeable at the beginning of a novel. Balzac's *Le Père Goriot* and *Eugénie Grandet* are good illustrations of this technique. If it is overdone, it may seem that the author is always butting in and that the characters are being manipulated in such a way that they appear to have no independent life of their own.

What often happens is that the viewpoint changes in the course of the novel, sometimes even on the same page, so that we may switch from being privy to the thoughts of one character to an exterior view of events. When examining the viewpoint of a novel, it sometimes helps if you imagine how part of a novel (or short story) might be presented as a film for TV or the cinema screen. The main thing is to think about the book and to respond actively to it. Which actors and actresses would you cast in each role and how would you advise them to play their part. Which episodes in the book would you leave out? Which events should be highlighted? Would background sounds or music be appropriate to key scenes taken from the book? How would the historical period be suggested by clothing or setting?

Many novels have been made into films and some are available on video which is very helpful since the latter can be watched and stopped with key events re-run and commented on (*see* appendix 3, pages 211–12). If you do have access to a video version, it can be used in several ways to improve your knowledge and understanding of a novel. You can examine and discuss how the actors or actresses interpret their roles; keep a note of any events that have been omitted and ask yourself if they should have been included; discuss whether the film adds to the book or changes it and why; and ask yourself if you would have treated the book in the same way?

Setting and background

Consider the value of the background in the story or novel you are reading. Does it play a dominant role or one that is hardly noticeable? Does the author sketch in a few features only, to create an impression, or are there long, detailed descriptions of defined places that give a sense of realism? Is the setting restricted to the way of life of a certain group of people? Sometimes features of landscape are described just for their beauty. At other times, an author might use aspects of background for symbolic purposes, to mirror the state of mind, or mood, of the characters. The 'wind-bent pines' and the 'brooding thunderstorms' of the Landes in Mauriac's novels and the intense heat of the Mediterranean sun in Camus's *L'Etranger* spring to mind.

Meaning

You should also consider the meaning of a novel in terms of an author's possible motives in writing it and any message he or she may have intended. Many writers are interested in highlighting a particular section of society from a critical rather than an approving point of view. If the group of people they depict is made to look ridiculous, or comic, then satire is being employed. Less often, a writer's motive is to celebrate or convey his delight about a period in life that has passed. Alain Fournier's *Le Grand Meaulnes* is partly about the lost experience of youth. Colette evokes the bitter-sweet emotions of awakening sexuality in *Le Blé en Herbe*. In his autobiographical trilogy, Pagnol celebrates a young boy's delight and fascination as he explores the natural world of Provence. Most novels have more than one motive and message. Voltaire's *Candide* sets out to ridicule the fashionable theory of 'total optimism' derived from the theories of the philosopher Leibnitz but it also reveals a young man coming to terms with human behaviour and finding eventually a way of coping with life. In *Madame Bovary*, Flaubert shows the dangers of romantic illusions promoted by novels but he also reveals his deep pessimism about most human endeavour.

You will be able to bring your own judgements to the novels or stories that you read because you come to the text with views, opinions and fantasies of your own. For example, as well as being delighted by Pagnol's descriptions of the Provençal countryside in *La Gloire de mon Père* and *Le Château de ma Mère* you might deplore the attitude towards shooting and trapping wild birds.

Case study of a novel: *Thérèse Desqueyroux* **by François Mauriac.**

(Page references are from the *Livre de poche* edition of the text.)

Anecdote In 1950, this novel was classed as eighth out of the fifty best novels of the first half of the nineteenth century. It was made into a film by Georges Franju in 1962. Mauriac writes in a very compact style. Almost any sentence is full of implications and allusions that have to be read carefully in order to understand the complete picture.

Structure

The story is, in part, about the attempted murder of a husband (Bernard Desqueyroux) by his wife, Thérèse. An inquiry is held but the case never comes to court because of insufficient evidence. The story also relates how Bernard treats his wife when the inquiry is over. It is a story about a crime but not in the conventional sense. The interest lies in motives for the crime that Thérèse does not fully understand herself. In this sense, she (and the reader) are the detectives. Interest is also sustained by learning what happens to Thérèse and how she copes with her isolation.

Chapters I–IX In a series of flashbacks, during the long coach and train journey back to Argelouse after the initial inquiry into the crime, Thérèse tries to reconstruct past events to understand why she tried to poison her husband and prepare herself for meeting him alone for the first time for some weeks. During this part of the book several events and episodes are related: Thérèse's childhood (pages 26–8); her friendship with Anne de la Trave (pages 27 and 35–7); her marriage to Bernard (pages 32–3, 38–42 and 43–5) and their honeymoon (pages 47–54); Anne's love affair with Jean Azévédo (pages 49–53), who is considered an unsuitable match by the rest of the family (page 57–8); Thérèse's role in bringing this liaison to an end (pages 64 and 67–72); her subsequent meetings with Jean Azévédo and their conversations (pages 83–90 and 92); the birth of her daughter, Marie (pages 104, 107 and 108); the events leading up to the poisoning of her husband (pages 110–14).

Chapters IX–XII These chapters relate her life in the relative confinement and isolation that Bernard subjects her to when she returns. Her health deteriorates to the extent that Bernard, having returned from a long holiday, is alarmed at her appearance (pages 162–3 and 168). Fearing possible scandal, he decides to let Thérèse live her own life in Paris (pages 168–9).

Chapter XIII Bernard has travelled to Paris with Thérèse. After a last unsuccessful attempt to explain her reasons for wanting to poison Bernard (pages 173–79), Thérèse is left alone to begin her new life.

The book has two time scales. The past, related in the flashbacks in chapters I–IX reconstructing Thérèse's life up to the inquiry; and the present with a starting point, just after the legal inquiry has ruled that there are no grounds for proceeding, and finishing as Thérèse disappears into the Parisian crowds. A further time scale of the future is suggested by the book since we do not know what life holds in store for Thérèse.

Characters

Main characters

Thérèse Desqueyroux (née Larroque)
Bernard Desqueyroux, husband to the former
Both are from families owning large areas of land in the Landes forest.

Thérèse is the main focus of interest in the novel. It is through her interior monologue that events are related. She tries to piece together and make sense of events in her life from childhood up to her marriage and attempted poisoning of her husband. We also listen to her thoughts later while she is a virtual prisoner at Argelouse and remain by her side until she disappears into the Parisian crowds. Thérèse is more gifted and intelligent than the people around her in whom (apart from Jean Azévédo), she finds no echo. She craves close human contact and understanding but cannot find this in her father, Anne de la Trave or Bernard. Consequently, she is introspective but cannot really understand herself without some reflection of herself from others and cannot make sense of her frustrations. Her mutilation of the photograph of Jean Azévédo, sent to her by Anne (page 61), illustrates well how repressed feelings surface and take hold of her almost by surprise.

She is also influenced by her family and social background. She has a taste for owning property and likes talking business with landowners (pages 39–40). She marries Bernard, partly because it is expected of her by the two families, but also because she likes the idea of adding to the family estates. Bernard also seemed to have more about him than most of the other men in the area (pages 32–3).

Bernard has a view of the world that is limited by the horizons of the Landes in which he lives. Although he has travelled, in order to broaden his experience, his life revolves around the work and pleasure that the forests of the Landes can provide. He likes eating, drinking and hunting. He is above all conventional: a creature of habit. He feels frustrated when Thérèse does not react or answer in the way he expects. He finds it difficult to cope with Thérèse's habit of talking in paradoxes. As a lover, he lacks sensitivity and the physical side of marriage does not make up for the couple's disparity in temperament and intelligence. Bernard worries about his health. This becomes something of an obsession, leading to the consultation with Pédemay and the prescribing of arsenic for his blood pressure.

Minor characters

M. Larroque is father to Thérèse and is involved in local politics. His main ambition is to become a *sénateur*. He is more interested in this ambition than in the happiness of his daughter whose conduct he sees as a possible hindrance to his career. His wife died giving birth while Thérèse was still very young.

Anne de la Trave is half-sister to Bernard through his mother's second marriage. Anne is not fully committed to friendship with Thérèse. They do not share common interests. Unlike Thérèse, Anne likes shooting birds, doesn't like reading, shows little curiosity about life, has strong maternal instincts and conforms, in the end, to the pattern the family have in mind for her by marrying *le fils Deguilhem*.

Jean Azévédo is the younger son of a well-off family but looked down upon, by the Larroque and the Desqueyroux clans, because he is Jewish and is reputed to suffer from tuberculosis. He is in fact reasonably healthy. He is shrewd, well-read, intelligent and describes with enthusiasm his life in Paris. He is able to stand back from life in the Landes and make judgements about it. He realizes that Thérèse's intelligence makes her a misfit in the circles in which she moves. There is an element of showing off in the conversations he has with Thérèse but the ideas he exposes her to are influential and act as a catalyst to her subsequent behaviour.

Tante Clara is the older sister of Thérèse's father. She is deaf and lives in the Larroque family home at Argelouse where she used to look after young Thérèse. Clara has sympathy for (and loyalty towards) Thérèse even though she doesn't understand everything that goes on. She spies on the conversation between Bernard and Thérèse when the latter returns from the inquiry, in chapter IX, and is relieved to see Thérèse smile (page 122). It is Tante Clara's sudden death that prevents Thérèse taking her own life (pages 140–1).

Mme de la Trave is Bernard's mother. She is only interested in the reputation of the family and she sees Thérèse mainly as providing an heir. She has no patience with Thérèse's cleverness and capriciousness.

M. de la Trave is a penniless spendthrift. He married the widowed Mme Desqueyroux and has tended to indulge his step-daughter Anne. He tends to agree with his wife and come out with the same kind of clichés.

Balion and Balionte are an elderly couple. They are tenant farmers (*métayers*) on Bernard's land, acting as faithful retainers and housekeepers to his family. They are given the task of looking after Thérèse while she is living in isolation at Saint-Clair. They carry out their task without showing any emotion.

Le fils Deguilhem is short-sighted and prematurely bald. He is seen by Bernard's family as a suitable match for Anne because of his wealth. He also speaks in clichés.

La grand-mère Bellade is Thérèse's grandmother whose first name is never mentioned by the family because of some scandal.

Le docteur Pédemay is Bernard's doctor; *Darquey*, the local pharmacist. Both these men are more concerned about damage to their reputations than the welfare of the people they serve.

Presentation of character

Mauriac does not describe the appearance of his characters. Often a word or two suffice to capture a physical impression. We know that Bernard is muscular, well-built but slightly overweight; that Anne's ears stick out when her hair is tied back; and that Thérèse's father becomes animated when he talks. We have almost no impression however of what Thérèse looks like: *on ne se demande pas si elle est jolie ou laide, on subit son charme*. Mauriac tends however to describe the physical gestures or attitudes that reveal a state of mind: Thérèse with an air of indifference opening almonds while Bernard inadvertantly swallows a double dose of Fowler's mixture; or (at the end of chapter I) M. Larroque 'pushing' Thérèse into the carriage. His characters also reveal themselves through their words and reactions. We find out all we need to know about Mme de la Trave through the collection of pros and cons that she has at the ready to deliver to all-comers when discussing the coming marriage of her son to Thérèse (page 38).

Viewpoint

For most of the novel, we tune into Thérèse's thoughts while she is alone and, therefore, see everything through her eyes. Her thoughts are sometimes presented directly in the first person (as in chapter VI) but more often in an indirect style. This creates the impression that it is Mauriac's voice we hear rather than Thérèse thinking for herself. There are other occasions where Thérèse could not be present as an observer (e.g. when Tante Clara is listening outside the door) or when she could not know what someone else was thinking (e.g. when an imaginary newspaper picture flashes into the mind of Bernard as he contemplates the poor state of his wife's health and appearance). The reader tends not to notice these discrepancies too much since the main focus of attention continues to be Thérèse.

Setting

The Landes landscape is not depicted in any great detail: pine trees; heather and bracken; a lack of water; sandy cart-tracks; clearings with hides for shooting migratory pigeons — but not much more. The remoteness of the setting, however, is referred to at many points. The nearest main town is the *sous-préfecture* of B. From there an hour's coach drive to Nizan station, then a long journey by train, followed by ten kilometres along rough tracks before you arrive at Saint-Clair. Argelouse is another ten kilometres further away along a track, after which there is nothing but forest and marsh land for eighty kilometres until you reach the sea. Most of the action of the novel takes place within a ten-kilometre circle encompassing Argelouse and Saint-Clair. Perhaps it is difficult for some readers to appreciate such remoteness. Total silence is one of the pervading impressions, broken only by isolated sounds like the barking of a dog, the hooting of an owl or crowing of cockerels. The loneliness and isolation of this *extrémité de la terre* have an undoubted influence on the mentality and attitude of the inhabitants and serve to strengthen the impression of living in a kind of prison.

Meaning

The meaning of this novel is not at all explicit. Mauriac seems to concentrate attention on the plight of a sensitive and intelligent individual, caught up by fact of birth, in a social and geographical setting from which escape is difficult. He seems absorbed too with the darker side of human behaviour that emerges from frustration whose cause is not clear to the individual concerned. He does not show approval for Thérèse's conduct but rather sympathy, pity and concern. The end of the novel seems inconclusive. Thérèse has not yet fully understood herself nor we her. We are left wondering what will happen to her and how she will cope with life. Mauriac also felt that he needed to go on with the story of Thérèse and he wrote several short stories and another novel, *La fin de la nuit*, that set out to do this. None of these works have the impact or the fascination of the initial novel.

Some work for you to do

1 Read Mauriac's *avant-propos* at the beginning of the text. Do you find the quotation appropriate? Does this and Mauriac's foreword shed any light for you on the meaning of the novel?

2 (pages 26–7) What impression do you have of the kind of person Thérèse appeared to be and what she was really like while she was at school?

3 (a) (page 39) Does Thérèse really 'adore' Bernard?
   (b) (pages 39–40) Why do you think she marries him?

4 (pages 40–1) What does this conversation between Bernard and Thérèse reveal about their ways of thinking? What do you think Thérèse means by her rejoinder to Bernard's previous comment: '*A vous de les détruire, Bernard*'.

5 (pages 46–7) Describe Thérèse's feelings towards the physical side of her relationship with Bernard.

6 (page 61) Describe the series of thoughts that go through Thérèse's mind as she flushes the pieces of photograph down the toilet.

7 (a) (pages 83–90) What effect does meeting Jean Azévédo have on Thérèse? Put into your own words what she means by; '*...le premier homme que je rencontrais et pour qui comptait, plus que tout, la vie de l'esprit*'.
   (b) (page 94) What do you understand by his claim that he feels that Thérèse has '*...une soif de sincérité*'.
   (c) (page 96) Do you think that Jean's offer to meet her in a year's time when she 'has found out how to free herself' has any importance for what happens later?

8 (a) (pages 109–10) Describe Thérèse's state of mind in the weeks leading up to the first temptation to poison her husband.
   (b) (pages 110–16) Is it possible to detect stages in her thinking about the act?

9 One chapter is devoted to Thérèse's imprisonment at Argelouse. What do we learn about her as a person from this section of the book?

10 (pages 173–80) What does this final conversation between Bernard and Thérèse reveal about both of them?

11 It has been pointed out that Mauriac often draws for his imagery on the animal world, referring particularly to those animals that are hunted or kept in captivity. Make a list of examples from the text with a comment on their effectiveness. Here are some to start you off: (page 33) Bernard as a batchelor is described as '*moins curieux des jeunes filles que du lièvre qu'il forçait dans la lande...*'. This image fits Bernard well because of his passionate interest in hunting; he is really more interested in chasing hares than girls. The latter nevertheless fall into the same category as prey. The chatter of the women in church at Thérèse's wedding is described as *caquetage* – 'clucking'. This word suggests the triteness of their conversation but also evokes the idea of the prison that Thérèse is about to enter and which is evoked in the next sentence.

Possible themes for essay questions:

1 **Character of Thérèse** Explain why she attempts to poison Bernard. Imagine that as a lawyer you have either to defend or to prosecute Thérèse. Prepare a case for or against (if two people, do both). This could be a class activity with a jury who listen to the evidence and then give their verdict.

2 **Character of Bernard** Describe the family unit (as represented by Mauriac) under the headings of marriage, children, wealth, religion, influence, attitude to others.

3 **Use of metaphor** Mauriac's world is full of violence, repression and cruelty shown by one individual to another. Examine Mauriac's use of images taken from the natural world.

2 Drama

Plays can be divided broadly into two categories:
(a) plays about people and the effect they have upon one another (psychological dramas)
(b) plays about society and its collective beliefs and the values that affect it at a particular time

Many plays reflect both these elements and the psychology of the individual comes into play with current issues of the day. Plays may be tragic and evoke emotions of anger, sympathy or sorrow. (The 'hero' or 'heroine' usually dies a violent death.) They may be comic and make us laugh at the behaviour of a particular individual or group of people. (The main characters usually marry each other.) Laughter works best when other emotions are not dominant. As soon as pity, sorrow or anger creep in we tend to stop laughing. For this reason the borderline between comedy and tragedy can be a delicate one.

You need to make your own synopsis of the events in a play. This is often made easier by the division into acts and scenes. Does the action take place over a relatively short period of time or is there a time lapse at some point? Is there a single main plot (or situation) around which events revolve or are there subsidiary plots enmeshed in the main one?

Characters

Divide characters into major and minor protagonists. Is the main psychological interest focussed on one person or on a group of people? Do the minor characters have any depth or are they only needed, at some point, for the development of the play. Do characters clash or do they complement each other? Are the motives for their behaviour clear or ambiguous? Make a character sketch of the main characters, finding your own words to describe features of their personality.

Action

This is the main feature of any play in terms of holding the attention of the audience. This is usually achieved by creating expectations, feelings of tension and suspense which resolve themselves in one or more climaxes in the action. There might be a gradual working towards one outcome or there may be several high points or climaxes with a sense in between. Anticlimax might be a central feature of a play. For example, in Beckett's *Waiting for Godot* expectations are created but never fulfilled.

Comedy

Comedy has its source in character and situation. Characters who make us laugh usually have one overriding obsession which creates a kind of rigidity in their personality. We laugh partly because we know how they are going to react, in certain situations, but also because their obsessed condition is likely to come into collision with the behaviour of more normal individuals: these clashes are funny. Comedy of situation usually has its origins in the efforts of characters to trick, outwit or deceive each other. Laughter is caused when plans go wrong, for one reason or another. Most comic plays exploit both character and situation. Molière's Harpagon, in *L'Avare,* is a good example of a man with an obsession of comic proportions but the efforts of his family and servants to outwit him also provide much of the humour. In Pagnol's *Topaze*, the hero's naïve dedication to the principles of *'la morale'*, as taught to French school children, collides several times with the views and behaviour of less scrupulous people. The changed and worldy-wise Topaze of Act IV is a less amusing person in many ways.

Studying seventeenth-century tragedies, by Corneille or Racine, presents a particular challenge. You need to become familiar with some of the literary and social conventions of that period to appreciate these plays fully. It is important to use a critical edition of the text with a good introduction.

Meaning

Because plays are designed to make an impact within the space of one to three hours of performance, their meaning (or message) is often closer to the surface and they are more likely to provoke an immediate reaction. The meaning (or worth) of a play is often on more than one level. Sartre's *Les Mains Sales* can be seen as an indictment of the Communist party's requirement of absolute adhesion to the party line, even though this may be changed to suit circumstances. On a philosophical level, it highlights the difficulty that the consciously willed act creates for an individual, determined to justify his existence. On a human level, it is concerned with the complexities of human relationships as seen in the father–son bond between Hoederer and Hugo.

Since plays are meant to be acted, rather than read, you can miss a good deal of their impact by just treating them as words on a page. You will find it profitable to examine selected scenes from the point of view of a stage director: decide on the positions of the actors; their movements; gestures; eye contact; tone of voice; and pauses in what they say. Some of these details may be broadly indicated in the stage directions but there will be a good deal of scope for improvisation and interpretation.

First of all, decide on the frame of mind of the characters at the beginning of the scene. Has this been influenced by events in the previous scene or is their attitude influenced by contact with each other? Decide on the positioning of the actors and on how they will move at the beginning of the scene. What do they do with their hands? Who are they looking at? What facial or bodily gestures might be appropriate? Do they speak slowly or quickly? Where might there be pauses in their speech? What tone of voice would they use? Are certain words emphasized by rise and fall of intonation? Once you begin to consider some of these features, you will discover that the scene can be broken down into shorter parts. This all works best if the scene can then be read or acted out by a group of people. You will find that by treating parts of a play, in this manner, they will begin to mean much more to you and you will remember them more vividly.

Many French departments, in universities and polytechnics, put on French plays from time to time, often choosing plays used as set texts. The local branch of ALL (*see* page 208) should be able to provide details. Many plays are available on video. Failing these possibilities, you could try and find other students working on the same play and organize play readings.

3 Poetry

Most Examining Boards offer poetry among the options for literary texts. Poems have the advantage of being shorter than plays or novels but, on the other hand, the language of poetry is more dense and the meaning more difficult to penetrate.

Poetry cannot be read solely in translation because it would not have the same impact. You should always read a poem several times before looking at a translation. There are some excellent parallel texts available. Avoid those that give a translation in English verse. The attempt to make each line rhyme, in English, usually distorts the meaning and thus serves no useful purpose.

Study techniques

1   Note first of all the way a poem looks on the page. Long-looking, regular length lines that rhyme are almost bound to be 12 syllable lines called alexandrines. Many plays by Corneille and Racine are written entirely in alexandrines; the style of declamation in these plays makes them very different on the stage. Alexandrines in poems may be divided into stanzas ('*strophes*' in French) of three or four lines. They may also be in pairs called couplets. A shorter line could indicate 6, 8, or 10 syllable lines. There may be a mixture of shorter and longer lines in a regular pattern. Poems made up of two four-line stanzas followed by two stanzas of three lines are called sonnets — a favourite form with many poets. Twentieth-century poetry may lack a regular pattern altogether, with lines of varied length that do not rhyme.

2   Make a note of the theme of each poem you read. This will rarely be the same as the title, if there is one. Nor will the theme be, for example, simply 'love' but some aspect of this emotion or attitude towards it. If a poem is mainly descriptive it may be coloured by a certain mood or atmosphere. Group themes together so that you can see which ones occur frequently and the different ways they are treated.

3   Look at the structure of the poem. It may be presented as a scene in miniature, with a stage setting, an atmosphere, speaking parts and action. Many of Verlaine's poems follow this pattern. The poem might be narrated by an anonymous person or the voice of the poet might be strongly present. If a poet is talking directly about his emotions, then the poem can be called lyrical. This is typical of the Romantic poets like Hugo, Musset and Lamartine.

4   The imagery of a poem (words and how they are used) is one of its most important aspects. Figures of speech are used to intensify meaning. Simile makes a direct comparison between one thing and another, and is usually signalled by the use of '*comme*', '*pareil à*' or '*qui ressemble*'. Metaphor omits the latter phrases so that comparison is implied rather than stated. For example: '*Je suis un cimetière abhorré de la lune*' (Baudelaire 'Spleen (2)', *Les Fleurs du Mal*)

Personification gives human characteristics to an abstract idea. Baudelaire turns '*ennui*' into a sinister hooka-smoking person in his poem '*Au Lecteur*' and there are numerous examples in his poetry of the use of personnification. Figures of speech may be: unusual, striking, dramatic, evocative or vivid; they may make a direct appeal to the senses of sight or touch; or they may appeal chiefly to the imagination.

5   Choice of words is also an important part of imagery. What they sound like is as important as their surface meaning. Look for the repetition of certain consonants (alliteration) and how harsh or soft, liquid sounds contribute to the meaning. If certain vowel sounds are repeated this is called assonance and is part of the musical effect of poetry. The latter are usually more prominent than consonant sounds in French poetry. Verlaine's poem '*Chanson d'Automne*' is a good example of the effectiveness of the above:

> *Les sanglots longs*
> *Des violons*
> *De l'automne*
> *Blessent mon cœur*
> *D'une langueur*
> *Monotone*

Which vowel sounds are prominent and which consonants? What effect do they contribute to? Is sound more important than the sense in this poem?

6   Rhyme is part of the overall sound attractiveness of poetry too. Try marking the ends of each line (a), (b), (c) and (d), to see if there is a regular pattern. If there is, then this part of the craftsmanship of the poet and enhances the total effect of the poem.

Explaining a poem: critical analysis

For this kind of examination task, you may be asked to discuss a poem under certain headings. It is likely that these will include some of the following:

(a) theme and title
(b) how the following contribute to the theme (poetical expression – use of dialogue, choice of vocabulary)
(c) poetic form (sonnet, length of line)
(d) poetic effects (rhyme, rhythm, imagery)

Here is an example of a well-known poem by Verlaine subjected to this kind of analysis.

Colloque sentimental

Dans le vieux parc solitaire et glacé
Deux formes ont tout à l'heure passé.

Leurs yeux sont noirs et leurs lèvres sont molles
Et l'on entend à peine leurs paroles

Dans le vieux parc solitaire et glacé
Deux spectres ont évoqué le passé.

–Te souvient-il de notre extase ancienne?
–Pourquoi voulez-vous donc qu'il m'en souvienne

–Ton cœur, bat-il toujours à mon seul nom?
Toujours vois-tu mon âme en rêve? – Non.

–Ah! les beaux jours de bonheur indicible
Où nous joignions nos bouches! – C'est possible.

–Qu'il était bleu, le ciel, et grand, l'espoir!
L'espoir a fui, vaincu, vers le ciel noir.

Tels ils marchaient dans les avoines folles
Et la nuit seule entendit leurs paroles.

Paul Verlaine, from *Fêtes galantes* (1869)

Theme

It is often a good idea to decide at this point only roughly what a poem is about, returning later for a closer definition, once you have examined it in other ways.

The theme at first glance, then, seems to be concerned with love. The title also reveals that it is about a conversation.

Structure or plan

Although you may not be asked to discuss specifically the structure of a poem, it is a good idea to discover if it has one. By doing this you will reveal other aspects of the poem.

This poem is devised rather like a playlet. The plan has three parts. The first three stanzas **introduce** us, through the eyes of a hidden and anonymous observer, to the setting and the characters (the grounds of an old château on a winter's night where two ghostly lovers are discussing their past); **the action** as the characters walk and speak; and **a conclusion** in the form of a fade-out as they disappear from sight and out of earshot. This plan is strikingly effective and simple. There is nothing else to distract our attention.

Note Many of Verlaine's poems take the form of a dramatized piece.

Poetic form

The poem is in the form of eight, ten-syllable rhyming couplets which suit the brief introduction and the conversation which follows.

The movement or unfolding of the ideas

A chill and lonely atmosphere is evoked by the first line. These are perhaps the grounds of a country mansion that was once the centre of a fashionable aristocratic lifestyle. The observer must have only just come upon this scene for the two characters are at first only *'deux formes'* gliding past as they talk.

As they turn and walk back we get a better view of them. Their faces are visible but they are not quite the faces of living people (line 3). The singling out of eyes and lips is both logical and eery: eyes and lips are important to lovers but these eyes are blank or hollow while the lips remain soft. We cannot yet hear all that they are saying (line 4), but a conclusion has now been drawn: they are two ghostly figures discussing the past and to emphasize the setting and atmosphere line 1 is repeated .

Lover A remembers their love affair with some enthusiasm as an *'extase'* (no ordinary affair this since *extase* in its original sense refers to an intense religious experience) and calls the other person *'tu'*. Lover B seems reluctant to be reminded and uses the *'vous'* form. Both questions remain unanswered, however, and hence excite our curiosity. Who were these two? If their affair was so special, why is one of them keen on remembering and the other not? Why the *'vous'* form of address to someone who was once very close? Members of the aristocracy would not usually use the *'tu'* form to each other in public.

Lover A remembers with delight their effect on the other person (again this was an exceptional relationship, line 10) since to see your lover's 'very soul' is unusual, even in dreams. Lover B is quite categoric in his or her response: *'non'*. There is no indication, however, of how this is said. Is the tone one of irritation or regret? Is it said hesitantly or firmly?

Lover A is not put off at all by this response since perhaps ghosts cannot re-experience emotion in their state: they can only recall it. Lover A continues with rapture to remember one of the sensual pleasures of their relationship, described not prosaically as a kiss but a 'joining of mouths'. This utterance from Lover A is in the form of an exclamation and not a question. He or she is now musing with delight. The sensual image produces a response in Lover B: something stirs in his or her memory – *'C'est possible'*. But how is this said? With pleasure, weariness or faint interest?

In line 13, Lover A continues his or her joyful review of the past with the memory of how promising life seemed — blue sky evokes the limitlessness of human expectations and dreams. Lover B reacts swiftly to this recollection; the sting in his or her voice is echoed by the *'i'* and *'u'* sounds and the *'s'* and *'f'* consonants. Black, a symbol of despair, takes the place of blue.

In the last stanza the pair carry on talking but move out of earshot, along the overgrown pathways of the château grounds.

Poetic effects

Imagery

There are strikingly few images used in this poem. The metaphor *'extase'* for love is unusual, being more normally associated with religious experiences. It fits readily here though with the possible religious connotations of the word *'colloque'* in the title (*see* below). The use of the phrase 'joining of mouths' is aptly sensuous, particularly in the context of the earlier mentioned 'soft lips'. The most memorable image is the metaphor of blue sky to evoke human aspirations and hopes. Blue sky broadens the discussion of these two lovers, beyond the confines of love, into the area of human desire for achievement and fulfillment. The image is familiar to the other person and he or she responds intellectually by personifying 'hope' and making it 'fly' before the storm of a darkened sky.

Vocabulary

There are a few unusual words such as *'colloque'* and *'indicible'* which are all the more striking because they are sparingly used. The combination of *colloque* and *sentimental* is unusual; a *colloque* is normally conducted on a subject of some seriousness, whereas *sentimental* suggests something, if not frivolous, then at least light-hearted. It also has connotations of emotions and nostalgia, in contrast to the intellectual flavour of *colloque*. This contrastive element is perhaps an echo of the two characters in the poem, one of whom seems full of pessimism and the other full of radiant memories. One of them reacts through feelings the other through the mind. There are a number of adjectives referring to sensory impression, particularly that of sight, and a few abstract nouns like *passé, bonheur* and *espoir*. The structure *te souvient-il*, instead of the more normal question form in speech *tu te souviens?* or *te souviens-tu?*, is interesting. The two latter forms might be used to **introduce** a subject for discussion. The use of the former suggests that the couple have indeed been reminiscing for some time before they were overheard. This impression is strengthened because speaker B uses it in his or her response: *Pourquoi voulez-vous donc qu' il m'en souvienne?*

Musical effects

The large number of *'s'* and *'l'* sounds lend the poem an overall musical quality. In lines 1 and 2, the repeated *'s'* sounds might evoke the whisper of half-heard conversation. The short syllables, *('t'* and *'i'* and *'e'* sounds) of line 7, suggest a lightness of character in the voice. By contrast, the *'ou'* and *'o'* sounds and the longer syllables suggest a more resonous tone of voice for speaker B. This impression is reinforced by the pompous sounding use of the 'vous' form. Lightness of tone is also suggested by the short words in lines 9 and 10. The repetition of *'b'* and *'d'* sounds in lines 11 and 12, could be evocative of someone mulling over old memories with satisfaction.

Rhythmic effects

Rhythm in French poetry derives from a natural break or caesura that occurs in the sense of a line, unlike English poetry where this effect is due to the alternation of stressed and unstressed syllables (*see* pronunciation, page 186). In French poetry, the word that occurs just before this break gains slightly more emphasis as does the word at the end of the line where the sense also traditionally pauses. The caesura can come anywhere in the line but often comes in the middle of a line. There could be more than one pause.

In line 3 there is a pause or caesura after *'morts'* so that it links rhythmically with *'molles'*. Both words are thus thrown into relief. In line 4 the caesura is slightly delayed with emphasis on the word *'peine'*. This creates the impression that we are straining our ears to catch what is being said. In line 9 there is a natural pause after *'Ton cœur'* throwing this word into prominence. The *'non'* of the next line is strongly emphasized since the break occurs just before it. Line 13 has a double break so that both *'bleu'* and *'grand'* are highlighted. In the next line, a similar effect is produced with *'fui'* and *'vaincu'*, more strikingly because here the two breaks are close together. Because of the sense, line 15 has a slight pause after *'tels'*. The lengthening effect on the rest of the line is suggestive of the motion of two figures walking away into the distance.

One last feature to mention is that of *'enjambement'*. The sense of a line of traditional French poetry is normally contained within the line. If this sense is carried across into the following line it is noticeable to a cultured French ear and can have an effect on the meaning. A noteworthy *'enjambement'* occurs here in lines 11 and 12. The effect is suggestive of someone being carried away by the excitement of memory.

Rhyme

In order to qualify as a rhyme words must end in two identical sound elements: *consonant + vowel, vowel + consonant*. Thus *'liberté'* rhymes with *'chanter'* but not with *'trouvé'* and *'père'* with *'vert'* but not with *'pire'*. If there is a third identical element the rhyme is said to be 'rich'.

There are four sets of rich rhymes in this poem. Can you spot them? The presence of rich rhymes suggests that this is a carefully crafted piece and these rhymes add to the general musical effect and beauty of the whole poem.

The subject of the theme can now be re-examined. It would not be fully accurate to say that this is a poem just about love. A whole life experience is suggested in the final exchange between the two lovers. There also seems to be a conflict in their view points. One of them is thoroughly disillusioned with their experience; the other can only remember happiness and pleasure. It is tempting to assign a sex to the characters. You will no doubt have formed your own opinion about this. One possibility is that they are the opposite sides of a single personality. Perhaps the theme is really bitter-sweet memories of life but the emphasis remains on the first element since this is the impression we are left with.

Note This analysis does not exhaust all the possibilities for discussion. You may well have other ideas yourself or the pictures the poem conjures up might be quite different. Talk these through with a friend or your teacher. Try learning the poem off by heart. This way you will make it yours so to speak and it will gain in depth of meaning as you say it over in your mind's eye.

4 *Comment étudier la littérature française en français*

Dans certains cas, vous serez obligé d'écrire en français sur un aspect de la littérature française. Pour savoir bien aborder cette tâche, certains exercices sont nécessaires. Voici quelques conseils préliminaires:

(a) Pour le premier texte, choisissez un livre d'un auteur moderne plutôt dans le style de la langue parlée. Voici quelques exemples:

Rochefort *Les Petits Enfants du Siècle*
Prévert *Poèmes*
Ionesco *Rhinocéros, La Leçon*
Beckett *En Attendant Godot*
Camus *L'Etranger*
Pagnol *Topaze*
Robe-Grillet *Les Gommes*

(b) Travaillez le plus possible avec un dictionnaire monolingue.

(c) Dès le début, prenez l'habitude d'écrire vos notes en français. Inutile de commencer en anglais avec l'idée de traduire cela plus tard en français.

(d) Etablissez des points de repère en fonction des remarques qui suivent.

Structure

Si possible discutez avec votre prof pour vous renseigner en avance sur le récit et les événements — où cela se passe-t-il, à quelle époque et qui en sont les personnages principaux? Sinon, trouvez dans un livre de critique un résumé du texte. Consultez, par exemple, les séries suivantes:

Profil d'une Œuvre, Hatier
Lire Aujourd'hui, Hachette
Théâtre et Mises en Scène, Hatier
et aussi les différents tomes de:
A Lagarde et L Michard *Les Grands Auteurs Français du Programme*, (17e, 18e, 19e, 20e, siècles), Bordas — the last volumes were published in 1969 and 1973 respectively.

Vous pouvez chercher ces livres dans votre bibliothèque ou les commander par le système de *'Inter Library Loans'*. Vous pourriez aussi les trouver ou les commander à la librairie Hachette de Londres ou à la librairie de l'université la plus proche. Dans des grands ouvrages, comme la collection Lagarde et Michard, il vous faudrait chercher le nom de l'auteur ou du livre dans le sommaire. En vous référant à la section correspondante, vous trouverez une description de la vie de l'auteur et de ses oeuvres principales, suivie d'un résumé des aspects importants de son œuvre puis des extraits commentés. Il faut prendre des notes sur ce qui vous semble intéressant ou important.

Au fur et à mesure que vous lisez les textes prescrits, prenez des notes sur ce qui arrive. Quand vous aurez lu tout le texte revenez en arrière et faites vous-même un petit résumé des événements en soulignant les moments importants, les grands épisodes, les actions déterminantes et le dénouement final. Notez la chronologie des événements et les sauts dans le déroulement de l'action ou les retours en arrière.

Les personnages

Faites une liste des personnages en les divisant entre personnages principaux — les héros ou les héroïnes — et ceux qui jouent un rôle secondaire. Pour chaque personne importante faites un portrait en signalant ses défauts et ses qualités. Trouvez dans le texte des exemples de son attitude, des pensées ou des jugements portés sur lui ou sur elle par d'autres personnages. Considérez les motifs qui ont déterminé leurs actes. Ces motifs sont-ils clairs ou ambigus? Est-ce que leurs actes trouvent leur origine dans la personalité de l'individu ou sont-ils dus à l'influence d'autres personnes? Est-ce que le caractère des héros ou des héroïnes change ou se modifie au cours du récit? Est-ce qu'il faut tenir compte de leur âge? Essayez de vous mettre à la place de tel ou tel personnage. Est-ce que vous auriez réagi de la même façon devant un problème identique? Finalement portez vous-même un jugement sur les personnages.

Les trouvez-vous sympathiques? Est-ce qu'ils sont à plaindre ou à condamner? Est-ce qu'ils méritent notre approbation ou notre réprobation. Illustrez votre opinion avec des références au texte. Quelles questions voudriez-vous leur poser si vous aviez la possibilité de les interviewer?

La mise en scène

Où se passe le récit et à quelle époque? Dans une région de France ou dans une grande ville? Dans quel milieu social est-il situé? De quelle valeur est la mise en scène: sans grande importance ou très importante? Les personnages vivent-ils en harmonie ou en désaccord avec leur environnement? Le milieu social a-t-il une influence sur leur manière de vivre? Sont-ils des privilégiés ou des défavorisés? Sont-ils relativement libres d'agir à leur guise ou se trouvent-ils en conflit avec la société? Quel rôle a joué leur naissance, leur éducation ou leur travail?

Qui raconte, qui 'voit' les événements qui sont racontés. S'il s'agit d'un narrateur anonyme ou extérieur, le récit sera mené à la troisième personne. Dans d'autres cas le récit sera à la première personne raconté par le héro ou l'héroïne comme par exemple dans *L'Etranger*, *Le Nœud de Vipères* ou *Les Petits Enfants du Siècle*.

La narration est liée au point de vue de l'œuvre. Le point de vue peut être celui d'un observateur externe qui se contente de constater les apparences sans pouvoir révéler les pensées des personnages. Il peut être interne par les yeux de quelqu'un qui participe à l'action mais qui donne nécessairement une interprétation subjective. Le point de vue peut être celui d'un narrateur 'omniscient' qui présente les faits sous plusieurs angles à la fois. Il lui est permis de passer sans obstacle d'une scène à une autre, de connaître le passé, le présent et le futur et de pénétrer toutes les pensées de ses personnages.

La description joue-t-elle un rôle important dans le livre? Le but de l'auteur est-il d'enchanter le lecteur par la beauté de la scène naturelle? Trouvez-vous ses descriptions poétiques? Quelle impression visuelle des paysages vous reste en mémoire après la lecture? L'auteur emploie-t-il la suggestion pour créer la mise en scène ou est-ce qu'il emploie une technique de photographie? Le résultat est-il un document de sociologie ou un film sur la nature avec flore et faune en abondance?

Le sens de l'œuvre

Le livre a-t-il un ou plusieurs thèmes? L'auteur a-t-il un message? Quelle société ou quel aspect de la société est-ce qu'il dépeint? S'intéresse-t-il à dénoncer, à accepter ou à approuver certaines attitudes? Est-ce qu'il cherche à en analyser les causes? Est-ce qu'il critique d'une manière directe ou est-ce qu'il présente les détails d'une manière objective? Le contexte historique est-il important pour bien comprendre le sens de l'œuvre? Le sens a-t-il une valeur aujourd'hui? Quelles sont vos réactions et vos réflexions? Sur quoi vous trouvez-vous bien informé après avoir lu le livre deux ou trois fois?

2 Planning and writing literary essays

Contents

1 Writing answers in French

Answers written in French will focus on the content of the books you have studied rather than on their literary and historical aspects. You will need to be able to describe the characters, their relationships to one another and the main events in the story. You will also be expected to describe your feelings towards the characters and your judgements on the ideas or certain aspects of the ideas presented by the author. You may have studied two texts on similar themes and be required to compare and contrast them. You may have selected one or two works from a list of books that revolve around a particular theme. Always read all the questions through before deciding which one to do. In thematic studies, all the questions may not be appropriate to all the books. Read the question you have chosen, carefully. It will usually ask you to do more than one thing, to explain or describe something and give your judgement. For example, on page 155:

Décrivez les personnages féminins de cette pièce (Anouilh: La Belle Vie). Les trouvez-vous sympathiques? (JMB, June 1990).

In this case, make sure you give space to both parts, usually in the proportion of 2 to 1. Even in a question like:

Quelle est votre impression des ennemis? (Cambridge, June 1990: Maupassant, Boule de Suif et autres contes de la guerre)

Your answer will contain more than one part because your impression will be divided inevitably between the good and bad qualities of the German soldiers occupying France (e.g. how differences in rank affect them and how they behave collectively and individually). With questions that ask for the candidate's personal response, it is a good idea to weave into the body of the essay such phrases as '*à mon avis*', '*je trouve que*' and '*selon moi*'. Bear all these points in mind when planning and writing your answer. Your answer should consist of:

(a) a brief introduction
(b) discussion in paragraphs that clearly treat particular aspects, putting two points of view if required, remembering to keep the most convincing or important points to last
(c) a brief conclusion (*see* pages 94–5)

If the question asks you to describe or relate, and then to give your own opinion you can either work in your own ideas with the description in each paragraph or devote a final section which is clearly devoted to giving your own viewpoint.

Marks are usually awarded weighted in favour of the content of the answer. Marks may also be awarded for the language used. The proportion is roughly 3:1. These two aspects go closely hand in hand. If you have had plenty of practice in discussing the texts in class, making notes on them in French and writing your own synopsis, you should be able to describe and give your own views without too much difficulty. A few incorrect genders and accents missing are not going to matter. Pay particular attention to tenses that you use. When you are describing someone's character, you will probably find yourself using the present tense. If you then refer to an incident or an event in the story, you are more likely to need a perfect or imperfect. If events before other events are mentioned you could need the pluperfect.

A comment in the Cambridge Board's report on the 1990 examination, in which the literature paper was entirely in French for the first time, is instructive to pupil and teacher:

> 'It was very encouraging that so many candidates could express themselves with fluency, sounding remarkably unhindered by linguistic constraints. It was also very clear that communication was least constrained where schools had provided a solid background of grammatical structures and an adequate descriptive and critical vocabulary.'

A brief vocabulary

Bonnes ou mauvaises qualités?

Lesquelles pouvez-vous attribuer aux personnages des textes que vous étudiez?

indépendant, assuré, confiant, agressif, brutal, résolu, humble, timide, modeste, souple (adaptable), *intelligent, habile, adroit* (clever, skilled), *maladroit* (clumsy, tactless), *incapable* (inept, useless), *rusé, malin* (cunning, crafty), *méchant* (malicious), *débrouillard* (resourceful), *sérieux* (earnest), *réfléchi* (serious, thoughtful), *limité, avoir l'esprit étroit/borné* (narrow-minded), *fantaisiste* (imaginative), *compréhensif* (understanding), *compatissant* (sympathetic), *charitable, chaleureux* (warm-hearted), *aimable, gentil, expansif* (out-going), *tendre* (loving), *innocent, naïf, impitoyable, sans pitié* (merciless), *sans scrupule* (unscrupulous), *sans pudeur* (shameless), *sadique, cruel, joyeux, gai* (cheerful), *amusant, avoir/manquer (de) le sens de l'humour, sombre* (gloomy), *mélancolique, triste, généreux, indulgent, avare, mesquin* (stingy), *honnête, malhonnête, menteur* (untruthful), *hypocrite* (hypocritical), *oisif, fainéant* (idle, lazy), *travailleur* (hard-working), *énergique, passif, soumis* (submissive), *anxieux* (insecure), *insolent, rude* (harsh, severe), *grossier* (rude, coarse), *vulgaire, bien-élevé* (well-mannered), *éduqué* (well brought-up), *prudent, impulsif, courageux, vaniteux* (vain), *menaçant, sinistre, optimiste, pessimiste, accepter son sort/réagir contre son sort* (accept/reject one's lot)

Petit vocabulaire critique

les personnages (the characters), *le caractère* (personality, character of one of the former — e.g. *il y a plusieurs personnages intéressants dans cette pièce, ils possèdent tous un caractère très différent*) *le héros, l'héroïne, jouer le rôle de* (play the part of), *un trait de caractère* (feature of character), *contradictoire, incompatible, contraster avec, faire une comparaison avec, on peut comparer X avec Y, le conflit des opinions, être attiré, séduit par X, tomber amoureux de Y, être rejeté par Z, être abattu, démoralisé* (be downcast, dejected), *cacher ses vraies intentions, les motifs, les mobiles* (motives)

un roman (novel) *la pièce* (play) *un conte* (short story), *un poème, dramatique, tragique, ironique, comique*

l'écrivain (writer) *le romancier/la romancière* (novelist), *l'auteur, l'écrivain, le dramaturge* (playwright)

dépeindre, *décrire* (describe, depict), *évoquer, fait penser à, rappeler* (evokes, makes you think of) *le récit* (the story), *l'action se passe, les événements se déroulent en* (action happens, events take place in), *l'intrigue devient complexe* (the action gets complicated), *le dénouement* (the outcome, conclusion), *atteindre un point culminant* (get to a climax), *un épisode qui attire notre sympathie/notre pitié, qui fait rire/pleurer une atmosphère tendue/détendue, décontractée* (a tense/relaxed atmosphere), *l'ambiance, la couleur locale* (local colour — details that create the sense of a place or time setting) *la mise en scène* (the setting, background), *réaliste, vraisemblable* (realistic, lifelike), *invraisemblable* (unrealistic, artificial)

une scène, *un épisode, un moment dramatique, des circonstances imprévues* (unexpected, unforseen circumstances), *une tournure imprévue* (an unexpected turn of events), *un retour en arrière* (flashback)

Model answer (with two points of view)

1 Faites le portrait de Madame Dalleray. Trouvez-vous son influence sur Phil plutôt bonne ou mauvaise? (*Le Blé en Herbe*, Colette)   *JMB A-Level, June 1990*

Possible answer

Phil recontre Mme Dalleray pour la première fois quand s'étant trompée de chemin elle lui demande des renseignements. Plus tard, il la revoit à Ker-Anna, la maison qu'elle avait louée près de Cancale, et il lui rend plusieurs visites.

C'est une femme mûre de 30–35 ans, aux cheveux noirs et aux yeux foncés. Elle aime porter des vêtements blancs et c'est pour cela que Phil la nomme 'la dame en blanc'. Il faut signaler que nous observons tous les détails sur Mme Dalleray par les yeux de Phil et donc nous n'avons que l'image que lui impose cette femme. On a l'impression d'une femme très assurée qui ne perd jamais son sang-froid. Tout ce qu'elle dit est bien pesé et même calculé. Dès la première rencontre avec Phil elle prend le dessus et il semble qu'elle joue avec lui et que ce jeu l'amuse. Se trouvant seule en vacances peut-être s'ennuie-t-elle un peu? Cette femme sensuelle aime brûler de l'encens dans la maison et se parfumer. Elle offre à Phil des boissons très fraîches et des fruits juteux. Elle est flattée par les attentions du jeune adolescent et amusée par sa maladresse. C'est elle qui prend l'initiative pourtant et joue la séductrice. Elle n'a pas d'illusions sur la profondeur des émotions de Phil. Vers la fin de son séjour pourtant, elle a l'idée d'obtenir de lui une confession de son amour, ou du moins, lui faire admettre qu'il sera triste quand elle sera partie. Mais à la fin elle n'ose pas l'obliger de peur d'être blessée.

(a) C'est par l'intermédiare de Mme Dalleray que Phil fait son apprentissage de l'amour sexuel et commence à découvrir la complexité du cœur féminin. **Je suis persuadé** que, sans cette expérience, Phil n'aurait pas eu le courage plus tard de prendre l'initiative avec Vinca et de lui faire l'amour. **Je trouve bon** que Phil découvre ces détails dans les bras d'une femme expérimentée. A mon avis, bien que Mme Dalleray soit une séductrice, son attitude envers le garçon révèle de la tendresse et de l'estime. **Je trouve qu'**elle est pleine de tact et qu'elle prend soin de ne pas blesser le jeune garçon. **Il me semble** qu'elle joue le rôle d'une mère autant que celui d'une amante. **J'approuve** pourtant le fait que leur liaison est courte. Si Mme Dalleray était restée disponible pour le reste des vacances, **je ne suis pas sûr** de ce qui aurait pu se passer entre Phil et Vinca. **A mon avis** c'est une décision volontaire de la part de Mme Dalleray de revenir à Paris sans lui dire adieu, pour faciliter le rapport qui va se développer entre ces deux jeunes personnes.

Je suis convaincu qu'il y a tellement de positif dans cette rencontre qu'il **est difficile de trouver trop de mal** dans l'influence que Mme Dalleray a exercé sur ce garçon de 16 ans. Je voudrais bien savoir si plus tard cette expérience sera simplement un souvenir heureux dans sa mémoire ou s'il désirera la répéter ou la raviver.

(b) Mme Dalleray sait bien ce qu'elle fait en séduisant ce jeune garçon. **Je crois qu'**elle s'ennuie en vacances et désire s'amuser. **J'avoue que je trouve un peu dégoûtant** l'idée qu'une femme mûre exploite ainsi un garçon de 16 ans. **C'est dommage** que ce soit là sa première expérience de l'amour. Tout est rendu trop facile pour lui. **Il vaudrait mieux** qu'il découvre les compléxités d'un rapport sexuel dans les bras d'une personne qui a le même âge que lui et qui partage le point de vue et l'attitude d'un adolescent. Ce serait du moins une découverte réciproque. **Je crois que** cette première expérience pourrait bien lui donner une fausse impression et influencer plus tard ses rapports avec le beau sexe. **J'ai le sentiment que**, une fois revenu à Paris, Phil pourrait éprouver un désir très fort de revoir la femme en blanc. Ce n'est pas pour rien qu'elle lui laisse son numéro de téléphone.

Je trouve donc difficile d'approuver l'influence que Mme Dalleray exerce sur Phil. Les impressions qu'elle laisse dans l'esprit de ce jeune homme vont revenir le hanter et peut-être même l'obséder.

A noter

(a) Les phrases en gras indiquent la manière dont on peut exprimer une opinion personnelle.

(b) Vous ne serez peut-être pas d'accord avec ni l'une ni l'autre des opinions exprimées à la fin de cette rédaction. Discutez ces conclusions avec votre professeur ou vos amis.

(c) The Board from which this question was taken assigns marks as follows (out of a total of 50): 35 for content; 15 for language. The 35 marks are split 20:15 (i.e. 20 marks for the factual response and 15 for the personal opinion).

2 Writing answers in English

Questions set in English usually require:
(a) an understanding and evaluation of the author's thought or technique
(b) some knowledge of social and literary history that helps you to appreciate the text better
This kind of answer gives less scope for personal reaction and puts more emphasis on reading about how other people have evaluated the works concerned and the aims and intentions of the writer when he was writing.

Questions are framed either as comments or quotations that contain a judgement followed by the invitation to discuss or evaluate. Most questions of this kind ask you to examine a judgement from two opposing viewpoints. You will need an introduction. This can take the form of re-stating in your own terms the two views to be discussed. For the main body of your answer you can use the model already suggested (*see* pages 94–5): a line down the middle of the page with for and against columns; number your ideas when you have roughed them out, in the order in which you will present them, putting the the most convincing ones last and your opinion in the second half of the essay. The conclusion should clearly state your final assessment.

One small but important technical point: when referring to the title of the work in your essay make sure you either underline this or put it between inverted commas.

Useful books:

R Hares, (1984), *Compo Lit! French Language Essay Writing*, Hodder & Stoughton
J Cruickshank (ed.), *French Literature and its Background*, Volume III 'The Late Nineteenth Century', (1969), 'The Twentieth Century', (1970), OUP
Studies in French Literature, Edward Arnold (series)
Look for critical editions of the works you are studying. They usually contain useful introductions.

Model answer

Read the question set and the answer. It is worth remembering that there is no 'perfect answer' to a literature question. Examiners often give high marks to very different attempts at the same question. It is important that your essay has a clear plan as outlined above and that one point leads logically into the next. Make it obvious that you know and understand the book you have studied by using clear references to the text and brief quotations when appropriate. Don't be tempted to throw in everything you know about the book or to try and make material from a previously done essay fit the exam question when it has no relevance. Examiners are constantly referring to this kind of fault in their reports.

1   'Molière's skill as a dramatist is evident not so much in his portrayal of individual characters as in the ways in which they are made to react to each other at particular moments.' Discuss with reference to *L'Avare*.   *Oxford and Cambridge A-Level, June 1990*

Possible answer

This judgement implies that Molière's characters are less interesting because of their individual personalities than they are through their interaction when brought into contact with one another. We are less involved in what they are and more absorbed in watching what they do.

All the characters in *L'Avare* seem to possess enough individuality both to make them credible as human beings and to win our approval, despite any faults they may have. Valère is devoted to Elise and is prepared to flatter (and play up to) Harpagon in order to be near her and fulfil his ambition of marrying her eventually. Elise and Cléante are supportive of one another in the difficult situation they face in Harpagon's household. Elise is defiant and impertinent towards her father when he reveals his marriage plans for her. The latter are so unreasonable that we cannot but feel sympathy for Elise. Cléante is something of a man about town and a gambler. He is head over heels in love with Mariane and has won her affection. Although he is rude to his father, telling him what he thinks of him in no uncertain terms, he has a reckless sense of humour that is appealing. Mariane is prepared to marry, against her own choice, to ensure her mother's financial situation even though she is really in love with Cléante. La Flèche tries to fulfill his double role (as coachman and cook) as best he can and tries to tell the truth. He is the only person who admits to an affection for Harpagon. Frosine lives by her wits and is prepared to lie and misrepresent facts to Harpagon. She wins our approval however when having got nothing out of him, she is ready to assist the course of true love for no financial reward.

Harpagon's character is somewhat more complex. There is just a hint in Elise's remark to her brother: '*Il* (Harpagon) *nous donne de plus en plus sujet de regretter la mort de notre mère*' to suggest that Harpagon was perhaps a different kind of person when his wife was alive. His avarice is of overwhelming proportions, however, and affects all his dealings with other people. Nevertheless, he is keen on marrying a young girl, despite both her lack of fortune and his age. He is vain and is easily flattered by Frosine who is wily enough to spot this weakness. He really does want to make a good impression when Mariane meets him for the first time. He goes as far as preparing a pretty speech to impress her. He keeps up appearances by maintaining a coach and horses and providing some food when his prospective bride comes to meet his family. An out and out miser might have made complete economies in all these areas. He offers sound advice to his son when he tells him to invest money won in gambling. On the other hand, he is perfectly obnoxious to both Elise and Cléante, telling Mariane that he will soon be rid of both and that '*mauvaises herbes croîent toujours*'.

All these details give some depth of interest to the characters but they might not provide any dramatic action in themselves. Also, our attention in *L'Avare* is not focussed on how people became as they are, or on what they might become in the future. Harpagon does not change at all during the play; nor does it seem likely that he will be very different when at the end he gets back his '*chère cassette*'. The main spring of the action is provided by the way in which the devices and desires of the characters clash and weave almost every time they are together on the stage.

This reaction can be clearly observed when we see Harpagon with his two children for the first time. Cléante has already told his sister about his love for Mariane so that when Harpagon broaches the subject of marriage, and mentions her name, Cléante and the audience jump to the conclusion that she is intended for the son of the family. Excitement builds, as Harpagon sounds out his children's opinion about the young lady, only to collapse in the astounding news that Harpagon intends to marry her himself.

While Cléante goes off to recover from the shock, Harpagon tries to deal summarily with marriage plans for his daughter. Her impertinence so defies him, however, that he is forced to engage Valère as umpire. Valère is then caught in the trap of his own hypocrisy and, although he wriggles and plays with words, he cannot escape the financial advantages of a marriage '*sans dot*' and finds himself obliged to read a moral lecture to Elise on daughterly obedience in a matter for which he has no stomach.

Next, we see a clash between a spendthrift young man, forced to borrow money to pay for his way of life, and a usurer — who not only lends at an extortionate rate but contrives to get rid of junk from his attic at the same time. The fact that they turn out to be Cléante and his father is a dramatic surprise for them (and the audience). Given what we already know about both these characters, it is not surprising that the sparks fly as they berate each other for their faults.

A little later Harpagon's vanity is a source of humour and reaction between characters when Frosine comes to discuss marriage arrangements with him. Frosine knows that to combat Harpagon's absorbing avarice, she must make Mariane seem as financially attractive as possible even though she hasn't a penny. Despite ingenious arguments, that center on Mariane's frugal way of life and her dislike of gambling, she fails to persuade him. She realizes though that something more important is troubling him about prospective wedlock. She seizes the initiative and succeeds in making him believe that Mariane really prefers old men. So the tables are turned. **She** now has Harpagon in her control and persuades him to walk up and down to display his manliness. She even manages to manipulate his vanity to the extent of making an attractive feature out of his cough. The situation is quickly reversed when she seeks financial reward for her services and, although she can still jerk the puppet's strings a little, Harpagon's money instinct asserts its own control of the situation.

There are moments in the play when Harpagon's love of money seems to bring him close to the edge of lunacy. This is particularly apparent when he raves about his lost '*cassette*' at the end of Act IV. In this scene, none of the other characters are present for him to react with. The fact that the audience are brought into the reactive process, prevents any tendency to an emotive impact in this monologue which might have been the case if we really believed we were watching a man entirely alone. The audience find Harpagon's ravings so ludicrous that they begin to laugh. He becomes suspicious at the noise and gradually the spectators become part of the action and are amused to be thus implicated as he leaves the stage to search for the thief.

Near the end of the play, we witness again Valère caught in the trap of his own deceit of Harpagon. Valère feels so guilty about his, as yet unrevealed, love for Elise that he readily jumps to the conclusion that this is what Harpagon means when he accuses him of a crime and of betraying him. The discussion at cross-purposes that follows is one of the most amusing episodes of the play. All the more so because love, in the minds of both men, assumes a different context (but to each a perfectly comprehensible one).

Almost any scene from *L'Avare* could be shown to depend to a great extent on character interaction. Molière does not rely on plumbing psychological depths to entertain the audience. The fast-moving action of the play springs from the details we have about the intentions and desires of the characters and the energy they expend as they come into contact with one another.

3 Context and commentary questions

Context questions are normally answered in English. You are asked to 'relate the passage to its context' or 'Identify the point at which this extract occurs'. This is followed by a series of tasks asking you to explain or comment on aspects of character or action revealed in the selected passage.

'Situating in context' means that you need to give sufficient detail for the significance of the extract to be understood within the context of the whole work. This is not an invitation to tell the whole story up to that point. You should ask yourself what would someone, with a broad knowledge of the work, have to know (about the characters and about what has happened so far) to be able to appreciate this scene or incident in particular. Quite often, the reason for the state of mind of the characters at the beginning of the extract is a good place to begin. What has made them like this? Why are they reacting in this way to what follows?

When referring to a play, it is not necessary to give the number of the act and scene from which the passage was taken. Something like 'Near the end of Act II' is quite adequate.

The other tasks usually relate only to the material in the extract itself. Make sure that your answer refers to this directly. Some Boards give the number of marks assigned to these tasks. Make sure you answer each part and be guided, as to length of answer and the time you need to spend on it, by the number of marks indicated. You are expected to be able to explain or comment by referring to the text, or show what it reveals about character or humour, but not to translate it!

Model answer

1 Place the following passage in its context (within the play *Les Mains Sales* by Jean-Paul Sartre). Why does Hoederer talk to Hugo in this way? What effect does this have on him? How well would this extract work on the stage? Comment on any other features of the passage which you consider important.

Hugo Lâchez ma main.

Hoederer (sans la lâcher) Suppose que je suis devant toi, exactement comme je suis et que tu me vises...

Hugo Lâchez-moi et travaillons.

Hoederer Tu me regardes et au moment de tirer, voilà que tu penses, 'si c'était lui qui avait raison?' Tu te rends compte?

Hugo Je n'y penserais pas. Je ne penserais à rien d'autre qu'à tuer.

Hoederer Tu y penserais: un intellectuel, il faut que ça pense. Avant même de presser sur la gâchette tu aurais déjà vu toutes les conséquences possibles de ton acte: tout le travail d'une vie en ruines, une politique flanquée par terre, personne pour me remplacer, le Parti condamné peut-être à ne jamais prendre le pouvoir...

Hugo Je vous dis que je n'y penserais pas!

Hoederer Tu ne pourrais pas t'en empêcher. Et ça vaudrait mieux parce que, tel que tu es, si tu n'y pensais pas *avant,* tu n'aurais pas trop de toute ta vie pour y penser *après. (Un temps.)* Quelle rage avez-vous tous de jouer aux tueurs? Ce sont des types sans imagination: ça leur est égal de donner la mort parce qu'ils n'ont aucune idée de ce que c'est la vie. Je préfère les gens qui ont peur de la mort des autres: c'est la preuve qu'ils savent vivre.

Hugo Je ne suis pas fait pour vivre, je ne sais pas ce que c'est que la vie et je n'ai pas besoin de le savoir. Je suis de trop, je n'ai pas ma place et je gêne tout le monde; personne ne m'aime, personne ne me fait confiance.

Hoederer Moi, je te fais confiance.

Hugo Vous?

Hoederer Bien sûr. Tu es un homme qui a de la peine à passer à l'âge d'un homme mais tu feras un homme très acceptable, si quelqu'un te facilite le passage. Si j'échappe à leurs pétards et à leurs bombes, je te garderai près de moi et je t'aiderai.

Hugo Pourquoi me le dire? pourquoi me le dire aujourd'hui?

Hoederer Simplement pour te prouver qu'on ne peut pas buter un homme de sang-froid à moins d'être un spécialiste.

Hugo Si je l'ai décidé, je dois pouvoir le faire. (*Comme à lui-même, avec une sorte de désespoir.*) je *dois* pouvoir le faire.

Oxford and Cambridge A-Level, June 1990

Possible answer

Note There are five parts to this question. No indication of mark allocation is given. Make sure you give adequate space therefore to each part.

(a) Hugo has volunteered to carry out the Communist party's plan to assassinate the party Secretary, Hoederer, because of the latter's avowed policy of collaborating with the invading Russian army and with right-wing political elements. Hoederer sees this as a temporary policy of compromise, prior to seizing power after the war, and is supported by a small group within the Party but opposed by the majority of 'pure' communists (of which Hugo is one). During this scene Hugo, a gun in his pocket and alone with Hoederer, has an opportunity to carry out his task. Hoederer knows that Hugo has a gun and, from the beginning of the scene, has been ready to prevent him from using it.

(b) Hoederer has suspected for some time that Hugo, his new secretary, has a secret purpose and has dropped hints to this effect on previous occasions. Just before this scene, Hoederer has found out (from Hugo's wife Jessica) that Hugo intends to use a revolver to kill him. Hoederer, thus forewarned, is tense from the start of this scene but he is also confident that, during their conversation, he can prevent any attempt to shoot him because he knows that Hugo is susceptible to rational argument. He also knows that Hugo is immature and hot-headed, that he is not a professional killer and that he has the intelligence to appreciate the consequences of his actions. He has explained his political motives to Hugo earlier and the latter could not successfully reject them. Hoederer also likes Hugo, in a fatherly sort of way, hence the offer to take him under his wing later.

(c) Hugo cannot face up to the act of killing Hoederer. Hoederer has **almost** no need to keep his hand on Hugo's during this scene. It is quite obvious that Hugo **is** thinking about the consequences of his act. When Hoederer accuses Hugo, and people like him, of wanting to kill because of their lack of love of life, he goes straight to the psychological heart of Hugo's problem and Hugo collapses into self-pity. Hoederer's fatherly tone has a clear effect and Hugo finds that this emotion gets in the way of the purpose he has tensed himself up for, hence his *'Pourquoi me le dire **aujourd'hui**?'*

(d) Since most of the play is a flashback, we know that at some point Hoederer will be killed. Dramatic tension springs therefore from wondering exactly when, and how, this will take place. This scene presents just this kind of rise and fall in tension and would work effectively on the stage. The audience would be aware of the strained frame of mind of both characters from their facial expressions and their movements. Hoederer seizes Hugo's hand to prevent him getting out his gun. While he keeps his hand there tension is maintained. It is removed at the psychological moment that Hugo allows his emotions to intrude into his reasoning.

(e) This extract contains the three main strands of interest in *Les Mains Sales*: the political theme (assassination for ideological reasons); the interplay of human feelings (the older–younger man relationship); but also elements of Existentialist philosophy (the consciously willed act which determines the right of an individual to life and shapes him or her as a person). Hugo wants desperately to prove his worth to the world, by killing Hoederer, but cannot come to terms with all the possible results of his action. His cry of being *'de trop'* illustrates the meaninglessness of life (from the Existentialist point of view) for a person who has not performed a consciously willed act. On another level, it shows that what Hugo wants desperately is to be valued by another human being.

Note Most plays and novels contain: moments of great tension; clashes of personality; and particularly funny incidents. This is where passages for context questions are most likely to be drawn from. You should make a habit of noting these as you read your set texts.

3 Coursework topic

Contents

Many Examination Boards offer the option of a topic, written in French, which is set against part or all of the written literature or background papers. Topic usually consists of 2 or 3 extended essays on a theme that you have researched. The essays are spread over the two years of the A-Level course. They are usually marked by your teacher and sent to the Board for moderation. This option has the advantage of being done in your own time without the pressure of an examination. It also gives a great deal of freedom of choice. However, the final pieces of work are not corrected by your teacher before being submitted; they are a reflection of your own efforts. The essays are marked for content, structure, language and accuracy and are usually weighted in favour of the first two elements. You need to check the requirements of your Board.

The following extract, from the Cambridge Board's Report of 1990, indicates clearly the qualities that ensure high marks in this area:

> The option of Course Work was clearly popular, and, for many candidates, produced high marks.
> The best pieces of work were characterized by original research, a high degree of personal

involvement, a very high standard of written French and neat and thoughtful presentation. It was clear that these candidates had been exposed to a wide variety of French source materials and that their learning had been strongly influenced by such exposure. Some candidates had carried out research in France and others had carried out surveys among fellow students.

There are two broad possibilities for topic work: it may be based on a literary text; or on some other subject of interest for research.

1 Book-based

This gives you the opportunity of treating a book you have read in a less formal and more lively way than the critical literary approach. Here are some possibilities:

1 Book review

Imagine that you are reviewing the book for a newspaper or magazine. Describe it **briefly** under the headings of **what, where, when,** and **who**. Say what you believe the author's intentions to have been in writing the book (e.g. to entertain, amuse, draw attention to some issue or problem, satirize) and how successful he has been in this and why, in your opinion. What tone does the author write in (e.g. light, amused, serious, embittered)? Is his or her opinion clearly evident or is it implied? Are details presented factually or are they exaggerated? Is it easy to identify with the main characters? Do you recognize them as types you have met or know of? What insight have you gained from reading the book? Would the book have a good or bad influence on readers? Say why you would, or would not, recommend others to read the book.

2 Interview

This could be the dialogue of an interview with one of the characters for radio or television. You would have to decide what series the interview was for and who the prospective viewers might be. This will both give you a purpose and an attitude to adopt for the interview. You could also think about the possible attitudes of the interviewer and interviewee. This kind of topic can go beyond what is actually stated in the text.

3 Diary extract

This would be from the diary of one of the characters. Decide on what period is covered by the entries in the diary. Again, what the character writes is based on the details of the book but you can go beyond this, to explore thoughts and feelings that are otherwise only suggested or perhaps even concealed.

4 Dramatized episode

This could be for film, television or radio. You should set yourself up as the *'metteur en scène'*, (producer and director), responsible for the details of the setting for the action. You can describe what the audience will see, what the camera shows at the beginning of the scene and thereafter. Describe where the characters are placed, how they are to move, what they are thinking and feeling, what tone of voice they use.

5 Report

This could be a report from a social worker, doctor or probation officer made at a given point in the book. It would try to be factual and unbiased, taking into account social conditions, environment and the influence of other people. It could outline what might happen if no action is taken and suggest what might be done.

6 Theme

This would deal with a theme or issue that underlies the story (e.g. social deprivation, crime, hopes and expectations of teenagers or life in an HLM). You would treat the book as a source of evidence and information that helps to build up a picture. It might prove helpful to draw upon other sources such as articles or statistics to fill out your picture.

7 Continuation of story

This would be based on imagining what might happen to one or more of the characters later in life. You would have to decide how long after, and use the book as a starting point, but otherwise there is a lot of scope here for exercising your imagination. You could, for example, interview a character much later in life, in the style of some TV programmes (think along the lines of a 'This is your life' presenter).

8 Documentary

This could be for radio or television and deal with part or the whole of the book. It could be a series of episodes to illustrate a way of life; how someone got over a critical period or the attitudes of a section of the community. You could concentrate on the presenter's monologue without giving the detail of everything the viewer sees.

9 Speech

This could be a talk or speech given by one of the characters to a specific audience (e.g. a self-help group, a group of pupils, a speech-day address, a television slot for personal opinion).
Note The above are merely suggestions and not meant to be restrictive.

2 Subject-based

This option offers the widest scope. However, you should avoid the pitfall of presenting a descriptive piece of writing that is closely based on details drawn from books. This usually leads to a regurgitation of what you have read and shows little intellectual processing. Historical, geographical and biographical themes can lend themselves to this approach. The important thing to remember is to set yourself a question to be answered, something to be proved or disproved or that has two sides to it or a particular slant.

A subject like *'Le tunnel sous la Manche'* is not so promising as *'L'Eurotunnel - les dangers et les avantages.'* *'La vie du Général de Gaulle'* sounds much less adventurous than *'Le Général de Gaulle — qu'a-t-il fait pour la France?'* Compare also *'La révolution de '68'* and *'La révolution de '68 — pourrrait-elle recommencer?.'* *'Mes vacances sur la Côte d'Azur'* and *'Les effets du tourisme sur la Côte d'Azur'*. The choice of title is very important and can be responsible for sending you in the right direction from the start.

Some subjects will be interesting because they are unusual or provoke comparisons. *'Le travail d'un garçon de café'* or *'La vie d'un fermier français'* would have a natural interest in this way.

Research done in France, in the form of opinion gathering, interviews or recordings, has the advantage of being authentic both in subject and in language. You can gain profit by including recorded and visual material in your study.

You could approach project work via your own interests and by getting in touch with clubs, societies or organizations in France or making a point of contacting someone while there on holiday. (*See* appendix 2)

If you are confined to seeking information without going to France, French radio and magazines could provide project material. For example, advertising on commercial radio stations or the pictures used for marketing through magazines.

Plan and presentation

It is helpful to bear in mind the advice of a beginning, a middle and an end to the plan of your study, and to pay attention to a clear introduction, paragraphing and a conclusion. Marks may not be given for presentation but 'how your finished study looks' is an indication of how much you have been involved in it and creates a positive impression. Pay attention to the following:

(a) Attractive title page (and binder if possible)
(b) Illustrations clearly labelled and positioned relevant to the text
(c) Pages numbered
(d) Footnotes or references where necessary, at the bottom of the page
(e) Contents list
(f) List of sources used (avoid using too many English sources. This can lead to anglicized French)

Note Avoid plagiarism! (This means copying from a source without acknowledging it.) Keep quotations brief and always give their source in a footnote.

Part V Oral and aural tasks

1 The oral examination

Contents

Depending on the Board, the oral examination carries from 20% to 25% of the total marks at A Level and from 30% to 40% at AS Level. It is, therefore, an important part of your work at A and AS Level.

The oral test lasts 15-20 minutes with most Boards, or 30-35 minutes in the case of the Oxford, and Oxford and Cambridge Boards. Some Boards provide the option of continuous assessment instead of, or combined with, a final oral test. This means that you can be tested orally at certain stages of your A-Level course.

Nearly all oral tests consist of some or all of three groups of tasks:

1 **Role-play** This involves getting information, resolving a problem or expressing opinions.

2 **Reporting tasks or discussion of material provided** Reporting task material is usually in English. Discussion may be based on a prepared topic, on a book or film, on a passage to be studied before the Examination or on a research area or personal experience. Depending on the Board, discussion may be related to, or exclusive of, topics prepared for the written paper. Check your Board's regulations carefully.

3 **General conversation**

Note You should check the following points about your oral:
(a) How long the test lasts
(b) How long the preparation time is. Some Boards give you a few days to prepare printed material for discussion when the latter is quite lengthy. Other Boards allow only about 20 minutes on the day of the test. The material is usually shorter in this case
(c) Whether dictionaries are allowed
(d) Whether or not you are allowed to make notes and refer to these during the test
(e) The tasks you will be required to carry out and what proportion of the test they represent

You should find all these details in the syllabus for your Board. You should also find a description of what skills the oral test is supposed to test and some indication of how marks are awarded.

Obtain from your library or send for copies of past oral papers. It can be helpful to get these from other Boards other than the one you are doing, particularly for role-playing tasks, in order to broaden the range of situations you might meet.

You should also try to obtain a copy of recent Examiners' reports. This will give you a clearer guide to what is expected of candidates.

1 Role-play

This task often comes first. Instructions are given in the form of a brief, which sets the scene and tells you what role you are going to play, and a task that gives you the information needed to play the role. It is important to do all the things you are asked to do in the task description. If these are not itemized, it is a good idea to underline and number each bit so that you work through them systematically. Jot down a phrase or a few words in numbered order to help you with each part. You will not have time, and neither is it a good idea, to write out everything you want to say. There is usually more than one way of saying things. The main thing is to communicate the information. Once you get into the swing of things, you will find yourself reacting more naturally and all you have to do is keep an eye on the items in the task.

Most role-play situations call for a bit of play acting. You may have to appear forceful or persistent, you may have to apologize, you may have to object to something, show surprise or even concern. Enter into the spirit of the situation and don't be intimidated by the Examiner. He or she will find their task much easier if they can provoke some reaction from you. During the brief exchange of the role-play, a change in attitude often takes place: somebody is convinced, reassured or conciliated; it usually ends on a friendly note. Keep all this in mind.

Exercices

The following exercises have a brief and a task description modelled on those you are likely to meet in an exam. This is followed by a series of phrases that the other person might use. You would not have access to these in an examination. They are provided here to help you practise the roles with another person. Some Examining Boards provide suggestions of this kind for the Examiner's use; (he or she will have worked out a series of possibilities in any case). They are not meant to represent the only things that might be said. There is always a great deal of room for invention and flexibility. Work with a partner and study one of the roles; take it in turns to play each one. Do not just try and translate the information in the task description. Try and add bits of natural language. A possible version of the first role-play is done for you as an example of this.

1 **Candidate's brief** You are spending a year at Grenoble University and have been asked to lead a group of French school children, 14-16 years old, who are spending a few days in the Isère region. They are being accomodated in the *cité universitaire*. They are not happy with things and a spokesperson comes to complain.

Task You counter all their complaints with excuses or explanations:
- The rooms are small because this is student accomodation not a hotel
- It isn't costing them very much
- You admit that the meals aren't very good but you will see what can be done
- If funds allow, you could all eat out at least once
- The weather is not your fault — it is to be expected in mountains
- Excursions were recommended to you but you will consult whole group about next ones
- You are not empowered to give refunds
- Anyway, two days is hardly long enough to form an opinion
- If the group go home on their own account they will have to pay own fare
- Not fair to you, your first experience of this kind of thing in France
- Reiterate that you will do your best
- End on a friendly note saying that the weather forecast for the next few days is a lot better

Spokesman's brief You will complain strongly on behalf of the whole group. You have a fairly long list of complaints (you can enlarge on the above). You are gradually persuaded by the group leader and end on a friendly note. You begin the exchange. The following are possible things to say. Try to fill them out as much as possible:

- *Je viens vous parler parce que nous, on n'est pas content, hein*
- *D'abord les chambres sont trop petites. On ne peut pas se réunir*
- *Les repas au réfectoire sont dégoûtants. C'est froid, il n'y pas de choix*
- *Manger en ville, c'est cher*
- *On ne peut pas aller tout le temps manger en ville*
- *Il fait mauvais temps, il pleut sans cesse depuis deux jours*
- *Les excursions ne sont pas formidables — deux fois un musée!*
- *On voudrait un remboursement de tout le voyage*
- *Il y en a beaucoup qui voudraient repartir chez eux*
- *Qu'est-ce que vous allez faire?*

Possible full exchange

Spokesperson Je viens vous voir, monsieur parce que nous, on n'est pas content du séjour, vous savez.
Leader Ah bon, qu'est-ce qu'il y a? Qu'est-ce qui ne va pas?
S Euh, d'abord les chambres sont trop petites. On ne peut pas se réunir.
L Mais, ici c'est une cité universitaire, vous savez, et pas un hôtel. C'est pour cela que le prix est si raisonnable.
S Et les repas au réfectoire sont dégoûtants. C'est toujours froid et il n'y a pas de choix. Et si on va manger en ville, ça revient cher.

L Pour les repas, je suis d'accord. C'est pas formidable. Je vais voir ce qu'on peut faire. On pourrait peut-être manger au moins une fois en ville, s'il nous reste de l'argent.

S Et puis il fait un sale temps depuis deux jours maintenant, il pleut sans cesse.

L Ecoutez, là vous allez un peu fort, hein. Ce n'est pas ma faute s'il pleut! Je ne peux pas contrôler le temps! Et puis à la montagne c'est souvent comme ça.

S Et les excursions, c'est pas formidable, hein? Deux fois un musée!

L On me les avait recommandés, mais... Ecoutez, je vais consulter le groupe pour la prochaine fois, hein?

S Il y en a qui voudraient un remboursement.

L Mais vous savez, je n'ai pas le droit de faire ça. Et puis il ne faut pas juger en deux jours. On est ici pour une semaine.

S Il faut dire que certains parlent de repartir chez eux.

L Bon, s'ils font ça, ils faut qu'ils paient leur voyage, n'est-ce pas. Je ne peux pas leur fournir un billet. Et ce n'est pas juste, pour moi, hein. Vous savez, c'est la première fois que fais ce travail.

S Bon, d'accord, je vais leur raconter ça et ce que vous avez dit.

L Dites-leur aussi que la météo prédit le retour du beau temps pour demain.

You will note that:
(a) Small details have been added
(b) Words like *écoutez, vous savez, bon, d'accord, mais* and *n'est-ce pas* have also been added
(c) The words *hein* and *euh* appear; they are a trifle inelegant but it suits the style of a conversation between two young people

2 **Candidate's brief and task** You are staying with the parents of your correspondant(e). Having heard about the famous cave paintings at Lascaux*, you try to persuade the father/mother to take you, and the family, by car to see them. For a variety of reasons they are not keen on going (e.g. already been, can't see real paintings anyway, too crowded on a Sunday, too far to drive, children car-sick/might misbehave, how about a day at the seaside instead?). You counter all these arguments as convincingly as possible and you end by persuading him/her because you might not have this opportunity again.

   *les peintures dans les grottes de Lascaux

Parent's brief The candidate begins the exchange. You start off by being quite against the idea. You gradually change your opinion because your visitor is being particularly persuasive. Here are some phrases you might use:
- *On y est déjà allé*
- *C'est pas la peine, on ne voit pas les véritables peintures. La grotte est fermée au public**
- *Il y aura du monde dimanche*
- *C'est loin, hein. On en aura pour deux heures en voiture*
- *Vous savez, les enfants sont insupportables dans la voiture*
- *Ils sont souvent malades*
- *On pourrait bien aller à la plage dimanche, non?*
- *Peut-être que vous avez raison — ça ne se voit pas en Angleterre, hein?*
- *Bien, je suis persuadé(e)/Vous m'avez convaincu(e) Il faut que vous vous occupiez des enfants, n'est-ce pas*
- *Ce sera votre faute s'ils ne sont pas sages*

   * Mais on a recréé la grotte et les peintures dans une exposition appelée 'Lascaux II'

Possible beginnings:
(a) On m'a parlé hier des peintures préhistoriques dans les grottes de Lascaux. Il paraît que c'est formidable. On pourrait y aller en voiture, non...
(b) Vous pourriez nous y emmener tous en voiture, dimanche?
(c) Je voudrais bien y aller. Serait-il possible d'y aller en voiture?
(d) On pourrait faire une excursion en voiture

3 **Candidate's brief** You arrive at a small railway station in the middle of France at 7.00 p.m., expecting to catch an overnight train to Montélimar where some friends are to pick you up by car at the station and give you a lift to Nice. They are expecting you to arrive at 10.00 a.m and have

arranged to wait for one hour only. The *syndicat* has given you times of trains. You have just enough money for a ticket since all the banks were closed today for the 15 August.

Task
- Ask for a single ticket, platform and time of train
- Express surprise and dismay when told the time of the next train to Montélimar
- Ask the attendant to double check
- Can he suggest an alternative route or a way out of the problem?
- All his suggestions won't work because of the money situation, your friends can't be contacted etc.
- Stress the fact that they will not wait
- Accept his final suggestions with thanks and ask where you could stay the night

Note The idea of surprise might be expressed by '*Mais... je ne comprends pas/Non, ce n'est pas vrai.... J'avais bien noté l'heure du train/vous êtes sûr/vous ne vous êtes pas trompé*'; and dismay by '*c'est embêtant/c'est incroyable/il y a une erreur, non?*'

Attendant's brief You begin the exchange. You are rather annoyed at first and dismissive of this person's problem but you gradually begin to feel a bit sorry for them. You realize that your initial suggestions won't work. Then you hit on a good idea. Here are some possible phrases and responses:
- *Bonsoir monsieur/madame, vous désirez?*
- *Ça fait 240 francs*
- *Quai numéro deux, départ demain matin à 5 heures 15*
- *Arrivée à Montélimar à 11h27*
- *C'est écrit ici, hein, noir sur blanc!*
- *Ah non, il n'y pas d'autre train*
- *Alors, vous avez un vrai problème*
- *Je suis désolé, mais je ne peux rien faire*
- *Ecoutez, vous pourriez passer la nuit à l'hôtel et revenir demain pour prendre le train*
- *Ou bien téléphonez à vos amis pour leur dire que vous serez en retard*
- *Bon, je vois bien que c'est embêtant pour vous*
- *Eh bien écoutez, je vais téléphoner à la gare de Montélimar et laisser un message pour dire à vos amis de vous attendre. Quelle voiture ils ont?*
- *Vous pouvez rester ici dans la salle d'attente*

4 **Candidate's brief and task** You are staying with a French family and giving English lessons to two boys aged 12 and 14. In return for this you are given your keep and spending money. You are becoming unhappy about the behaviour and attitude of your pupils. You ask to speak to the father about the matter.

Problems are the following:
- They arrive late or one of them is absent
- They don't do the work you have set them
- They don't pay attention and keep talking to one another; one of them is always making jokes
- Their friends keep phoning them or calling for them
- Be prepared to explain the methods you have been using — role-plays, games, reading texts, asking questions etc
- Ask the father if he will support you* by insisting on proper behaviour, regular attendance, (the hours of which you will both agree), and that they do their preparation
  * *Ça me gêne un peu de vous le dire, mais...*
- Also, you are embarrassed** to ask, but you have not yet received any spending money as agreed
  ** *Est-ce que je peux compter sur vous pour qu'ils fassent leur travail?*

Father's brief You appear surprised at first because you hadn't realized what was happening. You would like to know all the complaints. You would also like to make sure that your sons are not just bored or that the work is too difficult or too easy. Agree to a certain number of hours of lessons per day and to keeping an eye on the boys' work. Suggest an excursion with the family at the weekend. You apologize profusely about the non-payment of pocket money. It had slipped your mind! Here are some possible phrases and responses:
- *Vous voulez me voir, je crois*
- *Tiens! je ne savais pas ça*
- *Je n'étais pas au courant. Cela me surprend*

- *C'est parce que je ne suis pas ici pendant la journée*
- *Je vais m' occuper de ça, je vous assure*
- *Pouvez-vous me dire exactement ce que vous faites avec eux comme travail?*
- *Quelles méthodes est-ce que vous employez?*
- *Ce n'est pas un peu trop difficile/facile pour eux?*
- *Ils s'ennuient un peu, hein?*
- *Alors, c'est convenu, ... heures par jour le matin/l'après-midi, plus... heures de préparation*
- *Je vais surveiller ça, n'ayez pas peur!*
- *Ce week-end, nous pensons faire une excursion au bord de la mer. Est-ce que ça vous ferait plaisir de nous accompagner?*
- *C'est parfait*
- *Ah ça ! je n'y avais pas pensé. Je suis vraiment désolé. Vous auriez dû m'en parler plus tôt. Ne vous gênez pas une autre fois, hein*

5 **Candidate's brief** You are staying on a French campsite together with quite a few English families. The latter are not happy about a number of things on the site. Because you speak French better than they do, they ask you to voice their complaints to the owner of the site.

Task Be polite but firm*. The owner will have an excuse or explanation for everything
- Say who you are and why you have come
- The toilets and showers are dirty and not cleaned often enough
- Some of the drains are blocked
- Some of the electrical fittings — plug sockets (*les prises*) — are loose (*détachées*) and dangerous
- There is no supervision at the swimming pool
- There is a lot of noise after 10.00 o'clock, particularly from the disco
- Point out the dangers and risks of all this — health, safety, risks to children, older people can't sleep etc.
- The owner seems unconvinced until you threaten to complain** at the Mairie
- End by obtaining an assurance that certain things will be put right

  *Je vous assure que je n'exagère pas
  Je dois insister pour qu'on fasse quelque chose
  Je suis obligé de vous signaler
  Je regrette de vous dire que...
  Je répète, ce n'est pas une exagération
  Ce n'est pas raisonnable, voyons...
  Vous ne trouvez pas que j'ai raison?
  ** Je serais obligé(e) de porter plainte...

Owner's brief You give the impression that you do not take the person's complaints very seriously — you have had problems with British campers before! You can find an excuse or an explanation for all the complaints. You begin the exchange:

- *Je crois que vous voulez me voir*
- *Ah bon. Il me manque du personnel en ce moment, il y en a qui sont malades*
- *Il est difficile de trouver des remplaçants à présent*
- *Avec 2 000 campeurs, vous savez...*
- *L'électricien est en vacances. Les éboueurs sont en grève*
- *On n'a jamais eu d'accident dans la piscine*
- *Ils exagèrent un peu vos Anglais, non?/ Ce sont toujours les Anglais qui se plaignent!*
- *C'est un camping ici, on n'est pas à Colditz, hein!*
- *Après 10 heures il y a toujours un peu de bruit*
- *Il n'y pas de musique tous les soirs*
- *Vous n'allez pas porter plainte pour un rien!*
- *Que voulez-vous que je fasse?*
- *Bon, d'accord, je ferai nettoyer les toilettes/enlever les poubelles*
- *Je téléphonerai à un autre électricien*

6 **Candidate's brief** You are staying in Paris and the day before yesterday at about 5.00 p.m, you took a raincoat to the dry cleaners. You now find that you have lost the ticket. You go to the shop to collect your coat without being able to show the ticket.

Task Explain to the assistant what has happened and apologize*:

- Be prepared to describe the raincoat (e.g. colour, size, style) and say when you brought it in
- Doesn't the gentleman remember you, he served you?
- The first coat he brings is the wrong one. Yours is a light blue, with a belt
- Say you are sorry for the inconvenience you are causing him**
- Be pleased*** when he brings the right coat, and thank him
- You are staying at the Hôtel Continental, rue Victor Hugo. You have your passport with you
- Ask how much you owe, thank the assistant again and take your leave

> * *Je m'excuse/je regrette, mais...* or *Je suis désolé(e) mais...*
> ** *Je m'excuse de vous déranger, monsieur/madame*
> *** *C'est formidable, vous l'avez trouvé!*

Assistant's brief You are at first not very willing to cooperate and complain about customers always losing their tickets. You ask the candidate when the coat was left, a description (colour, size, style, with or without belt). You bring the wrong coat first and are not very pleased. Before handing over the right one ask where the person is staying and for some means of identification. Here are some possible phrases:

- *Mais vous savez c'est ce qu'ils disent tous! On perd tout le temps son billet*
- *Quand est-ce que vous l'avez laissé?*
- *Ah, non je ne me souviens pas de vous — je ne suis pas un ordinateur, moi!*
- *Décrivez-moi un peu votre imper, je vais tâcher de le retrouver*
- *Ce n'est pas le bon?*
- *Oh, il y en a des dizaines comme ça!*
- *Voilà, c'est bien le vôtre?*
- *Vous avez une pièce d'identité, une adresse à Paris?*
- *Ça fait 45 francs*
- *De rien, à votre service monsieur*

7   Candidate's brief Some friends have arranged to give you a lift on their way through Paris by car. You arrange to meet them very early in the morning near one of the slip roads to the *périphérique*. You have been waiting some time when you are approached by a policeman.

Task Your passport is at the bottom of your rucksack:

- Explain that identity cards are not required in Britain
- Explain what you are doing there, when you expect your friends to arrive etc.
- Be prepared to answer other questions about where you are heading for, who your friends are, what sort of car they have etc.
- A small packet in your rucksack contains some English cheese — a present for the family you are going to stay with
- The policeman is eventually convinced but you express dissatisfaction* with the way you have been treated

> * *Je trouve votre attitude/conduite un peu impolie*
> *Ce n'est pas poli, hein, de parler aux gens comme ça*
> *Ce n'est pas une manière de se conduire avec les visiteurs étrangers!*

Policeman's brief You are very suspicious of this person whom you have been watching for some time. The area is notorious for drug dealing. You are only slowly convinced of the person's innocence. You are genuinely baffled by the need to import cheese into France:

- *Contrôle d'identité, vos papiers s'il vous plaît*
- *Mais où sont-ils alors?*
- *Désolé, mais il faut que je voie ça*
- *Qu'est-ce que vous faites ici?*
- *Elle me paraît un peu bizarre, votre explication*
- *Comment vérifier ça?*
- *Qui sont-ils vos amis? Et leur voiture?*
- *Je vous surveille depuis un bon moment*
- *Il y a des trafiquants de drogue dans ce quartier, hein*
- *Ce paquet, qu'est-ce que c'est?*
- *Vous apportez du fromage en France! Ça c'est le comble!*

- *Bon, euh, ça a l'air d'aller. Vous pouvez partir*
- *Ecoutez! ce n'est pas ma faute, je fais mon boulot/travail, c'est tout*

Note The following role-plays are examples from Examination Boards:

8   Brief It is the last day of your holiday in Lausanne in Switzerland and you have bought an expensive book as a present for your parents. You return to the hotel, unwrap the parcel and throw away the receipt and wrapping paper.

   An hour later you flip through the book and discover that pages 56 to 75 are missing. On the following morning you return to the bookshop.

Task
- Ask to speak to the manager, explain what has happened and ask for a replacement copy. (He/she is unwilling to help since you have no receipt and anyway yours was the last copy in the shop)
- Persuade him/her that you did buy the book there and, since it is faulty, he/she should do something
- Request your money back in cash now and ask if there is another bookshop where you could buy another copy
- Say that you particularly want to replace the book and not purchase a different one, since it is exactly what you think your parents will like
- (The manager becomes more helpful now and promises to get you another copy within ten days.) Explain that you are returning home tomorrow. (The manager offers to post it on to you at the shop's expense.)

Oxford and Cambridge A and AS Level, June 1990

Note   As with most examination role-plays there are roughly 10 points that you need to make as candidate in this role which lasts 3–5 minutes, depending on the Board.

   To help you practise this role with a partner here are some suggested responses that the examiner might make:

- *Vous l'avez acheté quand?*
- *Vous avez la quittance/le reçu?*
- *Eh bien, je ne peux rien faire. Sans la quittance, vous savez...*
- *De toute façon, c'était le dernier exemplaire*
- *C'est la jeune fille là-bas qui vous a servi?*
- *Ah oui, en effet il y a l'étiquette du magasin en bas de la page*
- *Oui, je pourrais bien vous rembourser, mais c'est impossible de trouver ce livre dans un autre magasin*
- *Bon, écoutez , voici ce que je vais faire. Je ferai venir une autre copie dans 10 jours, d'accord?*
- *Bon, dans ce cas, je vous expédierai le livre aux frais du magasin*

9   Brief: You have applied to a London-based agency which interviews and selects both male and female 'au-pairs', matching them with appropriate French families.

Task
- Explain why you want the job (boys may have to combat certain preconceived notions). Give at least three reasons why you want to do this work and give examples of any relevant experience or skills.
- Ask about working conditions (hours, pay, time off — especially to attend language classes — insurance, accomodation etc.) and enquire particularly about apparently minor points (who pays the agency fee?) as well as about obvious ones such as who pays your fare there and back.
- Try to persuade the interviewer to place you with a family with just one child (about the same age as your little sister) in Lille, rather than with a family with three children in Dijon but be careful not to lose the job altogether)

Cambridge AS Level, June 1989

Here are some possible questions and statements that the examiner might use:
- *Vous pouvez m'expliquer pourquoi vous cherchez ce travail?*
- *Il y a peu de garçons qui veulent faire ça, n'est-ce pas*
- *Vous avez déjà quelque expérience de cette espèce de travail?*
- *Le nombre d'heures que vous travaillez varie un peu mais cela ne doit pas excéder trente heures par semaine*

- *Pour la répartition des heures il faut convenir avec votre employeur*
- *Pour les frais de l'agence c'est votre employeur qui paie*
- *C'est la famille aussi qui va vous rembourser les frais de voyage*
- *Bon, il y a une famille à Dijon avec trois enfants qui cherche quelqu'un pour le mois d'août... Ils ont exprimé une préférence pour un garçon...*
- *Vous partiriez en vacances avec eux, hein, en Bretagne*
- *Ou bien il y a quelqu'un à Lille, avec une fille seulement... elle a 7 ans... mais vous devriez rester à Lille, hein*

Note When working out your answer don't forget that you are being invited to **make things up**. You are not just telling the truth about yourself! So invent experience with younger children (e.g. your mother is a primary-school teacher and you have been helping her in school; you have often looked after your little sister; you run a local cubs group; you like organizing games for younger chidren; you **like** housework!).

10 Brief You have just landed at the Charles de Gaulle airport in Paris for a two-week holiday with French friends. You are waiting for your luggage (one large grey suitcase and a red and black sportsbag) to be returned to you at the appropriate collection point. After a while, it becomes apparent that something has happened to your luggage: all your fellow passengers have collected theirs and departed but your suitcase and bag are nowhere to be seen.

Task Explain the situation to the luggage attendant. Tell him/her that you were a passenger on flight AF 132 from London and that you handed in your bag and suitcase as requested when you presented your ticket at the check-in desk. Ask him/her to make enquiries. Answer all the questions that will be put to you regarding: size and colour of the luggage; identification tags; contents; name; and holiday address etc. Express your concern and annoyance, at the fact that everything you need for your holiday is in your luggage, and demand positive action.

Note
Whilst in France, you will be staying with *Monsieur et Madame Loubet, 275 rue de la République, Dijon.* The *'vous'* form of address will be used by both parties throughout this task.

JMB A and AS Level, June 1990

Here are some suggested questions or responses:
- *Je peux vous aider, Monsieur/Madame... vous avez l'air inquiet*
- *Vous êtes sûr(e) que vous avez bien regardé?*
- *Peut-être qu'un ami(ou quelqu'un d'autre) l'a pris, non?*
- *Vous êtes là depuis combien de temps?/Il y a longtemps que vous êtes là?*
- *Vous étiez sur quel vol?*
- *Eh bien, il faut continuer votre chemin et vous réclamerez vos bagages plus tard*
- *Alors, si je vais demander des renseignements maintenant vous allez perdre du temps, hein*
- *Il vaut mieux demander plus tard, non?*
- *Eh bien vous pouvez me décrire vos bagages s'il vous plaît?*
- *Votre nom était écrit dessus? Et votre nom, c'est...?*
- *Et dedans, qu'est-ce qu'il y avait?*
- *Et vous restez où en France?*
- *Bon, je vais voir ce que je peux faire*

2 Reporting tasks

The basis for this task in real life is having to explain to a French person, who does not read or understand English, the main points of a short piece of English text. The latter may be: a travel brochure; a newspaper item; an advertisement or other piece of publicity; or an account in English of something seen or witnessed. The latter may be accompanied by diagrams (e.g. in the case of an accident). The Examiner usually stays silent during this process.

Examination strategy

Marks are usually given for conveying a number of points (roughly 10 to 12, depending on the Board) and for quality of language and pronunciation. It is important therefore, when preparing, to underline the points you think are the main ones and to cover all these in your explanation. You will be given credit if you include them all, even though you may make some mistakes in French.

Conveying the information is partly a matter of knowing the vocabulary. Don't try to just translate the English. Sort out the points to be made first and jot down a word or a phrase in French to go with each one. Do not panic when you find words you do not know the exact French for. You will often find you can use a paraphrase or other words to get the meaning across. If you have been practising saying things in different ways, as already suggested, you will be more into the swing of this (*see* paraphrase, pages 125–7).

Note

(a) Here are some actual examples of references that managed to get the meaning across even though the French word was not exactly the right one:

the brain (*cerveau*) – '*Cette chose entre les deux oreilles*' – '*la tête*'
the man posted at the door (*le service de sécurité*) – '*l'homme à la porte/qui surveillait la porte*'
triggered an alarm (*a fait sonner l'alarme*) – '*Une cloche s'est mise à sonner*'
exotic foods (*nourriture exotique*) – '*produits de différents pays/de tous les pays du monde*' nourritures rares/recherchées'
shop assistant (*la serveuse*) – '*la femme dans le magasin/ qui servait/derrière le comptoir*'
the boot of a car (*le coffre*) – '*le derrière (l'arrière) de la voiture*' – '*la boîte de la voiture*'
7-day free trial guarantee (*essai gratuit pour 7 jours*) – '*on peut l'essayer pendant 7 jours, sans payer*'

(b) Here is an example of a candidate's brief, with the points in bold type and some examples of what you might say:

> You are looking **through the window** of your hotel room in Paris when you witness a raid on the bank opposite. Your attention is drawn by the **noise of breaking glass**. You see **two men emerge** through the glass door of the bank. **One** of them is **holding a gun**. They are **both masked** and are **wearing rucksacks** on their backs. **One is taller** than the other and **seems** as though he is hurt. They charge across the pavement **knocking over an old lady**, one gets on to a **motorbike** the other, the **taller one, gets into a waiting car**, a **Mercedes**, you think. It all **happens in a flash**.

Imagine you are describing what you saw to the police. You could use the past tense in your description but you could also use the 'vivid present'. Make sure though that you are consistent and stick to whichever one you started with:

> J'étais dans ma chambre à l'hôtel et je regardais par la fenêtre. Soudain, j'ai entendu un grand bruit de verre qui se cassait et j'ai vu deux hommes sortir de la banque en face. Un des hommes tenait un revolver à la main. Ils étaient tous les deux masqués et avaient des sacs à dos. Un des hommes était plus grand que l'autre et semblait blessé. En sortant de la banque, ils ont heurté une vieille dame qui est tombée par terre. Un des hommes est monté sur une moto et l'autre, le plus grand, a sauté dans une voiture qui attendait. C'était une Mercedes, je crois. Tout cela s'est passé très, très vite.

(c) If you had used the present tense you could have started:
> *Je suis dans ma chambre à l'hôtel, je regarde par la fenêtre et soudain j'entends le bruit...*

Study technique

1 You can practise this skill by taking any short news or publicity item, from the day's television or radio programmes, imagining that you have to tell a French person about them. By selecting items from as broad a range of sources as possible, and by sometimes working with a dictionary, you will broaden your vocabulary and experience of different areas of knowledge. You could also try making up in English short accounts of incidents witnessed as above. Shoplifting, break-ins, accidents and confrontations of various kinds are all likely material. It is more fun if you can work with a friend and have a bilingual dictionary handy. Try explaining a short item to your work companion who will take notes in English. If you do one item each, you can check back afterwards with the original to see how many details are correct and give each other a mark out of 10. If this activity is accompanied by asking in French, about things not quite understood, you will also be doing further valuable oral practice.

2 Although figures only sometimes occur in this kind of task, by including a few from time to time you can get valuable practice both in saying and understanding them.

Exercices

Here are some examples to be getting on with. You will have to cover up one half if you are working with a friend:

1   Est-ce que vous croyez aux coincidences?

Le Président Lincoln et le Président Kennedy ont été tous les deux assassinés. Voici quelques détails bizarres concernant leur vie et leur mort:

A   (a) Lincoln's secretary was named Kennedy and Kennedy's secretary was named Lincoln

   (b) Lincoln was elected president in 1860 and Kennedy was elected* president in 1960

   (c) The wives of the two men, Mary Lincoln and Jackie Kennedy, both had children who died while their husbands were living in the White House

   (d) Two of Lincoln's sons were named Edward and Robert. Edward died at the age of three whilst Robert lived on. Two of Kennedy's brothers were called Robert and Edward. Robert was assassinated whilst Edward lived on

   (e) Both presidents were with their wives, and both were shot in the head**. They both died on a Friday

   * *élu*

   ** *reçu une balle dans la tête*

B   (a) Lincoln's assassin, John Wilkes Booth, and Kennedy's alleged assassin*, Lee Harvey Oswald, were both Southerners in their twenties

   (b) Booth shot Lincoln while he was sitting in a theatre, then hid in a warehouse** Kennedy was shot from a warehouse; Oswald was found hiding in a theatre

   (c) Booth and Oswald were both killed before they could be brought to court***

   (d) Abraham Lincoln was succeeded by Andrew Johnson, born in 1808. John Kennedy was succeeeded by Lyndon Johnson, born in 1908. Both Johnsons had been senators before becoming president

   (e) The names Lincoln and Kennedy each contain 7 letters, Andrew Johnson and Lyndon Johnson each have 13 letters, and John Wilkes Booth and Lee Harvey Oswald each have 15 letters

   * *prétendu assassin*

   ** *un entrepôt*

   *** *avant d'être amené devant les tribunaux*

2   Voici une comparaison entre les possibilités offertes par deux stations de sports d'hiver:

A   Le massif de Ben Nevis (en Ecosse)   **B** St Moritz (en Suisse)

FACT FILE

- Ski pass £62 for six days in high season, £48 low season. Under 16's and over 60's, £42 high, £32 low
- Ski Packages, Midweek five-day packages, £100, which cover ski pass, tuition and ski hire and four hours' instruction daily
- Ski School: Six days, four hours daily, £50; two hours £33. Also individual tuition, £17 hourly. Also snowboarding, Telemark and ski touring
- Cross-country. Some high-altitude trails are available
- For non-skiers: Extensive walking trails, mountain biking, tennis, golf, fishing, swimming pool, gymnasium and cinema, all in Fort William
- Bed space: 70 hotels in the Fort William area with around 10,000 beds. Also self-catering chalets and some rooms in private homes
- Medical facilities: first-aid both at top and bottom of gondola station, full-time paramedic ski patrol. Hospital in Fort William
- How to get there: By air to Glasgow, Edinburgh or Inverness, then by road or train to Fort William (overnight sleeper from London)
- Information: Great Britain (0397 705825)

FACT FILE

- Ski Pass: Oberengadiner includes all lifts, swimming pool and public transport in area. 204 Swiss Francs for six days (low season 150). Children free up to six, then SF150. Beginners' Nursery lifts included in ski-school fee. Also points system available
- Ski School: Morning and/or afternoon classes available, SF182 for six days. Children up to 12 SF148. Individual tuition available, SF70 per hour. Also, ski touring, mono and surf
- Cross-country: Extensive (160km) for all levels. Also, floodlit track at Bad.
- For non-skiers: sleigh and toboggan runs, Cresta Run, horse riding, polo tournaments, golf on frozen lake, 120km of cleared paths. Also, pools, saunas, tennis, squash, English language cinema, shopping
- Bed space: 12,500, half of which is in hotels, rest in apartments
- Medical facilities: Doctors, dentists and fracture clinic in resort: Hospital at Samedan (6km)
- How to get there: Zurich airport, then either flight to Samedan, or road transfer (4 hours) or train, from anywhere in Europe, station in resort
- Information: Switzerland (82) 33147

Quelques mots et expressions

haute/basse saison – vacances de neige à prix forfaitaire – chalets indépendants – quelques chambres d'hôte – téléski pour débutants – leçons particulières – clinique sur place en cas de fracture

3   Cette semaine dans l'histoire du monde:

A   23 au 28 mars 1991   **B** 15 au 22 février 1991

THIS WEEK IN HISTORY

March 23, 1919: Benito Mussolini founded the Fascist Party in Italy.
March 23, 1956: Pakistan became a republic.
March 24, 1603: After the death of Queen Elizabeth I, the crowns of England and Scotland were joined under James VI of Scotland, who was to be known as James I of Great Britain.
March 24, 1848: Charles Albert, King of Sardinia, declared war on Austria.
March 24, 1972: The British government announced direct rule in Northern Ireland.
March 25, 1807: The slave trade was abolished in Britain.
March 25, 1815: Britain, Austria, Prussia and Russia formed a new alliance against Napoleon I of France.
March 25, 1924: King George II of Greece was deposed and a republic proclaimed.
March 25, 1957: The Treaty of Rome was signed by France, West Germany, Italy and the Benelux countries to establish the European Economic Community.
March 25, 1975: King Faisal of Saudi Arabia was assassinated in Riyadh by his mentally ill nephew.
March 26, 1953: Dr Jonas Salk announced the successful testing of a vaccine against polio.
March 27, 1802: Britain signs the peace of Amiens with Napoleon of France.
March 28, 1854: Britain and France declare war on Russia.
March 28, 1898: Germany passed an act allowing for a substantial expansion of its navy.
March 28, 1939: Madrid surrendered to General Francisco Franco, bringing to an end the Spanish Civil War.

THIS WEEK IN HISTORY

February 15, 1933: Giuseppe Zingara attempted to assassinate President Franklin Roosevelt in Miami.
February 16, 1937: Nylon, developed under the direction of Dr Wallace Carothers, was patented.
February 17, 1670: France and Bavaria signed a defensive alliance.
February 17, 1863: The International Red Cross was founded in Geneva.
February 17, 1934: King Albert I of Belgium was killed in a climbing accident.
February 18, 1965: The Gambia became an independent state within the British Commonwealth.
February 18, 1988: Boris Yeltsin was ousted from the ruling Communist Party Politburo.
February 19, 1803: The Act of Mediation restored independence to the Swiss cantons.
February 19, 1945: American troops landed on the island of Iwo Jima.
February 19, 1976: Iceland broke off relations with Britain over a fishing dispute.
February 20, 1437: James I of Scotland was murdered in Perth.
February 21, 1613: Michael Romanov was elected Czar of Russia.
February 21, 1916: The Battle of Verdun began in France during the First World War.
February 21, 1965: American militant black leader Malcolm X was murdered in New York.
February 22, 1828: Persia, and Russia signed the Treaty of Turkmanchai in which Persia ceded part of Armenia to Russia.
February 22, 1967: President Sukarno of Indonesia surrendered rule to General Suharto.

Quelques mots et expressions

A *l'autorité directe – le commerce des esclaves – un traité – la paix – capituler*

B *breveté* (patented) *– expulsé du parti – rompu les relations diplomatiques – céder une partie de – capituler*

4 Les résultats de deux sondages:

A Avez-vous confiance dans la police?

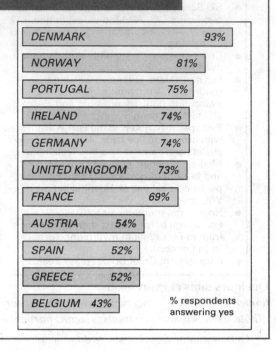

DO YOU TRUST THE POLICE FORCE?

The Belgians are the greatest sceptics in Europe, according to the confidence they express in society's institutions. The police, the military and the legal professions are all held in rock-bottom esteem. Less than half said that they had confidence in the police (*see* chart right) compared to 70 per cent for Europe as a whole, and less than a third trusted lawyers or soldiers. In Denmark, the police are extremely popular, with nine out of ten people expressing their confidence. The Portuguese seem almost complacent: a full three-quarters express confidence in the police and armed forces, and about 60 per cent have faith in the legal system and the media. Even the advertising industry is seen as relatively trustworthy, scoring a 40 per cent confidence-rating. The British reserve special hatred for their media: only 14 per cent hold confidence in the industry.

	%
DENMARK	93%
NORWAY	81%
PORTUGAL	75%
IRELAND	74%
GERMANY	74%
UNITED KINGDOM	73%
FRANCE	69%
AUSTRIA	54%
SPAIN	52%
GREECE	52%
BELGIUM	43%

% respondents answering yes

Quelques expressions utiles

les gens les plus méfiants de l'Europe – l'armée, les hommes de loi – un tiers se méfiait des militaires – presque tout à fait satisfait – la loi et les médias – l'industrie publicitaire – mériter sa confiance – détester les médias

B Seriez-vous prêt à retourner un objet perdu?

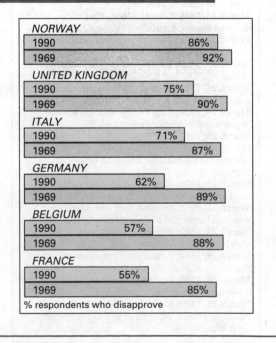

WOULD YOU RETURN LOST PROPERTY?

Europeans are becoming friendlier (towards each other at least), healthier and less dependent on hair oil, but they certainly do not appear to be getting more honest. The number of people who felt that they should return a lost item to its rightful owner has dropped from nine out of ten in 1969, to only seven out of ten now. In no single country did more people disapprove of the maxim 'finders keepers', although the Norwegians lost only a few percentage points. The French revealed the most dramatic slide: in 1969, 85 per cent believed that lost property should be restored. These days the figure is just 55 per cent, a drop of almost a third. Scandinavian countries are consistently more generous about returning lost property, and in the rest of Europe, only the Swiss have an honesty rating of more than 80 per cent.

	%
NORWAY	
1990	86%
1969	92%
UNITED KINGDOM	
1990	75%
1969	90%
ITALY	
1990	71%
1969	87%
GERMANY	
1990	62%
1969	89%
BELGIUM	
1990	57%
1969	88%
FRANCE	
1990	55%
1969	85%

% respondents who disapprove

Quelques expressions utiles

deviennent plus amical l'un envers l'autre – être en meilleure santé/ se porter mieux – la lotion pour les cheveux/capillaire – retourner à son propriétaire – approuver la maxime 'celui qui le trouve, le garde' – le plus grand changement se révèle chez les Français – les Scandinaves se montrent les plus généreux – un taux d'honnêteté supérieur à…

5 Deux publicités

A Stainsbury's fait du pain français

Stainsbury's have been baking french bread for many years.

But now, cooling down in our larger stores, you'll also find French bread with a capital 'F'. Because although Stainsbury's bake it, it's actually made in France.

With French flour, French yeast, French water and, dare we say it, French *savoir faire*. The dough is made in Lyon. We then ship it over to England and bake it in our in-store bakeries.

The bread that comes out is as French as any boulangerie could bake it. It has a light, airy texture, with a crisp 'eggshell' crust. And oh, the flavour!

(Close your eyes and you could be in a pavement café on Boulevard St. Germain.)

As well as the classic white baguette, we also bake a selection of other French breads and pastries.

You'll find *baguettes de campagne* (a brown version made with sour dough), *pain de campagne* (a short, cob-shaped loaf) and *petit pain boule* (small, but perfectly formed roll).

And if you want to know where the expression 'melt in the mouth' comes from, just try our butter croissants.

Like all Stainsbury's bakery products, our traditional French bread is freshly baked every day. Or perhaps we should say Frenchly baked every day.

Quelques mots et expressions

Depuis plusieurs années – du vrai pain français – Stainsbury's le fait cuire mais il est fait en France – la farine, la levure, l'eau sont françaises – la pâte – transporté – cuit sur place – le véritable pain français – léger et croustillant – et son arôme! – imaginez-vous – avec la baguette classique – baguette et pains de campagne et des petits pains – nos croissants fondent dans la bouche – comme tous nos produits boulangers – cuit tout frais tous les jours

B Arrêtez cette habitude dégoûtante. Arrêtez de fumer immédiatement!

Quelques mots et expressions

réussi pour des milliers de personnes – perdre l'habitude au bout de 5 jours – risque pour la santé – faire disparaître le besoin – sans douleur – grâce à ce traitement révolutionnaire développé aux Etats Unis – avaler un comprimé – supprimer votre désir de la nicotine – l'odeur et le goût des cigarettes deviennent rébarbatifs – regardez les statistiques – chaque cigarette raccourcit votre vie de cinq minutes et demie – une des causes principales des incendies – le succès est garanti ou vous serez remboursé

3 Study extracts

Study extracts usually take the form of passages, or other printed material, in French that you have to explain the gist of, expand on and/or answer questions about. You may have to select one from several and prepare this just before the oral exam or you may be given the material a week or so beforehand. Check the regulations of your particular Board.

You will need the skills of skimming, scanning and summary already referred to in the section on writing (*see* pages 85 and 118). Read the material several times and underline the main points, paying particular attention to the beginnings of paragraphs for the main ideas. The important thing in the exam, with this kind of material, is for you to take charge and be ready to tell the Examiner about it. Try to 'stand back' from the material and think of it as a whole rather than attempting to just read out bits of it. Be prepared to say what it is and what it is about. The title might not necessarily do this for you. For example:

(a) *C'est un article/une publicité/ une annonce/une brochure/un extrait/un dépliant qui concerne____/ qui traite de____*

(b) *Dans cet article/cette brochure il s'agit de____/il est question de____*

Then go on to give the main points. The following formula may be appropriate:

(c) ***D'abord** on signale que... **puis** on explique que... **ensuite** on cite l'exemple de... **enfin** on tire la conclusion que...*

The material is often chosen for its contemporary interest; issues for debate or disagreement may be raised. You should decide on what stance (or attitude) you are going to adopt beforehand and have a reason (or an example) that you can quote to back up your opinion. Don't forget that you do not have to tell the absolute truth, though if it is something you feel strongly about, you will find it easier to say why. It is also worth remembering that the Examiner is not there to test your knowledge or judge your opinion. He or she just wants to find out if you can express your views convincingly in French and defend or support them with evidence. You may even be able to turn the situation around a bit and ask the Examiner for his or her views! For example the following may be appropriate:

Moi, je suis d'avis que...
A mon avis on a raison/tort de dire que...
Je ne suis pas tout à fait convaincu que...
Ce qui est certain, c'est que...
Ce que je ne comprends pas, c'est que...
Ce qui est surprenant, c'est que...
Cela me surprend que ...
C'est un scandale! C'est une honte! C'est la faute du gouvernement/des hommes politiques...
On devrait faire quelque chose...
Il faut qu'on fasse quelque chose...
C'est une exagération de dire que...
C'est une situation/un problème préoccupant(e)/qui concerne tous les pays du monde

If you are going to say something like *Oui, c'est intéressant*, always be ready to add a reason or an example.

Model answer: short study extract

1   Les médias disent-ils vrai?
    Enquête réalisée du 1er au 15 septembre, auprès d'un échantillon de 2500 lecteurs de *Phosphore*, âgés de 14 à 18 ans

LES MÉDIAS DISENT VRAI			
En général, à propos des nouvelles qui sont diffusées dans les médias, est-ce que vous vous dites...			
	Presse (100%)	Radio (100%)	TV (100%)
Les choses se sont passées vraiment comme le média les raconte	8%	12%	19%
Les choses se sont passées à peu près comme le média les raconte	64%	66%	53%
Il y a sans doute pas mal de différence entre la façon dont les choses se sont passées et la façon dont le média les raconte	27%	21%	26%
Les choses ne se sont vraisemblablement pas passées du tout comme le média les raconte	1%	1%	2%

Possible answers

Ce tableau présente les résultats d'un sondage auprès des lecteurs d'un journal pour jeunes. Le but de l'enquête est de savoir s'ils croient ce qu'ils lisent dans les journaux, ce qu'ils entendent à la radio et ce qu'ils voient à la télé.

or

Dans ce tableau, on essaie de montrer ce que les jeunes pensent des informations présentées dans les journaux, à la radio, à la télévision: y croient-ils ou non?

On voit bien qu'en général ils pensent que les médias racontent plus ou moins la vérité, 64% à 53% le disent. Mais, ils croient moins la télé que les journaux.

Pour ceux qui croient absolument aux nouvelles racontées par les médias, c'est la télévision qui arrive en tête. On a peut-être plus tendance à croire ce qu'on voit.

Peu de jeunes croient que les médias ne racontent pas du tout la vérité.

Note Possible follow-up questions might be:
Pour savoir les nouvelles de la journée que faites-vous?
Pour vous, lequel des médias est le plus sûr? Pourquoi?
Quelles informations préférez-vous à la télé, à la radio? Et pourquoi?
Quel journal est-ce que vous préférez et pourquoi?

Exercices

Here are some examples to work on. Try explaining the gist to a friend. He or she will need to cover up one of the pieces while you do this. Check the details and figures afterwards:

1   (a) Le circuit de la drogue dans le monde

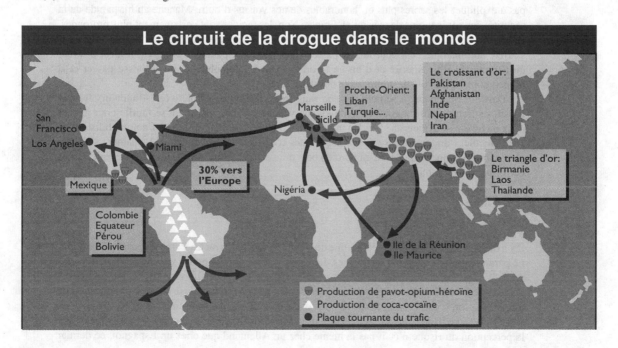

(b) La drogue en France — la consommation de l'héroïne

LA DROGUE EN FRANCE

Usagers: 150 000 environ (dont 2/3 d'héroïnomanes). Décès par overdose: environ 300 (uniquement les décès portés à la connaissance de la police).

Population atteinte: à 88% masculine. Age: 21-25 ans: 41%. 16-20 ans: 30%. 26-30 ans: 18%. 31-35 ans: 6,2%. 36-40 ans: 1,8%

La consommation d'héroïne (nombre de consommateurs)

Espagne	entre 80 000 et 120 000
Italie	80 000
France	80 000
Pays-Bas	20 000
RFA	12 300
Suisse	10 000
Autriche	3 000

(Source: *La Face cachée de l'économie mondiale* de Jean-François Couvral et Nicole Pless, chez Hatier)

2   Les Européens, sont-ils de bons conducteurs?

(a) Le gentleman conducteur

Le gentleman conducteur

Les automobilistes britanniques jouent fair-play, ils respectent dans l'ensemble plus les règles du jeu routier que nous. La répression implacable, la lutte très sévère contre l'alcool au volant et le permis à points, qui est retiré automatiquement après un certain nombre d'infractions, ne suffisent pas à expliquer les scores plus qu'honorables de nos voisins d'outre-Manche au hit-parade de la sécurité: deux fois moins de tués qu'en France. Non, les racines sont certainement plus profondes. La courtoisie comme le flegme british influent sur le comportement du conducteur anglais: il s'arrête automatiquement pour laisser passer les piétons aux passages protégés, il n'est pas rare qu'il remercie d'un sourire et d'un geste de la main l'automobiliste qui le laisse passer et il n'encombre pas la voie de droite (celle des dépassements).

Dans les bouchons, il ne perd pas son sang-froid. S'il bout de colère (c'est humain), il ne le laisse pas transparaître: pas de coup de klaxon vengeur, pas de malin qui se faufile pour gagner deux ou trois places dans une file. Un indice éclairant du rapport qu'entretient l'automobiliste avec son véhicule: l'ambiance cosy des publicités des constructeurs britanniques. La caméra s'attarde plutôt sur l'élégance du tableau au bord en bois brun et le moelleux des sièges de cuir, que sur les performances du moteur.

(b) Les Latins

Vous avez dit audace?

Il y a indiscutablement une manière latine de conduire. Les Alpes ou les Pyrénées passées, les règles ne paraissent plus tout à fait les mêmes. Les panneaux de limitation de vitesse paraissent retenir moins l'attention de l'automobiliste, les coups de klaxon intempestifs vous rappellent à l'ordre à la moindre hésitation. On a le pied sur l'accélérateur dès que le feu passe au vert, pas question de traîner! La loi, c'est souvent la loi du plus audacieux et chaque croisement est l'occasion d'un rapport de force. Une étude sur la traversée d'un carrefour simulée sur écran-vidéo a démontré que la perception du risque n'était pas la même chez un Allemand que chez un Espagnol, ce dernier étant nettement plus casse-cou. Etonnant, non?

Model answer: longer study extract

ANIMAUX DE COMPAGNIE
LES AIMONS-NOUS VRAIMENT?

Trente millions d'animaux de compagnie pour cinquante-cinq millions de Français! Notre pays est le premier en Europe, et au monde, à porter un intérêt aussi grand à près de dix millions de chiens, sept millions de chats, neuf millions d'oiseaux, cinq millions de poissons, lapins, tortues, souris et cochons d'Inde ... Voilà les Anglais, les Allemands et même les Américains largement distancés. Pourtant ... combien de chiens neurasthéniques restent enfermés et seuls toute la journée? Combien sont mal nourris, et même maltraités? Combien d'abandonnés, chaque été? Le nombre faramineux de nos amis à quatre pattes reflète-t-il l'amour ou l'égoïsme?

Peut-être l'avez-vous déjà rencontré, à Paris, dans le métro, du côté de la Chaussée-d'Antin. Il joue de l'orgue de Barbarie. Près de lui, trois boules de poils. Sur l'orgue, une chatte tigrée lovée dans un petit panier. A sa droite, une noire: à sa gauche, une grise frisottée. Sa musique chante la nostalgie, le bonheur. Le joueur d'orgue est né allemand. Il a choisi notre pays parce que, dit-il, 'c'est celui de La Fontaine et de ses fables pleines d'animaux.' Le poète ne fut pas le seul à les chanter: les animaux emplissent notre patrimoine culturel: de Goupil le renard à la chèvre de Monsieur Seguin sans oublier le Chat botté, plus qu'aucune autre littérature au monde, la nôtre glorifie le règne animal. Pour nos concitoyens, ce sujet allume souvent les passions. Témoin Fabien Gruhier, journaliste au Nouvel Observateur, qui, en février 1982, fut submergé par une masse de courrier — autant d'insultes que de félicitations — pour avoir fustigé la saleté canine des rues de Paris...

Les Français cohabitent de plus en plus avec les bêtes. Mais pourquoi? 'Nous avons besoin des animaux', assure le docteur Michel Klein.

Selon Guy Quéinnec, professeur d'élevage et d'économie à l'école vétérinaire de Toulouse, il existe trois conceptions: l'école éthologique, l'école utilitariste, l'école psychiatrique.

Pour l'école éthologique, posséder un chien est un critère d'affectivité sociale: aimer les chiens, c'est aimer les autres. Exemple, cet amour total, l'histoire soudaine entre un homme et un animal. Victor, artiste peintre, est un colosse: un double mètre, bon vivant. Il y a quelques mois, il aperçoit un garagiste en train de battre une jeune chienne qui se traîne avec peine. Victor menace le propriétaire: 'Salopard, je vous achète cette bête. Si vous refusez de me la vendre, je casse tout chez vous!' Depuis, Oona, plus douce qu'un agneau, est heureuse enfin et ne quitte plus son nouveau maître.

QUEL AMOUR?

L'école utilitariste estime que l'on possède un chien pour qu'il rende service: soit pour chasse, ou pour garder la maison. C'est surtout le cas en zone rurale. Ainsi, tous les ans, peu avant l'ouverture de la chasse, les demandes d'adoption augmentent dans les refuges de la S.P.A. 'C'est courant, explique-t-on là-bas: on vient chercher un chien, on s'en occupe, on le flatte, on le nourrit bien, pendant toute cette période. Puis une fois la chasse interdite on le laisse errer.' Parfois, on le garde, mais dans quelles conditions!

L'école psychiatrique, elle, pense que le chien aide à résoudre les difficultés personnelles du maître, problèmes de communication ou de maturité: à travers le chien ou le chat il recherche un éternel enfant ou une soumission qui puisse le gratifier.

Les bienfaits de la fréquentation quotidienne avec un animal de compagnie ne sont, c'est vrai, plus à démontrer. Les psychologues le savent: les enfants qui ont la responsabilité d'animaux sont plus équilibrés que les autres. Aussi, de plus en plus souvent, l'animal est-il présent à l'école. C'est un outil pédagogique qui initie l'enfant aux phénomènes de la vie. Le petit écolier apprend à soigner, à nourrir, à aimer les animaux et il en retire un bénéfice inestimable.

London Syllabus A-Level, June 1990

Answer plan

You will notice that this passage has a fairly clear stucture; an opening paragraph deals with the French obsession with pets in comparison to other nations and raises some issues. Then some examples are given of this obsession. Next, reasons are given for this behaviour. There are three main ones. The concluding paragraph ends on a positive note.

Here are some questions that an examiner might ask:

(a) On the article
- *De quoi s'agit-il dans cet extrait?/Quel est le sujet de cet article?*
- *Quelle différence est-ce qu'on remarque entre la France et les autres pays au sujet des animaux de compagnie?*
- *Quel est l'autre aspect de cette situation?*
- *Quelles sont les trois raisons pour avoir un animal?*
- *Que disent enfin les psychologues à ce sujet?*

(b) Arising from it:
- *Avez -vous un animal à la maison et pourquoi le gardez-vous?/Pourquoi n'avez-vous pas d'animal?*
- *Quels sont les avantages d'avoir un chat/un chien/un cheval etc?*
- *Quels problèmes existent actuellement avec les gens et leurs animaux?*
- *Si vous étiez au pouvoir que feriez-vous pour combattre ces problèmes?*
- *Devrait-on avoir un permis pour posséder un chien?*
- *Est-ce qu'on devrait proscrire certaines races de chien féroces ou dangereuses?*

Note All these questions require a longer answer than just *oui* or *non*. Always be prepared to answer the 'why' part of the question, particularly when a tired Examiner has left it out!

4 Talking about a prepared topic

A theme

This will usually be something you have been preparing for some time. Check carefully whether you are allowed to bring illustrative material to the exam and whether notes are permitted.

You will be allowed to give an introduction to your chosen subject but do not just recite a piece learned off by heart and sit back expecting the Examiner to be wildly excited about your subject and to ask all the questions. Take the initiative. First, say briefly what your subject is, why you are interested in it and how you went about the research. It helps if you then have just **three main** aspects that you can keep in your mind. By the time you have covered these, the examiner will have had time to relax a little and questions will have occured to him or her. They will also be impressed by the way you have organized the material!

Be prepared for open questions (**not** yes/no). Always have a reason or an example to back up what you are saying. Be prepared to respond to questions of the following kind:

Que feriez-vous si...?
Qu'est-ce que vous pensez de...?
Comment expliquez-vous cette attitude?
Que feriez-vous si vous étiez au pouvoir/Premier ministre?
Quels remèdes apporter à cette situation?
Qu'est-ce qu'on peut faire? Quelle solution proposez-vous?
Ne trouvez-vous pas que le gouvernement est...?
Que pensez-vous des gens qui disent...?
Pourquoi dites-vous que...?

A book or film

Essentially, this will be something you have chosen yourself and, whether you liked it or not, you should have something to say about it. You may be allowed to talk a little about the story but the Examiner will soon get on to other aspects. Be prepared to answer questions of the following kind:

Quel est le thème principal de ce livre (it is a good idea to have a category for the book: *c'est un roman/ d'aventure/policier/ de science fiction*)
C'est une histoire d'un/une...
Ce sont les aventures de...
Il y a plusieurs meurtres...
Cela se passe dans notre époque/au 19e siècle
C'est une aventure imaginaire/véritable
C'est raconté par l'auteur
Il/elle raconte ses expériences de...
Pourquoi l'avez-vous choisi?
Pourquoi l'avez-vous/ne l'avez-vous pas aimé?

Vous regrettez de l'avoir choisi? Pourquoi?

Quelle impression vous a fait ce livre/film?

Quel personnage vous a le plus frappé? (if you have found X or Y *sympathique* be prepared to say why)

Quel est le personnage-clef? (make sure you distinguish between *un personnage* — a character and *leur caractère* — their personality/character).

Quels moments/épisodes sont les plus mémorables/passionants pour vous?

Est-ce qu'il y a un message/une morale dans ce livre/film?

Selon vous, le sujet est-il important/sérieux/léger?

En le lisant/regardant est-ce que vous avez appris quelque chose?

Pourquoi l'auteur a-t-il écrit ce livre/tourné ce film?

General conversation

This aspect is found with all the Examining Boards. In theory it could be about almost anything but the following areas are favourite ones:

(a) Future plans for study and career

(b) Your hobbies and pastimes

(c) Your school/college and what you think of it

(d) Visits to France and your impressions of French life and people, making appropriate comparisons with life here. (You will probably have found the French *sympathiques,* but do be prepared to say why and what other qualities they possess! *See* list, literature section, page 155)

(e) Contemporary problems or issues that concern you and your ideas for overcoming them

(f) Any events that are occupying national or world attention at that time

Make sure you have run through all these possibilities and either asked yourself appropriate questions or worked through them with a friend.

Questions leading into these themes

(a) *Qu'est-ce que vous allez faire l'année prochaine?*

Vous avez l'intention de continuer vos études l'année prochaine?

Quels sont vos plans pour l'avenir?

Qu'est-ce que vous comptez faire dans la vie?

Pourquoi voulez-vous devenir_____?

(b) *Que faites-vous pendant vos loisirs?*

Le sport, c'est important pour vous?

Pourquoi? D'où vient cet intérêt pour_____?

Regarder la télé, c'est une perte de temps, non?

(c) *Que pensez-vous de cette école/ce collège?*

Etes-vous heureux/euse ici?

Si vous étiez le directeur/la directrice quels changements est-ce que vous apporteriez?

Quelles sont les qualités d'un bon prof?

Il faut avoir des règles, non?

Vous avez des privilèges comme élève en terminale?

Les élèves de sixième sont-ils bien discipliné(e)s?

(d) *Avez-vous visité la France (récemment)?*

Racontez-moi un peu votre visite

Quelles sont/étaient vos impressions des Français?

Comment avez-vous trouvé les Français?

La vie en France en quoi est-elle différente de celle en Angleterre?

La vie familiale en France est-elle différente de celle d'une famille anglaise?

Quelles différences avez-vous remarquées?

Quelles impresssions gardez-vous de l'école que vous avez visitée?

Faites quelques comparaisons avec votre école.

(e) *Il y a pas mal de problèmes dans la société actuelle, à votre avis quels sont les plus préoccupants?*

Que feriez-vous si vous étiez au pouvoir/premier ministre?

Quels remèdes y apporter?

C'est un problème insurmontable, non?

Quelles solutions apporter à long terme?

Challenging questions

You should also be prepared to be asked questions of a challenging or slightly controversial nature. The purpose of these is not to test out the content of your ideas but to see whether you can defend or support your point of view. Some of the questions above are of this kind:

C'est un problème insurmontable, non?
Il faut avoir des règles, non?

Other ways of doing this might be:

Moi, je trouve les jeunes trop/pas assez... vous ne pensez pas?
Les gens exagèrent/dramatisent ce problème, vous ne trouvez pas?
Est-ce que vous pensez sérieusement que...?
Vous avez dit que.... Vous ne pensez pas que vous exagérez un peu?
Ce n'est pas un métier pour une femme, voyons! /Peu de femmes réussissent dans ce genre de travail, vous savez

Your reaction should be to politely but firmly insist on your opinion, stating your reasons. You can say that you do not agree:
Vous avez tort
Ce n'est pas vrai
Je ne suis pas d'accord
Vous exagérez un peu, non?
Je dois insister

Or that you do not completely agree:

Je ne pense pas
Cela dépend
Cela dépend des circonstances/des cas
Jusqu'à un certain point vous avez raison
Je ne suis pas tout à fait d'accord
Je trouve difficile d'accepter cela

5 Ensuring success in the oral examination

The purpose of the oral exam is not to test your factual knowledge, on a variety of topics, but to provide an opportunity for you to show how much you can say in French. The Examiner will judge your ability to communicate naturally in French. To do this he or she will take a number of factors into consideration. Grammatical accuracy is only one of these elements. More important is your ability to keep going and get him or her involved in what you are saying. So arrive with the idea that you have something interesting to communicate. Do not come with the idea that you are just going to sit there and answer questions as they come. This makes it harder work for the Examiner. A skilfully led oral exam should consist of one-third or less Examiner talking and two-thirds or more of candidate speaking.

Factors taken into consideration are the following. They are usually presented in the form of a grid with a short description that covers a range within 2–3 marks:

(a) **Fulfilment of task** This applies to reporting, role-play or eliciting information tasks. It is important to do all the things included in the brief (see above). The description might range from 'Barest amount of information supplied' at the bottom of the scale, to ' most information supplied' near the top of the scale.

(b) **Fluency and responsiveness** These factors describe your ability to keep going without too much help from the Examiner. Near the bottom of the scale would be something like 'Examiner can only obtain very brief replies' to 'very fluent, occasional hesitation only' near the top of the scale.

(c) **Accuracy** This refers to grammatical accuracy — getting the right tenses, verb endings, agreements, genders etc.

(d) **Linguistic sophistication/range** These two terms include things like range of vocabulary and structures used and the ability to switch between tenses. If you stick to simple vocabulary, the present tense and short sentences without clauses, you will score less highly. A skilful Examiner will give the candidate the chance to use more than just the present tense. The rest is up to you. If you can work in a few subjunctives it does tend to impress. So instead of:

Il faut arrêter la pollution – Il faut qu'on fasse quelque chose pour arrêter la pollution.

Ce n'est pas possible – Je ne crois pas que cela soit possible.
Je ne suis pas d'accord mais je trouve que... – Quoique je ne sois pas d'accord, je trouve que...
Here are some typical responses in an oral exam to an Examiner asking about the candidate's school:

A *Examiner* Parlez-moi un peu de cette école. Vous êtes heureuse ici?
Candidate Oui. J'aime assez bien cette école. J'y suis restée cinq ans.
Examiner Qu'est-ce que vous n'aimez pas?
Candidate Les règles, je n'aime pas les règles.
Examiner Oui, expliquez.
Candidate Les règles sont stupides. En sixième (en terminale!) les règles, c'est embêtant.
Examiner Mais quelles règles est-ce que vous n'aimez pas?
Candidate On ne peut pas sortir quand les leçons... quand il n'y a pas de leçons.

B *Examiner* Parlez-moi un peu de votre école. Vous êtes heureuse ici?
Candidate Oui, oui assez heureuse. Il y a des choses que je n'aime pas et d'autres qui sont bien.
Examiner Par exemple?
Candidate Alors en terminale, quand on est en terminale il y des règles qui sont embêtantes. On ne peut pas sortir de l'école quand on n'a pas de leçons.
Examiner Oui, c'est tout?
Candidate Ça fait cinq années que suis dans cette école. Ça fait longtemps. J'ai beaucoup d'amis ici, mais je crois que maintenant... je voudrais partir.

You will note that candidate A uses short sentences, needs prompting to carry on and expresses one thought at a time. Candidate B is ready to explain her reasons without prompting, explains both aspects of the question and uses sentences with an extra clause. Candidate A communicates adequately but what she has to say is more limited and less interesting. Candidate B is more used to thinking aloud in French than Candidate A.

(e) **Phonetic accuracy** This refers to accuracy in pronunciation and intonation and how 'authentically' French you sound. Nearly all candidates at A Level could improve in this aspect. It is worth remembering that the more authentic you sound, the more faults in accuracy tend to be overlooked. It is a good plan, two to three weeks before the oral exam, to enlist the help of a French assistant(e) (or native speaker) and iron out pronunciation faults. Just getting rid of one or two can make a big difference to how you sound. Common faults are: pronouncing (or not pronouncing) final consonants; not giving nasal vowels the right pronunciation; not distinguishing between adjectival endings; an English type 'r' sound; making vowels into diphthongs (e.g. *donnei* instead of *donné;* not making liaisons where a French speaker would make them); and giving an English intonation pattern (strong stress on one syllable) — French words have equal stress on all syllables with a bit more emphasis on the last one. (*see* below).

2 Pronunciation

Contents

Some people find it easier to acquire an authentic pronunciation than others. This is partly a question of age. The younger you are, when exposed to a second language, the more likely you are to speak it like a native speaker. As you get older, your speech organs are more likely to get set in the groove of your first language and you find it difficult to make them adapt perfectly to new sounds. Another factor is the ability to mimic. If you can imitate one or two English regional accents, you are more likely to be good at reproducing the sounds of French. Mimicry is not necessarily linked to age. Another factor is undoubtedly the amount of time you have spent listening to and speaking French.

By the time you begin your sixth-form studies, you will have had the advantage of having started to learn French at least five years previously. There will still be a number of pronunciation points that need attention. Having a good pronunciation will enhance your performance in the oral exam and it will also give you satisfaction and confidence when in France. You will benefit from working with a native speaker or teacher who can iron out some of your difficulties.

You can also do a great deal on your own by listening to French radio and to tapes as well as taking every opportunity to practise speaking. If you have access to a language laboratory, in a local university or polytechnic, working with repetition exercise tapes will help a lot. These are usually tapes of continuous French, recorded with gaps for you to repeat in. You can achieve something of the same effect by just using these with an ordinary cassette recorder; the only difference being that you will not be able to listen to your own voice. If you have the text of what is recorded, you can also try reading over the voice on the tape with the volume turned down. This gives good intonation practice.

The main pitfalls in pronunciation are caused by the differences in sounds or features in the two languages. For example, the French find it very hard to make the two sounds represented by 'th' in English simply because they do not exist at all in French. The following are some of the main areas that cause problems for English speakers.

1 Intonation and stress

The patterns of French and English are very different in this respect. English has strong stress which can fall on any one syllable in a word. French has equal stress for each syllable, with a slight rise or emphasis at the end of the word. For example:

English	ad-min-is-**tra**-tion	com-pos-**it**-ion
French	ad-mi-nis-tra-**tion**	com-po-si-**tion**

You will also notice that the syllable break is different in both languages. French tends to end with a vowel sound; English with a consonant. This has the effect of putting the vowels in a prominent place in French and giving them more importance. The even distribution of stress in French makes the overall 'tune', or pattern, of the language sound very different to that of English with its constant beat of the stressed syllable. This is one reason why French poetry has a different sound to it and why the vowels tend to carry more musical effect.

Reading over a voice on tape as suggested is good practice but also make a conscious effort to eliminate the stressed syllable of English words, particularly when they are identical or almost so with French spelling.

2 Vowels

1 Diphthongs

A diphthong is a vowel sound made up of two vowels (e.g. English 'day' [dei] and 'now' [nau]). Eight out of the twenty English vowel sounds are diphthongs. French has sixteen vowels, none of them diphthongs. A common pronunciation fault is to give some French vowel sounds, particularly [e] and [ɛ], a double quality in words like j'**ai,** donné, arriv**ait.** When you pronounce a diphthong, your tongue moves slightly in the vowel position. The trick is to first feel this happening and then to try and stop it.

When some of our politicians speak French, you will often hear quite strong diphthongization; conversely, a French person speaking English might well do the opposite and pronounce 'day' as *des* and 'lay' as *lait.*

2 'Tense' vowel sounds

Two things are important when making vowel sounds:
(a) **tongue position** — whether the front or back is raised and how far it is up or down
(b) **the shape of the lips** — whether they are rounded, narrow-rounded or stretched apart

English vowel sounds require minimum movement of the lips and tongue whilst some French vowels require quite a lot. The main ones that cause difficulty are:

　(i)　**[i]** in words like *lit – appétit – île de la Cité – illisible* (illegible)

Note To make this sound correctly, the lips are stretched apart and the front of the tongue is raised to nearly touch the roof of the mouth.

　(ii)　**[y]** in words like *il a eu – j'ai pu – tu as voulu*

Note This time, the lips are narrow-rounded and protruded but the tongue is in the same position as for the previous vowel. You should hear a characteristic puff of air when this sound is made correctly. It's a bit like the action of blowing away a speck of dust!

(iii)   **[y]** often contrasts with the vowel **[u]** in a number of words. **[u]** is pronounced with the back of the tongue raised with lip-rounding but no protrusion. Can you hear the difference between the following:

tout – tu
roue (wheel) *– rue*
c'est vu – c'est vous
il s'est tu (he kept quiet) *– il sait* **tout**
lu – loup
une puce (flea) *– un pouce* (thumb),
au-dessous – au-dessus

If you are not sure, get a French speaker to say them for you, then practise yourself saying them in pairs. See if you can find other examples using the phonetic transcription in a dictionary.

3 Nasal vowels

There are none of these in standard English. There are four in French. A nasal vowel is pronounced by letting air flow through the nasal passage. If you want to check that you are pronouncing a nasal vowel correctly on its own, try pinching your nose. You should be able to feel a vibration through the top part of your nose. The following phrase contains the four French nasal vowels:

Un bon vin blanc

You will see that each vowel has a single '*n*' following it. In a dictionary transcription, nasal vowels have a little squiggle over the top.

(i)   The first vowel is the least common: *brun – lundi – un*. It causes least difficulty.
(ii)   The next one occurs in words like: *bon – ombre – melon – vont – sont – dont*.
(iii)   The next in: *plein – main – malin – fin – hein*. It is represented by the letters '*-ein*', '*ain*' and '*-in*'.
(iv)   The last occurs in: *vent – venant – deux ans – allemand – cependant*. It is represented by the letters '*-en*' and '*-an*'.
(v)   Confusion is caused sometimes by the different spellings that can represent the nasal vowels and also because of what is called 'denasalization'. All the above vowels lose their nasal quality:

(a)   when followed by another '*n*' or '*m*'

nasal	**non-nasal**
bon	*bonne*
dont	*donne*
an	*année*
mon	*monnaie*
colon (settler)	*colonne* (column)

(b)   when followed immediately by a vowel

nasal	**non-nasal**
fin	*fine*
plein	*pleine*
un	*une*
brun	*brune*
pan! (bang!)	*panne*

Try reading the words above aloud yourself. Get a French person to read them for you.

(vi)   The nasal sounds '*-on*' and '*-en/-an*' are often contrasted. Now try saying the following aloud:

vont	*vent*
dont	*dent*
sont	*sent/sans*
violon	*violent*
tromper (deceive)	*tremper* (soak)
long	*lent*

(vii)   Where the first syllable is '*in-*', '*im-*' and '*inn-*', '*imm-*' The rule is:
'*in*' or '*im*' + **consonant** (except n, or m) is pronounced as nasal in v**in**
'*inn-*' or '*imm-*' + **vowel** is pronounced non-nasally as in coll**ine**

ine, ime	*in, im*
innocent	*intelligent*
inégal	*intention*
inespéré	*ingénieur*
inadmissible	*inspirer*
imminent	*impossible*
immense	*imposition*
image	*insister*
inacceptable	*incapable*

Try reading the words above aloud. Find other examples.

Note You might also like to try the following:

A Melun (town) *il n'y pas de melons, mais il y a des moulins mêlant leur mélodie au bruit du ruisseau*

3 Consonants

1 Voicing

This is the vibration you can feel when you make a continuous 'zzzz' sound and place your finger on your Adam's apple. Many consonants can either be voiced with this vibration, or unvoiced as in a continous 'ssss' sound. Voiced consonants in French tend to be more fully voiced than in English. This applies particularly to the following:

(i)   **z** (sound in) – *zéro – maison – rose – chose*

(ii) **zh** (sound in) – *j'ai – Jean – gilet – rage*

(iii) **v** (sound in) – *vous – rêve – veuve – sauver*

Try to give these sounds more vibration in order to sound more French.

(iv) **[p]** This consonant is not pronounced with a following puff of air as in English. It sounds more like a 'b' sound to an English ear. The trick therefore is to think of a 'b' when pronouncing it. Try saying: *Paul part pour Paris* thinking of 'b's' instead of the '*p*'s'.

(v) **[r]** The main French '*r*' sound is made by raising the very back part of the tongue so that it nearly touches the uvular (the small flap hanging down at the back of the throat). This causes a vibration of air and of the uvular. Avoid the main English 'r' sound which is made by curling back the tip of the tongue towards the roof of the mouth. Try saying *rue de remarques* and *la route pour Paris* with all this in mind.

2 Liaison

One of the early basic pronunciation rules you probably learned was not to pronounce final consonants. But, you also found fairly soon that, in certain combinations of words, you **are** required to pronounce them. The latter cases are called **liaisons.** Leaving out liaisons, in common combinations, sounds very un-French. The simplest rules are the following:

(a) Liaison occurs in **noun phrases**, between the word before the noun and the noun:
les enfants – nos étudiants – vos intentions – ses idées – trois enfants – dix ans

It often occurs between a preceding **adjective and noun:**
mes anciens amis – ces dernières années – des enfants intelligents

(b) Around a verb:
nous allons – vas-y – allez-y – vous en avez – c'est un ami – c'est impossible – elle est ici

(c) After adverbs and prepositions + noun, adjective etc:
très intéressant – dans un mois – chez un ami – en anglais – sous un arbre – sans intérêt

(d) You can add to these some commonly used **set phrases:**
les Etats Unis – les Champs Elysées – petit à petit – de plus en plus – tout à coup – tout à fait – tout à l'heure – de temps en temps – mot à mot – moins en moins

3 Finally, here are some words that can cause difficulty. A rhyming word is given as a guide to pronunciation:
Adam (*le premier homme*) – **dent**

alcool – bol
Allemagne – campagne
allemand – banc
une aile (wing) – *elle*
ail (garlic) – *médaille*
album – homme (also like this are: *minimum*, *maximum*, *Rome* (*la ville*), *rhum* (*la boisson*))
baptême/baptiser ('*p*' not pronounced)
automne – tonne
démocratie (*cracie*)
poêle (frying pan/stove) – *voile*
un pneu (*p+n+eux*)
solennel (*-annel*)
soixante (*soissante*)
vieille (old woman) (*vi-ei-y*)
veille means the day before – the one with the two '*i*'s in it is human!

Further reading
R Martineau and J M McGivney, (1973), *French Pronunciation* , OUP

3 Listening comprehension

Understanding what someone is saying in French, when you can see them, is a lot easier than understanding a voice on tape, radio or phone. When you can't see the speaker, you miss many of the visual clues that help you to interpret what is being said.

Another factor is that when we 'listen' in English, we do not have to listen to every single word. We are able to guess at, or expect, certain meanings because we already know something about the subject being discussed and the order in which things might occur. We may be listening just to pick out certain details and ignore anything not connected with them. If you were listening to the national weather forecast, to find out if it was going to rain in your area tomorrow, you would probably keep half an ear monitoring the general run of what was being said but both ears would come into operation when you heard your region of the country mentioned and you would be on the alert for words like 'showers', 'patchy or prolonged rain', 'mainly dry', 'in the morning or afternoon' etc.

Listening comprehension in French is not such a relaxed affair. Your 'half an ear monitoring' system has to be fully alert **all the time** in case you miss something and doubly alert for the bit of information required, since it is not always possible to tell in advance at what point this might occur. You will probably only have two or three opportunities to catch what was said. This skill needs lots of practice (*see* pages viii–ix).

The other skill required is that of being able to take notes as you listen or during a pause. You are usually allowed to give your answers in note form. Dictionaries may or may not be permitted, depending on the Board. (*see* pages xi–xii)

The material for listening comprehension is usually taken from live sources such as radio news bulletins, advertisements, 'phone-ins', interviews and discussions. The material has always been carefully selected for level of understanding and speed and may have been edited or re-recorded. It will therefore be somewhat easier to understand than most things you may casually tune into on French radio.

Types of question set

These vary from Board to Board but are likely to include the following:
(a) Questions in English to be answered in English
(b) Questions in French to be answered in French
(c) Ticking true or false statements
(d) Filling in tables or grids relating to what was said
(e) Completing statements or filling in bits of missing text
(f) Summarizing in English

Some Boards make full use of the above but most use questions in English, with answers in English, as the main item.

A few minutes are usually allowed for studying the questions before hearing the tape. There are often pauses between items and at the end of sections. You are allowed to write an answer or make notes at any time. Some Boards provide space on the answer paper for making notes.

Examination strategy

1   Make sure you know the requirements of your particular Board with respect to: the layout of the paper; where and when pauses occur; what sort of questions to expect and whether dictionaries are allowed.

2   Read through the questions beforehand and underline the key words. This will help your eye while your ear is engaged in listening. If there are any numbers involved put a big 'N' to remind you, since these always require special concentration. Look at the number of marks awarded for each item, usually given at the end of each question. This will be a good guide to how many points are likely to be required and prevent you spending too much time on questions that obviously require just a single detail. You may find it helpful to highlight, in some way, those questions that have a high mark.

3   Some questions may involve a certain amount of deduction as well as giving facts from the text. In this case, take into consideration the theme of the passage as a whole and listen carefully for the part before and after where you think the answer is contained.

4   If answers are in English, it seems logical to take notes in English. Make these as brief as possible. If you don't understand a key word or phrase, and dictionaries are allowed, jot down an approximation so that you can look it up during a pause. Answers written in French are not usually penalized for grammatical error provided that they can be understood as French.

5   Use the space provided for notes. If you are writing on a blank sheet, divide your page in half, (left-side for notes in pencil, right-side for answers in ink — blue or black). Make sure you cross out anything you do not want to be included as a final answer. **Don't** use brackets.

6   Make sure that answers you write in note form in English: make sense; are unambiguous; and show that you have fully understood. Although answers don't have to be in note form, common sense often plays a part in giving an acceptable answer. Responses like 'Open 48 hours a day' and ' Since the 40th of July' (*London A and AS Level 1990*) could have been avoided if they had been read with a critical eye!

7   **Summary in English** You will probably hear the passage three times. Jot down French or English words as notes, during the first hearing, using the speaker's pauses at full stops as a guide line. Use these notes to give a framework to the summary in short phrases, leaving plenty of gaps. Use the second recording to fill in anything missing and make sure it makes sense. The third recording should be a check on the whole.

Examiners' reports, during the last two years, seem to indicate that listening skills are improving. There is a clear division between those candidates who have had sufficient practice and others who have not. Since questions in this part of the A-Level examination are closely defined, and relate directly to the spoken text, it is possible to gain full or nearly full marks. It is well worthwhile developing your skills in this area.

Finally, a comment on the listening test from the London Board's Report on the 1990 A and AS-Level examination. Having commented on some of the problems encountered, the Report stated:

> ....candidates put on a strong performance in this test. They were clearly well-prepared and had rehearsed examination procedures so as to be able to deal calmly with the mechanics of the test: note-taking; pauses; reading the questions; and so on. There were few occasions when marks were lost because a question had been carelessly read and there was evidence of considerable presence of mind in the longer passages where, despite misunderstanding initial details, candidates were able to make sense of subsequent material and score well, rather than panicking or losing the thread.

The cassette tape

The tape included with this book contains listening material in two sections. Side A has material taken mainly from French radio but also includes pronunciation practice and an anecdote. Side B has material and questions from Examination Boards as they appeared in recent examination papers. In order to include the maximum amount of listening material, the recordings on the tape are not presented as exactly as they would be in an examination (i.e. with pauses and repetitions). In order to simulate as closely as possible examination practice it is recommended that you do the following:

(a) Study the questions for a few minutes before listening.
(b) Listen to the whole of one recording without stopping the tape.
(c) Stop the tape yourself in appropriate places to write your answer.
(d) Listen once more to check what you have written.

Marks awarded for each question are given so that you can estimate the amount of material required for each answer.

You can either use the passages on this part of the tape as simulations of exam practice, or you can use them as listening practice with information to be extracted. In this case, you can listen to them as many times as you like, by stopping or replaying as required, without a time limit. A further exercise you can do is to transcribe the full text of part of any recording, stopping the tape as many times as you like. When you have transcribed part of the text, check it against the text of the recording in the appendix. Listen again while you follow the text and try reading over the voice on the tape as suggested earlier in this book.

Side A

Examples of spoken French in everyday life

I   In this extract you will hear a number of news headlines, broadcast in December 1990. Listen to the items once through without a break and complete the following tasks as you listen:

1   For each item, write down the name of the country where the event took place – or the town, if it happened in France.

2   Read through the ten headings below. There is one for each news item but they are not in the same order as on the tape. Listen to the recording again and number the items as they appear on the tape.
Gang shoot-out leaves two dead
Well-known company owner and his wife mugged in town centre
Gaza strip sealed off: arrests and expulsions
Bus strikes to continue
New Government to be formed
Frenchman third in downhill ski event
Calm returns to city after yesterday's disturbances
Tennis cup final tomorrow
No traffic hold-ups at end of winter break
Gales cause death and damage   [10]

3   Listen to the recording again and write down the French phrase that fits the English one below. There is one for each item in sequence.
suggested to a lawyer that he forms a government
after yesterday's riots
the Gaza strip
the winner of the event
match being played at the moment
funeral held of Lucien Toroloni
serious damage
well done, drivers!
attacked in town centre
a gang of hooligans   [10]

4 Listen to each news item again and put a tick next to those statements which are correct or a cross beside those that are incorrect.

Lech Walesa to form new Government
Unions claim 20 people died
600 Palestinians expelled
The winner was a Norwegian
Pete Sampras will meet Michael Chang in the final
Shoot-out was probably intended to settle old scores beween gangs
Latest figures give 73 dead
Motorists staggered their return home
Claude Taittinger's name appears on bottles of his champagne
One of the hooligans was armed with a knife   [10]

5 Listen once more to item number six.
What two events are referred to? What contrast is drawn between them.   [3]

6 Listen again to item number ten.
Explain the reason for the strike and say which bus routes are affected.   [7]

II France-Inter donne des conseils pratiques quant à la façon de soigner les animaux domestiques.

1 Répondez aux questions suivantes:

(a) En anglais
    (i)   What can some dogs be like (two characteristics)?   [2]
    (ii) In which two ways are cats different from dogs?   [2]
    (iii) What do you have to teach dogs to do if you *live in a town*?   [1]
    (iv) What should you persuade dogs not to do *when they are young*?   [1]
    (v)   What reason is given for doing this?   [2]
    (vi) What advice is given about barking?   [2]

(b) En français
    (i)   Quels chiens sont permis dans le métro ou l'autobus?   [2]
    (ii) Comment est-ce qu'on doit surveiller son chien dans le train?   [2]
    (iii) Quelle précaution doit-on prendre avant d'amener son chien
        chez des amis et pourquoi?   [2]
    (iv) Qu'est-ce qu'il faut fournir à son chat avant de le laisser pour le week-end?   [3]
    (v)   Si l'on est obligé de voyager avec son chat, quelles précautions doit-on prendre?   [2]

2 Comblez les blancs dans le texte ci-dessous:
Lorsque vous avez des invités, empêchez votre chat de s'installer sur leurs ——————- car beaucoup de gens sont allergiques à leurs ————— ou tout simplement ne les aiment pas. Si vous avez chez vous des animaux plus —————, pensez toujours à la tranquillité de vos amis ou de vos voisins. Après tout, ce n'est pas donné à tous d'aimer les————- blanches ou les —————! Et puis, évitez d'apprendre des ————— aux oiseaux parleurs, ils les retiennent facilement et cela risquerait de vous ————- devant des invités qui n'ont pas un grand sens de l'humour.

III The following is part of an interview with a former French soldier describing what life was like in a German concentration camp during the Second World War. The questions cover three sections of the interview.

Section 1 Répondez en anglais
  (i)   Age now of former soldier?   [1]
  (ii)   Captured when?   [1]
  (iii) Liberated when?   [1]
  (iv)   Name of *département* where captured?   [1]
  (v)   Name of town?   [1]
  (vi)   On which river?   [1]
 (vii)   He was captured at night? yes/no   [1]
(viii)   By Germans speaking French? yes/no   [1]
  (ix)   Weapon used in his capture?   [1]
  (x)   Was he alone? yes/no   [1]
  (xi)   He was taken straight to Germany? yes/no   [1]

(xii) How many prisoners were there in the transit camp?   [1]

(xiii) Name the two forms of transport between camps   [2]

(xiv) His final camp: is the town named? yes/no   [1]

Section 2 Complétez la transcription de cet extrait du texte de l'enregistrement et répondez en français aux deux questions.

A: Est-ce que cela vous a ——————— le sens de l'initiative dans le camp?

B: D'une façon générale on peut dire que le camp, on est ———————- sans rien, et par ——————- des uns et ———————, on était arrivé à reconstituer à l'intérieur du camp, absolument tous les ——————— dont on a besoin dans la vie sociale ——————- .

A: Vous pouvez donner un exemple?

B: Et bien il y avait un ———————, il y avait un théâtre, il y avait ———————-, il y avait du sport, du rugby, tous les sports étaient ———————.

A: Ahh...

B: Y compris le tennis. Il y avait ——————— des jardins potagers.   [10]

(i) Qu'est-ce que les prisonniers ont même réussi à fabriquer?   [1]

(ii) Nommez trois expositions montées par les prisonniers   [3]

Section 3 He now goes on to describe attempts to escape before and after the initiation of a daily parade by the Germans.

Answer in English:

(i) Name three ways of escaping before the parade was initiated   [3]

(ii) Give three ways the Germans used to prevent escape afterwards   [3]

(iii) What method of escape was eventually devised?   [1]

(iv) What help did the 'Libertas' organization provide?   [2]

(v) In your opinion, why does he believe that a third world war will not happen?   [2]

IV Summary in note form In the following news item you will hear about the plight of homeless families living in Paris. The item includes comment from a homeless mother and a primary-school teacher. Play the whole recording through without a break; then again, with a short pause after each piece of information required.

A First, read through the headings.

(i) Two more families are to join who?   [3]

(ii) Help provided by the Emmaus organization and how life is organized.   [5]

(iii) Why some families can leave from time to time.   [2]

B Interview with the mother Béatrice:

(i) What further details does she add about the daily routine?   [2]

(ii) What particular problems are there for Béatrice?   [3]

C Interview with school teacher Jean-Paul: Tick appropriate item.

(i) 150 children are able to attend school: true/false   [1]

(ii) Jean-Pierre has: (a) 35; (b) several; (c) 14 in his class   [1]

(iii) Main problem with these chidren is that they are: (a) violent (b) tired.   [1]

(iv) They become more alert at: (a) the end of the afternoon; (b) the beginning of the afternoon [1]

D Final question

How does the situation with the squatters stand as described by the news presenter at the end of the report?   [3]

V In this extract, Fabrice Lecantrac is talking about his impressions of Japan and the Japanese. You will also hear a Japanese person speaking French.

1 Questions in English:

(i) What recent event in Japan is referred to?   [1]

(ii) Why is Fabrice well qualified to talk about Japan?   [1]

(iii) Who did Fabrice meet recently?   [1]

(iv) Give two details about this person   [2]

    (v) How did the meeting come about?   [1]

    (vi) Give three details about the person's appearance   [3]

   (vii) Why does the interviewer think that Fabrice has been
influenced by the charm of this person?   [1]

  (viii) Was Akiko born just after or just before the end of the Second World War?   [1]

    (ix) Why does Akiko feel no resentment towards her stepfather?   [2]

    (x) What feature of the Japanese character is mentioned and what example is given?   [2]

    (xi) Describe the attitude of the Japanese towards the Americans after the atomic bomb.   [1]

   (xii) What positive and negative sides to the Japanese character does Akiko refer to finally ?   [2]

2 Listen to the next part of the interview and write down in French the phrases for which the English
equivalents are given below:

    (i) in effect have no memory

   (ii) on the other hand

  (iii) when it's over it's over

  (iv) in spite of the horrors they have experienced

   (v) the very next day

  (vi) the guns stopped firing   [6]

3 Voici une transcription de la prochaine partie de l'entrevue. Ecrivez dans les blancs les mots ou les
phrases qui manquent.

Et moi ce qui m'intéresse dans ce —————, outre cette particularité biographique qui fait que
cette femme est née après les bombes atomiques mais juste avant —————, alors que depuis
plusieurs mois la guerre était déjà ————— en Europe, et donc elle a connu depuis lors tout ce
développement du Japon, c'est le fait qu'elle ————— que, bien euh, après on est capable, on
est capable d'oublier et c'est vrai que c'est à mon avis l'une des forces du Japon et des Japonais de
—————, non pas en faisant table rase du passé, et disons sans s'attacher, se polariser sur des
choses matérielles. On peut très bien par exemple, quand on se balade à Tokyo, voir je ne sais pas,
————— assez laid inauguré avec un écriteau 'All new'– complètement neuf – et alors ça veut
dire que l'on a ————— peut-être une vieille maison en bois charmante qui était là. —————
—, si vous voulez on est capable de faire table rase mais en même temps on reste —————
japonais avec cette faculté de faire du neuf et d'aller de l'avant et c'est ainsi peut-être que l'on
arrive à cette ironie d'histoire que ————— de la deuxième guerre mondiale, enfin l'un des
vaincus, on arrive maintenant à porter ————— le trésor fédéral, le trésor fédéral américain,
mais tout ça ————— et sans rancune vis-à-vis des troupes victorieuses.   [12]

VI In the following recording, you will hear part of an interview with Pierre Fabre who has just published
a book on demonstrations. There are three sections. Listen to the complete text once without pausing.
Listen once more with a short pause to write the answer. Listen once more to the whole of each
section in order to check your work.

Section 1

    (i) Describe the three different types of demonstration in France defined by Pierre Fabre
and give an example of each   [6]

   (ii) What was the direct political effect of two particular demonstrations in France?   [2]

  (iii) Why were divorced fathers demonstrating?   [2]

  (iv) What did homosexuals hope to achieve through their demonstration?   [2]

Section 2 Complétez le résumé ci-dessous de cette section en rajoutant les mots qui manquent:

A: Vous citez le cas d'un jour de mars ————— où il y a une accumulation là pendant 2 ou 3 jours
assez extraordinaire.

B: Effectivement j'ai fait un reportage sur l'ensemble des manifestations qui ————— au ministère
de la —————. On s'aperçoit que sur une période de six mois l'an dernier il y en a eu une par
semaine. Alors, ces manifestations ne retiennent ... elles retiennent beaucoup moins l'attention du
public... au moins des journalistes, c'est-à-dire que le public en a sans doute beaucoup moins ———
—————, à moins qu'il ne se trouve sur le passage de la manifestation ou qu'il remarque telle ou
telle manifestation. Cela étant, le ministre qui est dans son ministère, il a ————— de cette
manifestation. Quand les manifestations deviennent nombreuses, il y a un effet de —————,
notamment d'ailleurs dans les crises, les grèves.   [6]

Section 3 Answer the following questions in English:
   (i) In what year did the right to demonstrate become part of the French constitution? [1]
   (ii) What distinction does the law make between a demonstrator and the
      organizer of the demonstration? [2]
   (iii) Explain carefully why Pierre Fabre believes the right to demonstrate is not as
      straightforward as most people think. [3]
   (iv) In what circumstances can the authorities ban a demonstration? [2]
   (v) What is the unknown factor in demonstrations? [2]

Les chiffres

VII Première partie
Vous allez entendre les résultats de trois jeux de pari nationaux:
(a) **Courses de chevaux - le tiercé** Pour gagner il faut prédire les trois premiers chevaux de la course
   et leur arrivée dans l'ordre ou dans un ordre différent. Pour *le quarté* il s'agit des quatre premiers
   chevaux. Vingt chevaux participent à la course.
(b) **Le tapis vert** Il faut deviner quatre cartes tirées au hasard.
(c) **Le loto** Il faut prédire six chiffres tirés au hasard.

   Dans chaque cas vous allez noter les chiffres des numéros sortants, le rapport pour le gagnant et la
   somme d'argent pariée (la mise)

(a) Le tiercé numéros gagnants: —————— rapport pour ——— francs, dans l'ordre
          ————— francs. Dans un ordre différent, —————— . [6]
   Le quarté: ————— rapport pour ————— francs dans l'ordre, ————— francs
     ————— centimes, et dans un ordre différent ————— francs et ——— centimes. [9]

(b) Le tapis vert: —————. [4]

(c) Le loto, premier tirage: ————— numéro complémentaire ———. [7]
   Deuxième tirage: ————— numéro complémentaire ——. [7]

Deuxième partie
Pour les chiffres qui suivent vous pouvez:
(a) la première fois écrire le chiffre après l'avoir entendu
(b) et la deuxième fois prononcer le chiffre avant la voix de la bande
Il faut signaler que ce sont des chiffres qui sont souvent confondus.

6, 600, 1606, 60, 66, 676, 550, 40, 14, 1404, 91, 1981, 1.005.599

1st, 6th, 11th, 21st, in the 16th century, in the 14th century, in 2500 BC

a thousand people, a third of the population, a quarter of his time, 500 ml that makes half a litre,
2%, 5%, 3,5%, 9,3%

Pronunciation practice

VIII Intonation
Remember equal stress on each syllable, slight emphasis on last:
possibilité – administration – postérité – technologie – attention – complication

Difficult vowels
[i] Lip stretching: *appétit – au lit – il lit la liste – Italie*
[y] Narrow lip rounding with puff of air for 'u': *aperçu – voulu – perdu – vendu – il a pu*

Vowel contrasts
[u] and [y]
*une roue – une rue, c'est vu – c'est vous, il sait tout – il s'est tu, au-dessous – au-dessus,
il est où? – il l'a eu.*

Nasals All French nasals are contained in the phrase, *Un bon vin blanc*
[œ̃] *lundi le vingt et un, aucun parfum, brun*
[ɔ̃] *un bon melon, ils ont, ils vont sur le pont*
[ɛ̃] *le vin, la main, bien, le dessein, assassin*
[ã] *le champ, un camp, deux ans, le vent*

Denasalization

bon – bonne, fin – fine, serein – sereine, brun – brune, dont – donne, plein – pleine, colon – colonne

Nasal contrasts [ã] [õ]

le vent – ils vont, long – lent, ils sont – ça sent, violon – violent, une dent – un don (gift)

in-, inn-/im-, imm-

innocent – intelligent, inespéré – ingénieur, inacceptable – incapable, imminent – important, immense – imprimé, inimaginable – intéressant

Voicing More 'buzz' than in English

[z]   *zéro, maison, rose, chose, pause*

[zh]   *les jeunes gens, un agent, la rage, une cage*

[v]   *un rêve, un veuf, une veuve, mauve*

Consonants [p] and [r]

[p]   *Paul part pour Paris, les petits problèmes, petit à petit*

[r]   *un rude hiver, rue de Rivoli, une route rurale*

Liaisons

(a) Noun phrases

les enfants, vos intentions, trois étudiants, dix ans, les idoles

(b) Adjective + noun

mes anciens amis, ces dernières années, de bonnes intentions

(c) Before or after verb

nous allons, ils ont, vous en avez, allez-y, c'est un ami, c'est impossible

(d) Adverb/preposition + noun/adjective

très heureux, dans un mois, chez une amie, sans intérêt, en anglais, trop important

(e) Set phrases

les Etats Unis, petit à petit, de moins en moins, de plus en plus, de temps en temps, tout à fait, à tout à l'heure

(f) A few words that can cause difficulty

l'Allemagne, allemand, une médaille, un agent, de l'argent, maximum, minimum, la démocratie, une femme, soixante, la veille (day before), *une vieille* (old woman), *de l'ail* (garlic), *une aile* (wing), *l'alcool, le baptême, l'automne, l'Europe, européen, européenne, évidemment, une grenouille, un oignon, solennel.*

IX Histore drôle Ecoutez cette histoire d'abord pour la comprendre mais aussi essayez de la mémoriser pour savoir la raconter à d'autres personnes.

X Annonces publicitaires *France- Inter*, octobre 1991

Avez-vous l'oreille fine? (*Have you got sharp ears?*) Ecoutez attentivement les deux annonces publicitaires suivantes et pour les mots soulignés, cochez (*tick*) celui que vous avez entendu.

(i) *A:* Vie de famille

     B: Vous avez un enfant de moins de six/seize ans et pour le faire garer/garder vous employez une assistante/assistant maternelle agréée. Nous, les allocations familiales/familières nous pouvons vous aider. Quelle que soit votre situation/stipulation familiale et le montant de vos revenants/revenus, nous prenons en charge les qualifications/cotisations sociales de l'URSAF. Alors si vous désirez en savoir plus, n'hésitez pas, tapez/frappez 36 15 code CAF. Vous voyez, vous faire aider à garder vos enfants, c'est aussi notre rouleau/rôle.

     A: Allocations familiales, ça vous met/fait la vie plus facile.

(ii) *A:* Un petit boulot/boule par ci, une bricole par là, un mois ici/aussi, un mois là-bas/par là, et caetera, et caetera. Quand on est jeune/jaune et qu'on veut travailler/trouver, on ne veut pas traîner pendant/pour des années et des années. L'Exojeune c'est la résolution/solution pour un jeune sans cotisations/ qualifications, d'entrer tout de suite dans la vie active/fictive avec un vrai salaire, un véritable emploi. Embaucher un jeune, ça n'est pas une large/charge.

     B: Pour en savoir plus sur l'Exojeune, contactez/contractez votre agence locale pour l'emploi. Compostez/Composez le numéro vert du ministère/ministre du travail sur le 05 10 10 10.

Side B

Texts from Examination Boards

Note The instructions which follow are not in the exact form used on the examination papers of the various Boards. They have been adapted to suit the arrangement of material on the tape.

I *London A and AS Level Syllabus A and B, June 1991*
Answer the following questions **in English**. Your sentences should give all **relevant** information but need not be in the form of complete sentences. You have three minutes to look through all the questions before you hear the French recording.
Cet exercice consiste en trois parties: la première partie comprend deux flashs et une annonce publicitaire, la deuxième partie est un reportage et la troisième est une interview.

Première partie: deux flashs et une annonce publicitaire. Vous écouterez chaque flash et l'annonce deux fois avec une pause. Ensuite mettez 1.30 – 2.0 minutes environ pour rédiger vos réponses.

(i)	How was the latest victim of the storms killed?	[2]
(ii)	What was he doing at the time?	[1]
(iii)	Why is the latest weather forecast a source of anxiety?	[1]
(iv)	At what time of the year was the advertisement broadcast?	[1]
(v)	What problem does this time present for parents?	[1]
(vi)	Give any two details of the item advertised?	[2]
(vii)	How did the crooks extort money from motorists?	[3]

Deuxième partie: un reportage sur une nouvelle entreprise appelée 'Tom et Flore'. Ecoutez une première fois et mettez quelques moments pour étudier les questions et écrire des notes. Ecoutez une deuxième fois et mettez quatre minutes pour rédiger vos réponses.

(vii)	What is the special service offered by the new firm 'Tom et Flore'?	[2]
(ix)	When is the service available?	[2]
(x)	Give **any three** details of the entertainment provided.	[3]
(xi)	How are they trying to obtain more publicity?	[2]

Troisième partie: Extrait d'une interview avec un Français qui travaille au Liban. Ecoutez une fois et mettez quelques moments pour étudier les questions et faire des notes. Ensuite écoutez une deuxième fois et mettez six minutes pour rédiger vos réponses.

(xii)	What two factors are making the teachers' lives impossible?	[2]
(xiii)	What is the children's attitude towards France?	[3]
(xiv)	Why is study difficult?	[1]
(xv)	What do we know of Houda's home circumstances?	[4]

II *Scottish Certificate of Education, French (Revised), Higher Grade – Paper 2, May, 1991.*
Listen carefully to the tape with a view to writing notes, in French, on the main points being made. Headings have been printed to help you organize your notes. You will have two minutes to study the headings before hearing the tape. Play the tape twice with an interval of one minute between the two playings. You may consult a French dictionary at any time.
Note You are not told how long to spend on finishing this question before doing the short essay [100-120 words] that follows. Total time for the paper is one hour. You should not therefore spend more than about 10 –15 minutes on the listening-test questions.

Vous allez écouter la bande deux fois. Eric nous parle de sa préparation au baccalauréat. Ecoutez la bande et prenez des notes en français, sur ce qu'il dit. Vous devez mentionner:

(i)	la section qu'il a choisie	[1]
(ii)	pourquoi il n'était pas content de ce choix	[1]
(iii)	pourquoi il est allé dans un lycée technique	[3]
(iv)	pourquoi sa section était un peu à l'écart des autres	[2]
(v)	l'attitude des autres élèves envers la section d'Eric	[2]
(vi)	ses expériences dans la classe de maths	[3]
(vii)	ce qu'il dit sur son professeur d'allemand	[5]

III *Oxford and Cambridge Schools Examination Board A and AS-Level, June 1991*
You have two minutes to read through the questions before you listen to the tape. After the first hearing allow a pause of two minutes. Listen to the tape once more with a short pause within the text. After the second hearing you have three minutes to complete your answers. You can write at any time and use a dictionary while the tape is not playing.

The recording is an extract from a radio report on illegal and unregistered labour. Here are nine statements relating to what you are about to hear. Five of them are correct; put a tick against those five, and do not put any mark against the others. Stop the tape for thirty seconds after *non-déclarée*.

(i) Le travail clandestin diminue d'année en année.
(ii) Le travail au noir rapporte l'équivalent de ce que gagnent 30 000 entreprises de taille moyenne.
(iii) Il y aurait plus de 800 000 personnes faisant du travail de façon clandestine.
(iv) Le nombre de travailleurs au noir ne comprend ni chômeurs, ni Portugais.
(v) La grande majorité des travailleurs étrangers non déclarés sont employés dans le bâtiment, l'agriculture, le textile et la restauration des garages.
(vi) Il y a très peu de travailleurs au noir sur la Côte d'Azur.
(vii) Le Ministère du Travail a l'intention de supprimer, dans la mesure du possible, le trafic de main d'œuvre.
(viii) Le travail au noir se répand dans tous les autres pays européens.
(ix) Le renforcement des verbalisations est une des premières mesures que compte adopter le ministre.

IV *Cambridge A-Level, June 1991*
Listen to the advertisements twice, with a short pause between them. Give yourself a minute at the end to complete and check your answers. *Répondez aux questions en français.*

Advertisement 1
(i) Entre quelles dates peut-on profiter de cette offre?
(ii) Quel est le prix de la mini-chaîne?
(iii) Notez les deux avantages de cette offre spéciale.

Advertisement 2
(iv) Que pouvez-vous assurer avec l'UAP? (4 choses)
(v) Nommez les deux grands projets européens dont l'UAP est l'assureur.

You will now hear two news items: the first about a change in the rules of volley-ball, the second about a plane hijacking in India. The first requires answers in **English** the second in **French.** Listen to each one twice, with a short pause in between. Give yourself three minutes to complete and check your answer after each one.

News Item 1
(vi) Why has it been decided to change the rules of volley-ball?
(vii) What is the normal procedure for scoring points?
(viii) What different procedure will be applied in the fifth set?
(ix) What is the highest score that can be obtained now in the fifth set?

News Item 2
(x) Sur quel pays l'avion a-t-il été détourné?
(xi) Sous quel prétexte a-t-il atterri?
(xii) Combien de passagers se trouvaient à bord de l'avion et combien de ces passagers étaient des étrangers?
(xiii) Quelle demande les pirates de l'air ont-ils faite?

V *JMB A-Level, June, 1991*
Item 1 In this recording you will hear a former French assistante, Nathalie, giving advice to a "would be " assistant.

(a) **Listening for gist**
Listen to the recording **once** in order to note, in English:
(i) Nathalie's overall attitude to her experience   [1]
(ii) **Three** reasons for this attitude   [3]

(b) Summary
Listen to the two sections of the recording beginning with:
(a) *Etre assistant...*
(b) '*Si je dois te parler de difficultés...*

After each section, summarize in English, the advantages and disadvantages which Nathalie mentions.
Listen once more to both sections with a pause at the end to check your work.
(a)   [6]
(b)   [5]

(c) Résumé en français
Vous allez maintenant entendre Nathalie en train de parler des qualités qu'elle considère nécessaires pour être un bon assistant. Un résumé incomplet de ce qu'elle dit se trouve en- dessous. Complétez le résumé en rajoutant les mots qui conviennent.

Ecoutez une fois sans pause, la deuxième fois avec des pauses pour vous permettre d'écrire les mots qui manquent et une troisième fois pour vérifier ce que vous avez écrit.

Lisez d'abord le résumé.

Selon Nathalie, pour être un bon assistant il faut être enthousiaste, bavard, patient, curieux et un peu acteur.

Enthousiaste parce que quand on mène une classe on doit —————————————————
Bavard parce qu'il faut —————————————————————————
Patient parce que les élèves ne font pas toujours ce qu'on voudrait ————————— et on est là pour les aider et pour être patient quand ——————————————————
Curieux du point de vue des élèves, parce qu'il faut savoir ————————————— et du point de vue personnel curieux —————————————————————

                                                [16]

Item 2 In this recording you will hear Patrick Olivier being interviewed about an autobiographical book which he has just published. Read through the questions then listen to the recording straight through without a break.

(a) Identifying information
Listen to the tape again in three sections with a short pause after each section to write brief but informative answers in English. Play the recording straight through and allow a short pause at the end to check your work.
Section (a)
  (i)   Give two ways in which the interviewer describes Patrick Olivier.   [2]
 (ii)   How does Olivier react to the interviewer's introduction?   [3]
Section (b)
(iii)   Describe the organization which Olivier joined in 1976.   [2]
(iv)   Why does he now disagree with the interviewer's description of him as a mercenary?   [2]
Section (c)
 (v)   What did Olivier do after Robert Mugabe's forces won the war in Zimbabwe?   [2]
(vi)   What were his reasons for doing this?

(b) Retranslation
Listen to the last part of the interview once more in **three** short sections. After each section write down, **in French**, the phrases for which the English equivalents are given below. Then listen to all three sections straight through so that you can check your work.
Section (a)
  (i)   I stayed an extra year.
 (ii)   in order to train the officers
Section (b)
(iii)   The white Christian West must be defended at all costs.
Section (c)
(iv)   not at all
 (v)   I feel I am partly African.

VI *Welsh Joint Education Committee A and AS-Level, June, 1989*
Candidates will be allowed a ten-minute break at the end of section two, before beginning section three.

Candidates will be allowed ten minutes to read the questions through before the tape is played and to make notes while it is being played. All questions are to be answered in English.

Section one

Listen to the conversations twice. Allow a pause of 30 seconds between the first and second time you listen. Allow five minutes after the second hearing to write your answers.

Note The French spelling of Marseilles is *Marseille*.

(a) While you are on a visit to France, you hear the following conversation between two of your French friends who have just taken the *bac:*

  (i) What is the girl's parents' reaction to what she has just told them?
     Explain this reaction. [2]
  (ii) Why does the girl say she has changed her mind about what she wants to do next year? [2]
  (iii) According to the boy, what are the disadvantages of working in a bank? [2]
  (iv) According to the girl, what are the disadvantages of a teacher's job? [2]
  (v) What arguments are used by the boy to try to persuade her to change her mind? [2]

(b) You are travelling in France in a car driven by your French friend's mother. She stops to give a lift to a young man who is hitch-hiking to his home in Marseilles. You hear the following conversation between the young man and your friend's mother:

  (i) What does the young man tell the woman about the origin of immigrants in Marseilles? [2]
  (ii) What problems does the young man say there are in Marseilles? [2]
  (iii) What does the young man say about the type of jobs done by
     immigrant workers in Marseilles? [4]
  (iv) How does the young man explain why many immigrants have come to Marseilles? [2]

Section two

There are **five** short news items. Listen to each one twice with a pause of approximately half a minute between the first and the second time. Then allow **one minute** after the second hearing to answer the question on that item.

Item one
  (i) How was Dominique Didier killed? When was his body found? [2]
Item two
  (ii) Where may you expect to find traffic jams this weekend? [2]
Item three
  (iii) How had the old lady lost her jewels? Where were they found? [2]
Item four
  (iv) Exactly when did the prisoner escape? [2]
Item five
  (v) Why will traffic in Valence be disrupted this weekend? [2]

Section three

Here is part of an interview with the French writer, Marcel Pagnol, first recorded some years ago and broadcast again recently on French radio as part of a programme about films which have been made recently of some of his works. Listen to the interview three times. (Allow a pause of **three minutes** between each listening. Allow a short pause of ten seconds between the second and third time you listen)

  (i) Why does the interviewer find it strange that Pagnol lives in Paris? [2]
  (ii) Pagnol says he is obliged to live in Paris for **three** reasons. What are these reasons? [3]
  (iii) Why does he say that he divides his time between Paris and the south of France? [4]
  (iv) What is the activity he takes part in while in the south of France
     and why is this activity particularly important there? [4]
  (v) What does Pagnol say about whether Parisians are more intelligent than
     people from other parts of France? [4]
  (vii) Pagnol gives a number of reasons why he no longer makes films. State **four** of these. [4]
  (vii) What sort of films does Pagnol say he is incapable of making? [1]
  (viii) What does the interviewer say about Pagnol and the 'Parisian landscape'? [1]
  (ix) Why does Pagnol say he chose the hills of the *Massif des étoiles* as a location for
     several of his films? [4]

(x) What does Pagnol say about the colours in the hills of the *Massif des étoiles* ?   [2]

(xi) What does he say about the rocks in the hills of the *Massif des étoiles* ?   [1]

VII *AEB A-Level, June 1990*

You will hear two brief news items, a publicity announcement and one longer piece: an interview. Listen to each item twice. Allow yourself half a minute to study the questions before listening to each of the shorter items. Allow a forty-five second pause in between to begin your answer and just over a minute at the end to complete it. For the longer item, allow one minute to read the questions, a minute and a half in between and four minutes at the end to complete your answers. You can make notes at any time during the reading. Your answers need not be in complete sentences.

Note Pay close attention to the number of marks given for each question as a guide to the amount of detail required.

Item one

(i) Who will be taking part in the protest march?   [2]

(ii) What is the subject of their protest?   [5]

Item two

(iii) Give details of the content of this news item.   [6]

Item three

(iv) Give details of the special offers which Ford is making on its cars
in this advertisement.   [7]

Item four: interview betwen Bernard Rigoulex and Hélène Dorlach

(v) Describe the problem outlined by Bernard Rigoulex at the beginning of the
interview.   [4]

(vi) Who is Hélène Dorlach and what action has she taken?   [5]

(vii) Bernard Rigoulex suggests that there has been a fresh outbreak of certain
forms of child abuse. Which does he specify?   [4]

(viii) What is Hélène Dorlach's reaction to this suggestion?   [2]

(ix) What measures are to be introduced?   [6]

(x) How will the specialist teams be able to respond?   [5]

(xi) How will the message of the publicity campaign be communicated?   [4]

Appendices

The following table provides a reference to regular verbs and most irregular ones. For simplicity's sake only the present tense is given in full. The past participles are given in **bold**, to attract the eye. Other tenses of the verb are given in the part most frequently needed. You should be able to work out the other parts of the tense by reference to the notes on the formation of tenses given in the grammar section.

Appendix 1: Verb table

infinitive/ present/ participles			perfect/ pluperfect	imperfect/ past historic	future/ conditional	present subjunctive
Regular verbs						
parler	je parle	nous parlons	j'ai parlé	il parlait	il parlera	que je parle
parlant	tu parles	vous parlez	j'avais parlé	il parla	il parlerait	que vous parliez
parlé	il parle	ils parlent				
finir	je finis	nous finissons	j'ai fini	il finissait	il finira	que je finisse
finissant	tu finis	vous finissez	j'avais fini	il finit	il finirait	que vous finissiez
fini	il finit	ils finissent				
entendre	j'entends	nous entendons	j'ai entendu	il entendait	il entendra	que j'entende
entendant	tu entends	vous entendez	j'avais entendu	il entendit	il entendrait	que vous entendiez
entendu	il entend	ils entendent				

'-er' verbs with peculiarities

Verbs in '-cer'

avancer	j'avance	nous avançons	j'ai avancé	il avançait	il avancera	que j'avance
avançant	tu avances	vous avancez	j'avais avancé	il avança	il avancerait	que vous avanciez
avancé	il avance	ils avancent				

(A cedilla always comes before an '-a', '-o' or '-u' only. See also *commencer, menacer*, and others.)

Verbs in '-ger'

arranger	j'arrange	nous arrangeons	j'ai arrangé	il arrangeait	il arrangera	que j'arrange
arrangeant	tu arranges	vous arrangez	j'avais arrangé	il arrangea	il arrangerait	que vous arrangiez
arrangé	il arrange	ils arrangent				

('-ge' always before an '-a' or '-o'. Also *ranger* – to tidy, *venger* – to avenge, *songer* – to dream, think and others)

Verbs in '-yer'

payer	je paie	nous payons	j'ai payé	il payait	il paiera	que je paie
payant	tu paies	vous payez	j'avais payé	il paya	il paierait	que vous payiez
payé	il paie	ils paient				

('-y' changes to '-i' before a mute [unpronounced] '-e'). The forms *je paye, tu payes, je payerai* are also found. Similarly *nettoyer* – to clean, *essuyer* – to wipe, *s'ennuyer* – to be bored **but** alternative in '-y' not normal)

jeter	je jette	nous jetons	j'ai jeté	il jetait	il jettera	que je jette
jetant	tu jettes	vous jetez	j'avais jeté	il jeta	il jetterait	que vous jetiez
jeté	il jette	ils jettent				

('-tt' before mute ending. Note the future and conditional)

Infinitive/ present/ participles			perfect/ pluperfect	imperfect/ past historic	future/ conditional	present subjunctive
appeler	j'appelle	nous appelons	j'ai appelé	il appelait	il appellera	qu'il appelle
appelant	tu appelles	vous appelez	j'avais appelé	il appela	il appellerait	que vous appeliez
appelé	il appelle	ils appellent				

('-*ll*' before mute '-*e*')

Changing accents

mener	je mène	nous menons	j'ai mené	il menait	il mènera	qu'il mène
menant	tu mènes	vous menez	j'avais mené	il mena	il mènerait	que vous meniez
mené	il mène	ils mènent				

('-*e*' becomes '-*è*' before mute ending, Note the future and conditional. Also *amener* - to bring, *emmener*- to take along, *lever, geler* - to freeze, and a number of others)

espérer	j'espère	nous espérons	j'ai espéré	il espérait	il espérera	qu'il espère
espérant	tu espères	vous espérez	j'avais espéré	il espéra	il espérerait	que vous espériez
espéré	il espère	ils espèrent				

('-*é*' becomes '-*è*' before mute '-*e*'. Note the future and conditional. Also like this *répéter*)

Most common irregular verbs

aller	je vais	nous allons	je suis allé	il allait	il ira	que j'aille
allant	tu vas	vous allez	j'étais allé	il alla	il irait	que vous alliez
allé	il va	ils vont				

s'asseoir	je m'assieds	nous nous asseyons	je me suis assis	il s'asseyait	il s'assiéra	que je m'asseye
s'asseyant	tu t'assieds	vous vous asseyez	je m'étais assis	il s'assit	il s'assiérait	que vous vous asseyiez
assis	il s'assied	ils s'asseyent				

avoir	j'ai	nous avons	j'ai eu	il avait	il aura	que j'aie
ayant	tu as	vous avez	j'avais eu	il eut	il aurait	qu'il ait
eu	il a	ils ont				que vous ayez
						qu'ils aient

battre	je bats	nous battons	j'ai battu	il battait	il battra	que je batte
battant	tu bats	vous battez	j'avais battu	il battit	il battrait	que vous battiez
battu	il bat	ils battent				

(Also like this are: *combattre* - to combat, *abattre* - to knock down, *rabattre* - to push, force back. **Note** *bâtir* - to build is a regular '-*ir*' verb so *je bâtis, j'ai bâti* etc.)

boire	je bois	nous buvons	j'ai bu	il buvait	il boira	que je boive
buvant	tu bois	vous buvez	j'avais bu	il but	il boirait	que vous buviez
bu	il boit	ils boivent				

connaître	je connais	nous connaissons	j'ai connu	il connaissait	il connaîtra	que je connaisse
connaissant	tu connais	vous connaissez	j'avais connu	il connut	il connaîtrait	que vous connaissiez
connu	il connaît	ils connaissent				

(The circumflex appears only before '-*t*'. Also like this: *paraître, apparaître*)

courir	je cours	nous courons	j'ai couru	il courait	il courra	que je coure
courant	tu cours	vous courez	j'avais couru	il courut	il courrait	que vous couriez
couru	il court	ils courent				

craindre	je crains	nous craignons	j'ai craint	il craignait	il craindra	que je craigne
craignant	tu crains	vous craignez	j'avais craint	il craignit	il craindrait	que vous craigniez
craint	il craint	ils craignent				

(All verbs in '-*aindre* '-*eindre*, '-*oindre* follow this pattern, only the vowel '-*e*', '-*i*''or '-*a*' changes. Other verbs are: *peindre* - to paint, *éteindre* - to put out, extinguish, *restreindre* - to restrain, *contraindre* - to constrain, *joindre* - to join etc.)

Infinitive/ present/ participles			perfect/ pluperfect	imperfect/ past historic	future/ conditional	present subjunctive
croire	je crois	nous croyons	j'ai cru	il croyait	il croira	que je croie
croyant	tu crois	vous croyez	j'avais cru	il crut	il croirait	que vous croyiez
cru	il croit	ils croient				
croître	je croîs	nous croissons	j'ai crû	il croissait	il croîtra	que je croisse
croissant	tu croîs	vous croissez	j'avais crû	il crût	il croîtrait	que vous croissiez
crû	il croît	ils croissent				

(This verb has a circumflex over the '-*i*' whenever it might be confused with *croire*. *Croître* means 'to grow'. Other verbs like this are *accroître* - to increase, and *décroître* - to decrease. You are most likely to meet them in the third persons singular and plural, present tense.)

devoir	je dois	nous devons	j'ai dû	il devait	il devra	que je doive
devant	tu dois	vous devez	j'avais dû	il dut	il devrait	que vous deviez
dû	il doit	ils doivent				
dire	je dis	nous disons	j'ai dit	il disait	il dira	que je dise
disant	tu dis	vous dîtes	j'avais dit	il dit	il dirait	que vous disiez
dit	il dit	ils disent				

(Also like this are *interdire* - to forbid, *prédire* - to foretell, *médire* - to speak ill of, slander, *contredire* - to contradict. But the latter have *vous médisez, vous prédisez, interdisez* and *contredisez* for second person plural present tense.)

dormir	je dors	nous dormons	j'ai dormi	il dormait	il dormira	que je dorme
dormant	tu dors	vous dormez	j'avais dormi	il dormit	il dormirait	que vous dormiez
dormi	il dort	ils dorment				

(Also like this: *s'endormir* - to fall asleep.)

écrire	j'écris	nous écrivons	j'ai écrit	il écrivait	il écrira	que j'écrive
écrivant	tu écris	vous écrivez	j'avais écrit	il écrivit	il écrirait	que vous écriviez
écrit	il écrit	ils écrivent				

(Also *décrire* - to describe, *prescrire* - to prescribe, *proscrire* - to proscribe, ban, *s'inscrire* - to sign on, enroll, *circonscrire* - to circumscribe.)

envoyer	j'envoie	nous envoyons	j'ai envoyé	il envoyait	il enverra	que j'envoie
envoyant	tu envoies	vous envoyez	j'avais envoyé	il envoya	il enverrait	que vous envoyiez
envoyé	il envoie	ils envoient				

(Note the change '-*y*' to '-*i*' before mute '-*e*'.)

être	je suis	nous sommes	j'ai été	il était	il sera	que je sois
étant	tu es	vous êtes	j'avais été	il fut	il serait	qu'il soit
été	il est	ils sont				que vous soyez
						qu'ils soient
faire	je fais	nous faisons	j'ai fait	il faisait	il fera	que je fasse
faisant	tu fais	vous faites	j'avais fait	il fit	il ferait	que vous fassiez
fait	il fait	ils font				

(Also *satisfaire* - to satisfy, *contrefaire* - to counterfeit.)

falloir	il faut		il a fallu	il fallait	il faudra	qu'il faille
fallu			il avait fallu	il fallut	il faudrait	

(Only exists in the third person singular and there is no present participle. Do not confuse with ***faillir*** - to fail, which you will meet mainly in the perfect tense to mean - to nearly do something, e.g. *il a failli se noyer* - he nearly drowned, *j'ai failli tomber* - I almost fell.)

fuire	je fuis	nous fuyons	il a fui	il fuyait	il fuira	qu'il fuie
fuyant	tu fuis	vous fuyez	il avait fui	il fuit	il fuirait	que vous fuyiez
fui	il fuit	ils fuient				

(Also *s'enfuir* - to run away.)

Infinitive/ present/ participles			perfect/ pluperfect	imperfect/ past historic	future/ conditional	present subjunctive
lire	je lis	nous lisons	il a lu	il lisait	il lira	qu'il lise
lisant	tu lis	vous lisez	il avait lu	il lut	il lirait	que vous lisiez
lu	il lit	ils lisent				
mettre	je mets	nous mettons	il a mis	il mettait	il mettra	qu'il mette
mettant	tu mets	vous mettez	il avait mis	il mit	il mettrait	que vous mettiez
mis	il met	ils mettent				

(Also *commettre* - to commit, *compromettre* - to compromise, *permettre* - to permit, allow, *promettre* - to promise, *soumettre* - to submit.)

mourir	je meurs	nous mourons	il est mort	il mourait	il mourra	qu'il meure
mourant	tu meurs	vous mourez	il était mort	il mourut	il mourrait	que vous mouriez
mort	il meurt	ils meurent				
naître	je nais	nous naissons	il est né	il naissait	il naîtra	qu'il naisse
naissant	tu nais	vous naissez	il était né	il naquit	il naîtrait	que vous naissiez
né	il naît	ils naissent				
ouvrir	j'ouvre	nous ouvrons	il a ouvert	il ouvrait	il ouvrira	qu'il ouvre
ouvrant	tu ouvres	vous ouvrez	il avait ouvert	il ouvrit	il ouvrirait	que vous ouvriez
ouvert	il ouvre	ils ouvrent				

(Also *couvrir* - to cover, *offrir* - to offer, *souffrir* - to suffer. Unusual past participles - *couvert, offert, souffert.*)

partir	je pars	nous partons	il est parti	il partait	il partira	qu'il parte
partant	tu pars	vous partez	il était parti	il partit	il partirait	que vous partiez
parti	il part	ils partent				

(*Servir* is the same - *je sers, nous servons* etc., except that it has **avoir** in compound tenses.)

plaire	je plais	nous plaisons	il a plu	il plaisait	il plaira	qu'il plaise
plaisant	tu plais	vous plaisez	il avait plu	il plut	il plairait	que vous plaisiez
plu	il plaît	ils plaisent				

(Not easily confused in fact with the next verb. You will often hear: *Ça vous a plu?* - Did you like it?)

pleuvoir	il pleut		il a plu	il pleuvait	il pleuvra	qu'il pleuve
plu			il avait plu	il plut	il pleuvrait	
pouvoir	je peux (puis)	nous pouvons	il a pu	il pouvait	il pourra	qu'il puisse
pouvant	tu peux	vous pouvez	il avait pu	il put	il pourrait	que vous puissiez
pu	il peut	ils peuvent				
prendre	je prends	nous prenons	il a pris	il prenait	il prendra	qu'il prenne
prenant	tu prends	vous prenez	il avait pris	il prit	il prendrait	que vous preniez
pris	il prend	ils prennent				

(Also *apprendre* - learn, *comprendre* - to understand, *surprendre* - to surprise.)

produire	je produis	nous produisons	il a produit	il produisait	il produira	qu'il produise
produisant	tu produis	vous produisez	il avait produit	il produisit	il produirait	que vous produisiez
produit	il produit	ils produisent				

(Also *conduire* - to drive, *construire* - to construct, *introduire* -to introduce, *réduire* - to reduce, *séduire* - to seduce, *traduire* - to translate.)

recevoir	je reçois	nous recevons	j'ai reçu	il recevait	il recevra	qu'il reçoive
recevant	tu reçois	vous recevez	j'avais reçu	il reçut	il recevrait	que vous receviez
reçu	il reçoit	ils reçoivent				

(Also *apercevoir* - to notice, *concevoir* - to conceive.)

résoudre	je résous	nous résolvons	j'ai résolu	il résolvait	il résoudra	que je résolve
résolvant	tu résous	vous résolvez	j'avais résolu	il résolut	il résoudrait	que vous résolviez
résolu	il résout	ils résolvent				

Infinitive/ participles	present/		perfect/ pluperfect	imperfect/ past historic	future/ conditional	present subjunctive
rire	je ris	nous rions	j'ai ri	il riait	il rira	que je rie
riant	tu ris	vous riez	j'avais ri	il rit	il rirait	que vous riiez
ri	il rit	ils rient				

(Also *sourire* - to smile.)

savoir	je sais	nous savons	j'ai su	il savait	il saura	qu'il sache
savant	tu sais	vous savez	j'avais su	il sut	il saurait	que vous sachiez
su	il sait	ils savent				

sentir	je sens	nous sentons	j'ai senti	il sentait	il sentira	qu'il sente
sentant	tu sens	vous sentez	j'avais senti	il sentit	il sentirait	que vous sentiez
senti	il sent	ils sentent				

(Also *ressentir* - to feel, experience, *consentir* to consent.)

suffire	je suffis	nous suffisons	j'ai suffi	il suffisait	il suffira	qu'il suffise
suffisant	tu suffis	vous suffisez	j'avais suffi	il suffit	il suffirait	que vous suffisiez
suffi	il suffit	ils suffisent				

suivre	je suis	nous suivons	j'ai suivi	il suivait	il suivra	qu'il suive
suivant	tu suis	vous suivez	j'avais suivi	il suivit	il suivrait	que vous suiviez
suivi	il suit	ils suivent				

tenir	je tiens	nous tenons	j'ai tenu	il tenait	il tiendra	qu'il tienne
tenant	tu tiens	vous tenez	j'avais tenu	il tint	il tiendrait	que vous teniez
tenu	il tient	ils tiennent				

(Also *appartenir* - to belong, *contenir* - to contain, *maintenir* - to maintain, *soutenir* - to uphold, support, *retenir* - to retain.)

vaincre	je vaincs	nous vainquons	j'ai vaincu	il vainquait	il vaincra	qu'il vainque
vainquant	tu vaincs	vous vainquez	j'avais vaincu	il vainquit	il vaincrait	que vous vainquiez
vaincu	il vainc	ils vainquent				

(Also *convaincre* - to convince.)

valoir	je vaux	nous valons	j'ai valu	il valait	il vaudra	qu'il vaille
valant	tu vaux	vous valez	j'avais valu	il valut	il vaudrait	que vous valiez
valu	il vaut	ils valent				

venir	je viens	nous venons	je suis venu	il venait	il viendra	qu'il vienne
venant	tu viens	vous venez	j'étais venu	il vint	il viendrait	que vous veniez
venu	il vient	ils viennent				

(Also *convenir* - to agree, *prévenir* - to forewarn, *revenir* - to return, se *souvenir* - to remember.)

vivre	je vis	nous vivons	j'ai vécu	il vivait	il vivra	qu'il vive
vivant	tu vis	vous vivez	j'avais vécu	il vécut	il vivrait	que vous viviez
vécu	il vit	ils vivent				

(Also *survivre* - to survive.)

voir	je vois	nous voyons	j'ai vu	il voyait	il verra	qu'il voie
voyant	tu vois	vous voyez	j'avais vu	il vit	il verrait	que vous voyiez
vu	il voit	ils voient				

(Also *revoir,* and *prévoir* - to foresee.)

vouloir	je veux	nous voulons	j'ai voulu	il voulait	il voudra	qu'il veuille
voulant	tu veux	vous voulez	j'avais voulu	il voulut	il voudrait	que vous vouliez
voulu	il veut	ils veulent				

Appendix 2: Useful addresses and references

Alliance Française
Offers a wide range of courses, both intensive and
long term, in London and in France.

1 Dorset Square
London
NW1 6PU

Association for Language Learning (ALL)
The major organization for those interested in learning
and teaching languages. Language days, lectures, films
etc. Contact main office for address of your local branch.

16 Regent Place
Rugby
CV21 2PN

Association of Language Export Centres (LX)
Provides links and language services between further
and higher educational establishments and exporting
companies. Contact main office for details of local branches.

PO Box 1574
London
NW1 4NJ

Authentik Language Learning Resources Ltd
Publication of collected French news items
with audio tape. (Also German, Spanish)

27 Westland Square
Dublin 2
Ireland

BBC
The BBC publishes in the spring of each academic
year a programme of language broadcasts:
Living Languages.

BBC Education
London
W5 2PA

Also of interest: *List of residential courses*
based on BBC series and the series *Europeans*
compiled from foreign television stations.

BBC Book Enquiries
Room A3116
Woodlands
80 Wood Lane
London
W12 0TT

British Film Institute
A film and video library that has French titles

21 Stephen Street
London
W1P 1PL

British Institute in Paris
Resource packs (including cassette) for London A-Level syllabus
topics + others. Available from **London Office**

Senate House
Malet Street
London
W1E 0HU

Central Bureau (CBEVE)
A national office resonsible for providing information
and advice on all forms of educational visits and exchanges
with other countries. Many services: school and class
linking; pen-friends etc. and publications; *Working holidays*
Young Visitors' Pupil Exchange News and others.

Seymour House
Seymour Mews
London
W1H 9PE

3 Bruntsfield Crescent
Edinburgh
E10 4HD

16 Malone Road
Belfast
BT9 5BN

Centre National de Documentation Pédagogique
Textes et documents pour la classe. Project work for
French secondary pupils

31 rue de la Vanne
92120 Montrouge
France

**Centre for Information on Language
Teaching and Research (CILT)**
A national organization providing a vast amount of
information on all aspects of language learning.
Send for list of lists. Most of the latter are free.

20 Bedfordbury
London
WC2N 4LB

Commission of the European Communities
Various publications, posters and maps. Information on
education, training and youth exchanges

London Office
8 Storey's Gate
London
SW1A 3AT

Council of Europe
Many publications, reports, some available from Strasbourg
others from Sales Agents or publishers.

Publications section
F 67006
Strasbourg
France

HMSO Agency Section
51 Nine Elms Lane
London
SW8 5DR

Dial-Search
Check list and guide to radio stations in Europe.
Publication available from:

G Wilcox
9 Thurrock Close
Eastbourne
East Sussex
BN20 9NF

La Documentation Française
A government department that produces dossiers on
various aspects of French life

29-31 quai Voltaire
75340
Paris

Francoscopie — Les Français: *Qui sont-ils
où vont-ils. Gérard Mermet.* An A-Z reference to the
French and their way of life. Regularly revised.

Larousse

French Embassy Cultural Department
Bureau d'action linguistique et Service de documentation
Information on exchanges, school links, pen-friends
Information on many aspects of French society

23 Cromwell Rd
London
SW7 2EL

188 Oxford Road
Manchester
M13 9GP

BAL Ecosse
7 Bowmont Gardens
Glasgow
G12 9LR

Food and Wine from France
Main source of information and publicity on this subject.

Nuffield House
41 Piccadilly
London
WIV 9AJ

Government of Québec
Posters and information sheets.

Documentation Dept
59 Pall Mall
London
SW1Y 5JH

Institut français
A wide range of cultural activities: theatre; films;
exhibitions; lectures; secretarial courses. Membership
available. Also video and film lending service.

17 Queensberry Place
London
SW7 2DT

13 Randolph Terrace
Edinburgh
EH3 7TT

Le Journal des Journaux
*Utilisation du journal pour l'enseignement
de la langue et de la civilisation.* Publishes
an index to a selection of articles from French
press arranged under subject headings.

Département Presse
Centre international d'études pédagogiques
1 avenue Léon
Perrault
F-92311
Sèvres
France

National Council for Educational Technology
Information on task-based learning of languages with IT.

Science Park
Coventry
CV4 7EZ

Olympus Satellite TV
Collection of TV news items with explanations,
background information, exercises.

University of Oxford
Language Teaching Centre
41 Wellington Square
Oxford
OXI 2JF

Oxford University Delagacy of Local Examinations
Resource packs on a number of background
and literary themes. Information on request.

Ewert Place
Oxford
OX2 7BZ

Que sais-je? *Presse Universitaire de France.*
A French series covering a wide range of topic areas.
Distributed by:

European Schoolbooks
Ashville Trading Estate
The Runnings
Cheltenham
Gloucestershire
GL51 9PQ

Quid
A yearly analysis of events in France with statistics
and addresses of organizations. Distributor in Britain:

Grant and Cutler
55-57 Great Marlborough Street
London
W1V 2AY

Summer Academy
List of study holidays at British Universities.

Summer Academy
School of Continuing Education
The University
Canterbury
Kent
CT2 7NX

La Vie Outre-Manche
*Le magazine en français pour les lecteurs
du Royaume-Uni.* Many bilingual texts with
accompanying audio tape.

8 Skye Close
Maidstone
Kent
ME15 9SJ

World Radio and TV Handbook
Details of programmes worldwide.

Billboard, New York
Distributed by Fountain Press
Windsor

Appendix 3: A-Level set texts

This is a list of many of the texts that have been prescribed for A Level. Those marked '**F**' and '**V**' are available respectively as films or videos from the Institut Français (*see* address on page 210). Those marked '**VSP**' (*voir sur place*) can be viewed at the Institute.

Alain-Fournier: *Le Grand Meaulnes* (1913) **F**

Anouilh: *Antigone* (1946); *L'Alouette* (1953); *L'Invitation au Château* (1941)

Balzac: *Le Père Goriot* (1834-5); *Eugénie Grandet* (1833); *Le Curé de Tours* (1832); *Le Lys dans la Vallée* (1835) **VSP;** *Pierrette* (1832) **VSP;** *Le Cousin Pons* (1847) **VSP**

Bazin: *Vipère au Poing* (1948); *Le Cri de la Chouette* (1972) **VSP**

Beaumarchais: *Le Barbier de Séville* (1775) **V;** *Le Mariage de Figaro* (1784) **V**

Beauvoir: *Les Belles Images* (1966) **V**

Beckett: *En Attendant Godot* (1952); *Fin de Partie* (1957); *Dis Joe* (1966) **VSP** *Tous Ceux Qui Tombent* (1957) **VSP;** *Oh les Beaux Jours* (1975) **VSP**

Bosco: *L'Enfant et la Rivière* ((1956)

Camus: *La Peste* (1947) **F;** *L'Etranger* (1942) **F**

Cesbron: *Chiens Perdus Sans Collier* (1954)

Cocteau: *La Machine Infernale* (1934) **V**

Colette: *Le Blé en Herbe* (1923); *La Maison de Claudine* (1922)

Constant: *Adolphe* (1816)

Corneille: *Le Cid* (1637); *Cinna* (1640); *Polyeucte* (1641)

Duhamel: *Le Notaire du Havre* (1933)

Duras: *Moderato Cantabile* (1958)

Ernaux: *La Place* (1983)

Etcherelli: *Elise ou la Vraie Vie* (1967)

Flaubert: *Madame Bovary* (1857); *Un Cœur Simple* (1877)

France: *L'Ile des Pingouins* (1908)

Genevoix: *Lorelei* (1978)

Gide: *La Symphonie Pastorale* (1919) **F;** *La Porte Etroite* (1909)

Giono: *Regain* (1930)

Giraudoux: *La Guerre de Troie N'aura Pas Lieu* (1935); *Amphitryon '38* (1929)

Ionesco: *Rhinocéros* (1976); *La Leçon* (1951); *Les Chaises* (1952); *Le Roi se Meurt* (1962); **V;** *Tueur Sans Gages* (1974)

Joffo: *Un Sac de Billes* (1973)

Lainé: *La Dentellière* (1974) **F**

Maupassant: *Boule de Suif ou autres contes* (1880); *Au Champ* (short story) **VSP;** *Mont Oriol* (1887) **VSP;** *Une Histoire Vraie* (short story) **VSP**

Mauriac: *Thérèse Desqueyroux* (1927) **F;** *Le Mystère Frontenac* (1933) **V;** *Génitrix* (1923); *Le Nœud de Vipères* (1932) **V;** *Un Adolescent d'Autrefois* (1969) **VSP**

Mérimée: *Carmen* (1852); *Colomba* (1841)

Michel: *L'Agression* (1967)

Modiano: *Une Jeunesse* (1981)

Molière: *Le Bourgeois Gentilhomme* (1670) **V;** *L'Avare* (1668) **V;** *L'Ecole des Femmes* (1662) **V;** *Don Juan* (1665) **VSP;** *Le Médecin Malgré Lui* (1666); *Le Misanthrope* (1666)

Musset: *On Ne Badine Pas Avec L'amour* (1834)

Pagnol: *Topaze* (1928); *La Gloire de mon Père* (1957); *Le Château de ma Mère* (1976)

Prévost: *Manon Lescaut* (1731)

Racine: *Phèdre* (1670); *Andromaque* ((1667); *Bérénice* (1670) **V;** *Brittanicus* (1669)

Robbe-Grillet: *Djinn* (1981); *Les Gommes* (1953)

Rochefort: *Les Petits Enfants du Siècle* (1969)

St Exupéry: *Pilote de Guerre* (1942); *Vol de Nuit* (1931)

Sagan: *Bonjour Tristesse* (1954)

Sartre: *Les Mains Sales* (1948); *Les Jeux Sont Faits* (1947) **F** *Huis Clos* (1944); *Kean* (1987) **VSP**

Touati: *Et Puis Je Suis Parti d'Oran* (1985)

Tournier: *Vendredi ou la Vie Sauvage* (1967)
Troyat: *Viou* (1980); *La Tête sur les Epaules* (1951); *Grandeur Nature* (1936)
Vailland: *325 000 Francs* (1965, 1977); *Un Jeune Homme Seul* (1977)
Vercors: *Le Silence de la Mer et autres contes* (1942)
Voltaire: *Candide* (1759)
Zola: *La Bête humaine* (1890) **F**; *L'Assommoir* (1877); *Germinal* (1885)

Note: This does not exhaust the possibilities. Contact also:

British Film Institute (*see* address, page 208)
Grant and Cutler Ltd 55-57 Great Marlborough Street, London W1V 2AY
A la Page 7 Harrington Road, London SW7 2DT
DUFVC 55 Greek St, London WIV 5LR
Video City 117 Notting Hill Gate, London W11
Video Palace Perwick St, London WI
Video Club Français PO Box 618, London SW13 ODF

Appendix 4: Texts referred to in this book

Books referred to in the text

Dictionaries

Collins-Robert Eng.-Fr., Fr.-Eng Dictionary, 2nd edition, (1987), Collins, one volume
Dictionnaire du Français Contemporain, (1970), Larousse (monolingual), one volume
Dictionnaire de la Langue Française, (1975), monolingual, two volumes
Dictionnaire des Synonymes, (1991), Larousse, monolingual
Petit Larousse Illustré, (1992), Larousse, dictionary and encyclopedia (monolingual)
Claudie Cox, (1988), *A Pocket Dictionary of Contemporary France*, Berg.
C W E Kirk-Greene, (1981), *French False Friends*, Routledge and Kegan Paul

Grammar Books

H Ferrar, (1973), *A French Reference Grammar*, 2nd edition, OUP
J E Mansion, (1952), *A Grammar of Present Day French*, 2nd edition, Harrap
L Byrne and E Churchill, (1956), *A Comprehensive French Grammar*, 3rd edition, Blackwell
W Rowlinson, (1991), *French Grammar*, OUP

Writing

R Hares and G Elliot, (1984), *Compo! French Language Essay Writing*, Hodder and Stoughton
    (*see also* Literature sections of the book)
J Aitchison, (1987), *Words in the Mind*, Blackwell

Other publications

Phosphore — Le Magazine des Années Lycée, Mensuel, Bayard Presse Jeune, Paris
The European, Weekly publication

Bilingual texts

Les Langues Pour Tous. Presse Pocket (series)
La Vie Outre-Manche (*see* appendix 2, page 210)

Literature

Profil d'une Œuvre, Hatier (series)
Lire Aujourd'hui, Hachette (series)
Théâtre et Mises en Scène, Hatier (series)
A Lagarde et L Michard, *Les Grands Auteurs Français du Programme 17e, 18e, 19e, 20e siècles*, Bordas
    (series)
J Cruickshank (ed.), *French Literature and its Background* (vols 2-4), OUP (series)
Studies in French Literature, Edward Arnold (series)
R Martineau and J M McGivney, (1973), *French Pronunciation*, OUP

Appendix 5: Tape transcripts

Side A: Examples of spoken French in everyday life

I Grands titres: *France Inter,* février 1991

(a) Le reste de l'actualité à l'étranger. En Pologne, le Président Lech Walesa propose à un avocat de soixante ans, Ian Olsekski, de former un gouvernement pour remplacer celui de Tadeusz Mazoweski.

(b) Au Maroc, le calme semble être revenu à Fez après les émeutes d'hier. Deux morts selon les syndicats et apparemment une centaine d'interpellations. L'armée marocaine continue de patrouiller dans la ville.

(c) En Israël, fermeture de la bande de Gaza et plusieurs interpellations dans les milieux islamistes; on estime que c'est une vague d'arrestations sans précédent qui s'est produite: quatre cents... pardon, quatre activistes palestiniens ont été expulsés et six cents arrestations en tout.

(d) Deux mots de sport. En ski, en descente à Valgardenna, en Italie, le Français, Luc Alfan, s'est classé troisième. C'est son premier podium en coupe du monde. Le vainqueur de l'épreuve, c'est le Norvégien Skardale.

(e) En tennis, la finale de la coupe du grand Chelem, qui se déroule à Munich, en Allemagne, opposera demain l'Américain Pete Sampras au vainqueur du match Gilbert–Witon qui se joue en ce moment. Sampras a battu son compatriote Michael Chang.

(f) La violence, encore et toujours en Corse. Deux hommes sont morts ce soir dans une fusillade à Propriano. Ils ont été tués à coups de fusil de chasse. Il s'agit tout simplement d'un règlement de compte entre truands, compte tenu de la personnalité des victimes. Par ailleurs les obsèques de Lucien Toroloni ont été célébrées aujourd'hui en présence de plusieurs centaines de personnes émues et recueillies.

(g) La tempête sur l'Irlande et le sud-ouest du Royaume Uni, de très importants dégâts et trente-sept morts d'après les derniers chiffres.

(h) Les retours des vacances d'hiver sur les routes. Bravo, les automobilistes, vous avez étalé vos arrivées dans les grandes métropoles et vous vous êtes épargné le pire.

(i) Claude Taittinger, patron du champagne qui porte son nom et son épouse, agressés chez eux en plein centre de Reims, par des gangsters qui emportent six cent mille francs d'argent et de bijoux.

(j) Encore des perturbations demain sur les cinq lignes d'autobus parisiennes touchées par une grève depuis vendredi soir. Un mouvement déclenché par l'agression d'un conducteur par une bande de voyous à bord de son autobus; l'un des voyous étant armé d'une hachette. Les agents ont voté ce soir pour la poursuite du mouvement, cela concerne les lignes 32, 48, 60, 75 et la Petite Ceinture donc les autobus de Paris.

II Reportage: *France-Infos,* 1 mars 1990

Les Animaux de Compagnie font partie de notre vie, de notre famille, mais eux aussi doivent être bien élevés. Les chiens peuvent être turbulents et bruyants, alors que les chats sont plus discrets et relativement autonomes. Il faut promener les chiens plusieurs fois par jour, leur apprendre quand ils sont tout petits, à faire leurs besoins dans le caniveau si vous habitez en ville. Le chien doit apprendre aussi la signification du mot 'non'. Quand il est encore tout petit, dissuadez-le de vous faire des gentillesses en vous sautant dessus, sinon il sera tenté de continuer lorsqu'il aura sa taille adulte, et quand il est mouillé, c'est très désagréable. Pour lui faire perdre cette mauvaise habitude, repoussez-le fermement, en disant non, avec énergie. Il faut aussi lui apprendre à ne pas aboyer n'importe où et quand. Laissez-le aboyer contre les inconnus, car les aboiements dissuadent les cambrioleurs, mais apprenez-lui à s'arrêter dès que vous lui direz non. Dans le métro ou l'autobus, seuls les chiens d'aveugles ou les petits qui entrent dans un sac, sont admis. En avion, les chiens de moins de 6 kilos peuvent voyager en cabine, au-dessus de 6 kilos ils doivent être mis dans la soute. En train, tout est permis, mais le chien doit se coucher à vos pieds, et ne pas déranger vos voisins de compartiment. N'arrivez jamais à l'improviste chez quelqu'un avec votre chien. Si vous êtes invité, lui ne l'est pas forcément, demandez la permission avant de l'emmener. Les personnes qui ont des chats ou des chiens ne verront peut-être pas d'un bon œil arriver un invité à quatre pattes sur lequel ils ne comptaient pas, et qui risque de se battre avec leurs animaux. Apprenez-lui aussi de ne pas réclamer de la nourriture à table.

Les chats, beaucoup plus casaniers, préfèrent rester seuls le week-end, plutôt que de changer leurs habitudes. Laissez votre chat avec de la nourriture, de l'eau et une litière propre, et il sera parfaitement heureux. S'il doit voyager, mettez-le dans un panier. Les chats n'aiment pas être en laisse, et s'il est nerveux, donnez-lui un léger sédatif. Il n'embêtera personne avec ses miaulements. Lorsque vous avez des invités, empêchez votre chat de s'installer sur leurs genoux, car beaucoup de gens sont allergiques à leurs poils ou tout simplement ne les aiment pas. Si vous avez chez vous des animaux plus exotiques, pensez toujours à la tranquillité de vos amis ou de vos voisins. Après tout, ce n'est pas donné à tous d'aimer les souris blanches ou les pythons! Et puis, évitez d'apprendre des grossièretés aux oiseaux parleurs, ils les retiennent très facilement et cela risquerait de vous embarrasser devant des invités qui n'ont pas un grand sens de l'humour.

III Interview: *Radio Prévert,* Convalin, Pays de la Loire
Section 1
A: Vous êtes un ancien prisonnier de la guerre de 39–45, n'est-ce pas?
B: Exact.
A: Vous avez quel âge?
B: 76 ans.
A: Et vous avez été prisonnier en quelle année?
B: En 1940.
A: Et libéré en quelle année?
B: En 1945.
A: Et où avez-vous été fait prisonnier?
B: Du côté…, dans l'Aisne, exactement près de Guise, une ville qu'on appelle Guise, qui est sur l'Oise.
A: Et comment avez-vous été capturé?
B: Par les Allemands, en pleine nuit, sur le coup je pensais que c'était des Anglais, parce qu'on ne voyait rien du tout, et comme ils me parlaient anglais, moi je me suis présenté, pensant rencontrer des Alliés, et puis ils m'ont mis le revolver sous le nez, en me disant de lever les mains en l'air. Et voilà.
A: Vous étiez officier, oui?
B: J'étais officier, j'avais quelques hommes avec moi.
A: Et vous avez été transporté immédiatement en Allemagne?
B: Oh non, on a été acheminé, on a été, on a été repris, on a fait… on nous a indiqué une direction à suivre. On s'est regroupé avec d'autres prisonniers, on s'est retrouvé dans un immense camp, du côté d'Hirson, on était au moins 4 ou 5 mille. Ensuite, on nous a transportés en camion, et finalement on a abouti à Bastogne, et de Bastogne on nous a transportés par les trains jusqu'à Trêves, et de Trêves ensuite on… par les trains, on nous a transportés jusqu'au camp où nous sommes restés pendant 5 ans sans sortir.

Section 2
A: Est-ce que cela vous a développé le sens de l'initiative dans le camp?
B: D'une façon générale on peut dire que le camp, on est arrivé sans rien, et par l'initiative des uns et des autres, on était arrivé à reconstituer à l'intérieur du camp, absolument tous les organismes dont on a besoin dans la vie sociale normale.
A: Vous pouvez donner un exemple?
B: Et bien il y avait un cinéma, il y avait un théâtre, il y avait l'université, il y avait du sport, du rugby, tous les sports étaient pratiqués.
A: Ahh…
B: Y compris le tennis. Il y avait même des jardins potagers.
A: C'est vrai.
B: Et on a fabriqué, avec des, des, des denrées qu'on recevait dans les colis, il y en a qui fabriquaient même l'alcool, avec du sucre et du raisin.
A: Ah, très intéressant.
B: Il y avait des expositions organisées par des corps de métier. L'EDF avait son exposition, les Chemins de Fer avaient organisé leur exposition, le livre, une exposition de livres, une exposition de fromages de France, une exposition sur les vins de France, etc., etc., ça ne finirait pas de raconter tout ce qui s'est fait.

Section 3

A: Est-ce que vous avez essayé de vous évader?

B: Tout le monde a essayé de s'évader.

A: Et comment?

B: Et bien, il y avait des organis… le meilleur syst… différents procédés, ça avait été trouvé, au départ, qu'on réussit en général parce que la parade n'était pas prévue par les Allemands, et certains sont partis dans des, dans des cercueils, d'autres sont partis un vélo à la main, faisant le salut à celui qui lui tenait la porte, parce qu'il y avait des ouvriers qui travaillaient dans le camp, en se mêlant à eux. Et finalement tous ces systèmes-là ont été abolis parce que très tôt il y a eu des barbelés autour du camp, avec des chiens policiers, avec des barbelés électrifiés, des miradors qui nous surveillaient jour et nuit, avec des projecteurs jour et nuit, avec des projecteurs la nuit, des mitrailleuses en permanence, braquées sur tout ce qui pouvait se passer le long des barbelés, une main courante pour nous empêcher d'approcher des barbelés de trop près, etc., si bien que le procédé plus normalement utilisé pour préparer des évasions, c'était de creuser des tunnels.

A: Ah...

B: Alors il y avait une organisation qu'on appelait 'Libertas' qui tenait à jour la géographie, la topographie souterraine du camp, pour que, quand on voulait creuser un tunnel, qu'on sache, qu'en creusant en telle direction, on risquait de faire découvrir d'autres tunnels, alors il fallait partir dans une autre direction.

A: Très bien. Et vous qui êtes né pendant la Première Guerre Mondiale, quelle est votre attitude vis-à-vis de la situation mondiale actuelle? Est-ce qu'il est possible d'imaginer une autre guerre mondiale?

B: Ah, comme celle-là, non. D'ailleurs la preuve, c'est que tous ceux qui ont fait une guerre, la dernière guerre, prenez le Japon, prenez les Américains, prenez les Allemands, prenez les Russes surtout, ceux qui ont été les plus... qui ont le plus souffert de la guerre, eh bien, sont incapables de faire une guerre comme ça, c'est inimaginable, que des peuples entiers arrivent maintenant à s'affronter comme ça, c'est fou!

IV Reportage: *France-Inter,* 1990

Présentatrice: Deux familles avec des enfants ont encore été expulsées hier d'un hôtel du 2e arrondissement de Paris. Deux familles qui vont probablement rejoindre les 300 expulsés qui vivent depuis six semaines Place de la Réunion dans le 20e arrondissement, Nicolas Poincaré.

Nicolas Poincaré: Cela fait maintenant 41 jours qu'ils vivent dans ce square au milieu de la Place de la Réunion, exactement depuis ce matin du 2 mai, où la police a expulsé les squatteurs de la rue des Vignobles et de la rue de la Fontaine-au-roi. Des tentes offertes par Emmaus, sont dressées en cercle, avec au milieu celle qui sert de cantine. Environ 500 repas sont servis chauds chaque jour. La vie est organisée, il y a des tours pour les tâches ménagères et pour les gardes de nuit, on craint une intervention de la police. En réalité il n'y a pas 300 personnes chaque nuit, les familles obtiennent de temps en temps des nuits d'hôtel payées par la préfecture. Lorsque l'hôtel n'est plus payé, ils reviennent sur la place. Ainsi Béatrice, une jeune mère de trois enfants, qui vit sous la tente depuis maintenant 10 jours.

Béatrice: Alors, on a un coin cuisine, on a des surveillants, quoi, on fait des tours de garde, chacun son tour, on a des gens qui viennent nous soutenir, et tout quoi. Il y a Emmaus qui nous amène à manger, il y a une grande tente, et il y a les gazinières, la vaisselle, et tout quoi.

Nicolas Poincaré: Alors ces derniers temps la météo n'a pas été très bonne?

Béatrice: Non, pas très. D'ailleurs 'y a des enfants qui sont malades, quoi. Bronchite, grippe. Tout le monde est fatigué, hein, à un moment ou un autre, on craque, hein. Même moi, j'ai craqué.

Nicolas Poincaré: Sur les 150 enfants qui n'ont plus de logement, un certain nombre continuent à se rendre à l'école. Ils sont par exemple 14 à l'école communale la plus proche. Jean-Pierre, un instituteur de 35 ans, en a plusieurs dans sa classe.

Jean-Pierre: Bon, ce qui était dur, c'était les premiers jours, hein, quand ils ont été expulsés, et donc ils étaient totalement perdus. Parce qu'ils ont vécu ça sous forme d'une grande violence. Puis là ils se sont... ils se sont un peu réfugiés dans l'école. Bon, ils sont assez fatigués le matin, quoi, ils sont assez fatigués, certains dorment à moitié, et c'est en début d'après-midi, ou disons vers 10 heures qu'ils commencent, bon, à avoir une activité, quoi.

Nicolas Poincaré: Après plusieurs discussions infructueuses avec la mairie de Paris, et avec la préfecture, les expulsés n'ont maintenant plus aucun rendez-vous. Une manifestation de soutien est prévue jeudi à Paris.

V Reportage

Présentatrice: Fabrice Lecantrac, bonjour.

Fabrice: Bonjour.

Présentatrice: Nous parlerons aujourd'hui du Japon. Je rappelle qu'hier il y a eu lieu le couronnement de l'empereur du Japon, Akito, c'est bien ça...

Fabrice: Oui, oui.

Présentatrice: Et que vous nous présentez différentes images de la vie... et des Japonais, puisque vous revenez d'un voyage à Tokyo. Alors, vous avez rencontré une jeune femme qui s'appelle Akiko, elle... elle habite à Tokyo?

Fabrice: Elle habite à Tokyo, c'est une femme de 45 ans, elle va vous dire exactement... un peu, elle va parler même de sa biographie, c'est une femme de 45 ans, un de mes amis français, l'écrivain Jean Peyrol avec qui elle avait travaillé, m'avait conseillé de prendre contact avec elle, et c'est une... une Asiatique je dirais assez typique, euh, pas très grande, souriante, à la voix chantonnante, enfin comme beaucoup... comme beaucoup d'Asiatiques...

Présentatrice: Vous avez un sourire fendu jusqu'aux oreilles en le disant, on sent déjà que le charme a opéré.

Fabrice: Et alors c'est une dame, une dame charmante donc que j'ai rencontrée, et qui m'a raconté un petit peu sa... sa vie et je trouve que... derrière sa vie, en filigrane, s'inscrit un petit peu, à la fois l'histoire du Japon et puis en même temps un jugement, un témoignage sur ce formidable développement du Japon.

Akiko: Je m'appelle Akiko Aisauwa. Je suis née en mille neuf cent quarante-cinq, la veille de la fin de la guerre, de la deuxième guerre mondiale. Mon père est mort à cause de la guerre. Comme ma mère s'est remariée après, je ne savais pas que mon père n'est pas mon vrai père. Comme je... je n'ai pas connu jusqu'à vingt ans la vérité de... sur mon père, ça ne m'a pas marquée, ça ne m'a pas influencée. Mais euh, comme... comme beaucoup d'autres, qui sont nés en mille neuf cent quarante-cinq et vivent aujourd'hui, on se rend compte que pendant ces quarante ans depuis la guerre, la société japonaise a changé euh... à une vitesse vraiment incroyable. Ce qui est très intéressant c'est le caractère des Japonais: on oublie tout très facilement. Quand un événement se produit, on en parle beaucoup pendant des jours, et puis on oublie soudain. Et cette tendance se révèle dans le fait qu'on ne parle pas de la guerre. On n'évite pas d'en parler. On a oublié. C'est tout. Cette tendance se retrouve en Corée, en Chine, au sud de l'Asie. Ce que les Japonais ont fait ça restera toujours comme blessure de... de peuple. Et vis à vis des Américains, la bombe atomique, j'ai l'impression que les Japonais n'ont pas de rancune. Ça c'est deux côtés... bon côté, mauvais côté, on oublie ce qu'on a fait et aussi on peut pardonner très facilement.

Présentatrice: Fabrice Lecantrac, est-ce qu'on peut généraliser, est-ce que effectivemnent les Japonais sont sans mémoire?

Fabrice: Ils ne sont pas sans mémoire parce qu'il y a trop de valeurs et de traditions auxquelles ils croient et qui sont complètement intériorisées. Mais en revanche, c'est vrai qu'ils ont cette faculté très asiatique de tourner la page, quand c'est fini c'est fini. Et c'est ça qui explique chez d'autres Asiatiques, par exemple les réfugiés vietnamiens ou cambodgiens, leur faculté de...

Présentatrice: D'adaptation?

Fabrice: Ils arrivent à se réinsérer malgré les horreurs qu'ils ont vécu. Et les Japonais finalement ont beau avoir beaucoup souffert et également fait souffrir pendant la guerre. Quand l'empereur, le père de celui-ci, enfin Hirohito, a déclaré qu'il faut accepter l'inacceptable, eh bien du jour au lendemain, mais même d'une seconde à l'autre, les armes se sont tues, et les Américains ont pu finalement arriver et s'installer au Japon sans qu'un seul coup de feu, une seule bavure ne viennent ternir cette fin de guerre. Et moi ce qui m'intéresse dans ce témoignage, outre cette particularité biographique qui fait que cette femme est née après les bombes atomiques mais juste avant la capitulation, alors que depuis plusieurs mois la guerre était déjà terminée en Europe, et donc elle a connu depuis lors tout ce développement du Japon, c'est le fait qu'elle dise que, bien euh, après on est capable, on est capable d'oublier et c'est vrai que c'est à mon avis l'une des forces du Japon et des Japonais de se tourner vers l'avenir, non pas en faisant table rase du passé, et disons sans s'attacher, se polariser sur des choses matérielles. On peut très bien par exemple, quand on se balade à Tokyo, voir je ne sais pas, un cube béton assez laid inauguré avec un écriteau 'All new'– complètement neuf – et alors ça veut dire que l'on a démoli peut-être une vieille maison en bois charmante qui était là. De ce côté-là, si vous voulez, on est capable de faire table rase mais en même temps on reste très profondément japonais avec cette faculté de faire du neuf et d'aller de l'avant et c'est ainsi peut-être que l'on arrive à cette ironie d'histoire que le pays vaincu de la deuxième guerre mondiale, enfin l'un des vaincus, on arrive maintenant à porter à bout de bras le trésor fédéral, le trésor fédéral américain, mais tout ça sans animosité et sans rancune vis-à-vis des troupes victorieuses.

VI Interview *France-Inter,* février 1990

Section 1

A: Alors, Pierre Fabre, en France quelle est la véritable fonction de la manifestation, sa valeur je dirais, en termes d'efficacité?

B: Je dirais que... il ne faut pas parler sous cette forme de la manifestation parce que... lorsqu'on commence à regarder la multitude des manifestations en France, ces manifestations n'ont pas du tout le même statut et que... il vaudrait mieux parler des différents types de manifestation... il y a des manifestations qu'on dirait routinières – je pense à certains premiers mai qui donnaient l'impression que la fonction était...

A: On était obligé quoi!

B: Oui, une fonction de souvenir, une fonction peut-être moins importante que des manifestations de crise. Vous avez cité les manifestations étudiantes de '86 et la manifestation sur l'école privée, l'école libre...

A: Dans les deux cas, hein, dans les deux cas, on a fini par changer le ministre.

B: Absolument. C'est à dire que ces manifestations ont une efficacité, ont...

A: Ou en tout cas politique, hein, c'est le cas avec les écoles libres.

B: Voilà. Puis on a toute une série de manifestations qui sont des manifestations qui cherchaient à imposer une nouvelle revendication, qui peut-être, dans certains cas, était celle de peu de gens au départ. Je pense aux pères divorcés voulant garder leurs enfants.

A: Ou les manifestations pour l'avortement, des manifestations qui ont été... les premières manifestations des homosexuels qui cherchaient à faire reconnaître leur existence, un statut et donc en même temps, à se faire reconnaître, à se rassembler dans une action politique...

B: Solidarité cimentée dans une manif!

Section 2

A: Vous citez le cas d'un jour de mars 1989 où il y a une accumulation là pendant 2 ou 3 jours assez extraordinaire.

B: Effectivement j'ai fait un reportage sur l'ensemble des manifestations qui aboutissent au ministère de la Santé. On s'aperçoit que sur une période de six mois l'an dernier il y en a eu une par semaine. Alors, ces manifestations ne retiennent... elles retiennent beaucoup moins l'attention du public, au moins des journalistes, c'est-à-dire que le public en a sans doute beaucoup moins connaissance, à moins qu'il ne se trouve sur le passage de la manifestation ou qu'il remarque telle ou telle manifestation. Cela étant, le ministre qui est dans son ministère, il a un écho de cette manifestation. Quand les manifestations deviennent nombreuses, il y a un effet de pression, notamment d'ailleurs dans les crises, les grèves.

Section 3

A: Alors, l'attitude des pouvoirs publics – quelle est la politique aujourd'hui, si vous en avez connaissance, à l'égard de ces manifestations? C'est admis, c'est dans la constitution, enfin quand même, ça peut tourner mal.

B: Alors, je vous suis et réponds en disant que c'est dans la constitution, parce qu'il y a effectivement le droit de la manifestation qui est assez curieux. On pense tous que la manifestation est un droit constitutionel et que nous avons tous le droit de manifester. En réalité le droit de manifester est un droit très particulier qui date de 1935, après le 6 février 34, qui est un droit d'autorisation administrative, de déclaration administrative permettant à l'autorité d'accepter ou non la manifestation, qui distingue entre l'organisateur de la manifestation, qui peut être, lui, poursuivi, alors que le manifestant ne peut pas l'être. Enfin, c'est un droit extrêmement particulier, c'est-à-dire que l'autorité administrative doit, si elle a le sentiment qu'elle ne maintiendra pas l'ordre, interdire la manifestation. C'est donc ce système curieux d'interdiction qui suit peut-être une déclaration de manifestation. Donc, c'est un droit décalé par rapport au sentiment qu'on en a. Tout le monde pense que la manifestation est un droit effectivement constitutionel et ce n'est pas encore le cas. Ce le sera d'ailleurs peut-être. Je crois que l'attitude des pouvoirs publics est marquée par le fait que les manifestations sont imprévisibles. On ne peut jamais savoir à l'avance, quand on lance une manifestation, quel va être son déroulement. Si la manifestation se déroule mal, et il y a eu récemment la mort d'un homme, et donc dans ce...

A: Malekrouskine.

B: Malekrouskine à Amiens, et l'année suivante...

A: Effectivemnent, il y a eu un mort...

B: Lucien Barbier. Dans ce cas-là, le sens de la manifestation va complètement changer.

VII
1ère partie: Résultats des jeux de pari

Pour terminer, le tiercé quarté plus, disputé aujourd'hui à St Cloud. Pour le tiercé il fallait jouer le onze, le dix-huit, le dix-sept, rapport pour 6 francs dans l'ordre-neuf mille, sept cent cinq francs, dans un ordre différent – mille neuf cent quarante et un francs. Pour le quarté plus c'était le onze, le dix-huit, le dix-sept et le huit, rapport pour 8 francs dans l'ordre, cinquante-cinq mille, cinq cent quatre-vingt quatorze francs et quarante centimes et dans un ordre différent mille neuf cent quatre-vingt-dix francs et quarante centimes. Le tirage du tapis vert, dame de pique, dix de cœur, dame de carreau et as de trèfle. Enfin, le premier tirage du loto ce soir c'était le un, le douze, le quinze, le vingt, le vingt-huit, et le trente, numéro complémentaire le trente et un. Le second tirage, le six, le neuf, le vingt-deux, le vingt-quatre, le vingt-sept, et le trente-deux, et le numéro complémentaire c'était le vingt et un.

2ème partie: Les chiffres

six, six cents, seize cent six, soixante, soixante-six, six cent soixante-seize, cinq cent cinquante, quarante, quatorze, quatorze cent quatre, quatre-vingt-onze, l'année mille neuf cent quatre-vingt-un, un million cinq mille cinq cent quatre-vingt-dix-neuf.

le premier, le sixième, le onzième, le vingt et unième, au seizième siècle, au quatorzième siècle, deux mille cinq cents ans avant Jésus Christ (2500 av. J-C).

un millier de personnes, un tiers de la population, un quart de son temps, cinq cents millilitres ça fait la moitié d'un litre, deux pour cent (2%), cinq pour cent (5%), trois virgule cinq pour cent (3,5%), neuf virgule trois pour cent (9,3%)

VIII Intonation

Remember equal stress on each syllable, slight emphasis on the last:
possibilité – administration – postérité – technologie – attention – complication

Difficult vowels

[i]   Lip stretching: *appétit – au lit – il lit la liste – Italie*
[y]   Narrow lip-rounding with puff of air: *aperçu – voulu – perdu – vendu – il a pu*

Vowel contrasts

[u] and [y]
une roue – une rue, c'est vu – c'est vous, il sait tout – il s'est tu, au-dessous – au-dessus, il est où? – il l'a eu.

Nasals All French nasals are contained in the phrase, *Un bon vin blanc*

[oe]   *lundi, le vingt et un, aucun parfum, brun*
[ɔ̃]   *un bon melon, ils ont, ils vont sur le pont*
[ɛ̃]   *le vin, la main, bien, le dessein, assassin*
[ã]   *le champ, un camp, deux ans, le vent*

Denasalization

bon – bonne, fin – fine, serein – sereine, brun – brune, dont – donne, plein – pleine, colon – colonne

Nasal contrasts [ã] [ɔ̃]

le vent – ils vont, long – lent, ils sont – ça sent, violon – violent, une dent – un don (gift)

in-,inn-/im-,imm-

innocent – intelligent, inespéré – ingénieur, inacceptable – incapable, imminent – important, immense – imprimé, inimaginable – intéressant

Voicing More 'buzz' than in English

[z]   *zéro, maison, rose, chose, pause*
[zh]   *les jeunes gens, un agent, la rage, une cage*
[v]   *un rêve, un veuf, une veuve, mauve*

Consonants [p] and [r]

[p]   *Paul part pour Paris, les petits problèmes, petit à petit*
[r]   *un rude hiver, rue de Rivoli, une route rurale*

Liaisons
(a) Noun phrases
   les enfants, vos intentions, trois étudiants, dix ans, les idoles
(b) Adjective + noun
   mes anciens amis, ces dernières années, de bonnes intentions
(c) Before or after verb
   nous allons, ils ont, vous en avez, allez-y, c'est un ami, c'est impossible
(d) Adverb or preposition + noun or adjective
   très heureux, dans un mois, chez une amie, sans intérêt, en anglais, trop important
(e) Set phrases
   les Etats Unis, petit à petit, de moins en moins, de plus en plus, de temps en temps, tout à fait, à tout à l'heure
(f) **A few words that can cause difficulty**
   l'Allemagne, allemand, une médaille, un agent, de l'argent, maximum, minimum, démocratie, une femme, soixante, la veille (day before), *une vieille* (old woman), *de l'ail* (garlic), *une aile* (wing), *l'alcool, le baptême, l'automne, l'Europe, européen, européenne, évidemment, une grenouille, un oignon, solennel.*

IX Histoire drôle

Je vais vous raconter l'histoire de mon bon ami, M. Camembert. C'était une personne qui avait la passion des voyages. Il avait voyagé un peu partout et avait vu presque tous les beaux coins du monde, mais il n'était jamais allé au désert du Sahara. Alors un jour le désir lui a pris de visiter cette région. Après s'être installé dans son hôtel il a fait une petite promenade dans les alentours. Il faut dire qu'il était un peu déçu. Le désert n'était pas tellement intéressant. Ça avait l'air très plat. Il n'y avait que du sable et quelques palmiers. Le lendemain il commençait vraiment à s'ennuyer. Puis, il a remarqué, sous un palmier, assis par terre, un Arabe qui gardait des chameaux et devant lui une affiche, 'Promenades à chameaux'.

'Bon,' dit M. Camembert, 'je vais faire une petite promenade pour m'amuser.'

Une fois assis sur l'animal l'Arabe lui explique que pour faire partir le chameau il faut dire 'ouf' et pour l'arrêter il faut prononcer le mot 'pouf'. M. Camembert crie 'ouf' et bien sûr, la bête part au petit trot. M. Camembert est maintenant très content. Il voit au loin dans le désert. Il y a des palmiers et des collines et le chameau va de plus en plus vite. Mais, il faut savoir que le désert du Sahara n'est pas tout à fait plat. Il y a des collines et parfois de grandes collines avec des ravins. Tout à coup notre héros remarque que son chameau s'approche d'un endroit dangereux. Au bord du chemin il voit un écriteau 'Danger! Précipice!' Quel est le mot pour arrêter cette bête? M. Camembert n'arrive pas à se le rappeler et le chameau est maintenant tout près du bord du ravin. Juste au dernier moment il se rappelle la formule. 'Pouf' s'écrie-t-il. Le chameau s'arrête tout court au bord même du précipice. Et M. Camembert, baigné de sueur mais soulagé, s'exclame 'ouf'.

X Annonces publicitaires: *France-Inter,* 28 octobre 1991

1 *A*: Vie de famille
   B: Vous avez un enfant de moins de six ans et pour le faire garder, vous employez une assistante maternelle agréée. Nous, les allocations familiales nous pouvons vous aider. Quelle que soit votre situation familiale et le montant de vos revenus, nous prenons en charge les cotisations sociales de l'URSAF. Alors si vous désirez en savoir plus, n'hésitez pas, tapez 36 15 code CA Vous voyez, vous faire aider garder vos enfants, c'est aussi notre rôle.
   A: Allocations familiales, ça vous fait la vie plus facile.

2 *A*: Un petit boulot par ci, une bricole par là, un mois ici, un mois là-bas, et caetera, et caetera. Quand on est jeune et qu'on veut travailler, on ne veut pas traîner pendant des années et des années. L'Exojeune c'est la solution pour un jeune sans qualifications, d'entrer tout de suite dans la vie active avec un vrai salaire, un véritable emploi. Embaucher un jeune, ce n'est pas une charge.
   B: Pour en savoir plus sur l'Exojeune, contactez votre agence locale pour l'emploi. Composez le numéro vert du ministère du travail sur le 05 10 10 10.

Side B: Texts from Examination Boards

I *London, June 1991*
Flash

La tempête fait une nouvelle victime. A Chéraud dans les Pyrénées Atlantiques un homme de 43 ans est mort après avoir été projeté au sol par une forte rafale de vent alors qu'il travaillait sur son toit. M. Démoy était en train de clouer des tuiles justement arrachées par le vent au moment de l'accident. Les toutes dernières prévisions météo de Jean Breton sont plutôt inquiétantes: il annonce une nouvelle aggravation du vent et des orages. La nuit prochaine risque d'être le point culminant de la tempête.

Annonce publicitaire
– La semaine de la rentrée, pour les parents c'est la semaine la plus chère de l'année.
– Savez-vous quel est le budget pour un enfant de huit ans? Au moins 250 francs. Et cette somme sera dépensée en 2 jours!
– Voilà pourquoi Mammouth s'attaque au budget rentrée.
– Un exemple: pour un enfant de huit ans, le jogging brodé entièrement lavable à la machine, 89 francs, prix Mammouth.
– Oui, 89 francs le jogging. Quand Mammouth s'attaque au budget rentrée, ça vaut vraiment le déplacement!

Flash
Dans le Jura, trois faux gendarmes, âgés de 19, 24, et 34 ans, effectuaient des contrôles routiers et contraignaient les automobilistes à leur verser 20 francs pour des infractions. Les vrais gendarmes sont intervenus après les plaintes des conducteurs qui s'étaient fait voler.

Reportage
Présentateur: La société 'Tom et Flore' a été créée tout récemment par quatre jeunes très dynamiques. Sa spécialité? L'organisation et l'animation de goûters pour enfants de 3 à 12 ans. A partir d'un simple coup de fil, les animatrices 'Tom et Flore' préparent en 48 heures le goûter, le spectacle de votre choix. Elles s'occuperont des enfants tout l'après-midi, les mercredis et les samedis. Autres possibilités: les équipes de 'Tom et Flore' peuvent aussi s'occuper des enfants pendant une cérémonie ou une réception de mariage. Les explications de Constance de l'Exegenia, responsable de la société.
Constance: Nous leur proposons toute une décoration de fête, ce qui permet de donner aux lieux un air d'anniversaire pour que les enfants soient très bien accueillis. Nous les accueillons en musique, nous les maquillons, nous les déguisons éventuellement et nous proposons donc des jeux suivant l'âge des enfants avec des marionnettes, des professionels de magie et ils sont ravis, ils adorent ça. Alors pour avoir plus de pub, nous recherchons des contacts avec des sociétés alimentaires de biscuits, de bonbons pour avoir un type de collaboration possible que nous pouvons faire ensemble. Et nous cherchons aussi des contacts avec des sociétés organisatrices de salons puisque nous lançons également une nouvelle activité qui est l'animation des enfants dans les salons et les lieux publics.

Entrevue
Professeur: La situation là-bas est très, très dure. Les professeurs enseignent dans des conditions très, très, très ingrates puisqu'il y a les bombardements, surtout ces cinq derniers mois, et en plus ils ne gagnent que 500 francs par mois pour vivre leur... leur propre famille. Donc, euh... la situation devient vraiment... impossible.
Présentateur: Mmm. Comment... comment se passe la classe?
Professeur: Euh, on enseigne la littérature et la langue françaises. Ces jeunes appellent toujours la France leur mère et aspirent toujours à découvrir notre propre pays, la France.
Présentateur: Ce sont des jeunes qui viennent de... de toutes confessions?
Professeur: Toutes confessions... toutes confessions confondues sans discrimination. Ils sont super. Moi je vis avec eux une histoire d'amour... et vraiment que ce soit les musulmans, les jeunes druzes et les jeunes chrétiens, on vit là-bas le vrai visage du Liban.
Présentateur: On arrive à étudier quand même, malgré les bombes?
Professeur: Eh bien on arrive difficilement puisqu'il n'y a pas d'électricité, du tout. On... ils passent leurs examens à la bougie. Et puis... il n'y a pas... d'eau. Je vous donne un exemple concret: vous allez après déduire vous-même. Et bien j'arrive en classe de première, n'est-ce pas. Et soudain j'interroge Mlle Houda. Houda s'effondre par terre. Je vais près d'elle. je lui dis 'Mais qu'est-ce que tu as?' Et elle me dit 'Je suis l'aînée de sept euh... enfants, monsieur. Il faut nourrir les deux derniers. Maman ne peut pas acheter le lait puisque deux kilos de lait en poudre valent vingt jours de salaire. Et nous n'avons plus de salaire puisque depuis le blocus papa a été licencié'.

II *Scottish Higher, May, 1991*
Eric: Moi j'ai fait une section économique et littéraire... c'est à dire que j'ai étudié de l'économie ... un peu... même beaucoup de mathématiques... des langues vivantes... l'anglais, l'allemand... euh ... enfin toutes sortes de sujets... c'était très général... c'est... je ne voulais pas faire cette section... je voulais faire une section avec une troisième langue vivante... avec de l'espagnol... mais je n'ai

pas pu parce qu'il n'y avait plus de places dans le lycée où je voulais aller, alors j'ai été dans un lycée technique… au départ j'étais… très malheureux… je ne voulais pas y aller… euh… mes parents m'avaient proposé d'aller dans un lycée privé… dans un lycée à vingt kilomètres de chez moi… mais ça ne me disait trop rien… je me suis dit que j'allais essayer quand même… mais j'ai passé trois excellentes années dans ce lycée… on était une classe un peu particulière… on était un peu à l'écart du reste du lycée qui préparait des sections… pour être techniciens… pour être mécaniciens… ou… pour être cuisiniers aussi… donc c'était un peu particulier… on n'était pas très bien vu par le reste du lycée qui pensait qu'on était des personnes très riches….

Enfin moi, en maths, j'avoue que je dormais… les maths ne m'ont jamais intéressé… j'ai toujours été nul… je n'ai jamais rien compris aux maths… donc en général j'étais au dernier rang… je dormais… et pendant les interrogations, les tests, je regardais sur la copie de… de mon ami….

Mais… euh.., je crois que, au lycée, le professeur que j'ai le plus détesté, c'était pas mon professeur de maths… c'était mon professeur d'allemand… qui était… euh… qui était affreux… c'était quelqu'un qui détestait les élèves… et je trouvais que l'allemand était très difficile… mais c'était… c'était très difficile… tout particulièrement avec un prof qui n'aime pas ses élèves… qui n'aide pas… qui crie beaucoup… et fait des commentaires… euh… pas très agréables pendant une heure.

III *Oxford and Cambridge, A and AS-Level, June, 1991*
Reportage

Présentateur: Et puis ce matin, au journal officiel, un arrêté qui nous a bien intéressés: le renforcement de la lutte contre le travail clandestin, ce que l'on appelle plus communément le travail au noir et qui, ces deux dernières années, a pris des proportions considérables: 40% de plus en 86 et en 87. Brigitte Garambole.

Brigitte Garambole: Imaginez ce que gagnent en une année 30 000 entreprises de taille moyenne. Et bien, c'est exactement ce que rapporte le travail au noir: trente milliards en 1987. Un véritable mode parallèle de la finance qui selon l'INSEE concernerait 800 000 personnes, un chiffre certainement très en deça de la réalité. D'autant que les formes de travail au noir évoluent. Au bricoleur du dimanche et atelier de confection clandestin s'ajoute aujourd'hui le marchandage de main d'œuvre essentiellement portugaise entre entreprises européennes ou encore l'utilisation par des sociétés de travail temporaires de main d'œuvre non-déclarée. On évalue à 10% le nombre de chômeurs inscrits mais exerçant un travail clandestin. A eux seuls, le bâtiment puis l'agriculture, le textile et certains secteurs, tels que la restauration ou les garages, regroupent plus de 86% des travailleurs étrangers en situation irrégulière. Les régions les plus touchées, toujours les mêmes, l'Ile de France et la Provence, les Alpes, la Côte d'Azur. Le Ministère du Travail à travers une mission de lutte contre le trafic de main d'œuvre, a donc décidé de renforcer ses moyens de contrôle, notamment en s'élargissant à l'Europe, mais également par une première mesure immédiate, le renforcement des verbalisations.

IV *Cambridge A-Level, June, 1991*
Publicité 1

Cap sur Continent. Ecoutez, écoutez, de la fin de juin jusqu'au 3 août opération images et son dans les hypermarchés Continent. Ouvrez grand vos oreilles, en ce moment la chaîne hi-fi stéréo est à 750 francs chez Continent. Oui, 750 francs la chaîne hi-fi, garantie 2 ans, et en plus, pendant la période de cette offre spéciale, livraison à domicile gratuite. Pour l'audio vidéo c'est tout vu, cap sur Continent, bien entendu.

Publicité 2

L'UAP quel sera votre avenir et celui de votre famille, votre maison, votre voiture? Assurez-vous avec UAP. UAP est aussi l'assureur de grands projets européens, le tunnel sous la Manche, Eurodisneyland. Aujourd'hui UAP augmente son capital et vous invite à vous associer à un assureur européen exceptionel. Pour 620 francs l'action UAP. Souscrivez vous-même ou par votre intermédiaire financier habituel. Attention, souscrivez vite! UAP.

Flash 1

Nouvelles règles pour le volley-ball. Les dirigeants de la fédération internationale du volley-ball ont décidé que le cinquième set d'un match sera désormais joué selon le principe du tie-break. Ceci afin de raccourcir la durée du match et de faciliter ainsi les retransmissions télévisées. Les quatre premières manches se joueront selon le système classique, c'est à dire qu'une équipe ne pourra marquer un point que sur son service. Dans le dernier set, en revanche, le point sera compté quelle que soit l'équipe au service. Pour limiter la durée les sets en cas d'égalité à 15 – 15 ne pourront pas excéder les 17 points, même si la différence n'est que d'un point.

Flash 2

Un Boeing de Indian Airlines a été détourné hier sur Lahore au Pakistan alors qu'il faisait route entre Delhi et Srinagar près de la frontière entre l'Inde et le Pakistan. L'appareil a atterri sur l'aéroport de la ville pakistanaise sous le prétexte qu'il était à court de carburant. A bord de l'avion se trouvaient cent onze passagers, dont une quinzaine d'étrangers. Les pirates de l'air qui se réclament du mouvement nationaliste Sikh ont exigé la libération de six membres de leur organisation emprisonnés en Inde. Selon certaines informations une centaine de Sikhs auraient été assassinés en Inde récemment. Hier après-midi soixante-six passagers, surtout des femmes et des enfants, ont été libérés.

V *JMB A-Level, June, 1991*

1: French 'assistante'

Nathalie: Ah, toi aussi tu veux être assistant en Angleterre? Ah, je suis sûre que tu voudrais que je te donne des conseils, c'est ça. Bon, écoute je vais t'en parler un petit peu. Euh, si tu préfères, être un assistant, ça demande pas mal de choses, déjà ça demande un an de ta vie où tu arrêtes tes études et où tu es carrément intégré dans le pays. Moi je suis partie en Angleterre et j'avoue que ça m'a beaucoup, beaucoup, beaucoup apporté. Si tu préfères c'est… je pense que c'est vraiment une expérience inoubliable. Bien sûr c'est difficile si tu n'es jamais parti de chez toi mais si jamais tu es parti, vraiment, ça t'apporte encore plus de choses. En plus, bon, j'ai peut-être pas mal de chance. C'est à dire que je travaillais dans deux lycées, qui étaient à Sheffield, et les deux lycées m'intéressaient, bon, mais il y en avait un que je préférais. Et si tu veux je travaillais avec des jeunes qui avaient entre seize et dix-huit ans, c'est à dire des premières et des terminales. Et c'était franchement très agréable parce qu'ils aimaient vraiment le français, ils avaient choisi de le faire, ils étaient donc intéressés et donc les cours avec eux devenaient pas seulement des cours mais un plaisir. Et, en plus, dans les écoles où j'étais les professeurs, enfin plus dans une autre, les professeurs étaient assez dynamiques et ils avaient... les jeunes avaient vraiment un niveau très convenable. Etre assistant c'est aussi peut-être en profiter pour se faire de nouveaux amis, c'est à dire que tu rencontres des Anglais, des gens, et euh tu rencontres aussi d'autres assistants, par exemple les autres assistants allemands ou italiens peut-être. Donc là aussi c'est enrichissant parce que tu parles avec des gens que tu n'as jamais rencontrés, que tu n'as jamais vus et tu deviens… des fois tu deviens amis même. En plus, bon, un avantage qui est vraiment très, très important, et c'est pour ça aussi que je l'ai fait, c'est que ton anglais devient vraiment très bon, c'est à dire que là, tu parles tous les jours, tous les jours anglais avec les gens autour de toi, dans la ville, à chaque fois tu parles anglais, et je vais te dire mieux, tu arrives même à rêver en anglais. Tu penses en anglais bien sûr, mais tu rêves aussi en anglais. Ce n'est que quand tu fais des cours que tu parles français, autrement ce n'est que de l'anglais. Et ça franchement c'est très bon, il n'y a rien de tel pour apprendre une langue que d'être dans le pays, ça tu le sais. Si je dois te parler de difficultés, les difficultés majeures que j'ai eues ça a été euh, peut-être d'être loin de ma famille, de mes amis, parce que, bon, ces gens-là, tu les aimes, et tu aimerais peut-être que des fois ils soient avec toi. Mais le fait est que c'est peut-être une bonne occasion pour leur dire de venir te voir et de connaître l'Angleterre. Je pense que c'est ce qu'il faut faire. Tu peux les inviter. L'autre difficulté a été pour moi bien sûr le temps, euh… parce ce que je vais dire que tout le soleil, le soleil m'a vraiment manqué et le froid a été vraiment assez rude cette année-là, et j'ai vraiment souffert du froid. Mais tu oublies, tu oublies ça, tout passe. Voilà en gros ce que j'avais à te dire sur mon expérience.

Continuation

Si je dois te résumer un peu les qualités que tu dois avoir pour être assistant, je te dirais qu'il faut être enthousiaste, bavard, patient, curieux et un peu acteur quelque part. Enthousiaste parce que c'est toi qui mène une classe, toi qui dois sourire et montrer ton énergie, bavard parce qu'il faut aimer parler, pour toi et pour les autres. Patient peut-être parce que les élèves ne font pas toujours exactement ce que tu voudrais qu'ils fassent, mais, bon, de toute manière ils apprennent quand tu es là pour les aider, et pour être aussi patient quand ils ne comprennent pas quelque chose. Curieux, curieux il faut que tu le sois envers les élèves. Savoir ce qui les motive, leurs problèmes, mais aussi pour toi, c'est à dire curieux de la civilisation anglaise, curieux des gens, curieux de tout. Essaie de t'enrichir au maximum.

2: Interview

Présentateur: Face à moi un mercenaire, ce que l'on appelle un mercenaire, Patrick Olivier qui vient d'écrire *Soldat de Fortune* aux éditions Gérard Hubervillier avec la collaboration de Thibaut Doiron. Est-ce que ça vous a gêné que je vous présente comme un soldat perdu tout d'abord?

Patrick: Non, non je ne suis pas gêné parce que… toutes les causes que j'ai pu défendre sont… ont été des causes perdues.

Présentateur: Est-ce que c'est pour ça que cela vous a attiré dès le départ, est-ce que vous saviez qu'elles allaient être perdues?

Patrick: Non. Au départ je ne pensais pas qu'elles seraient perdues mais, peut-être inconsciemment au fond de moi-même j'y allais parce que... finalement il n'y avait pas d'aboutissement possible que finalement perdre.

Présentateur: Alors on va essayer de reprendre les choses au point de départ, 67 par exemple, où vous aviez 26 ans, vous êtes un jeune Tourangeau un peu monarchiste déjà.

Patrick: Oui, absolument.

Présentateur: Vous décidez de combattre auprès des Rhodésiens.

Patrick: Oui.

Présentateur: Des Rhodésiens qui tentent de sauvegarder leur indépendance.

Patrick: Oui.

Présentateur: Donc vous allez du côté blanc, face aux millions de noirs et vous arrivez en Rhodésie et vous vous engagez dans une troupe peu connue mais pratiquement la dernière troupe à cheval au monde que l'on appelle les Greys Scouts et c'est là que vous allez pour la première fois devenir un mercenaire, c'est à dire vous êtes un étranger qui vient s'engager auprès d'une armée qui n'est pas celle de votre pays.

Patrick: Oui, mais euh c'était une armée irrégulière une armée extrêmement britannique, même plus britannique que les Britanniques d'après les Rhodésiens, et donc je suis rentré et j'ai souscrit à un engagement ce qui fait que, au début de mon aventure je n'étais pas ce que l'on peut à proprement parler appeler mercenaire.

Présentateur: Vous étiez un soldat régulier.

Patrick: J'étais un soldat régulier dans une armée irrégulière qui se battait pour un...

Présentateur: Contre la guérilla.

Patrick: Contre la guérilla, oui.

Présentateur: Bon. Il se trouve que... au terme de cette, euh de cette guerre, on sait comment ça s'est terminé.

Patrick: Absolument oui.

Présentateur: Et on vous a proposé de... de devenir tout d'abord citoyen rhodésien et d'être engagé dans cette armée euh...

Patrick: Absolument.

Présentateur: Cette armée d'indépendance.

Patrick: Oui. Alors ce qui s'est passé c'est qu'en 1980, lorsque l'indépendance est arrivée, lorsque le Premier ministre Robert Mugabe a été élu, après les accords de Londres, euh il a fallu changer l'armée. Beaucoup de cadres rhodésiens, européens ont quitté pour partir en Afrique du Sud et d'autres sont restés et j'étais parmi ces gens-là parce que je n'ai jamais oublié que j'étais français et que mon pays aussi depuis la fin de la guerre 39–45 a été engagé sur différents territoires outre-mer et a toujours laissé derrière elle des personnes qui lui avaient fait confiance. Le dernier exemple en date est ce qui s'est passé en Algérie avec les Harkis. Donc je me suis dit, moi français, rhodésien dans ce petit pays... euh me battant avec... dans une unité multiraciale. Je voulais faire en sorte que les... eh bien que ces Africains m'aient à leur côtés dans un moment qui serait difficile, donc je suis resté une année supplémentaire pour former les cadres de la nouvelle armée nationale du Zimbabwe.

Présentateur: Est-ce que votre idée c'est la même qu'ont les gens qui pensent qu'il faut défendre à tout prix l'Occident blanc, l'Occident chrétien?

Patrick: Non, pas du tout moi je suis... vous savez, on ne passe pas sept ans en Afrique sans aimer ce continent et aujourd'hui je me sens un peu africain.

VI *Welsh Joint Education Committee A and AS-Level, June, 1989*
Section one:
Conversation (a)

Jacques: Mais, Suzanne... qu'est-ce qu'il y a ? Tu n'as pas l'air content ce matin.

Suzanne: Je viens de dire à mes parents que j'ai en assez d'étudier... que je ne veux pas aller à la fac... après les vacances... mes parents sont déçus... ils veulent que j'aille à la fac.

Jacques: Mais, Suzanne, Pourquoi tu ne veux pas aller à la fac? Tu as toujours dit que tu voulais être prof. Qu'est-ce que tu vas faire alors?

Suzanne: Travailler dans une banque... comme Jeanne... Ella a trouvé un bon poste au Crédit Agricole l'année passée après le bac. Maintenant elle peut s'offrir de jolis vêtements, des vacances à l'étranger. Moi aussi je veux gagner de l'argent sans être obligée d'attendre trois ou quatre ans. J'ai presque dix-neuf ans... je ne veux pas passer toute ma vie à étudier.

Jacques: Mais, Suzanne... travailler dans une banque, ce n'est pas toujours très intéressant... on a de longues heures de travail... très peu de vacances... et les clients ne sont pas toujours gentils.

Suzanne: Et si on est prof! Ça, ce n'est pas toujours intéressant non plus!Le niveau est si bas... les élèves ne s'intéressent pas à leurs cours... il sont souvent indisciplinés... même violents dans certains collèges... et les profs ne sont pas bien payés.

Jacques: Mais, si tu vas à la fac, tu n'es pas obligée d'être prof.

Suzanne: Mais des études de lettres, à quoi est-ce que ça sert si on ne veut pas être prof?

Jacques: Mais il y a beaucoup d'autres possibilités... dans le commerce, par exemple... tu aurais un meilleur choix d'emplois.

Suzanne: C'est exactement ce qu'ont dit mes parents... ah, je ne sais pas... je vais réfléchir.

Conversation (b)

Dame: Alors, monsieur, vous habitez Marseille... c'est une ville que je ne connais pas, mais on dit qu'il y a énormément de problèmes à cause des immigrés. Il y a beaucoup d'Algériens, n'est-ce pas?

Jeune homme: Les immigrés ne sont pas tous des Algériens, vous savez, madame... il y en a beaucoup qui sont d'origine européenne... des Italiens, des Portugais, des Espagnols..

Dame: Il y a des problèmes, quand même?

Jeune homme: C'est vrai qu'il y a des problèmes, madame, mais ce n'est pas seulement à cause des immigrés, vous savez.... Il y a un fort taux de chômage... et il y a une crise de logement.

Dame: Mais c'est parce qu'il y a tant d'immigrés que le taux de chômage est si élevé et qu'il y a une crise de logement!

Jeune homme: C'est ce qu'on dit… mais ce n'est pas vrai... les immigrés occupent surtout des emplois qui n'intéressent pas les Français.

Dame: Ah, vous croyez?

Jeune homme: Mais oui, madame… des emplois dangereux et mal payés. Dans la construction, par exemple. Parce qu'il y a une crise du logement à Marseille on est en train de construire beaucoup de grands immeubles dans la banlieue... et c'est justement pour travailler dans ces chantiers que les immigrés viennent à Marseille.

Dame: Ah, oui, peut-être… je n'y avais pas pensé.

Section two
Flash 1

Un professeur de Lyon, Dominique Didier, âgé de 45 ans, qui passait ses vacances dans le massif de l'Oisans dans les Alpes, a fait une chute mortelle au cours d'une randonnée hier matin. Son corps n'a été retrouvé qu'en fin d'après-midi.

Flash 2

Peu de bouchons à prévoir sur les routes du week-end, seulement quelques difficultés localisées, soit sur les grands axes habituellement embouteillés, soit à proximité des stations de vacances. Attention surtout aux gendarmes: ils seront de nouveau nombreux au bord des routes.

Flash 3

Gendarmes et policiers à Bergerac ont retrouvé, après huit jours d'enquête, les bijoux d'une vieille dame, victime d'un cambriolage. Ces bijoux étaient cachés dans un endroit inhabituel – à l'intérieur d'une machine à laver.

Flash 4

Un prisonnier de la prison des Baumettes, en détention pour vol aggravé criminel, s'est évadé hier, peu après six heures du matin. Ce prisonnier, de nationalité algérienne, est parvenu à scier un barreau de sa cellule et à franchir le mur d'enceinte de la prison en nouant des draps.

Flash 5

En raison de la course cycliste nocturne qui se déroulera ce soir, la circulation à Valence sera interrompue sur le boulevard Gambetta, dans les deux sens, entre l'avenue Victor Hugo et l'avenue de la Gare de 20 heures à 3 heures.

Section three
Interview

Présentatrice: Marcel Pagnol, vous êtes un régionaliste… c'est à dire que l'action de vos pièces, de vos romans et de vos films se déroule dans le Midi... en Provence. Pourquoi vivez-vous à Paris?

Pagnol: Je suis obligé de vivre à Paris à cause de ma profession, à cause de l'Académie et à cause de mes amis. Au bout de six mois de Paris, je ne puis plus y rester. Je retourne dans le Midi où je pense que je vais retrouver un bonheur définitif. Au bout de trois mois dans le Midi, j'en ai assez et je reviens à Paris avec le plus grand plaisir. Je me trouve bien partout, mais jamais longtemps.

Présentatrice: Quelles sont vos activités parisiennes et quelles sont vos activités méridionales?

Pagnol: Dans le Midi, je cherche des sources; c'est une manie... une passion. J'en ai trouvé plusieurs dans des endroits où l'eau est infiniment précieuse, comme dans les massifs des Alpes Maritimes. Là, les paysans sont prêts à défendre leur eau à coups de fusil.

Présentatrice: Ecrivez-vous dans le Midi?

Pagnol: Non, très peu. C'est à Paris qu'on écrit. Il y a un climat particulier à Paris qui fait que les gens sont plus intelligents qu'ailleurs. Je ne dis pas que les Parisiens soient plus intelligents que les autres... je dis que les provinciaux qui viennent à Paris sont plus intelligents et plus actifs que ceux qui restent en province.

Présentatrice: Avez-vous un projet de cinéma?

Pagnol: Non. Je n'ai plus mes studios; je n'ai plus mes laboratoires; je n'ai plus d'agence de distribution. Un film coûte un prix exorbitant... et, avec la crise du cinéma, on ne peut pas récupérer cet argent en France seulement. Il faut faire des films internationaux, c'est à dire des films à grand spectacle, que je suis incapable de réaliser.

Présentatrice: Les paysages ont beaucoup compté dans votre vie. A lire vos souvenirs on sent que le paysage parisien ne vous inspire pas vraiment.

Pagnol: Le grand paysage de ma vie, c'est vrai, se trouve là-bas dans le Midi. C'est le Massif de l'Etoile .. et les collines qui vont d'Aubagne à Aix-en-Provence avec au fond Sainte Victoire et la Sainte Baume. Là, l'air là-bas est d'une qualité particulière parce qu'il n'y a aucune espèce d'humidité, ce qui fait que les photographies que l'on prend sont toujours extraordinaires, toujours très belles. C'est pourquoi j'ai tourné plusieurs films dans ces collines... *Angèle, Regain, Le Puisatier.* Les couleurs n'y sont pas du tout dures, pas du tout italiennes. Les rochers, par exemple, ne sont pas blancs, ils sont bleutés; les verts ne sont pas éclatants non plus. C'est un paysage assez doux mais aux formes rudes.

VII *AEB, June, 1990*

Flash 1

Les professions libérales, elles, descendent aujourd'hui dans la rue. Médecins, huissiers, pharmaciens, experts comptables, ou architectes défileront cet après-midi de la République au Palais Royal à Paris. Ils protestent contre l'augmentation des cotisations des allocations familiales adoptées en décembre par le Parlement.

Flash 2

Le coup de colère de Lionel Jospin alors que les professeurs de second degré s'apprêtent à faire grève demain. Le ministre de l'éducation frappe du poing sur la table en condamnant ceux qui envisagent de refuser de donner leurs notes aux élèves. Les jeunes, dit-il, n'ont pas à être pris en otage.

Flash 3

En juillet partez en diesel pour le temps des vacances. Ford met des modèles diesel aux prix des modèles essence. La Fiesta CL diesel est au prix de la quatorze cent CL essence. Les Escorts ET DIA sont au prix des quatorze cent DIA à l'essence. Chez Ford le diesel au prix de l'essence, c'est vraiment le moment d'en profiter. Et en plus, chez Ford, les prix sont bloqués jusqu'au quinze juillet. Les modèles 89 sont au prix des modèles 88 sur toute la gamme Ford.

Entrevue 4

Bernard Rigoulex: Il y a en France, selon les estimations sérieuses, cinquante mille enfants maltraités d'une façon ou d'une autre et de ces mauvais traitements il en meurent en moyenne deux par jour. Hélène Dorlach, Secrétaire d'Etat chargée de la famille, a présenté hier au Conseil des Ministres un plan de protection de l'enfance, plan qui devrait, sinon fait disparaître totalement ces drames, du moins aider à en réduire sensiblement le nombre. Alors notre invitée ce matin, Hélène Dorlach, bonjour!

Hélène Dorlach, il ne se passe guère de jours sans qu'on apprenne que des enfants ont été victime de violence, d'assassinat mais aussi de viol, d'inceste, de vices en tous genres, abandon et caetera. J'ai l'impression qu'il y a une recrudescence de ces violences contre les enfants.

Hélène Dorlach: Je ne pense pas qu'il y ait une recrudescence, mais effectivement on en parle d'avantage. En plus la conscience sociale a évolué.

Bernard Rigoulex: Alors, Hélène Dorlach, parlons du détail de votre plan d'action. Première grande mesure c'est... ce serait de mieux coordonner la protection judiciaire et la protection sociale de ces enfants. Alors on sait bien qu'en France il y a souvent dans ce domaine des blocages, des lenteurs administratives, des problèmes de coordination. En quoi ça va consister de débloquer tout ça?

Hélène Dorlach: Effectivement le gouvernement a décidé de s'attaquer très fortement à tous les disfonctionnements. Un des disfonctionnements, vous le soulignez, c'est quelquefois le manque de coordination ou tout au moins de rapidité dans la coordination entre la protection judiciaire et la protection sociale qui sont en France les deux axes de la protection des mineurs, d'où nécessité de changer la loi, de changer le code.

Bernard Rigoulex: Deuxième mesure donc, Hélène Dorlach, sans doute la plus spectaculaire, un service d'accueil téléphonique à la chaîne nationale, qui fonctionnera, je crois, vingt-quatre heures sur vingt-quatre, trois cent soixante-cinq jours par an, tout le temps tout le temps tout le temps, l'anonymat sur une garantie, vous allez donner ce numéro de téléphone à tous les enfants et en leur disant quoi?

Hélène Dorlach: Oui, effectivement, on se rend compte que beaucoup de retard, beaucoup de retard dans le signalement des enfants maltraités vienne du fait que les gens, même les mieux intentionnés, même les professionnels, ne savaient pas où signaler. Est-ce que l'on doit signaler à la justice? Est-ce que l'on doit signaler à l'aide sociale? D'où l'idée de créer ce numéro d'écoute nationale qui sera largement connu, qui fonctionnera vingt-quatre heures sur vingt-quatre et trois cent soixante-cinq jours par an. Et à l'écoute de ce numéro il y aura des gens tout à fait formés, je crois que ça il faut le dire, extrêmement spécialisés, qui sont capables de faire le tri dans l'urgence, d'écouter, de donner des réponses, et de savoir après s'il faut avertir, soit immédiatement en cas d'urgence absolue, des services de justice, soit, s'il s'agit plutôt de donner des conseils, avertir les services d'aide sociale à l'enfant.

Bernard Rigoulex: Alors, Hélène Dorlach, vous prévoyez aussi d'amplifier la campagne nationale de prévention des abus sexuels envers les enfants, qu'est-ce que vous allez faire de plus?

Hélène Dorlach: Eh bien cette campagne qui va être généralisée à la suite d'expérimentations effectuées dans deux départements qui ont été tout à fait positives, cette campagne va être généralisée en faveur des enfants de six à douze ans. Elle sera précédée des sensibilisations du public et elle s'appuiera sur un large volontariat de ceux qui la feront, sur le patronariat total et surtout elle ne pourra se faire qu'avec l'accord des familles. Il y a des documents vidéoscopiques, il y a des brochures d'information qui sont destinés à la fois aux adultes et à la fois aux enfants, et, bien entendu, pour être présentés aux enfants, expliquer le mode d'emploi, et nous comptons en particulier sur les enseignants et une circulaire interministérielle est en cours de signature.

Index

A Level French Cassette

If you have purchased a copy of our Study Guide
for A Level French and would like to buy the
accompanying cassette, please complete the order
form below and return it to:

**Letts Educational Ltd
Aldine House
Aldine Place
London W12 8AW**

Telephone 081-740 1111

Forenames (Mr/Ms) _____

Surname _____

Address _____

_____

_____

Postcode _____

Please send me the following:

	Quantity	Price (incl VAT)	Total
A Level French C90 cassette	_____	£4.00	_____
Add postage – UK & RoI 75p for each cassette			_____

I enclose a cheque/postal order for £ _____
(made payable to Letts Educational Ltd)

Or charge to Access/Visa card No. ☐☐☐☐☐☐☐☐☐☐☐☐☐☐☐☐☐☐

Expiry date _____

Signature _____